Production, Entrepreneurship, and Profits

Shih-Yen Wu

Basil Blackwell

First published 1989

Basil Blackwell Inc.
3 Cambridge Center
Cambridge, Massachusetts 02142, USA

Basil Blackwell Ltd
108 Cowley Road, Oxford, OX4 IJF, UK

Library of Congress Cataloging in Publication Data

Wu, Shih-Yen.
Production, entrepreneurship, and profits/Shih-Yen Wu.
p.   cm.
Bibliography: p.
ISBN 1-55786-028-9
1. Production (Economic theory) 2. Industrial organization
(Economic theory) 3. Entrepreneurship. 4. Resource allocation.
5. Profit. I. Title.
HB241.W83 1988
658.1'55—dc 19   88-27482
                                                                              CIP

British Library Cataloguing in Publication Data

A CIP catalogue record for this book is
available from the British Library.

Typeset in 10 on 11½ pt Times
by Times Graphics, Singapore
Printed in Great Britain

Contents

Preface

The purpose of this book is to study the allocative role played by the entrepreneurs and the firm in a competitive market economy. Traditionally the market is viewed as the allocator of resources. The attainment of our goal requires us to demonstrate that the entrepreneur and the firm indeed perform an intrinsic allocative function as well as to show how the allocative responsibility is apportioned between the entrepreneur–firm and the market.

The attention given by economists to the study of entrepreneurship has fluctuated considerably over time. This is because their attention shifts among the various fundamental economic issues which involve the entrepreneur to varying degrees. The classical economists' concern over capital accumulation and economic growth led them to pay special attention to the capitalist entrepreneur. The neoclassical economists' preoccupation with the theories of value, distribution, and equilibrium under the condition of certainty enabled them to relegate the entrepreneur to the sideline. Recently, the revival in the interest of uncertainty has again thrust the entrepreneur to center stage.

Despite the regained prominence, no general theory involving the entrepreneur has emerged. The literature offers many specialized theories, each based upon a specific activity of the entrepreneur. These activities include the discovery of profit opportunities, risk-bearing, innovation and so on. If we were to construct a comprehensive theory involving all the well-known entrepreneurial roles, the resulting theory would become too complex to be manageable.

In this book we reduce the complexity of the theory by basing our analysis on two observations: (a) entrepreneurial services are not tradeable; (b) the nature of these services changes with the market environment that the entrepreneur faces. With this perspective, we easily incorporated the entrepreneurial activities into a general economic theory without having to enumerate the various roles played by the entrepreneurs. This theory describes a process by which the cooperative entrepreneurs organize for production and share profits. The theory that we advocate offers a more realistic description of the capitalist economy since it describes both the cooperative activities of the entrepreneurs within the firm and the noncooperative activities of agents in the markets. Through both cooperative and noncooperative activities, the available resources are channeled by the entrepreneur and the market into their employment.

In this book a literary approach is used rather than mathematical modeling. We chose this method in order to concentrate on describing the structure of the entrepreneur-centered economic system unencumbered by digressions on solution concepts necessary for mathematical modeling. The mathematical model will be presented in a subsequent volume. Moreover, a clear verbal presentation of the entrepreneur-centered economy will make this volume accessible not only to all professional economists but also to inquisitive undergraduates and interested lay persons.

No ideas can grow out of a vacuum. This is particularly true for this book. My debt to the long line of literature is evident; it is acknowledged in chapters 2, 3 and 4. I also received help from many people. Colleagues and friends have read different chapters and offered many helpful comments and encouragements. These individuals include Michael Balch, Paul Fellows, Arjo Klamer, Donald McCloskey, Gerald Nordquist, Andrew Policano, Barbara Solow, and Thomas Saving. I owe a particular debt of gratitude to my graduate students Roderick Beck, Yue-Shan Chang, Meten Cosgel , Shu-Ying Li, Cheng-Zhong Qin, and Xiang-He Wang who read the various versions of this book and offered many helpful comments. Xiang-He Wang also served as my research assistant when chapter 7 was written, and Cheng-Zhong Qin served in the same capacity and helped me to prepare the mathematical appendix. In addition, two undergraduate students, William Bulmer and John Z. Smith, also read the manuscript and, by their comments, helped me to improve its clarity. John Smith, together with Jennifer Wu, also assisted me with the tedious task of preparing the footnotes and the bibliography.

I also wish to thank Marguerite Knoedel for her uncanny ability to decipher my illegible handwriting and cheerfully transform it into flawless pages. Her many years of faithful service are greatly appreciated. Finally, I wish to thank my family for their support and encouragement. I hope that they will share my joy in the publication of this volume.

Shih-Yen Wu
Iowa City, Iowa

1

The Role of the Firm, Entrepreneur, and Profits in Economic Theory

When people live together there exist obvious advantages in acting cooperatively, dividing up the work, and sharing its fruits. Cooperation makes it possible for each individual to avoid doing everything for himself. It allows the members of society to exploit comparative advantages in production and to reap the benefits resulting from the division of labor and the economies of large-scale production associated with modern technology.

Specialization, however, also makes one man's enjoyment rely upon another man's work. The opportunistic nature of man and his distaste for work may make his commitment to work undependable. Cooperative efforts can be sustained and productive activities can be brought into a state of harmony with society's interest only through some institutional arrangements: the adoption of rules and regulations to guide production and distribution. Because such institutions affect the extent of economic activity as well as the relative share received by the members of society, economists and social philosophers have devoted a great deal of time and effort to studying how different social, political, and economic institutions affect human want-satisfying activities.

People's tastes vary widely and their endowments differ. Therefore it is natural to assume that, if individuals were allowed to pursue their own self-interest when producing together, mere chaos would result. A "cooperative outcome" can be sustained only when members of the society act in concert. A social goal must be established. The attainment of the goal needs deliberate execution of plans. This view clearly underlies eighteenth-century mercantilism, which advocated the creation of national wealth as the supreme objective of the states and advocated the primacy of national power. The nineteenth-century German nationalists, neomercantile institutionalists, and present-day communists all subscribe to this view.

1

Diametrically opposed to the collective view of cooperative behavior is the individualistic view. The individualist believes that in a proper setting the effect of cooperation can be achieved with members of the society acting individualistically in a noncooperative manner. The view was inspired by Newton's discovery of the natural law, but emerged politically only as a reaction against mercantilism. The physiocrats, Richard Cantillon and Dudley North for example, insist that all human activity is subject to the regulation of a "natural order in the social sphere." They attempt to show how individual economic activities motivated by self-interest in the marketplace are indeed consistent with the "natural order." Adam Smith forged these insights into a remarkable proposition. Smith admitted that human activities are motivated by self-love: "It is not from the benevolence of the butcher, the brewer, or the baker, that we expect our dinner, but from their regard to their own interests. We address ourselves, not to their humanity but to their self-love, and never talk to them of our necessities but of their advantages" (Smith, 1937, p. 14). Assuming that men are rational beings, knowing their preferences and capable of making calculations necessary to pursue their self-interest efficiently, Smith went on to assert that "each man is the best judge of his own interests" and should as far as possible be allowed to pursue these interests. In a competitive market environment, man is "led by an invisible hand to promote an end which was no part of his intention. Indeed, by pursuing his own interest he frequently promotes that of the society more effectually than when he really intends to promote it" (Smith, 1937, p. 14). In the words of Frank Knight, "the apparent chaos of competition, the welters of buying and selling, are resolved or transmuted into an orderly system of economic cooperation by means of which, under individual freedom in contrast to central direction, the community's wants are supplied and its wealth increased" (Knight, 1971, p. 9). The Smithian theme is taken further by Hayek, who advocates that spontaneously created social institutions resulting from interactions of free man can further social aims better than the consciously designed institutions. Hayek says: "Nations stumble upon establishments which are indeed the result of human action but not the result of human design; and that the spontaneous collaboration of free man often creates things which are greater than their individual minds can fully comprehend" (Hayek, 1948, pp. 6–7).

The Smithian proposition can be decomposed logically into two parts. First, individual pursuits of self-interest in the marketplace do not lead to chaos; instead they lead to a state of equilibrium where individuals' interests are made consistent. Second, the equilibrium is socially desirable. The validity of these propositions depends crucially upon the market environments within which production and exchange take place, the nature and extent of the division of labor, and the degree of competition in the commodity and factor markets. As we will see, these factors also crucially determine the type of agents needed in the economy to coordinate production.

In the early stage of economic development specialized "producers" as such do not exist. The household serves for both consumption and production. It seldom trades factors of production. Division of labor in the economy takes the form of product specialization alone. Each household, using resources under its disposal, undertakes to produce a specific good or service. The household sells the good or service it has produced for money, using the proceeds to purchase the goods and services needed for consumption. In this simple economy there exists only one level of exchange activities, namely, the exchange of the finished products in the market.

It is relatively easy to visualize that in such a market environment the competitive market alone can be relied upon to coordinate production and consumption efficiently. Given the resource endowment and the production technology, the household converts inputs into outputs. Through the market the households exchange finished products with each other. The market determines the price of the products and the household determines the quantity of each product produced and consumed. In this manner all available resources are allocated through the market mechanism. Since society is nothing more than the aggregation of households, and since exchange between a buyer and a seller is always mutually beneficial, the market outcome must be socially desirable.

As the market expands and the production technology becomes more advanced, division of labor extends from product specialization to include specialization in tasks. Each individual is no longer responsible for the production of an entire product; many individuals jointly carry out the tasks in the long chain of productive activities leading to the creation of a given consumable good or service. The individual then uses the income thus derived to purchase the goods and services needed for consumption. Intimately associated with such a specialization in tasks is the functional division of labor. As the economy advances, the land, labor, capital, and entrepreneurial services are increasingly provided by different individuals. The factor markets have become active.

When specialization in tasks and functional division of labor are present in the economy the problem of coordinating production becomes more complex. Because individuals now sell productive services instead of finished products, production activity takes place outside the household. Someone outside must coordinate the transformation of the various inputs into outputs and then market them. Firms thus emerge as separate production entities.

Now the market economy comprises two classes of agents: the

consumer and the firm. The consumer is endowed with preferences and endeavors to maximize his utility.[1] The firm's objective, however, is not readily apparent. It is the subject of considerable controversy. Some believe that the firm is organized to maximize profits and others insist that it is organized to maximize sales; other notions are also possible. It becomes unclear whether the efficiency of the market system is impaired by firms, and whether the market is still capable of producing a socially desirable outcome.

It took economists nearly two centuries to formally establish that the Smithian proposition is valid in a competitive economy where the capitalist-owned firm is the basic production unit. The proof involved three stages. First, Jevons, Menger, and Walras showed what it means for an agent to act in his own interest, and then Walras demonstrated that in a competitive market environment there do exist equilibrium prices for goods and services. The issue of the existence of a competitive equilibrium has been further refined in recent years by Arrow, Debreu, and McKenzie.

Second, in order to show social optimality some notion of efficient use of resources had to be proposed. With the assumption that society is an aggregation of individuals, two efficiency criteria were proposed: the utilitarian and the Paretian. By assuming that the marginal utilities of income of the individuals are comparable the utilitarian is able to assert that the interest of the community is the sum of the interests of its members. He therefore advocates "the greatest happiness for the greatest number," which can only mean the maximum of summed utility. Many economists, however, question the plausibility of interpersonal comparisons of utility. Pareto provided an efficiency criterion enabling social outcomes to be ranked without reliance on such comparisons. He asserts that a social outcome is efficient if there does not exist another outcome which is unanimously preferred by all its members, a notion of efficiency widely adopted by economists today.

Third, modern welfare economics, under the guiding hands of Bergson, Hicks, Samuelson, and Arrow, established the relationship between the outcome of the self-interest-seeking behavior of Walras and the socially efficient allocative outcome of Pareto. This body of theory is referred to as the neoclassical theory of the competitive economy.

Neoclassical economic theory is erected upon a particular economy where all markets (including a full set of contingency markets) exist and are perfect. There are in it two sets of agents, the consumer and the firm. The consumers own both the resources and the firms; they supply all inputs required for production, receive all dividends distributed by the firm, and consume all the final goods and services produced. The firms, in contrast, are simple analytical constructs –

they are dimensionless production units. The firm is assumed to be owned and managed by the capitalists in a capitalistic economy. Further, the existence of firms is taken for granted and their number is assumed to be fixed. The capitalistic economy, supported by property rights and legally enforceable contracts, operates through a system of interrelated markets to determine production, distribution, and exchange of goods and services.

In a complete market environment, all agents are assumed to behave noncooperatively with each other and to pursue their own objectives in the marketplace: the consumer acts to maximize his utility subject to a budget constraint and the firm seeks to maximize its profit. In order to maximize utility the consumer equates the marginal rate of substitution of each pair of commodities with their price ratios. In order to maximize profit, the firm employs each factor of production to the extent that its marginal value productivity is equal to its market price. Thus, guided exclusively by prices both within and without the firm, resources are allocated in an impersonal market environment. Demand and supply interact in the market, and a state of equilibrium will emerge.

As long as the economy is perfectly competitive, even though all agents behave noncooperatively to pursue their own objectives, the end result is socially desirable. The reason for this remarkable result is simple. In a competitive market, the ability of any seller to sell at a special price is constrained by the fact that the consumer can buy elsewhere; competition therefore acts to protect consumers from exploitation. Competition among sellers also forces each producer to adopt the most efficient method of production, and provides incentives for firms to produce the goods and services desired by the consumers. Through competition the consumer, within the income available, attains the highest level of satisfaction. Because social welfare is the collective welfare of the consumers, competition also leads to a result which is consistent with the interests of society at large. Consequently, the competitive market not only affords each agent the complete freedom to choose but also in the end reconciles the diverse interests among its participants. Finally, the market is appealing because it is simple: prices alone are sufficient to serve as signals to guide the individual agent's action. The only untidy and troublesome thing is that the neoclassical economy fails to guarantee an equitable distribution of income. This shortcoming, however, creates no serious problem for the self-confident neoclassical. Inequity can be corrected through lump-sum taxes and subsidies. Since lump-sum transfers of initial endowments do not affect the individual's incentive to work, it corrects the inequality without producing any side effects. There is no need to tamper with the market process.

The neoclassical economist thus views the economic system as being coordinated by the price mechanism and treats the society not as an organization but as an organism. In the words of Sir Arthur Salter: "The normal economic system works itself. . . . Over the whole range of human activities and human needs, supply is adjusted to demand and production to consumption, by a process that is automatic, elastic and responsive" (Coase, 1937, p. 387). The phrase "the normal economic system works itself" does not mean that the market participants do not make choices. It simply means that, for a given market situation, both the market transactions and the firm's decisions on inputs and outputs are guided by the same set of prices. Based upon these prices each agent is forced to make the "right choice" which is perceived to be the same by all. This implies that, given all resource endowments and production technology, the market through the price mechanism determines the quantity of each input employed, the quantity of each output produced, and the prices of all inputs and outputs. In other words, there exists a universal rule of the market and this rule renders suboptimal any agent's attempt to employ resources in an idiosyncratic way. The market alone directs the flow of social resources.

Because the firm does not possess a separate internal decision rule in neoclassical theory, it makes no independent contribution to the market outcome. Therefore the firm is not an alternative to market coordination in production but merely an extension of the market. To put it differently, firms are on "automatic pilot." If the market is allowed to work unimpeded, all available resources are allocated as before, with the households serving as the basic decision units. As in the simpler economy, the households view exchange as mutually beneficial; the market is again able to allocate the resources in a socially optimal way. This faith in the market leads to the doctrine of "laissez-faire, laissez-passer." Some social philosophers go so far as to claim that the pursuance of self-interest is a precondition for the attainment of optimal social welfare, thus making selfishness a necessary virtue. Some such worldly philosophy has evidently gained a wide following in America today.

Two features characterize the neoclassical economy. First, in this full information market environment, entrepreneurs and firms play no role in resource allocation. The production policy of any firm is determined by market demand and by the technology of production. The market outcome is determined totally and automatically by the market process. The firm's role is purely passive, and the entrepreneurial activities are said to be limited to the situation in which market disequilibrium exists. Since firms are managed by owner–entrepreneurs, if profit rates among the various productive ventures differ the entrepreneurs will move quickly to take advantage of the profit opportunities. In the end a new equilibrium prevails, the rates of return are equalized among all productive endeavors, and profit vanishes. When profit vanishes, the entrepreneurial function also vanishes. Since the neoclassical economic theory is concerned primarily with equilibrium analysis, the neoclassical economy is left without entrepreneurs and profits. Second, the neoclassical economy lacks the internal dynamics for change. Once an equilibrium is reached, without the assistance of any intermediary agents, the market itself allocates resources inexorably. In the words of Schumpeter "a perfect circular flow" exists and the economy will continuously reproduce itself (Schumpeter, 1934, chapter 1.) If the economy should experience any change, the change must be brought about by exogenous factors. Changes such as population growth, technological innovation, shifts in tastes, and so forth are all outside the economic system. Because changes can only take place by way of exogenous shocks, we cannot look to the economic system to explain basic economic phenomena and issues such as investment activities, accumulation of capital, and business fluctuations, not to speak of such grand matters as the long-term prospect of the capitalistic system. On these the neoclassical economic theory is mute. This characteristic of the neoclassical theory stands in sharp contrast with classical, Marxian, institutionalist, and Schumpeterian economics, which consider the internal dynamics of an economy to be a major concern of the economist.

It must be concluded that, even though the theory has provided a formal support for Adam Smith's intuitive propositions, it is of little practical use. It has failed on two major fronts. First, it does not provide a faithful description of the prevailing economy. Casual empiricism reveals that the entrepreneur and the firm play a vital role in resource allocation. Firms are not dimensionless entities; the size and the internal structure of the firm contribute crucially to the allocative outcome. Second, the creation of surplus and the accumulation of wealth based upon the profit motive serve as the basic driving forces for economic activities. By not giving entrepreneurs and profits a central place in economic theory the neoclassical theory robs itself of the descriptive and explanatory power and removes the elements that generate the internal dynamics of the market system. As a consequence, we can no longer hope to understand the interplay of market forces and use the market to explain the sequential occurrence of important economic events.

In addition, the neoclassical model is not deemed to be useful because of another serious deficiency: it is not robust enough to be extended to an economy where some contingency markets are absent. In an incomplete market environment, an individual investor must use his own implicit contingency prices, given the firm's production policy, to evaluate the firm's worth. The firm, however, must rely on all individual shareholder's implicit contingency prices in order to evaluate its own worth and to select its production policy. To be specific, the firm is assumed to use a weighted average of its shareholders' contingency prices in each state of the world to evaluate its own worth in that state of the world. The weights used are the proportion of the firm's share that each individual investor holds. This is the way that the firm coordinates production and interacts with the consumer and the resource owner. The economy will again reach an equilibrium.

The existence of such an equilibrium, however, depends crucially upon the fact that the firm knows the true implicit contingency prices of its shareholders. Since a market mechanism to induce the shareholders to reveal their implicit contingency prices truthfully does not exist, the firm will not be able to select a production plan that will be unanimously agreed upon by all its shareholders. Lack of such unanimity cripples the ability of the privately owned firms to coordinate production, and prevents the neoclassical economy from reaching an equilibrium and from reproducing itself. Thus the inability to obtain contingency prices destroys the neoclassical version of the capitalistic economy. Neoclassical theory is not robust.

These shortcomings of neoclassical theory force us to search for a better alternative. In order to progress beyond neoclassical theory we need to formally take account of the fact that the market is not perfect. Economists have long recognized the imperfections of markets and have identified four causes of these imperfections: monopoly, externality, public goods, and uncertainties. The failure of markets invariably leads to a decreased use of markets and to the reliance on nonmarket means of resource allocation. The presence of market uncertainties, in particular, is responsible for a class of market failures inducing a variety of market activities and causing the emergence of many business and social institutions that would otherwise be redundant in a complete market environment. Paradoxically, in an uncertainty-regnant market environment some contingent markets are reluctant to come into existence; markets become incomplete.

When uncertainty exists and the markets are incomplete, the conversion of inputs into outputs ceases to be a routine matter. Resource owners no longer hold unanimous opinions on what to produce, how to produce it, and what quantity of each good should be produced. In a given choice situation, not all agents in the market agree objectively about what constitutes the right choice. The lack of unanimity signifies the disappearance of the universal market rule; the market breaks down. A special individual must break the impasse and assume the responsibility for production.

This individual is called the entrepreneur. The entrepreneur in an uncertain market environment performs a creative act in the same way as an artist, an essayist, or a scientist. The entrepreneur is a creative person who converts inputs into outputs efficiently or who produces outputs which he believes will give greater satisfaction to the consuming public. Since the consumer's tastes are subject to change and the outcome of any productive activity is uncertain, the entrepreneur's task is not routine. The entrepreneur must use judgement to make production decisions and take the associated risks. Thus he must be a person who has confidence in his judgement and believes that he possesses the ingenuity to solve problems, and he must be a person with the spirit of venture and the capacity to endure and persevere. The entrepreneur must have the desire to accumulate or to act altruistically, to see that progress is made, and to do things that are different and novel. Above all, he is a person driven by the freedom to do things his own way and to set and achieve his own goals. Because the outcome of production is uncertain, the value of the entrepreneurial services cannot be ascertained *ex ante*. With the entrepreneur insisting on doing things in his own way, no one will be willing to hire his services at a predetermined price. The entrepreneur, must therefore initiate production and claim the residual as his reward. The promise of a positive expected profit at equilibrium therefore constitutes an essential inducement for the entrepreneurial services in the profit sector. Further, in a complex economy where division of labor is beneficial, the entrepreneurial service must be pooled for joint production. It follows that in order to describe and explain the functioning of the economy it is necessary that entrepreneurs, firms, and profits be formally incorporated into an economic theory.

The attempt to incorporate entrepreneurs, firms, and profits is, of course, not new. However, no viable new theory has emerged. The failure stems from the fact that entrepreneurs, firms, and profits are introduced into the formal theory in a piecemeal fashion, and that the concept of equilibrium is taken unaltered from the neoclassical economies. Commonly, entrepreneurs are studied independently of the firm, theories of the firm are constructed with casual reference to the entrepreneur, and analyses of equilibrium are conducted without considering the role played by entrepreneurs. In addition, the nature of profits remains elusive to the economist. How does profit differ from returns to capital? Is it a reward to risk-bearing, perception of market opportunities, or innovation and progress? Does it vanish in a state of equilibrium? Because the issues of the entrepreneur, the firm, profits, and equilibrium are closely interwoven it is not surprising that such a piecemeal approach fails to yield results. In order to construct a mutually consistent general theory involving entrepreneurs, firms, profits, and equilibrium, the common thread must be identified. The common thread is the entrepreneur.

To construct a viable theory we need to ask the following questions related to the entrepreneur. What makes entrepreneurs behave the way they do? What goals do entrepreneurs pursue? Why must they pursue these goals through a firm? What is the nature of the resultant market equilibrium and the consequence on resource allocation? Only in this manner can the problems of the entrepreneur, the firm, profits, and equilibrium be dealt with simultaneously and the roles played by each in economic theory be properly understood.

In this book we develop the theme that in the presence of market uncertainties a market for entrepreneurs can never be established. Entrepreneurial services are therefore not tradeable. Since entrepreneurial services are not tradeable but are essential for production, they must be put into use by the entrepreneurs themselves. In other words the entrepreneur must initiate his own employment and then take the initiative to organize the other factors of production. The entrepreneur thus differs from the other factors in that he is self-mobilizing, self-driven, and self-employing. Whenever a single entrepreneur's effort is not sufficient to make production possible, entrepreneurs must join hands to make production a common task by forming a firm. A firm is thus a coalition of entrepreneurs. The combining of entrepreneurs in a firm and the relationship among them give the firm a distinct internal structure and character.

The point we wish to emphasize is that production takes place as a consequence of a society-wide cooperative game played by the entrepreneurs. The entrepreneur's objective is to receive a share of the value of the game to be revealed as an equilibrium outcome. Since the entrepreneurs make the production and equilibrium possible, the role of the entrepreneur does not vanish in the state of equilibrium. Moreover, in order to induce the entrepreneurs to play the game through production, the return to the entrepreneurs must be positive in equilibrium. In this way entrepreneurs, firms, and profits are formally integrated.

The entrepreneur-centered theory of the competitive economy stands in sharp contrast with neoclassical theory. The existence of the firm is not taken for granted: it is a result of the market outcome. The entrepreneurs behave cooperatively within the firm, while all agents act noncooperatively in the market. This is how the entrepreneurs and the market codirect resources. Through competition the economy will arrive at an equilibrium. The resulting equilibrium, however, is different from the neoclassical steady state. The entrepreneurs do not vanish at equilibrium. In addition, there is no tendency for profits of different business enterprises to equalize and vanish at equilibrium. The equalization of profits is a phenomenon associated with an economy where the firms are managed by owners and profits are deemed to be returns to capital. Since capital investments among different business ventures are comparable, competition will insure that at equilibrium the rates of return to capital are equalized among all business endeavors. In an economy where the firms are coalitions of entrepreneurs the result is different. Since entrepreneurial talents are unique and returns to their services are not known *ex ante*, there does not exist a way of measuring the worth of entrepreneurial services and hence of measuring the corresponding value of each enterprise. Since profits are the residual yield to the incomparable enterprises, it follows that profit rates of different enterprises are also incomparable. Consequently, there is no tendency for profits of the firms to converge, let alone vanish, at equilibrium.

Furthermore, there is a fundamental difference between the income to tradeable factors and the income to the entrepreneur. The former is contractual in nature and the latter is a residual. The behaviors of factor owners receiving contractual returns and entrepreneurs receiving residuals differ sharply. The tradeable factor owners look to productivity as a source of income. Entrepreneurs earning a residual income, however, look to opportunities created by market changes as well as their current productivities as sources of income. They equate changes with opportunities and insist that only through changes does a rapid accumulation of wealth become possible. It is the entrepreneur's desire for rapid accumulation that stimulates economic activities and supplies the dynamics of capitalism. Since uncertainties prevail in the marketplace and the entrepreneurs must base their current actions on the expectations of the future, planning becomes necessary. However, plans of the individual agents may be inconsistent with the aggregate outcome; since adjustment of discrepancies is costly and time consuming, economic fluctuation becomes the common state of affairs. Furthermore, since entrepreneurial actions are based upon expectations and expectations change swiftly, fluctuation caused by "expectational discrepancies" may lead to a spiral. The willingness of entrepreneurs to take chances for profits is therefore the primary cause for all internal dynamics and instabilities in the capitalistic economy.

Entrepreneurs also cause market environments to evolve. Because the entrepreneurs are reluctant to accept the status quo they propel the economy into constant change. Since entrepreneurs are owners of resources whose services are not tradeable, what constitutes entrepreneurial services also obviously depends upon the market environment within which production takes place. Different imperfections in the marketplace will induce different sets of entrepreneurial activities.

In other words, since entrepreneurs must organize into firms in order to carry out production, the nature of market imperfections must also determine the characteristics of the firms, that is their ownership structure, size, and internal organization. For example, the presence of imperfections in the labor market may force the laborers to play an entrepreneurial role, giving rise to labor-managed firms. Similarly, the presence of imperfections in capital markets may force the capitalist to assume the entrepreneurial role, giving rise to owner-managed firms. Market imperfections may also induce some of the firm's activities to bypass markets entirely and will therefore affect the internal organization of the firm. When many imperfections in the factor markets exist stimultaneously, different types of firms with different internal organizations are found.

Because firms with different ownership structure and internal organization arise as a result of the responses of entrepreneurs to different market environments, we naturally expect that different firms will allocate resources in a different manner. Specifically, in the early stage of economic history, when the factor markets were not developed, to produce anything at all the entrepreneur had to gain control of all the required resources through nonmarket means. The entrepreneur was a self-sufficient all-inclusive resource owner. As the market for industrial labor developed, labor relinquished the entrepreneurial role and the entrepreneurs shed the labor function. Later, when the capital market was developed, the capitalists relinquished their entrepreneurial role and the entrepreneurs shed their financing function. Control of the production initiative and production process was now left entirely in the hands of the pure entrepreneurs. Complete functional specialization had taken place.

Thus the extent of the market at any given time defined the entrepreneurial role. However, the entrepreneur yearned unceasingly to improve his lot, and therefore initiated improvements in the market environment and in economic and social institutions. The nature of this evolution in market activities and industrial organizations is examined in chapter 9. The entrepreneur's behavior and the socio-economic institutions have evolved together over time. The entrepreneur's activities not only benefited himself but also, through the improvement of the market institution, enhanced the welfare of others. As the labor and the capital markets improved, the exploitation of labor and the risk to the capitalist lessened. These improvements, in turn, increased the economy's productive power and contributed indirectly to the consumer's welfare.

A capitalist economy has both for-profit and not-for-profit firms. When the entrepreneurs of a given coalition seek pecuniary returns, the resultant coalition of entrepreneurs is a for-profit firm. However, when the entrepreneurs of a given coalition seek nonpecuniary returns, the resultant coalition of entrepreneurs is a nonprofit firm. These nonprofit firms include hospitals, schools, theaters, and museums. The for-profit and nonprofit firms intertwine in the marketplace; they compete in the same factor markets. Generally, the nonprofit firms produce goods and services that are essential to the society but are shunned by the profit-oriented firms. Since the provision of these goods and services is essential to society's wellbeing, the proper mix of entrepreneurial activities in the two sectors is essential. The supply of entrepreneurial services in the nonprofit sector obviously depends on the ethical and cultural setting of the society. What constitutes a proper mix is clearly a value judgement. The society must first adopt an ethical standard. Given a set of social ethics, a desired mix of entrepreneur services can be achieved only if the entrepreneur class collectively adheres to this ethical standard.

Because the entrepreneur-centered theory integrates entrepreneur, firm, and profit into a single analytical framework, recognizes endogenous sources of change, and embraces nonprofit production entities, it apparently affords greater descriptive realism. Moreover, it also forces us to modify our perception of the nature and scope of economics. By formally recognizing the entrepreneurial element, the functioning and the outcome of the market now depend on human behavior. Social welfare can no longer be achieved automatically through the market with an "ideal market structure." Since the entrepreneur can devote efforts either to pursuing profit or to pursuing nonprofit goals, the achievement of collective welfare depends crucially on conscious human effort. A society's welfare now hinges on the quality, vision, and purpose in its entrepreneurs, and on complementary social institutions. In short, the entrepreneur-centered theory of the capitalistic economy changes the central concern of economics.

NOTES

1 Throughout the book the generic pronoun "he" is used. This usage is not gender specific.

2

The Heritage

Although writings about consumption, production, exchange, and money appeared in ancient times, modern economic analysis is a heritage of classical and neoclassical economics. The central concern of the two schools, however, is different. Classical economics paid special attention to economic development and its effect on the relative wellbeing of the various social classes. Neoclassical economics, in contrast, is static in nature. It centers its attention on investigating how the market alone, through the price mechanism, allocates resources and examines how the resulting market equilibrium affects the wellbeing of the individual. In this chapter we provide a skeletal summary of the development of the major results in classical and neoclassical economics relevant to the theme of resource allocation. Since the scopes of classical and neoclassical economics are much broader than issues involving resource allocation, this summary is necessarily limited. It is designed to show, within the realm of resource allocation, how classical ideas lead to the development of neoclassical economics, and how the latter, in turn, contribute to the present work on production, entrepreneurship, and profits.

THE CLASSICAL LEGACY

The classical school was inaugurated with the publication of *The Wealth of Nations* by Adam Smith in 1776. Although Smith's forerunners, such as William Petty, Dudley North, Richard Cantillon, and David Hume, had made important advances in studying the operations of the market, the determination of value and interest rate, the role of money, and the importance and the advantages of trade, it was Adam Smith who integrated these fragmented pioneering efforts into a systematic and scientific inquiry. He dealt carefully with all

14

major economic problems of his day. These problems included the psychology of motivation and the functioning of the market, division of labor and the accumulation of capital, the determination of value and the distribution of income, the advantage of trade, the principle of taxation, economic development in Europe, and many more. Unemployment and business cycles were the only topics of importance omitted by Adam Smith since they were not pertinent to his time. *The Wealth of Nations* is truly monumental in scope and content. It serves as a point of departure for all subsequent economic inquiries and sets the agenda according to which flow two centuries of fruitful research on the market economy.

The primary aim of the classical economists was to investigate the source of a nation's wealth and to analyze the long-run consequences of economic development, especially its effect on society's welfare. Adam Smith and his followers believed that the wealth of a nation is identical with its annual produce. Smith identified labor as the source of wealth and then used the famous pin factory example to illustrate how division of labor increases productivity.

In Adam Smith's view, division of labor takes place naturally in a market environment. Trade permits labor to specialize and to exploit the advantage of division of labor. The market is seen not only as a vehicle for enhancing productivity but also as an efficient allocative institution which is best suited for coordinating economic activities and offers the best chance for rapid economic growth. Adam Smith's description of the self-adjusting market process is indisputably the crown jewel of his analysis. The market adjusts automatically through the price mechanism which brings about the production of goods and the distribution of resources. In the short run, prices, wages, profit, and rent are determined in the market by demand and supply. The businessman, motivated by self-interest, allocates resources to where profit is highest; the laborer, also motivated by self-interest, seeks work which offers him the highest wages. These self-interests are held in check by competition (the invisible hand). In the end, profit is reduced to a "normal level" across industries and labor is employed in places where society most appreciates its efforts. Thus the pursuance of self-interest by individuals in a competitive economy leads to a state of equilibrium where all individuals' interests are made consistent.

In order to support these contentions, the classical economist had to construct a body of theories known as the theory of value and the theory of distribution. The theory of value explains how the price of a commodity is determined. Only after the prices of commodities are determined will it become possible to evaluate the extent of economic growth. The theory of distribution is composed of a set of laws that govern the division of the nation's produce among its constituents. It

is on the basis of this division of the nation's produce that the effect of
development is evaluated.

The Theories of Value

Since Adam Smith took labor as the source of wealth, his natural
inclination was toward a labor theory of value. Thus, said Smith, "The
real price of everything, what everything really costs to the man who
wants to acquire it, is the toil and trouble of acquiring it" (Smith,
1937, p. 30).[1] Yet he observed that his labor theory of value conformed
with neither the observed price phenomenon nor the price mechanism
of his market system. The price of a commodity often deviates
markedly from the amount of labor used to produce it, and the market
price of a commodity fluctuates constantly despite the fact that the
labor used in producing it remains the same. This inconsistency also
led him to advocate a theory based upon the cost of production.
Accordingly, he declared that the value of a commodity is determined
by the cost of labor, capital, and land that must be incurred in order to
produce it (Smith, 1937, p. 50). Adam Smith assumed that in any
economy there exist average rates of wages, profits, and rent which are
all deemed to be natural. When a commodity is sold at a price which is
just enough to compensate the worker, the capitalist, and the landlord,
then it is sold at its natural price (Smith, 1937, p. 58). Adam Smith
recognized that in practice a commodity is not always sold at its
natural price. Changes in market demand and supply cause the short-
run market price of a commodity to fluctuate. Such deviations,
however, are temporary. In the long run, through competition, the
market price tends to gravitate to the natural price, which is thought to
be independent of demand forces and is determined solely by the cost
of production.

Among the followers of Smith, David Ricardo and Karl Marx
championed the labor theory of value while Nassau Senior and John
Stuart Mill supported the cost theory of value.

Labor Theory of Value   In order to establish the labor theory of value,
Ricardo and Marx had to overcome some obstacles. First they had to
explain and justify the discrepancies that often exist between the
exchange value and the market price of a commodity, and second they
had to show that land and capital are not factors of production and
therefore do not serve as determinants of value. Ricardo and Marx
sidestepped the first obstacle by accepting Smith's distinction between
the short-run market price and the long-run natural price. Because
Ricardo and Marx were mainly concerned with the long-run tendency
of an economy, they simply acknowledged the existence of the

discrepancy between market and natural prices as a matter of fact and proceeded to show that the natural price of a commodity is indeed determined by the quantity of labor embodied in it.

The kernel of Ricardo's deductive argument used to establish his labor theory of value is his theory of "differential rent." According to Ricardo, rent ceases to exist on the margin of production; thus land ceases to be a cost of production. Only the quantities of labor and capital determine value. Having eliminated land as a factor of production, there was still the task of denying capital any productivity of its own. There were two alternative approaches. The first treated profit, the payment to capital, as equal to the value of labor embodied in the capital, and the second treated profit as an unmerited reward for ownership. Ricardo took the first approach and Marx the second. In Ricardo's view, capital is not a source of value because it represents the embodiment of past labor and thus lacks any productivity of its own. Labor is therefore left as the sole source of value.

Karl Marx attempted to establish the labor theory of value in a different way. He began by observing that the capitalist sells the commodity based upon the "exchange value of labor" but pays laborers only "the use value of labor": a surplus is created. Marx devoted considerable effort to demonstrating that his surplus value doctrine is consistent with the labor theory of value. He started by distinguishing between "constant capital" and "circulating capital" denoted by c and v respectively: c represents the embodiment of labor such as machines and raw materials used up in production; v primarily comprises the wage fund which is used to support the workers. To say that labor alone creates surplus value is to say that v alone is transformed into labor power and thus creates a surplus, denoted by s. Let the exchange value of a commodity be denoted by p, where $p = c + v + s$. Marx defined the rate of surplus by $s/v = s'$ and the organic composition of capital by $c/v = g$. Then, it is evident that $p/v = 1 + g + s'$. To establish the consistency between the surplus value doctrine and the labor theory of value, we need only show that, for any pair of commodities A and B, $p_A/v_A = p_B/v_B$. Marx arrived at this conclusion by observing that labor tends to move from low wage areas to high wage areas, and the producer tends to use production techniques as efficient as those used by his competitors. Consequently $s'_A = s'_B$ and $g_A = g_B$. Hence, $p_A/v_A = p_B/v_B$ is always true.

Although both Ricardo and Marx each managed to offer a labor theory of value, neither approach is wholly successful. The major stumbling block is their inability to explain away the fact that the rate of profit to the producer is dependent upon the capital structure of the enterprise. This dependence casts doubts on the assertion that capital is not productive and labor alone determines value.

Cost Theory of Value   In order to formulate the cost theory of value, we must first identify the factors of production. Only after these factors are known will it become possible to determine the total cost of production of a commodity and hence its value. Most followers of Adam Smith agreed with him that there were three factors of production – labor, land, and capital – and believed that wage, rent, and profit were the components of the cost of production. Since Smith did not justify the selection of labor, land, and capital as the factors of production, the classical economists endeavored to accomplish this task.

The classical economists took it as self-evident that labor was a factor of production. Their discussion about labor centered around the wage fund theory of wages. The wage fund theory stated that the demand for labor depended on the size of the wage fund and the supply on the size of the work force. Therefore wages could not rise (fall) unless there was an increase (decrease) in the aggregate funds set aside to employ labor or a decrease (increase) in the number of workers for hire. No outside influence, such as government policy, could alter this fact.

According to the classical economists, land is endowed by nature, is scarce, and is subject to the law of diminishing returns. They generally accepted Ricardo's law of rent, and treated rent as a return to the scarcity of land. Because industries must compete with one another for the use of a given piece of land, a price – rent – must be paid in order to secure its use. Therefore rent becomes a cost of production.

The classical economists also followed Adam Smith and treated capital as an accumulated stock which is divided into two parts – circulating capital and fixed capital. Unlike Smith, who treated capital as a mere surplus, some classical economists endeavored to show that capital is productive. Nassau Senior advocated that capital was not merely the embodiment of past labor but that it also included natural materials and abstinence. Senior believed that in order to bring capital into existence, it was necessary for someone to abstain from unproductive consumption. Since it was the capitalist who must abstain from current consumption so as to make accumulation and production possible, the capitalist must be "repaid for it by his appropriate remuneration, profit" (Senior, 1965, p. 93). John Stuart Mill adopted this view wholeheartedly and believed that profit comprises three parts – interest, insurance, and wages of superintendence. Profit was a reward for the abstinence, risk and exertions implicit in the employment of capital (Mill, 1976, p. 416).

With the factors of production identified, the cost theory of value advocates concluded that the value of a commodity is determined by the cost of labor, capital, and land that must be incurred in order to produce it.

Theories of Distribution

Classical economists generally followed Adam Smith and believed that a nation's produce was divided among the owners of labor, land, and capital. Even though many of them propounded the labor theory of value, they did not find it inconsistent to have the nation's produce distributed to the three social classes in the form of wages, rent, and profit. This attitude was influenced by the belief that production and distribution were governed by distinct principles.

Specifically, Smith and his followers supplied many theories of wages, of which the wage fund theory enjoyed the greatest popularity. A society was believed to possess a pool of wage fund which was accumulated from the nation's produce and from savings. The demand for labor depended upon the size of the wage fund. At any given moment in time, the average real wage rate was determined by the size of the wage fund and the number of workers in the work force.

Labor, just as any other commodity, had a natural price. "The natural price of labour is that price which is necessary to enable the labourers, one with another, to subsist and to perpetuate their race, without either increase or diminution" (Marx, 1967, p. 93). The market price of labor, however, might rise above or fall below the natural price of labor. If the market price should rise above the natural price, an increase in birth rate and a decrease in mortality rate will cause the population to increase and hence depress real wages. Conversely, if the market price should fall below the natural price, a decline in birth rate and a rise in mortality rate will return the real wage to its natural level.

The classical economists also offered various theories of rent. Adam Smith viewed rent as a case of monopoly pricing of a costless item that exists in a limited quantity. However, most classical economists adhered to the Ricardian theory of differential rent. Ricardo first defined rent as "that portion of the produce of the earth which is paid to the landlord for the use of the original and indestructible power of the soil" (Ricardo, 1951, p. 67). Since this is a typical "scarcity rent" definition made in the tradition of Smith, Ricardo needed to convert it into a differential rent concept. He did this in the following manner. An increase in the population increases the demand for food. Greater demand for food implies that either land of lower quality is brought into cultivation or that a greater amount of capital–labor is applied to the existing land. If it is assumed that marginal land does not pay rent, the first alternative implies that the intramarginal land will yield a surplus which is appropriated by the landlord in the form of an extensive rent. If it is assumed that applying greater capital – labor to a fixed amount of land will lead to diminishing returns on capital – labor, the second alternative implies that an intensive rent will emerge since capital – labor is paid according to their marginal product. Since both extensive and intensive use of land are subject to the law of diminishing returns, in order for the landlord to maximize his rent income the extensive and intensive rents must be equal at equilibrium. Thus, by applying the law of diminishing returns, Ricardo arrived at a concept of differential rent.

In addition, classical economists proposed many theories of profit. The advocates of the labor theory of value naturally viewed profit as a surplus. Recognizing the fact that surplus is not identical with profit, Ricardo separated profit and rent by noting that, since marginal land does not pay rent, surplus on marginal land therefore represents pure profit. In contract, Marx paid little attention to decomposing rent, interest, and profit from the surplus.

The advocates of the cost theory of value, however, regarded profit as a return to a distinct factor of production. Because the capitalist and the entrepreneur were viewed as one and the same, profit was treated as a reward to the capitalist either for abstinence or for his capital investment. From the first point of view profit was equivalent to interest, and from the second point of view it included interest since capital could be borrowed. The disentanglement of interest from profit was never resolved.

Long-run Tendency

The classical economists generally believed that economic development augments both circulating and fixed capital. Increases in circulating capital augment the wages fund. Money wages will rise as a result. This rise in wages invariably encourages the population to multiply. Population growth, however, yields different consequences for different economists.

The optimistic Adam Smith believed that an increase in population also promotes finer division of labor and hence increases productivity. This increase in labor productivity always outstrips the increase in population, thus leaving the laborer a higher standard of living. Moreover, economic development also brings about accumulation in capital stock. Since increasing capital stock intensifies competition among the capitalists, economic development also depresses the rate of profits. Finally, Smith believed that economic development causes the price level to rise (Smith, 1937, p. 250). Since rent is viewed as a differential surplus and a higher rent is the result of a higher price, rent must also increase with economic progress. Economic development thus causes wages and rent to rise and profit to fall.

The pessimistic Ricardo and Marx believed that economic development depressed not only profit but also wages. Ricardo based his analysis on the decreasing marginal productivity of land. Thus growth in population brings less fertile land into cultivation and causes rent and food prices to rise. The rise in food (wage good) prices offsets the rise in money wage: the net effect is to leave the real wages at the subsistence level. Moreover, because money wages and profit are inversely related to each other, an increase in money wages implies a decrease in profit. Consequently, economic development has the effect of increasing rent and money wages, keeping real wages at the subsistence level and forcing profit downward.

Ricardo's long-run analysis thus stands in sharp contrast with the optimistic conclusion reached by Adam Smith. In Ricardo's world, society becomes more antagonistic. The interests of the landlord clash with those of the laborer and the capitalist, and in turn the interests of the laborers and capitalists clash with each other. In addition, Ricardo also holds the view that the internal dynamics of the market cannot sustain continuous economic growth. Since economic development for ever causes an increase in population and rent and a decrease in profit, the profit will eventually become so low that it ceases to provide incentive for the capitalist to work for further growth. The stationary state will emerge. In this state of things, labor lives on subsistence, profit is at a minimum level, and the landlord captures the bulk of the surplus. The economy once more returns to the state it had experienced under feudalism.

Marx arrived at a similar pessimistic conclusion from another angle. He based his long-run analysis of the market economy on contradictions which exist within the capitalist system and on the system's propensity to increase the organic composition of capital over time. Capital and labor are antagonistic because labor is subjected to exploitation by the capitalists who keep wages at the subsistence level. In addition, not only are capital and labor inherently antagonistic, but capitalism is programmed for ultimate self-destruction. The capitalist, in the process of creating surplus value, must increase the use of capital. Marx believed that in the process of economic development there is a tendency to increase the organic composition of capital, that is, the ratio between constant and circulating capital. If it is postulated that the relationship among profit π, surplus s, circulating capital v, and constant capital c is $\pi = s/(c + v)$, and that only circulating capital contributes to surplus, it is evident that economic development entails a falling rate of profit. In addition, in order to sustain growth, the capitalist must sell his product. The ability of the consuming mass to consume is unfortunately limited by their high unemployment and low wages. This insufficient demand causes a further decline in profit. The capitalist, in a quest for surplus, is forced to introduce further capital-intensive methods of production and thus is caught in the long-run internal contradiction existing in the capitalistic system. This vicious circle, instead of leading the economy to the Ricardian stationary state, leads it to a perpetual decline in profit and the "mesmerization of the workmen." In the end, both the exploiter and the exploitee are put in a state of despair. Capitalism gives way to socialism.

These pessimistic views were buffeted by J. S. Mill who felt that the falling rate of profit did not necessarily spell disaster. Because social progress also lowers risks in capital investments, the capitalist will still be interested in investing his money for production. Nonetheless profit rate must reach a lower limit; the continuing decline in profit will eventually lead the economy to a stationary state. Mill's stationary state differs from that of Ricardo in that everything saved through abstinence by the capitalist is employed and every increase in capital is capable of providing additional employment to labor. Through Say's law, the economy will be kept at the full employment level (Mill, 1976, p. 748). As the economy grows, the working class will increase their "intelligence, education and love of independence." These changes in the workers will ultimately restrict population growth to the extent that the workingman's lot will be improved (Mill, 1976, p. 728).

Conclusion

The early aim of the classical economists was to investigate the source of a nation's wealth, the market process, and the long-run consequence of economic development. The later emphasis, however, had shifted to the development of the associated value and distribution theories. The attempts to solve these theoretical problems were by and large unsuccessful. Toward the end of the classical era, the precise nature of the market process remained elusive to the classical economists. In addition, the precise long-run effect of the market economy was also unclear. The classical economists failed to reach a consensus on whether the self-adjusting market is capable of promoting harmony or whether it only leads to a conflict of interests among members of the various social classes. In the realm of value theory, neither the labor theory of value nor the cost theory of value was free from internal contradiction. The advocates of the labor theory of value failed to establish unequivocally that labor is indeed the sole source of value. The champions of the cost theory of value, however, failed to identify and to characterize clearly the factors of production. Moreover, the age-old paradox regarding the "use value" and the "exchange value" remained a phenomenon to be taken for granted rather than explained. The same confusion also existed in the realm of distribution. The classical economists used distinct principles to explain wages, rent, and profit. Wages are determined by the wage fund and the size of the population; rent is either a residual or is determined by the differential fertility of land. Profit is either a residual or a reward to abstinence. Moreover, the relationship between the value theory and the distribution theory was not well understood. They stood as separate bodies of theory.

In short during the twilight years of the classical era, a major building block for a coherent body of economic theory was still missing. The literature leaves us with the impression that there existed only chaos and disorder. Hindsight tells us that the missing block has to do with understanding the role that demand played in determining value and realizing that the values of outputs and inputs are determined by the same principle. Although J. S. Mill had already pointed the way, the burden of developing a coherent theory was passed on to the neoclassical economists.

NEOCLASSICAL SYNTHESIS

The plight of classical economics can be traced to its neglect of the influence of demand on value. However, even during the height of the classical era there were economists who insisted that utility does affect value. The most important contribution on this subject matter was made by J. H. Gossen (1810–1858). His ideas are summarized in what are known as Gossen's laws.

1   The value of any unit of a given quantity of good is appraised by its marginal unit; therefore the value of any individual unit is equal to its marginal utility.
2   In order to maximize utility, an individual must distribute his income among goods so that the last unit of money spent on each good brings him equal satisfaction.

Unfortunately these ideas were offered before their time. Gossen's pioneering efforts received little attention for more than two decades.

During the 1870s, the classical school's grip loosened. Almost simultaneously the suppressed idea burst into the open. William Jevons (1871), Carl Menger (1871), and Leon Walras (1874) independently formulated the theory of exchange value based on the principle of diminishing marginal utility. These developments not only contributed further to the understanding of how utility helps to determine value, but each idea also sowed the seed for further development. Soon the marginal principle was extended to the realm of production, distribution, and welfare economics. These developments took place by way of a series of syntheses. The first synthesis used the marginal principle to determine demand and supply which were then used to establish the proposition that demand and supply jointly determine value. The second synthesis integrated production, value, and distribution theories into a single body of theory under the marginal principle. The recognition of utility's role in determining value also shifted the economist's concerns about welfare from social classes to individuals. The third synthesis revolved around integrating the value–distribution theory with welfare economics. Through these syntheses the intuitive ideas of classical economics were transformed into a coherent body of theory. This body of theory, known as the neoclassical theory, treated economic outcomes as a result of the interrelated network of economic activities based upon the equimarginal maximization principle and verified Smith's conjecture that the market and the price mechanism can indeed allocate resources in an orderly and efficient manner. In this section we first describe the evolution of neoclassical economics and then provide a characterization of the neoclassical theory and assess its accomplishments and shortcomings.

The Evolution of Neoclassical Economics

In this section, we summarize the development of the various syntheses which culminated in the formal establishment of Adam Smith's intuitive proposition: in a self-adjusting market environment, agents guided by their self-interest and checked by competition will not only carry out activities that are consistent with each other but will also promote social welfare.

The First Synthesis: The Marginalist Revolution and the Theory of Value Jevons, Menger, and Walras independently derived the "utility – scarcity theory of value" on the basis of diminishing marginal utility. The utility function was assumed to be cardinally measurable and additive; the marginal utility of a good was a decreasing function of the quantity of that good possessed (scarcity). In this way, Jevons, Menger, and Walras not only developed the concept of diminishing marginal utility by rediscovering Gossen's first law but also were able to solve the age-old "water and diamond paradox." Because the supply of water is so abundant and the supply of diamonds is so limited, the marginal utility derived from water is small and that derived from diamonds is large. Since the value of a commodity is determined by the value of its marginal unit, the value of diamonds exceeds that of water even though the total utility derived from water far exceeds that derived from diamonds. The value of a commodity is therefore jointly determined by utility and scarcity.

In order to yield theoretical importance, this subjective value of the individual must be extended to the market value which relates to price. Jevons and Walras did so by recognizing that the market prices of individual commodities are linked together by the "law of substitution." Through the law of diminishing marginal utility they both concluded that the individual will continue to trade units of a given commodity for units of another as long as the marginal utility per dollar derived from the one good exceeds that of the other. This principle led to the rediscovery of Gossen's second law. Cost of production determines supply, supply (scarcity) determines the final degree of utility, and the final degree of utility determines value.

It is now well known that the utility–scarcity theory of value is incomplete. Just as Smith and his followers had ignored demand and emphasized that value is determined by cost alone, the utility–scarcity advocates were eager to refute the classical theory and had gone so far as to deny that the cost of production had anything to do with value. A complete theory must include both demand and supply influences. In order to reconcile these two viewpoints, the concept of demand and supply schedules had to be developed. Although Cournot had already developed such schedules in a monopoly market setting, it was Marshall who performed this important feat.

Marshall's synthesis was carried out using his well-known "scissors metaphor," which illustrates that both market price and value are determined through the interaction of the appropriate demand and supply forces. Market demand curves are the horizontal sums of individual demand curves which are built up from the individual's marginal utility function by a liberal use of the *ceteris paribus* assumption. Market supply curves are built up from cost curves of representative firms. In the short run, when some productive factor cannot be varied in quantity, market price is determined by short-run supply and demand. In the long run, when all factors are variable, normal price or value is determined by long-run supply and demand. The long run is not a chronological time period but an analytical device – an abstraction. The long-run value is one which would be attained if all adjustments in the system were permitted to work themselves out. Thus, through the period analysis, Marshall ingeniously integrated the marginal methodology and put the marginalists' analytical innovation squarely within the tradition of classical economics.

Despite Marshall's enormous accomplishment, his work was not exempt from further correction and refinement. One of the first of his analyses to fall was his cardinal and additive utility function which stated that the utility of a good depended solely upon the quantity of that good consumed. Through the efforts of Edgeworth (1881), Fisher (1925), Pareto (1971), Slutsky (1965), and Hicks and Allen (1934) it became known that ordinal utility was sufficient to derive the individual's demand curve. In order to derive the demand curve, the consumer is no longer assumed to have a unique utility function but only a preference function. This demand theory, together with its equivalent – the revealed preference demand theory (Samuelson, 1947) – constitutes the present-day classroom treatment of modern demand theory.

The Second Synthesis: Marginal Productivity and the Theory of Distribution The second synthesis is intimately associated with the development of the marginal productivity theory of distribution. Despite the fact that the nature of the allocative process in the product and factor markets is the same, it is something of an enigma that neither Jevons nor Menger nor Walras had developed an explicit theory of distribution based upon the marginal principle. The application of the marginal principle to production and distribution was worked out under the banner of the marginal productivity theory of distribution, associated most closely with John Bates Clark (1889). Clark began his analysis by assuming that the factor proportion in the firm's production function is not fixed but variable. Therefore the contribution of each factor can be separated out on the basis of its marginal productivity. Since the factors of production cannot be used to satisfy consumer's wants directly, the demand for a factor is a derived demand which depends upon the marginal productivity of the factor as well as on the value of the product that the factor helped to produce. The marginal productivity theory of distribution asserts that, in a competitive market environment, each factor of production will tend to receive a return which is determined by and is equal to the value of its marginal product.

It is now well known that the marginal productivity theory of distribution had erred in believing that demand alone determined the price of an input. Again, Marshall is credited with having seen clearly the role played by both demand and supply in determining the input price. The theory of distribution is nothing more than using the demand and supply apparatus to determine the factor prices. Since the prices paid for the use of the factors represent the income to the owners of the factors, the determination of the factor prices also determines how the products are distributed.

The distribution theory based upon the marginal principle cannot be viewed as a viable theory until it is demonstrated that payments to the factors according to their respective marginal productivity would exhaust the product. Although attempts were made at the outset by J. B. Clark (1889, 1891) to show that this was indeed the case, a satisfactory solution was not found until more than four decades later.

The first meaningful attempts to establish the so-called adding-up theorem were offered independently by Wicksell (1901) and Wick-steed (1894, 1910, p. 529). They did so on the assumption that the production function is linearly homogeneous. In this technological environment, factors of production are employed in a fixed propor-tion determined by their market prices; that is, as the factor prices are determined in the market the proportion of their employment in production is determined accordingly. Moreover, under the assumed production technology, the proportion of the factors employed in turn determines the marginal and average productivity of these factors at all scales of operation; that is, regardless of the scale of production the marginal productivity of each factor remains the same. Each factor's contribution to the total output is therefore equal to its marginal productivity times the number of units of that factor employed. The total output is the sum of the contributions of all factors. If payment to the factors of production is determined by the value of the marginal product of each factor, it is evident that, in equilibrium, payment to the factors of production would indeed exhaust the value of the total product.

However, it is evident that the validity of a theory built upon such a narrow foundation cannot be trusted. When production exhibits the property of variable returns to scale, payment to factors according to their respective marginal productivity will in general not exhaust the product but will leave a residual. A residual results because the total output depends not only on each factor's own marginal productivities but also on the interactions among the cooperative factors. If an increase in the employment of one factor also increases the marginal productivity of another, the payment to each factor on the basis of its own marginal productivity will undercompensate its owners. The residual represents the value of the product derived from all these uncompensated cross-effects. Unless the add-up theorem applies to regimes involving more general production functions, the validity of the marginal productivity theory is impaired.

Schneider (1935, pp. 19–21) and Samuelson (1947, p. 86) indepen-dently saw the correct solution to the Wicksell and Wicksteed problem. Schneider and Samuelson observed that Wicksell and Wicksteed had placed undue emphasis on the importance of the production function and on the firm's internal equilibrium condition when considering the problem of distribution, and had neglected the impact of the market forces in determining the equilibrium condition for the firm. Schneider and Samuelson then demonstrated that, even if the production function is not linearly homogeneous, the total product of each firm will indeed be exhausted through interfirm competition and the entry and exit of firms whenever the factors are paid according to their respective marginal productivity and the industry has reached a long-run equilibrium. This is because the commodity price at the long-run industry equilibrium is equal to the firm's long-run marginal and average cost of production.

The establishment of the marginal productivity of distribution not only enabled us to see that the nature of the demand for all factors of production is based upon the same marginal principle, but also made us realize that through the process of imputation the production function serves as a link between product and factor markets and their prices and thus between the theory of value and the theory of distribution. This realization brought about the neoclassical integration of the theories of production, distribution, and value into a single theory based upon the marginal principle. The neoclassical economists did so under the assumption that all agents are motivated by self-interest and act with full knowledge of all relevant information about the market. Given the production function and the supply functions of the factors of production, cost functions can be constructed. Given the production function and the demand functions for the products, the demand functions for the factors of production are determined. The cost functions together with the demand functions for the products determine the prices of the products and the quantity produced. The demand functions for the factors of production together with the supply functions for the factors determine the factor prices and the quantity used. The former belongs to the realm of the theory of production and the theory of value. The latter belongs to the theory of production and the theory of distribution. This integration of the theories of production, distribution, and value constitutes the second neoclassical synthesis.

The Third Synthesis: General Equilibrium and Social Welfare Although partial equilibrium analyses enable us to see how values for inputs and outputs are determined in each market, they have not shown the full power of the market process. In order to demonstrate that the self-adjusting market is capable of rendering the various conflicting interests of the market participants consistent, we must show the process by which the interconnected markets can be brought into equilibrium simultaneously. The need for such an effort was recognized by both Cournot and Marshall; however, it was Walras (1954) who undertook to carry out this task.

Walras constructed a mathematical model to study the nature of a general equilibrium. In this model there are two sets of agents – the consumer and the producer. The consumer maximizes his utility by allocating his income among m commodities, and the producer maximizes his utility by allocating his capital among n factors of production. Walras assumed (a) that both the product and the factor markets are competitive, and (b) that as more is consumed the agent's marginal utility derived from each good decreases. He sought to describe how markets are interrelated and to show that, given the necessary data, a mutually consistent set of prices exists for the m goods and n factors which will bring each and every market into equilibrium simultaneously.

The Walrasian model consisted of three sets of structural equations and a set of auxiliary equations. The structural equations include (a) the product demand equations, each of which states that the quantity of the good demanded is a function of the prices of all m goods and n factors in the economy, (b) the factor supply equations, each of which states that the quantity of the factor supplied is a function of the prices of all m goods and n factors in the economy, and (c) the production function, which is represented by an $n \times m$ fixed production coefficient. The structure equations depict the nature of the mutual dependence among all markets in the economy. Each household enters into the market twice, once as a consumer of the finished product and once as a supplier of factors of production. Likewise, each producer enters into the market twice, once as a buyer of inputs and once as a supplier of outputs. The auxiliary equations, however, state the conditions that exist at equilibrium – the price of a commodity is equal to the average cost of producing the commodity.

Since Walras was interested only in determining the relative prices among the commodities and the factors, he arbitrarily selected the price of one good as the numeraire. Therefore there exist $2m + 2n - 1$ variables, representing m quantities and $m - 1$ prices of the commodities, n quantities, and n prices of the factors. Walras also observed that the total amount earned by the households in supplying the factors must always be equal to the total outlay for consumer goods (the Walras law); therefore there is one redundant equation. Walras assumed that the remaining $2m + 2n - 1$ equations are independent and concluded that a unique solution exists for the prices and quantities of the m goods and n factors. Note that, because the total demand and total supply of a factor is equal, this equilibrium represents a full employment equilibrium.

Walras's pioneering work needed refinement. To begin with, we know that counting the number of equations and unknowns is not sufficient to guarantee the existence of a general equilibrium. In addition, since Walras's equilibrium was obtained with very special utility and production functions, it was necessary to investigate the existence of such an equilibrium under more general functional forms. Sophisticated general equilibrium models, incorporating the modern demand and production theories, were first developed in the 1940s by Wald and von Neumann, and were later perfected in the 1950s by Arrow, Debreu, and McKenzie. The Arrow–Debreu–McKenzie economy is a static economy with complete certainty: it comprises two sets of agents – the consumers and the firms. The consumer is endowed with preferences that obey the axioms of modern utility theory.[2] The firm is owned by capitalist shareholders; it employs a general production technology and operates under nonincreasing returns to scale. Assume that (a) each consumer is endowed with a sufficient amount of tradeable commodities which insure him at least a subsistence standard of living, (b) externality and indivisibility are abent in the economic system, and (c) the functional relations in the economy satisfy certain mathematical conditions needed to guarantee that the agents can carry out their maximization programs. The general equilibrium theory shows that the agents in a competitive market environment, each acting individualistically in pursuing their self-interest, can indeed bring about a mutually consistent equilibrium. A competitive equilibrium consists of a set of prices, production allocation, and consumption allocation such that (a) each consumer maximizes his utility at these prices subject to the income constraint implied by these prices, his initial endowment, and his profit shares, and (b) each firm chooses from its production set a production plan which maximizes profits. In addition, aggregate consumption is feasible in that it does not exceed the sum of the outputs produced and the initial endowments. The existence of such an equilibrium assures us that the competitive economy is not a logically inconsistent system.

Because the consumer's life spans more than one period and the production of a good invariably takes several periods to complete, economic agents are forced to plan for their future. Consequently, each agent's decision problem is multiperiod in nature. The fate of his future not only depends on his own action but also is shaped by circumstances beyond his knowledge and control; decisions involving the future are therefore necessarily made under uncertainty. In the light of this consideration the static certainty models of Arrow, Debreu, and Mckenzie appear to be inadequate. However, it turns out that neither expanding the decision horizon to more than one period nor recognizing the presence of uncertainty in the marketplace will invalidate the conclusion reached in the models of Arrow (1971c, chapter 4), Debreu (1959, chapter 5), and McKenzie (1959) if the contingent market is complete. Formally, a complete contingent market is one where the number of independent securities is equal to the number of states of nature.

Under the more general complete market environment, a commodity is described by its physical characteristics, the date at which it is available, and the particular state of nature that must be realized in order for the delivery of the commodity to take place. Let there be Q goods, T periods, and S states of nature. We now describe a commodity by a triplet (q,t,s) where $q = 1,\ldots, Q$, $t = 1,\ldots, T$, and $s = 1,\ldots, S$. With each (q,t,s) is associated a price p_{qts} which is nothing more than a contractual price to the producer stipulating that a unit of good q will be delivered to the buyer in period t if the state s is obtained. If s does not occur in period t nothing is delivered to the buyer. However, the price P_{qts} must always be paid by the purchaser in order to secure a guarantee of delivery at time t if state s occurs. Suppose that all contingency markets exist and that the contingent commodity prices are determined competitively in the marketplace. All decisions concerning current and future consumption and production can be made at once. The consumer will choose an optimal consumption portfolio for all periods in his decision horizon. The firm in this market environment now faces a deterministic price for its product in each period. The price of its product in a given period is equal to the market contingent prices of its product in that period summed over all states of nature. Based on these deterministic prices that the firm faces in all periods, it chooses an optimal rate of output for each period. The presence of a complete set of contingent markets thus implies that the mathematical structure of the general equilibrium problem for a competitive economy is the same whether uncertainties are present or absent. The existence of a general equilibrium is therefore guaranteed by the Arrow–Debreu–McKenzie solution concepts.

Having shown that a general equilibrium exists in a competitive economy, we are satisfied that the self-adjusting market with a host of agents each acting individualistically to pursue his own interests can, through competition, bring about a mutually consistent outcome. In other words, at the going market prices each buyer of a commodity has bought all that he wants to buy and each seller of a commodity has sold all that he wants to sell. In this way, the self-interests of all agents are reconciled with each other.

Although markets have yielded a mutually consistent outcome to the agents, it remains to be seen whether this outcome is socially optimal. In order to judge how socially desirable a given state of the economy is, it is necessary to construct a social ranking over any set of the states of the economy. Since the 1870s, economists have abandoned the notion that the purpose of the economy is to increase the nation's wealth and have given up the concern of the relative wellbeing of the various social classes. Instead, they have embraced the notion that the purpose of the economy is to enhance the welfare of the consumer. Accordingly, the measurement of the desirability of any economic action is based upon its consequence as reflected in the preferences of the individuals that make up the society. Under this view, there are no "social goods" over and above the "individual goods" which affect the individual's preference rankings. Preference rankings over the states held by consumers alone are used as primary data in constructing the social ranking.

In this ethical framework, the individual would evaluate the state of the economy on the basis of how it affects his own self-interest. First of all, he would not want the scarce social resources to be wasted. Second, he would want the economy to produce goods and services that he likes and then allocate as many of these goods and services to him as possible. In other words, the individual's welfare depends first on the manner in which the scarce resources are employed and second on the way in which society's outputs are distributed.

Because society is composed of many individuals, it is inevitable that their interests clash. The problem in establishing a social ranking must thus center around the issue of how the interests of the various individuals are compared and aggregated. The establishment of a social ranking depends crucially on the nature of the utility functions. To put it another way, since the 1870s welfare judgements have been based on some form of utilitarianism. In this setup any social ranking will depend crucially upon the utility structure that governs the individual choices and the utility structure used to judge the optimality of the market outcomes. The development of welfare economics can be divided into three stages which will be referred to as old welfare economics, new welfare economics, and recent developments.

The earlier writers on welfare economics accepted the utility structures of Jevons, Menger, and Walras, and built their welfare theory on three pillars: (a) cardinal measurement of utility, (b) diminishing marginal utility, and (c) interpersonal comparisons of utility. Their analysis culminated in the work of the Cambridge School of economists – Marshall, Pigou, and Kahn. The Cambridge School reached the conclusion that perfect competition leads to optimal production and exchange. Since individuals' utilities are comparable, the total social welfare is found by adding together the utilities of all individuals in the society. Assume that the marginal utility of income is similar for all individuals. Then the production and exchange optimum leads to maximum welfare of the society if the distribution of income is relatively even. Based upon this analysis, the Cambridge economists advocated equal distribution of income as a means of achieving maximum social welfare.

Since the introduction of the ordinal utility theory, most economists have been skeptical about accepting interpersonal comparisons of utility. This skepticism leads to the investigation of social ranking consistent with the ordinal utility principle. Because the consumer theory postulates that a well-behaved preference ranking for the individual satisfies completeness, transitivity, and reflexiveness, efforts have been made to establish a social ranking of the states of the economy satisfying these same properties.

One of the first attempts to construct a social ranking without reliance on interpersonal comparisons of utilities was made by Alfredo Pareto (1971). Pareto observed that, even though one is reluctant to engage in interpersonal comparisons of utility, one may nonetheless still make social welfare judgements whenever unanimity exists in evaluating the alternative states of the economy. According to Pareto, a state of the economy is said to be dominated if there exists another feasible state preferred by all members of the society. Using this notion of dominance, a notion of optimality can be defined. Any state of the economy is said to be Pareto optimal if it is not dominated by any other feasible state of the economy.

When individuals' preferences conflict within a society, it is important to observe that the Pareto optimum is not unique. We typically find that many states in a set of feasible states of the economy are Pareto optimal. Moreover, each Pareto optimal position is associated with a specific distribution of income. Consequently, to say that a state of the economy is Pareto optimal is not to make a very strong statement. In fact, when we merely rely on Pareto optimality, we have abandoned any judgement on the distribution of income. In this sense, Pareto optimality is merely an efficiency principle. If the economy is not in a Pareto-optimal state, then there exists an alternative state which is judged by all individuals to be superior to the current state. Clearly, it is not efficient to be in the current state where resources are being wasted. As an efficient principle, Pareto optimality is a necessary but not a sufficient condition for welfare maximization. Since welfare economics deals with social optimality, it must have something to say about equity. Before we turn our attention to the question of equity, we will first examine the relationship between general competitve equilibrium and Pareto optimality.

It has been shown by Arrow (1951) that there exists a close relationship between competitive equilibrium and Pareto optimality. This relationship is stated formally by the following pair of theorems.

1   Every competitive equilibrium yields a Pareto-optimal state.
2   Every Pareto-optimal state can be achieved as a competitive equilibrium provided that the initial endowments are appropriately distributed.

Since Pareto optimality does not imply social optimality, the first theorem does not imply that the competitive economy will resolve into a socially optimal and ethically just state. The modern general equilibrium analysis merely provides a rigorous statement on the competitive market's ability to allocate resources efficiently. There is nothing in the competitive process that could be relied upon to guarantee distributive justice.

Although the competitive economy does not automatically lead to an ideal social optimum, nonetheless it is not incompatible with distributive justice. The second theorem on welfare economics implies that the issues concerning efficiency and equity can be dealt with separately. Since any distribution deemed to be equitable can always be achieved by a lump-sum transfer of initial wealth, the theorem suggests that in order to achieve equity without loss of efficiency the preferred strategy is to adjust the initial endowment instead of tampering with the market process. In this way, even though the market system cannot by itself guarantee an outcome that is both efficient and equitable, with minimum outside interference on endowments the market can nonetheless achieve an efficient outcome consistent with the prescribed equity norm.

Because the Pareto criterion is incapable of making equity judgements, economists have endeavored to extend the scope of the Pareto ranking to include distributive considerations. The social welfare function was constructed in an attempt to find a unique social optimum. A social welfare function maps individuals' preference rankings into a social ranking. It was hoped that by selecting the appropriate social welfare function, a unique social optimum could be obtained. However, it was discovered that a whole set of social rankings could be constructed, each differing in the way in which weights are assigned to the individual preferences. Assigning weights to the individual's preference is tantamount to engaging in interpersonal comparisons of utility. Since interpersonal comparisons of utility are prohibited under the ordinal utility framework, the social welfare function advocates have failed to secure a desired unique social welfare maximum.

The existence of such a social welfare function was shown in principle to be impossible by Arrow (1963a). He proved that, given the individuals' preference profiles and excluding dictatorial rules and rules based on interpersonal comparisons of utility, there is no method which can be relied upon to always derive a consistent ranking of states having the properties of completeness, transitivity, reflexiveness, and "independence of irrelevant alternatives."[3] The proposition that universal social rankings which always meet the above widely acceptable rules are impossible is shared by most welfare economists, despite some criticisms of the axiom of "independence of irrelevant alternatives."

As a result of Arrow's investigation, the attempt to construct complete rankings of all possible social states has been abandoned. Welfare economists have shifted their attention to two fronts. At first, they proposed social choice theories in an attempt to derive sufficiency criteria which would enable society to choose among specific alternative policies, and made efforts to construct partial orderings with the effect of extending the scope of the Pareto ranking. This effort has been associated with the compensation principle originally proposed by Kaldor (1939) and Hicks (1939). For a given change in policy, if the gainers can afford to make lump-sum compensations to the losers in a way which will leave everybody better off, then this change represents a Pareto improvement. Since the willingness to make and to accept a certain amount of payment is dependent upon the comparison of the marginal utilities of income of the gainer and the loser at a specific initial distribution of income, the compensation principle is found not to be free from interpersonal comparisons of utility.

This lack of success leads the economist to cast doubt on the policy relevance of the Pareto principle. In the first place, it has been realized that the Pareto principle itself is not devoid of value judgement. In applying the Pareto criterion, the consumers' tastes are commonly assumed to be independently determined. Suppose instead that they are mutually dependent. Then changes which will make all individuals better off take on a different meaning. "Better off" can now be measured in "absolute terms" or in "relative terms." The choice of how "better off" is to be measured is, of course, a value judgement. Furthermore, doubts are also cast on the validity of the second welfare theorem. In practice it is not possible to bring about an optimal distribution of income through lump-sum transfers. The reason is that the market fails to supply the information necessary to carry out such transfers. We have seen earlier that the market cannot by itself bring about an equitable distribution of income. An agent outside the market system is needed to accomplish this goal. Yet, in order to make social welfare maximum decisions, the agent needs information concerning all individuals' ability, tastes, etc. However, this information is known only to the individuals themselves. If the individual understands the principle that governs the lump-sum transfer scheme, whenever this information tends to go against his own interests concerning his initial endowment of resources, he would have the incentive to act strategically by concealing or distorting the information needed to implement the optimal transfer. Only when mechanisms used to implement a policy are "incentive compatible" will the market be immune to individuals who manipulate in their own favor.[4]

The presence of the incentive problem yields two important implications. First, it is no longer possible to separate the issues concerning efficiency and equity. Second, the economy faces not only the customary resource constraints but also incentive constraints. Pareto efficiency ceases to be a necessary condition for welfare maximization. This realization forces us to accept the reality that policy considerations necessarily involve interpersonal comparisons of utility.

Recognizing that making interpersonal comparisons of utility is inevitable, economists have shifted their efforts to investigating ways of incorporating interpersonal comparisons of utility into the ordinal utility framework. This recent development is associated with Sen (1970), d'Aspremont and Gevers (1977), and Hammond (1979), and is surveyed by Arrow (1977) and Hammond (1985). The new theory specifies utility functions which allow the profiles of the individual utility functions to be compared in the ordinal sense and hence make sense of the statement "the individual i in state x is better off than the individual j in state y." With this ordinal comparison, it becomes possible to integrate interpersonal comparisons of utility into the formal social choice framework introduced by Arrow. Moreover, if the interpersonal comparisons reflect certain ethical principles, the choice based upon this social welfare function will also be equitable. Since the development of the literature is still in its early stage, we must wait to discover the full implication of this new perspective on welfare economics.

CHARACTERISTICS OF NEOCLASSICAL ECONOMICS

In an attempt to integrate production, value, and distribution into a single analytical framework and to examine the welfare consequences of the competitive economy, the neoclassical economists have shifted their attention from production to include demand and from the welfare of the state to that of the individuals. With the initial endowment of resources assumed as given, they investigate the market process and examine the nature of the market equilibrium. From a set of equilibrium conditions, these economists deduce how individuals' interests are served by the market. The essence of the neoclassical economic theory can be summarized as follows.

The consumer and the firm are taken as two basic decision units in the economy. Because of the neoclassical economist's utilitarian orientation, the consumers are given center stage. They own both the resources and the firms, supply all inputs required for production, receive all dividends distributed by the firm, and consume all the final goods and services produced. The firm, in contrast, is a simple analytical construct – a dimensionless production unit. Its existence is taken for granted. In a complete market environment, all agents are assumed to behave noncooperatively with each other and to pursue their own objectives in the marketplace: the consumer acts to maximize his utility subject to a budget constraint and the firm its profit. In order to maximize profit, each factor of production is employed to the extent that its marginal productivity is equal to its market price. Thus, guided exclusively by prices both within and without the firm, resources are allocated in an impersonal market environment. A state of full employment equilibrium will emerge and, in addition, this equilibrium is Pareto optimal.

It is also evident from this statement that the neoclassical economists have abandoned the concerns of the wealth-creating process, instead centering their attention on the conditions required for the efficient allocation of existing resources. Shifts in emphasis, such as those mentioned above, inevitably give neoclassical economics a certain special character. In this section, we examine some of these characteristics and assess their implications.

Firms Are Owned by Capitalists

Generally, there are two ways through which the production and distribution of goods and services can be carried out. First, the owners of all the relevant factors can act cooperatively to select, through bargaining, a production policy and a distributive rule. In this case, the factor services are allocated collectively by the resource owners using a nonmarket means. Second, some capitalists can organize the firm and become its owners. The capitalist owners then carry out a production policy by hiring the required factors of production and claim the residual.

Under the collective ownership regime (i.e. the bargaining regime), the production policy and the distributive rule do not reflect solely the marginal productivities of the factors; the marginal productivity of each factor merely serves as a reference point for bargaining. An agent's bargaining power, in general, exceeds the amount warranted by the factor's marginal productivity if the resources he owns have attractive opportunities to be employed elsewhere. In addition, in a bargaining environment, a resource owner not only bargains for his income derived from production, but also bargains for other non-pecuniary benefits which are made possible through a coalitional arrangement. Because each agent strives to maximize his utility through the formation of a firm, the resulting production policy and distributive rule reflect the utilities of all the cooperative agents. These outcomes are "coalitional specific" and can only be determined in a subjective manner.[5]

The allocative outcome under the capitalist owner-managed regime is totally different. Under the condition of certainty or in a complete market setting under uncertainty, each owner's interest can best be served by maximizing the firm's residual. Regardless of the composition of the owners' utility functions, an increase in the size of the firm's residual increases the value of the firm which, in turn, increases each shareholder's income and thus his utility. The owners, in order to maximize the firm's residual, will hire each factor to the point where the market price of the factor is equal to its marginal productivity.

When all factor markets are present and are perfect, the bargaining solution cannot be sustained. This proposition can be demonstrated in the following manner. When all markets are present, all goods and services, including the firm's shares, can be exchanged in the market-place. In the presence of a perfect capital market there exists an opportunity for any member of the collectively managed firm to sell his share of the firm. The market price of the firm's share reflects the current net surplus of the firm, while the maximum price of the firm's share depends on the potential net surplus of the firm. If the present members of the collectively managed firm consume perquisites, the perquisites cause the payment to members to be different from their respective marginal productivity. This, in turn, causes the firm's surplus to be lower than the possible maximum determined by the rule of employing factors according to their marginal productivity. The surplus value yielded by the firm is therefore lower than its potential. The potential owner of the firm would be willing to pay more for the firm's share than its current market value because he can increase the surplus of the firm by hiring factors of production in the marketplace and paying them according to their marginal productivity, thus yielding a greater surplus and a financial gain. Competition will ensure that the firm's ownership will change hands. The objective of the new share owners will be directed to increasing the net surplus of the firm.

It is now evident that whenever all factors of production are traded in competitive markets where certainty or complete contingent market prevails, the firm will ultimately be managed by the capitalist owners. Since the firm has many capitalist owners, this form of organization is viable only if all owners always agree on a single production policy. We will demonstrate that this indeed is the case.

In order to facilitate this task, we follow the literature by using a special case of the Arrow–Debreu model which we presented in the previous section. The basic ingredients of this model are given below.

The economy comprises I consumers and J firms, indexed respectively by $i = 1, \ldots, I$ and $j = 1, \ldots, J$. Their decision horizon involves two periods, the present and the future, indexed by 0 and 1. The present is known while the future is uncertain. However, there are a finite number of states of nature in the future, indexed by $s = 1, \ldots, S$.

Associated with each consumer is a consumption plan represented by an $(S+1)$-dimensional vector $x^i = (x_0^i, x_1^i, \ldots, x_S^i,)$, where x_0^i denotes his current consumption and x_s^i denotes his future consumption in state s. Consumer i's preferences are represented by a utility function $u^i(x^i)$ which reflects his time preferences, probability beliefs, and attitudes toward risk. Consumer i is endowed with an $(S+1)$-

dimensional vector of the good denoted by $w^i = (w_0^i, w_1^i, \ldots, w_S^i)$ and a J-dimensional vector of ownership shares denoted by $\bar{\theta}^i = (\bar{\theta}^{i1}, \ldots, \bar{\theta}^{ij})$, where $\bar{\theta}^{ij} \geq 0$ for all i and j and $\Sigma_i \bar{\theta}^{ij} = 1$ for all j. The consumer's problem is to choose the consumption plan which maximizes his utility subject to his budget constraints, which we will identify in each market situation.

Similarly, associated with each firm j is a production plan represented by an $(S+1)$-dimensional vector $\mathbf{y}^j = (y_0^j, y_1^j, \ldots, y_S^j)$, where y_0^j denotes the present input committed by the firm and y_s^j represents the output realized by the firm in state s. Let the convex set Y^j represent the technologically feasible productions of firm j. The firm's problem is to choose a production plan $\mathbf{y}^j$ in Y^j which maximizes its profit to be defined in each market situation.

Generally the agent's preferences, endowments, and incomes are different in different periods and in different states of nature. These differences force the agent to choose his consumption in each period and state on the basis of the relevant budget constraint. The resulting consumption pattern for the agent can hardly be deemed optimal. In order to achieve an optimal consumption program, the agent needs to shift his resources between periods and states so as to align his resources with his preferences. There are many financial instruments that the agent can employ in order to carry out the intertemporal and interstate arbitrage. Since our present interest is to examine the issues associated with owners' choice of a production policy, we will center our attention on showing how the presence of a complete set of stock markets enables the shareholders to trade shares and thus reach a unanimous production policy. Here, with one commodity universe, a set of stock markets is said to be complete if the number of independent stocks is equal to the number of states of nature.

In the neoclassical economy, consumers own the firm. Because the firm's profit is state dependent, the consumer's dividend income is also state dependent. In general, the consumer's initial endowment of shares and his income stream do not provide the consumer with the most desirable consumption pattern. In an economy with stock markets, the consumer will trade ownership shares and reallocate his resources between periods and states. Since there is a complete set of security markets, the consumer is able to reallocate his resources freely between periods and states and then choose a portfolio of ownership shares which enables him to maximize his utility subject to the overall resource constraint.

In order to see how the consumer arrives at his consumption–investment decision, let us first denote ρ_s^i as consumer i's marginal rate of substitution between his current consumption and his consumption in state s. ρ_s^i can also be interpreted as the implicit contingent claims price which consumer i is willing to pay for a unit of income to be delivered if and only if the state s occurs. Let $\pi_s^j (y_s^j)$ denote firm j's profit in state s when its output is y_s^j, and let P^j denote the market value of firm j. It is well established in the literature that, given $\mathbf{y}^j = (y_0^j, y_1^j, \ldots, y_S^j)$ and $P_j, j = 1, \ldots, J$, consumer i's optimal portfolio satisfies the condition

$$\Sigma_s \, \pi_s^j (y_s^j) \, \rho_s^i = P_j \qquad j = 1, \ldots, J$$

This condition states that, given the market value of the firms and their state distribution of profits, consumer i will select his portfolio of ownership shares in such a way that the weighted sum of the profits derived from the firm in each state of nature is equal to the market value of that firm. The weights used are consumer i's own implicit contingent claims prices.

From the firm's point of view, the above equilibrium condition also implies that the firm's market value depends on the individual consumer's implicit contingent claims prices. Thus the firm's production decision must be guided by these prices. Since there are I consumers, the question is whose implicit prices the firm should use in order to evaluate its market value. Fortunately, when a complete set of stock markets exists, the implicit price in each state of nature is the same for all consumers. The reason is simple. Let the firms' production plans $(y^1, \ldots, y^J)$ and their state distribution of profits $(\pi^1, \ldots, \pi^J)$ be given. Let firms' market values be determined in the stock market. The consumer, as described earlier, will select his optimal portfolio to satisfy the relationship

$$\Sigma_s \, \pi_s^j (y_s^j) \, \rho_s^i = P_j \qquad j = 1, \ldots, J$$

Since there is a complete set of stocks, $S = J$. This implies that the state distribution of profits $(\pi_1^1, \ldots, \pi_1^J), \ldots, (\pi_S^1, \ldots, \pi_S^J)$ for the firms is linearly independent. Based upon a well-known theorem in algebra, we can conclude that $\rho_s^i = \rho_s$ for all i.[6] In other words, given the firms' production plans and their market prices, at equilibrium all consumers have the same implicit contingent claims price in each state of nature. It is therefore immaterial whose implicit prices are used to guide the firm's production decision.

Another issue must be resolved before the firm can legitimately use the existing implicit contingent claims prices to guide its production policy. This issue stems from the fact that the consumer's implicit contingent claims prices depend on the aggregate market output level. If a change in the firm's output level, through its effect on the market output level, also changes the implicit contingent claims prices, these prices cannot be trusted to guide the firm's production policy. In a competitive market environment, however, each firm perceives that its own output constitutes only an insignificant fraction of the total market output and a change in its production policy will have an imperceptible effect on the prevailing implicit contingent claims prices. Consequently, each firm will take the prevailing implicit contingent claims prices as given and select an output policy which maximizes its market value.

In short, we see that the effect of arbitrage through the complete set of stock markets is the emergence of a complete set of contingent claims prices. These prices will guide the consumer to reallocate his income among periods and states so that his expected utility is maximized subject to an overall budget constraint. These same contingent claims prices also enable the firm to convert its state distribution of profits into a well-defined aggregate level and to guide the choice of a profit-maximizing production plan. Because the firm is owned by the consumers, any firm which is committed to a profit-maximizing production policy will provide each of its shareholders with a maximum income which, in turn, will enable the consumer to attain the highest utility. In the end, all utility-maximizing consumers–shareholders will agree unanimously with the firm's production plan. This unanimity among shareholders also signifies that the owner-managed firm is indeed a viable production organization.

Market Alone Allocates Resource

Although owners share the management of the firm, neoclassical economics assigns no allocative role to either the owner–entrepreneur or the firm.

In order to establish the validity of this proposition, we need only show that at equilibrium all prices, including returns to the owners and organizers of the firm, are determined objectively by the market. We have already demonstrated in the last section that in a competitive economy the quantity and price of each factor employed and each product produced as well as the optimal size of each production unit are determined impersonally by the market forces which reflect the consumer's tastes, the prevailing technology, and the resource endowments of the economy. In order to establish the desired proposition, we need only show that even the returns to the owners of the firms are determined by the markets. This statement is trivially true for the constant-return industries where returns to the owners are identically equal to zero. We now center our attention on examining an economy including increasing-cost industries.

Assume that some economies of scale in production exist. The presence of increasing-cost industries implies that the opportunity to organize firms is limited by the size of the market (Stigler, 1951, pp. 185–93). Once the marginal firm is organized, it prevents the others from doing the same. This is why the organizers of the firm are often referred to as promotional entrepreneurs. The promotional entrepreneurial role, however, is short lived. It vanishes from the market scene as soon as the promoters, through capitalization of the firm, capture the promoter's profit.

The promoter's profit is determined in the capital market. Through the entry and exit of firms, the market arrives at an optimal number of firms and reaches a long-run equilibrium. At the long-run equilibrium the marginal firm receives no surplus while the intramarginal firm receives a quasi-rent. Given market demand, the quasi-rent for each firm is determined by the production technology and the distribution of the scarce resources (Marshall, 1953, pp 622–3).

The residual, which is distributed to the owners, includes two components: the first represents the partial (current) recovery of the rent which was paid out to the firm's organizers, and the second is the interest payment to the owners' investment. Since the amount of rent is determined at the margin through the entry and exit of firms, the more efficient firm will command a higher rent. At equilibrium the rent earned by the firm must be treated as a cost of production. Consequently, wages, interest payments, and rent together exhaust the value of the product. All factors of production are then employed in accordance with their marginal productivity (Samuelson, 1957, p. 894). This is a typical result for a Marshallian firm.

Because equilibrium occurs instantaneously in a perfect market where certainty (or complete contingent markets) prevails, the present value of each firm's quasi-rent stream is known as soon as the firm is organized. Since the capital market is also perfect, the capitalized value of each firm is also known at once. The promoter can thus convert the firm's quasi-rent stream into present wealth, known as the promoter's profit. Once this conversion has taken place, quasi-rent becomes a cost item in the same way that wages and interest payments are cost items. The new shareholders will now receive a payment equivalent to that of an interest payment. Since all prices, including that of the promotional entrepreneur's return, are determined in the market, production policy is determined once more by the objective rule – each factor is employed to the point where the price of the factor is equal to its marginal productivity. Thus the presence of the organizers in no way affects the allocation of society's resources. The organizers simply perform no allocative role.

Thus, under the market environment assumed, the market forces interact in an impersonal manner to determine both the employment of inputs and the distribution of the products in accordance with the marginal principle. Because markets are competitive and impersonal, the owner of each factor is certain that, through the market, his resources can earn a return commensurate with their worth. Therefore competition will force all factors of production to be exchanged in the market. In addition, competition will also dissolve any collusive arrangement among the agents and will force them to act individualistically. Consequently, no nonmarket special agent is needed to control the production process. Furthermore, the firm does not possess separate internal decision rules; it makes no independent contribution to the market outcome. Thus the firm cannot be viewed as an alternative to market coordination in production but merely as an extension of the market (Cyert and Hedrick, 1972, pp. 398–9). Markets alone allocate resources.

Economy without Endogenous Growth

The neoclassical economy lacks a mechanism for generating endogenous changes. Therefore it is not surprising that we cannot deduce from neoclassical economic theory "laws of change of the capitalist economy" similar to those derived by the classical economists. In the neoclassical framework, any such changes must originate from a source outside the market system. Given any exogenous shock, neoclassical economics describes how the economy adjusts to a new equilibrium. If the exogenous change should persist over time, these changes will induce a growth phenomenon. Careful inspection of the neoclassical growth theories invariably reveals that these growths are driven not by factors generated from the internal dynamics of the market system but rather by changes originating outside the system. In what follows, we use two growth models to illustrate this point.

The first model is due to Morishima (1977, chapter 6) who constructed a Walrasian growth model by extending Walras's one-stage model to a two-stage temporary equilibrium model[7] involving today and tomorrow. He showed that a temporary equilibrium exists at each point in time and that the sequence of these equilibria traces out a path which can ultimately be used to construct a Walrasian theory of motion of the capitalist society (Morishima, 1977, p. 7).

Morishima's temporary equilibrium model also consists of a set of structural equations (inequalities) and a set of auxiliary equations (inequalities). The major difference between this model and the one-stage Walrasian general equilibrium model is the presence of variables and relationships that link the two periods. The structural equations include the following:

1 the matrices of the production coefficients and the matrices of the inventory coefficients;

2   the demand functions for the commodities which include consumption goods, capital goods, capital services for production, land and labor, inventories for consumption goods, inventories for capital goods, and bonds (the demand for each of these commodities is assumed to be a function of the prices of the consumption goods, the prices of the inventory services of the consumption goods, the prices of land and labor, the bond price, and the full employment national income);

3   the price and cost relations for consumption and capital goods such that the total profit is not negative.

4   the Walras law, that is, the total sum of the values of all excess demands in the economy equals zero.

Assume that the endowments of land and labor, the stocks of capital goods for production, and the stocks of consumption goods and capital goods for inventory purposes are given. At the beginning of the first period, the market determines, by carrying out *tâtonnement*, the equilibrium values of the prices of the commodities, the interest rate, the quantities of consumption goods and capital goods produced, and the amount of investments in terms of the new capital goods installed and inventories of the consumption goods and capital goods accumulated. In the state of equilibrium, all resources are fully employed and the full employment level of national income is realized.

Assume that the temporary equilibrium is "strongly stable" in each period, that is, the fluctuations of the values of the variables during the process of arriving at the equilibrium do not affect the equilibrium values. Then the state of the economy over time can be described by a sequence of temporary equilibria. Since the investment in consumption goods and capital goods made in one period becomes the stock of these goods in the next period and there is a natural growth of labor forces over time, the economy's initial endowments and accumulated stocks change over time. With new endowments and accumulated stocks, the economy carries out the *tâtonnement* in the second period and will arrive at a new temporary equilibrium in that period. Because the endowments in land and labor and the quantity of the accumulated stocks at the beginning of the second period differ from those at the beginning of the first period, the temporary equilibrium established in the second period is necessarily different from that established in the first period. In this manner the economy moves forward from one period to another.

Based upon this line of thinking and the implicit assumption that the population grows over time, Morishima presents Walras's conjecture which states that as the economy progresses if the respective quantities of a given type of land-service (T) required for the manufacture of single units of (A), (B) , (C), (D)...(K), (K'), (K'').... were invariably fixed, then the multiplication of final products and new capital goods would be absolutely limited by the existing quantity Q_t of this type of land. In general it is possible to employ smaller and smaller quantities of land-services per unit of output of consumers' goods and new capital goods provided that larger and larger quantities of the services of capital goods proper are used. Whence the possibility of indefinite progress.... The indefinite multiplication of products can only take place to the extent that capital-services can be substituted more and more for land-services though never wholly replacing them (Walras, 1954, pp. 382–3).

In production entrepreneurs will pay higher rents, but they will employ less land-services in the manufacture of their products. They will pay lower interest charges, but they will employ more capital-services. Thus costs of production will remain approximately the same as they were before and will be equal, or very nearly equal, to selling prices.

The land-owners, workers and capitalists, in their role as consumers, will sell less land-services, but they will sell them more dearly. They will sell more capital-services, but they will sell them less dearly. Thus they will have nearly the same income as before, and they will, on the whole, be able to buy at least the same quantity of the same products at approximately the same selling prices which will continue to be equal, more or less, to the costs of production....

Based upon these arguments, Walras proposed the following two laws. First: "In a progressive economy, the price of labour (wages) remaining substantially unchanged, the price of land-services (rent) will rise appreciably and the price of capital-services (the interest charge) will fall appreciably." Secondly: Because the prices of capital services fall while the prices of capital goods, equal to their cost of production remain almost constant, "in a progressive economy the rate of net income [hence, the rate of profit] will fall appreciably" (Walras, 1954, pp. 390–1). (Morishima, 1977, pp. 97–9)

Thus, in this manner, Walras arrived at a law of motion for the capitalist economy similar in spirit to those arrived at by the classical economists. There is a fundamental difference, however, in the source of energy that fuels the changes in these economies. In the classical economy, the source of change is the capitalist and his desire to accumulate wealth. The activities associated with profit acquisition generate endogenously the market dynamics which cause the economy to move forward. In the Walrasian economy, the source of change is entirely different – it is the population growth. If the rate of population growth is zero, then the accumulation of stocks will eventually cease. The economy will reach a state which Schumpeter called a circular flow equilibrium. All progress will cease to take place. Since population growth is not endogenously determined in the marketplace, the Walrasian neoclassical economist cannot look to the market to provide an explanation for economic growth and development. In this sense, classical and neoclassical economics are fundamentally different. The former is intrinsically dynamic and the latter is static.

The second model is a neoclassical monetary growth model developed by Tobin (1965), Johnson (1967) and others, which has been carefully summarized by Stein (1971). This neoclassical macrogrowth model is characterized by the facts that the rate of capital formation is identically equal to the planned savings and that all markets are always in equilibrium regardless of the price changes.

The model seeks to analyze the rate of growth in output per effective labor force caused by changes in the supply of money. Let $Y(t)$ and $N(t)$ respectively denote the output and the supply of effective labor force in period t. The model thus analyzes how changes in the supply of money affect $y(t) = \hat{Y}(t)/N(t)$. Tobin has found that the rate of growth in output per effective labor force is a function of the ratio of capital to effective labor, i.e. $y(t) = f\{K(t)/N(t)\}$, where $K(t)$ denotes the capital stock available in period t. The analysis thus reduces to the investigation of how changes in the money supply affect the capital intensity.

Monetary policy can affect the time profile of the capital intensity as well as its steady state equilibrium value in a full employment economy if it can shift either the consumption function or the net production function.[8] To do this, a change in the money supply must produce a real-balance effect through real balance as a consumer good or a producer good. Real balance is a consumer good whenever it provides utility to the consumer. The literature justifies this claim by asserting that (a) large real balances provide leisure to the consumer since they economize on the transaction cost, (b) it is safer to hold real balances than capital, and (c) holding real balances facilitates intergeneration transfer of wealth to the next generation. Real balance is a producer good whenever money generates productive services complementary with labor and capital, that is, whenever real balances enter into the production function. Money is assumed to enter into the production because it performs a productive role by reducing the transaction costs in production. Expansion in the supply of money in this environment will necessarily affect the time profile of capital intensity and thus the growth in the rate of output per effective labor. There is some controversy, however, regarding the issue of whether monetary expansion will affect the steady state capital intensity, but this does not concern us here. Presently, we only wish to observe that the growth induced by the monetary expansion in this model originates outside the market system. To be sure the monetary authority's decision to expand the money supply may have been a response to the market need. Yet because the decision to respond is made by an independent agent other than the market, in order to explain economic growth we must first provide an explanation of why the monetary authority chooses to expand the money supply in a specific manner. Growth is induced by a monetary expansion and cannot be viewed as having been produced by the internal dynamics of the market system. The neoclassical monetary growth model again describes an economy which lacks the law of motion inherent in the capitalistic economy. The neoclassical economy is therefore intrinsically static.

CONCLUDING REMARKS

The outlooks of the classical and neoclassical economists on the role of economics are fundamentally different. The classical economist's major concern is the creation of a nation's wealth. He views the market as inherently productive, for "production is a result of division of labor" and "the extent of division of labor is limited only by the size of the market." Moreover, the market is also inherently dynamic: an endogenous force exists that propels the economy forward. The classical economist examines whether this dynamic force will lead to an improvement in the welfare of a society. Unfortunately, classical economists have failed to offer coherent theories to support their contentions. Their major blunder is the adherence to the cost theory of value in general and the labor theory of value in particular. In doing this, the classical economists are prevented from seeing that there does exist a unified theory of value, production, and distribution, and from developing a viable theory of development. Instead, they are forced to settle with specialized value and distribution theories and to deal with the various internal contradictions. This lack of cohesiveness eventually caused the demise of the Classical School.

The neoclassical economists rescue economics from its abyss by discovering the universality of the marginal principle. They are able to integrate the theories of value, production, and distribution into a unified theory and establish formally the validity of the Smithian

proposition which states that the pursuance of self-interest by individuals in a competitive market environment leads to a state of
equilibrium where all individual interests are made consistent.

With the change from the classical to the neoclassical era, economists also shift their attention from "the creativity of the market" to
"the efficiency of the market." Under the premise that all present and
future markets do exist and are perfect, the neoclassical economists
arrive at the conclusion that the market alone is able to allocate the
endowed resources efficiently and thus deny an allocative role to any
agents in the market.

Entrepreneurs and firms are both passive agents in this economic
environment. Moreover, since the market is efficient, given the
resource endowments, it will necessarily explore all opportunities and
settle on the one which is optimal, both for now and in the future.
There is no possibility for improvement and change. If the economy
should experience any change, this change must be brought about by
exogenous factors. Changes such as population growth, technological
innovation, shifts in tastes etc. are all outside the economic system.
Because changes can only take place through exogenous shocks, we
cannot look to the economic system either to explain basic economic
phenomena such as investment activities, accumulation of capital,
and business fluctuations, or to deal with issues such as the long-term
prospects of the capitalistic system. Neoclassical economic theory is
mute on these vital topics.

Casual empiricism reveals that the entrepreneur and the firm play a
vital role in resource allocation and that the size as well as the internal
structure of the firm contribute crucially to the allocative outcome. In
addition, evidence also strongly suggests that the profit motive indeed
serves as a driving force to generate endogenous growth. These
observations imply that the neoclassical theory is incongruent to
reality. Perhaps the most serious indictment of neoclassical economics
is its inability to cope with uncertainty. In this case, not only the reality
of the model comes into dispute, but the very existence of an
equilibrium in neoclassical economy is also called into question. In the
following two chapters we will first show how the neoclassical model
fails to cope with uncertainty and then summarize the various
attempts in the literature to deal with problems that neoclassical
economics has failed to address.

NOTES

1 Smith distinguishes "measure of value" from "determinant of value." He
  selected the wage unit as the unit of social accounting of wealth since in his

view "labor is the only universal as well as the only accurate measure of value" (Smith, 1937, p. 36) and wages are invariant over time.

2 The consumer's preference on the commodity space is assumed to be complete, transitive, monotonic, continuous, and convex.

3 The independence of irrelevant alternatives states that if some individual ordering is removed as irrelevant, the social ordering must not be affected as a result.

4 An arrangement among a given group of agents is said to be incentive compatible if there does not exist an incentive for any agent to deviate from the arrangement as long as all other agents adhere to the agreement.

5 We have more to say about this subject in chapter 6.

6 The system of equations $\Sigma_s \pi_s^i \rho_s^i = P_j, j = 1, \ldots, J$, can be written in the form $\pi\rho = P$. Since $J = S$, π is of full rank; the inverse of π thus exists. Hence, $\rho = \pi^{-1}P$. Because the right-hand side of this equation is independent of i, ρ is independent of i.

7 We will study the temporary equilibrium model more carefully in chapter 6.

8 The net production function represents the economy's ability to produce for consumption.

3

Lack of Neoclassical Equilibrium in Incomplete Markets

It was shown in the preceding chapter that either under certainty or under uncertainty with complete markets a competitive equilibrium exists in a neoclassical economy; in addition, this equilibrium is Pareto optimal. However, such a conclusion cannot be reached in an incomplete market setting. Markets are said to be incomplete in a one-commodity universe whenever the number of independent financial instruments falls short of the number of states of nature. The factors that contribute to the incompleteness of markets will be examined in chapter 5. Here we will take it as given and survey the literature which leads toward the establishment of the above-mentioned proposition.

EARLY CONCERNS

Knight criticizes the neoclassical theory by pointing out its failure to distinguish actual competition from perfect competition, with the former taking place in a market where uncertainties prevail and the latter in a market where uncertainty is absent. Knight begins his analysis by making a clear distinction between risk and uncertainty. He declares, "The practical difference between . . . risk and uncertainty, is that in the former the distribution of the outcome in a group of instances is known . . . while in the case of uncertainty this is not true . . ." (Knight, 1971, p. 233), and then concludes that the presence of risk does not invalidate the result of the neoclassical model. According to Knight, "Even though the business man could not know in advance the results of individual ventures, he could operate and base his competitive offers upon accurate foreknowledge of the future if quantitative knowledge of the probability of every possible outcome can be had. For by figuring on the basis of a large number of ventures (whether in his own business alone or in that of business in general) the

50

losses could be converted into fixed costs" (Knight, 1971, pp. 198–9). Thus, as long as the probability law of an event is known, the decision-maker can always convert risk into a fixed cost through insurance. Consequently, there is no reason to consider production activities under risk as different from those under certainty. This analysis clearly anticipates the Arrow–Debreu complete market argument.

The impact of uncertainty on production activities, however, is far from trivial. Uncertainty arises because production requires time; during the production process either supply or demand may change abruptly. It is this unpredictable change, occurring after production decisions are implemented but before the results of productive activity are accomplished, that is responsible for the transformation of a certain environment into an uncertain one. In Knight's words:

> At the bottom of the uncertainty problem in economics is the forward-looking character of the economic process itself. Goods are produced to satisfy wants; the production of goods requires time, and two elements of uncertainty are introduced, corresponding to two different kinds of foresight which must be exercised. First, the end of productive operations must be estimated from the beginning.... Second, the wants which the goods are to satisfy are also, of course, in the future to the same extent, and their prediction involves uncertainty in the same way. (Knight, 1971, pp. 237–8)

The presence of this somewhat exogenously given uncertainty destroys the market's capability to coordinate joint production. Under an uncertain market environment, in order to commit resources for joint production each resource owner must possess some expectations about the future market events. These expectations about the future events are formulated by converting market uncertainties into subjective probability statements. Once such a transformation is made by each resource owner, there remains the question of how much resource each owner is willing to commit for production. The magnitude of this commitment depends upon the individual's wealth, his subjective risk assessment, and his attitude toward risk. Because there exists great diversity among resource owners regarding these determining factors, we should not be surprised to find that, for a given production project, the "optimal resource commitments" of the resource owners will, in general, not be consistent with each other under the prevailing production technology. From Knight's point of view, "men differ in their ... intellectual capacity to decide what should be done. In addition, there must come into play the diversity among men in degree of confidence in their judgment and powers and in disposition to act on their opinions ..." (Knight, 1971, p. 269). Consequently, there does not exist a unanimously acceptable production plan and joint production will not take place. Thus, under uncertainty, the market alone will not be able to coordinate joint production.

Although diversity in the resource owner's expectations about market events destroys the market's ability to coordinate joint production, paradoxically the very existence of these diversities provides opportunities for gain to entrepreneurs who could make production possible. Knight emphasizes that the key to overcoming the lack of consistent resource commitment is to be found in the entrepreneurial role. The Knightian entrepreneur is a capitalist who seeks profit from ever-changing market environments and is not afraid to make decisions and bear risk. In modern parlance, this follows because the individual with the greatest wealth endowment, best information, sharpest judgement about market events, and least risk aversion is willing to commit the greatest amount of resources for production compared with his fellow resource owners who possess opposite attributes. More importantly, there is an opportunity for profit for this high-output-preference individual if he can find a way of inducing the low-output-preference individuals to increase their resource commitment to production.

The Knightian entrepreneur is a high-output-preference resource owner who simply accepts all market uncertainties by organizing a firm and thus makes production possible. Hence, according to Knight, production takes place under the system where ". . . the confident and venturesome 'assume the risk' or 'insure' the doubtful and timid by guaranteeing to the latter a specified income in return for an assignment of the actual results" (Knight, 1971, pp. 269–70). Moreover, in Knight's conception, risk-bearing and decision-making are inseparable. This led Knight to state, "With human nature as we know it, it would be impracticable or very unusual for one man to guarantee to another a definite result of the latter's action without being given power to direct his work" (Knight, 1971, p. 270). In this manner, the market activities are split into two tiers – production and exchange. Production takes place under the direction of an authoritative capitalist entrepreneur. Through imputation and competition, the market orchestrates the exchange activities and channels resources into their most efficient usages.

However, Knight's resolution of the market failure is incomplete. It is limited to the case where the firm is owned and controlled by a single proprietor. Suppose that a firm is owned and controlled by many capitalist entrepreneurs. Since the capitalists are also endowed with different preferences and resources, their subjective optimal production plans will also be different. This lack of unanimity among the shareholders will again prevent joint production from taking place.

Knight has merely shifted the disagreement among all resource owners to that among the capitalist owners (shareholders) but has not successfully restored the market as an effective resource allocator.

Knight did not deal seriously with this version of the unanimity problem; he sidestepped the issue by allowing the capitalist owners to delegate their decision prerogative to the manager. According to Knight, the capitalist entrepreneur performs two distinct functions: exercising responsible control and bearing risk. While the risk-bearing role is vested solely in the entrepreneurs, the control function can be delegated. By shifting from a many-owners control situation to a single-person managerial control situation, the unanimity problem is naturally resolved. No attention was paid either to the question of how it is possible to amalgamate controls vested in all the owners into the hands of a single manager or to the question of how this transfer of control reconciles the self-interest of the shareholders. Instead, Knight shifted his attention to the issue of whether the delegation of the control function impairs the integrity of the capitalist entrepreneurs. Although his conclusion is negative, it nonetheless sowed the seed for the controversy later waged under the banner of "separation of ownership and control" in modern corporations, a topic we will explore in the next chapter.

The unanimity issue lay dormant until the early 1970s. It resurfaced when economists realized that it was not possible to investigate the firm's production and financing decisions independently of each other (Diamond, 1967). Simultaneous investigation of these decisions forces the economist to inquire how shareholder unanimity can be obtained.

THE BASIC ISSUE OF STOCKHOLDERS' UNANIMITY

The absence of some security markets impedes arbitrage. The inability to arbitrage forces the agent to make choices under the constraints imposed by conditions associated with a specific time or state of nature, and thus leaves him with a multiplicity of budget constraints. In addition, it also prevents agents from acquiring all information relevant to decision-making and forces them to evaluate market situations in a subjective manner. This observation has led to doubts on the possibility that all shareholders of a firm can reach a commonly desired production policy.

In the extreme case where no security exists, income is completely state dependent. There is no opportunity for the consumer to shift his income from one state to another. The consumer's utility derived in each state of nature depends solely on income obtained in that state.

For example, let there be two states of nature 1 and 2. The incomes in the two states are m_1 and m_2 respectively. Assume that the marginal utility of income in state 1 exceeds that in state 2. It is therefore to the advantage of the consumer to transfer some of his income from state 2 to state 1. In the absence of any security, no mechanism to effect such a transfer exists; the consumer is forced to face a separate budget constraint in these states. His expected utility derived from consumption under this set of constraints clearly does not reach its potential. Suppose now that there is a single stock y which yields a state distribution of returns y_1 and y_2, where $y_1 > y_2$. Based upon this state distribution of returns, the consumer, by purchasing the stock y, can increase his resources in state 1 and decrease them in state 2, thus enhancing his expected utility. In the presence of only one stock, the consumer's ability to transfer income from one state to another is limited, however. This limitation is imposed by the fact that the shareholder's fraction of claim to the firm's profit is the same for both states of nature. Although the presence of a state-dependent profit facilitates arbitrage, the fixed fraction of claim to the firm's profit still leaves the consumer with a distinct budget constraint in each state of the world. The state distribution of returns for the one stock could rarely adequately adjust the consumer's income in the two states to the desired level. Hence, despite an increase in the consumer's expected utility, it still falls short of its highest potential.

In order to guarantee the consumer with the highest utility warranted by his total command of resources, there must be two securities. Let the second security z yield z_1 and z_2 respectively in the two states of nature. The consumer can now trade y and z to achieve any desired configuration of income in the two states. He will choose the configuration which enables him to attain the highest expected utility.

The principle deduced from the example of a two-state universe can be extended immediately to an S-state universe. When the number of independent securities falls short of the number of states of nature, the consumer can only shift his resources from one state to another in a limited way as defined by the state distribution of returns of these securities. He is left to face a distinct budget constraint in each state of nature. Suppose that there are K independent securities, where $K < S$. The state distribution of returns of the K securities defines a K-dimensional hyperplane in S-dimensional vector space. The consumer can arbitrage among points on this hyperplane without impediment. If the optimal consumption bundle should locate at any place other than points on this hyperplane, the consumer cannot attain it. Thus when $K < S$ the consumer can only achieve a suboptimal consumption program. Only when the number of independent securities equals the number of the states of nature will the consumer be able to use his resources to attain the highest expected utility.

Having examined the nature of arbitrage through the use of securities, we will now examine the problems inflicted by the absence of some of the security markets.

Decision Problems in Incomplete Markets

Despite the fact that the lack of some security markets hampers the consumer's ability to arbitrage and leaves him to face a multiplicity of budget constraints, the nature of the consumer's choice problem remains intact. Given the firms' market values and their state distribution of profits, the consumer will select his portfolio of shares and consumption bundles so that his expected utility is maximized subject to his budget constraints.

Recall that P^j and $\pi_s^j(y_s^j)$, $s = 1, \ldots, S$, denoted firm j's market value and its state distribution of profits respectively. In order to maximize his expected utility, the consumer, as in the complete market case, will adjust his portfolio, that is, his implicit contingent claims prices ρ_s^i, $s = 1, \ldots, S$, to equate his subjective imputed value $\Sigma_s \rho_s^i \pi_s^j$ of firm j with the market price p^j of firm j, $j = 1, \ldots, J$. Because the market is incomplete, that is, $J < S$, the vectors $\pi_1, \ldots, \pi_J$ are now linearly dependent. Based on a theorem in algebra, the coefficients ρ_s^i, $s = 1, \ldots, S$, in the above linear equation system are not unique. This implies that at equilibrium different consumers assign different implicit contingent claims prices to each state of nature. With different implicit contingent claims prices, the consumers' tastes are disguised and cannot be extracted from the stock market prices.

The inability to uncover consumers' preferences from the stock market prices is grievous to the firm. The incomplete markets rob the firm of the market-determined contingent claims prices which are needed to help the firm to evaluate its state-dependent returns. Thus the firm can no longer pursue a production policy which maximizes its market value through the use of existing market prices. An alternative must be found.

In the literature it is suggested that the firm could arrive at a production policy by formulating estimates of the market-determined contingent claims prices. It offers two possible estimators, both requiring the knowledge of the individual's implicit contingent claims prices for each state of nature. Let $\hat{q}_s$ denote the estimate of q_s, $s = 1, \ldots, S$. The first estimator uses a particular individual's implicit contingent claims price in each state as a surrogate for the market contingent claims price for that state, that is, $\hat{q}_s = \rho_i^s$, $s = 1, \ldots, S$. Based on this estimator,

$$P^j(i) = \Sigma_s \rho_s^i \pi_s^j$$

The second uses a weighted average of all the firm's shareholders' implicit contingent claims prices in each state as a surrogate for the market contingent claims price in that state; the weights used are the fraction of the firm's shares that each shareholder owns. Let θ^{ij} denote the fraction of firm j's stock held by consumer i; then

$$\hat{q}_s = \Sigma_i \theta^{ij} \rho_s^i \quad s = 1, \ldots, S$$

Based on this estimator,

$$P^j = \Sigma_s (\Sigma_i \theta^{ij} \rho_s^i) \pi_s^j$$

Both these estimators are the subject of considerable controversy. Neither of them will always yield a production policy for the firm that will be agreed upon by all its shareholders. According to the first estimator, the value $p^j(i)$ of the firm is individual specific because the implicit contingent claims prices are different for different shareholders. It is apparent that there is no way that the firm can select a production policy on the basis of maximizing $P^j(i)$ which will meet the approval of all its shareholders. The result of the second estimator is not much better. According to this method, firm j uses $\Sigma_i \theta^{ij} \rho_s^i$ as the estimate of the market contingent claims price in state s. Although the value of the firm

$$P^j = \Sigma_s \Sigma_i \theta^{ij} \rho_s^i \pi_s^j$$

is not individual specific, unanimity is still not guaranteed because

$$\Sigma_i \theta^{ij} \rho_s^i \not\equiv \rho_s^i$$

for all i. Thus, regardless of how the firm arrives at its production plan, there is no consensus among its shareholders regarding the value of the firm. It is now not possible for the firm to find a production policy that will receive unanimous endorsement by all its shareholders. Production breaks down. In addition, even if a firm's production policy perchance did meet the approval of all the shareholders, the difficulty does not end here. A change in the firm's production plan will generally induce the consumers to adjust their portfolio and hence their implicit contingent claims prices.[1] These changes will, in turn, lead the firm to change its production plan. Thus the use of some form of the consumers' contingent claims prices to guide the firm's production is meaningful only if this sequence of adjustments will eventually lead to an equilibrium where each firm's production policy meets the approval of all its shareholders. The condition needed for such an equilibrium will be discussed later in this chapter. In the next section we will examine some special cases where it is not necessary for the firms to know all the shareholders' implicit contingent claims prices when making profit-maximizing production decisions.

SPECIAL CASES WHERE UNANIMITY IS POSSIBLE

Unanimity exists in special cases either because the technology underlying production in the economy or the consumers' preferences satisfy certain special conditions. The former is known as the spanning condition and the latter requires that the consumer's utility depends solely on the mean and variance of his portfolio returns.

Spanning and Production Decisions

Production satisfies the spanning condition whenever a firm's production plan or a change in its production plan can be expressed as a linear combination of the existing production plans; that is, every firm's production plan or change in its production plan is contained in the space spanned by the production plans of the existing firms in the economy. Because changes in each firm's production do not affect the economy's overall productive capabilities, the spanning condition implies that any change in a firm's production decision will not alter the set of the state distribution of returns available to the entire economy. This result further implies that the market value of a firm or a change in its market value can be expressed as a linear combination of the market values of the existing firms in the stock market. In other words, when production satisfies the spanning condition, information about the consumers' preferences on portfolio choices is embedded in the current stock market prices. The investor, knowing the production technology, can use the prevailing stock market prices instead of the market contingent claims prices or their estimates to evaluate any change in the firm's production plan. Since the security market prices are public information and are known uniformly to all investors, any change in a firm's production plan which increases the value of the firm in terms of the prevailing security prices will meet the unanimous approval of its shareholders. As a result, under production spanning, individual investors or firms can sidestep the need to know the market contingent claims prices and simply use the market security prices to guide their activities.

Even though there is no longer a need to gain information on the market contingent claims prices, ironically, when the production spanning condition is satisfied, this information becomes readily available. As the spanning condition is satisfied, the planned production lies within the existing market capability and a distribution of returns is priced uniquely by all shareholders. Any individual-specific or firm-specific contingent claims prices can now be used as a surrogate for the market contingent claims prices. They all lead to the same evaluation of the firm's production plan.[2]

Thus we see that when the production spanning condition is satisfied, every change in a firm's production plan can be unambiguously evaluated by all its shareholders. These shareholders will either unanimously accept or reject a given change in the firm's production policy. This is not all. In a competitive market, the firm perceives that a change in its level of production will not perceptibly affect the total supply of returns (outputs) in each state of nature. Moreover, a firm's change in its level of production will affect neither other firms' perception of their market value nor each shareholder's perception of his demand price for the shares. As a consequence, each firm will take all other firms' market values as given and pursue a production policy which maximizes its own market value, and each consumer will take the market value of all firms as given and pursue a program which maximizes his utility subject to his budget constraints. The interaction between the consumer and the firm in the competitive market will result in a set of market clearing prices in both the goods and the security markets, and thus will lead the economy into a state of equilibrium. This equilibrium is referred to as the Ekern–Wilson equilibrium (Ekern and Wilson, 1974).

The Ekern–Wilson equilibrium is, in general, not equivalent to the Arrow–Debreu equilibrium which is arrived at in a complete set of contingent claims markets. The reason for this is that the spanning condition is pertinent only to the production sector of the economy under a set of initially given prices. Spanning implies that the output produced by each firm in each state of nature can just as well be produced by the other firms in the economy. It also implies that any feasible aggregate distribution of returns generated in an economy can be produced by redistributing the available resources among the existing firms. If the available production technology spans the same space as that spanned by the existing securities, the ability to produce any feasible output by the existing firms will in no way help the economy to break out of the restrictions imposed by the lack of stock markets. All production spanning does is to offer the economy another avenue to perform the necessary arbitrage. The economy can now obtain a given feasible consumption program in two alternative ways. First, given the initial endowment of stocks, the economy can obtain this program with firms adjusting their production plans. Second, given the firms' production plans, the economy can attain this program through consumers adjusting their portfolios. Thus production spanning simply implies that any feasible consumption program which is achievable through portfolio selection can also be achieved by production adjustments. Unless the existing production plans span a space which contains a proper subspace spanned by the existing securities, production spanning in no way vitiates the constraints imposed by the lack of the required security markets. Thus, despite production spanning, there is still no mechanism in the incomplete market setting which provides the consumer with the exact amount of monetary return in each state of nature which allows him to obtain a superior consumption program associated with the Arrow–Debreu equilibrium. Consequently, the Ekern–Wilson equilibrium is different from the Arrow–Debreu equilibrium.

This statement is not invalidated by Roy Radner's observation. According to Radner (1974), if the consumers' consumption sets are also spanned by the return vectors of the firms, the Arrow–Debreu equilibrium is sustainable by the Ekern–Wilson equilibrium. Because the Ekern–Wilson equilibrium is obtained under a set of initially given stock prices while all prices are determined endogenously in the Arrow–Debreu economy, it remains to be true that these equilibria are not identical.

Mean–Variance Utility and Production Decisions

Stockholders' unanimity is thought to be possible not only because of the special condition underlying the production technology of the economy but also because of the special nature of the consumer's preferences. Unanimity is possible, according to the literature, whenever shareholders value only the mean and the variance of their portfolio returns. However, the establishment of this proposition is not straightforward. It requires the aid of a very strong assumption: all consumers have identical portfolio opportunities and assign the same probability distributions of returns associated with the various portfolios.

When the consumer is interested only in the summary characteristics of returns instead of the entire distribution of the returns, it becomes simpler to convert the firm's distribution of returns into aggregate values. Under the mean–variance regime, in order to compute the value of a firm it is no longer necessary to know the state contingent claims prices; a single price of risk will suffice. The price of risk in the present case is the marginal rate of substitution between the mean and the variance of the portfolio returns. Because this marginal rate of substitution is individual specific, the price of risk is individual specific. Given this price of risk, the consumer can compute his imputed value of the firm. Since the consumer is risk averse, his imputed value of the firm is simply the mean value of the firm's returns minus the price of risk times the risk incurred by including the stock of the firm in question in his portfolio. The above-mentioned risk is represented by the covariance between the returns of the firm in question and those of the other firms appropriately weighted by their respective shares. Symbolically,

$$v_f^i = \bar{x}_f^i - \rho^i \sum_{f' \in F} \mathrm{cov}^i(x_f, x_{f'})$$

Because the price of risk is individual specific and the distributions of returns of stocks involved are subjective, the value of the firm derived by the different shareholders is also different. The chance of establishing the above-mentioned proposition now rests upon the phenomenon that in a market economy where individuals' subjective prices of risk differ, trading risks among them can bring about mutual gains. Such a trade also tends to equalize the individuals' prices of risk and to convert them into a single market price. The process of carrying out such a trade is described by the capital asset pricing model (CAPM) (Sharpe, 1964; Fama, 1971). In the remainder of this section we first describe the structure of the CAPM, then explain how risk is traded in the market, and finally show how the trading of risk leads to stockholders' unanimity on the value of the firm.

Structure of the Capital Asset Pricing Model   The CAPM adopts the standard two-period temporary equilibrium format. The consumer allocates his resources between current consumption and a portfolio of investments whose market value in the second period determines his consumption level in that period. As usual, the consumer is assumed to be risk averse and to be an expected utility maximizer. The distinguishing feature of the CAPM is that portfolios are ordered by their mean and variance only and are not directly related to the states of nature. Portfolio A is said to dominate portfolio B if A yields a greater mean and exhibits a smaller variance on returns than B. However, the mean–variance criterion provides only a partial order and is incapable of ranking a portfolio against another which has both greater (or less) mean and variance. Thus the mean–variance criterion can only separate all feasible portfolios of a consumer into two sets: the dominated and the undominated. The undominated set, which is represented by the northwest boundary of the feasible set in the (σ, μ) plane, is commonly referred to as the efficient set. It is important to note that, whenever the consumer is risk averse, his efficient portfolio frontier is concave toward the variance axis. In addition, because consumers face different portfolio opportunities and assign different probability distributions to returns associated with the various portfolios, their efficient portfolio sets are different. The crucial feature underlying the CAPM is that all consumers face an identical efficient portfolio set. This requires the assumption that all consumers have the same portfolio opportunities and hold homogeneous expectations on the probability distributions of returns associated with these portfolios.

Given the consumer's preferences, he strives to select from his efficient portfolio set a portfolio which maximizes his expected utility. In figure 3.1 $I_1^a, I_2^a, \ldots$ and $I_1^\beta, I_2^\beta, \ldots$ are the indifference curves for a and β, and ℓ is their common efficient portfolio frontier. The optimal portfolios for a and β are represented by the points M and N respectively, where each individual's indifference curve is tangent to the efficient portfolio frontier. Because the consumers' tastes differ, they select different optimal portfolios.

Trading of Risk   The selection of different portfolios by the individuals reflects the difference in their subjective price of risk. It is evident from figure 3.1 that a is more risk averse than β and the marginal rate of substitution of mean for variance is greater for a than for β. This means that the subjective price for risk is relatively high for a and low for β. Let these prices be denoted by ρ_a and ρ_β respectively. A mutual gain can be achieved if a can sell risks to β. This transaction is accomplished by permitting β to sell a bond bearing a fixed interest rate to a, say at the rate r where $\rho_\beta < r < \rho_a$, and then to use the proceeds to buy the portfolio N. The investors a and β now hold a new portfolio involving both debt and equity. For clarity, we will henceforth refer to the equity portfolios, e.g. M and N, as pure portfolios and to the combined debt–equity portfolios as mixed portfolios.

Whenever it is possible to borrow and lend an unlimited amount at a fixed interest rate r, β can achieve any linear combination of returns

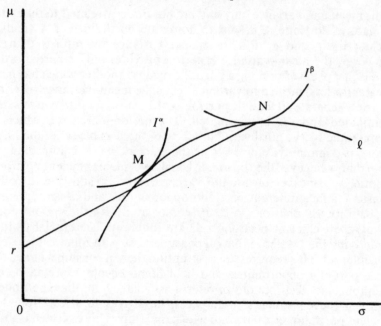

Figure 3.1

through the formation of a mixed portfolio represented by a point on the line r N. From this perspective, β clearly regards the pure portfolio N as suboptimal. Any pure portfolio represented by a point southwest of N on the line ℓ is now superior to N. β will opt to shift to such a portfolio. Likewise, in the presence of unlimited lending and borrowing opportunities at the fixed rate r, a finds that the pure portfolio M is no longer optimal. He now prefers a portfolio represented by a point northeast of M on ℓ. Concomitant with these adjustments in the pure portfolios of a and β, the demand and supply of bonds will also change. These changes, in turn, cause the interest rate to adjust. All these adjustments will cease whenever both the equity market and the bond market are simultaneously in equilibrium. In this equilibrium situation all consumers, independent of their tastes, select a common pure portfolio e and trade bonds at the equilibrium market interest rate r_e. Differences in individuals' tastes are now solely reflected by the composition of the mixed portfolio, that is, the proportion of bonds and e which the individuals buy. The more risk-averse individuals, e.g. a, will hold both bonds and e, while the less risk-averse individuals, e.g. β, will borrow to invest in e. In doing so, both a and β enjoy a

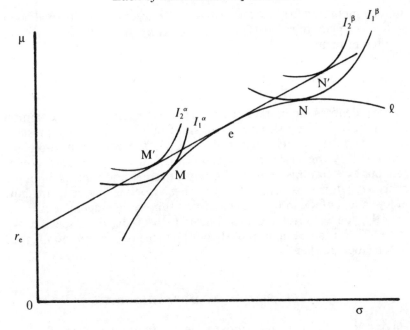

Figure 3.2

higher utility level than they can attain before risk is traded. Their equilibrium choices are shown in figure 3.2, where a selects the mixed portfolio M' and β selects the mixed portfolio N'. The market price of risk is now represented by the slope of the line $r_e e$.

Stockholders' Unanimity Having examined the market process leading to the equalization of the investors' subjective price of risk and the selection of a common pure portfolio for all the investors, it is now simple to demonstrate that all consumers will assign the same value to each firm in the stock market. Recall that the individual i's subjective value of a firm f is given by

$$v_f^i = \bar{x}_f^i - \rho^i \sum_{f' \in F} \mathrm{cov}^{\,i}(x_f, x_{f'})$$

where the first term on the right-hand side of the equation represents i's subjective evaluation of the expected returns of firm f and the second term represents his subjective evaluation of the risk contributed by including firm f's stock in his investment portfolio evaluated by his own price of risk ρ^i. The CAPM converts the value of a firm into a different form:

$$v_f^i = \bar{x}_f - \rho \operatorname{cov}(x_f, x_m)$$

where ρ denotes the market price of risk and x_m denotes the common pure portfolio. The risk associated with firm f's stock now represents the contribution of its stock to the risk of the common portfolio x_m evaluated by the price of risk ρ. Because all investors hold homogeneous expectations on portfolio opportunities and returns, both the expected returns of firm f and the risk associated with it are now independent of the individual investor's subjective judgement. Consequently, the value of the firm ceases to be individual specific. All investors thus agree unanimously on the value of the firm established in the stock market.

THE PROBLEM IN INCOMPLETE MARKETS

Having seen that it is only under special situations that the firm can base its decisions on information contained in stock market prices, we must now examine efforts that have been made to base production decisions directly on the preferences of the firm's shareholders. In this regard, Drèze (1974) proposed a shareholders' equilibrium model and Grossman and Hart (1979) proposed a production-exchange equilibrium model. Both models suggest that the manager uses the firm-specific implicit contingent claims prices to calculate the firm's market value. Recall that the firm-specific contingent claims price in each state is a weighted sum of the individual shareholders' implicit contingent claims prices in that state. The Drèze model differs from the Grossman–Hart model in that the former uses the *ex post* ownership fraction while the latter uses the *ex ante* ownership fraction as weights to calculate the firm's market value. Both models agree that the manager pursues a production policy which maximizes the market value of the firm, i.e. a weighted sum of the firm's future production stream. Since these models differ only in form and not in spirit, in this section we will essentially summarize the Drèze model.

Drèze based his analyses on the observation that, when the markets are incomplete, the stock ownership structure introduces a certain rigidity into the economy. The rigidity stems from the fact that, regardless of which state of nature obtains, the individual shareholder's claim to the firm's profit is fixed at the proportion determined by the fraction of the ownership shares that he possesses. As we have seen earlier, because the ownership shares are fixed at the same level in all states of nature, the consumer in incomplete markets is unable to adjust his resources among the different states in order to achieve the best consumption program. In technical terms, this rigidity renders the feasible set of the stock ownership program nonconvex. According to Drèze, this lack of convexity places severe restrictions on the ability of the economy to adjust toward an equilibrium in a decentralized market setting. In fact, it is not immediately clear how a suitable equilibrium can be defined. Consequently, a solution concept must be devised first.

In devising such a concept, Drèze partitions the economy into two connected parts: the production sector and the financial sector. He finds that the equilibrium concept in each of these sectors is well defined. In order to weld the equilibria in the two sectors into a single equilibrium, Drèze proposes a process which successively reallocates resources through the production decisions of the firm in the production sector and through the exchange of shares among the consumers in the financial sector. Guided by the principle of individual rationality and Pareto optimality, this sequence of adjustments will eventually lead the economy into a shareholders' equilibrium. Drèze's idea is described under the headings of pseudo-equilibrium for the firm, portfolio equilibrium for the stock market, and stockholders' equilibrium for the economy.

Pseudo-Equilibria for the Firm

Consider a stock ownership program denoted by $(\bar{X}, \bar{Y}, \bar{\theta})$, where $\bar{X}$, $\bar{Y}, \bar{\theta}$ respectively denote the equilibrium consumption, production, and shareholding configurations in the economy. Let $\bar{\theta}$ and the production policies of all firms other than firm j be fixed. Firm j can generate an alternative production policy in its production set Y_j. This change is made possible with the concomitant adjustments of consumers' current consumptions. A change in firm j's production policy thus induces a set of feasible allocations for the economy. Clearly the utility level of the consumer is also affected by firm j's adjustment in production. Over the set of feasible allocations, shareholder i prefers a production plan y^j over another production plan $\hat{y}^j$ if and only if the former yields for him a higher utility than the latter. This phenomenon leads Drèze to define a Nash–Pareto optimality criterion for the firm. Given the ownership structure of firm j represented by $\bar{\theta}_j$, the production plan $\hat{y}^j$ is Pareto optimal if there does not exist in Y^j any other production plan which is preferred to $\hat{y}^j$ by at least one of its shareholders and is indifferent to $\hat{y}^j$ by all others. We need to show that there does exist such a Pareto-optimal program for production.

Drèze establishes that there indeed exists at least one such Pareto-optimal program on the set of aforementioned feasible allocations. He accomplishes this by observing that the firm's production plans determine simultaneously the dividends paid and hence the consumption of all shareholders. The choice of firm j's production plan $(y_1^j, \ldots, y_S^j)$ is thus comparable with the choice of a vector of S public goods. Since well-known solution concepts exist for public goods problems, this concept is used to establish the existence of a Pareto-optimal program for the firm's production problem. In the present context, equilibrium means that there exist a set of implicit contingent claims prices for the individuals, i.e. $\rho_s^i, s = 1, \ldots, S$ and $i = 1, \ldots, I$, and a set of firm-specific contingent claims prices $q_s^j = \Sigma_i \theta_{ij} \rho_s^i, s = 1, \ldots, S$ and $j = 1, \ldots, J$, such that the following hold.

1　　Based upon the prices q_s^j, $s = 1, \ldots, S$, the firm j, $j = 1, \ldots, J$, is able to choose a production plan which maximizes its expected profit.

2　　Based upon the prices ρ_s^i, $s = 1, \ldots, S$, the consumer i, $i = 1, \ldots, I$, finds that his existing portfolio of shares θ^i and the firm's production policies $(y^1, \ldots, y^J)$ indeed enable him to attain the maximum utility.

In order to accept this equilibrium as one which meets the condition that each firm's shareholders will unanimously accept the firm's production policy, we must address the unanimity issue raised earlier. We recall that this issue arises because each shareholder evaluates the firm's production plan by using his own implicit contingent claims prices, i.e.

$$p^j = \Sigma_s \rho_s^i \pi_s^j (y_s^j) \quad i = 1, \ldots, I$$

Since $\rho_s^i \neq q_s^j$ for all i and s, how can it be possible for the firm to choose a production plan which maximizes

$$P_j = \Sigma_s \Sigma_i \theta_{ij} \rho_s^i \pi_s^j (y_s^j)$$

and is unanimously endorsed by all its shareholders? Drèze resolved this problem by making the internal activities of the firm more complex and giving the manager an extra nontrivial function. In addition to performing activities such as collecting information about the states of nature and solving maximization problems, the manager must now elicit shareholders' preferences and find a way of discovering the shareholders' implicit contingent claims prices. More importantly, the manager is given the power to mediate the shareholders' interests "through taxation." A change in firm j's production plan can either increase or decrease the individual shareholder's valuation of the firm. Let $\Delta P^j(i)$ denote stockholder i's subjective change in firm j's value. It is evident that $\Delta P^j(i)$ is positive for some i and negative for others. The manager of the firm is now given the responsibility of transferring the current period income from shareholders who favor the proposed production change to those who oppose it. Clearly, all shareholders can be made better off after such income transfers if and only if $\Sigma_i \Delta P^j(i) > 0$. Changes in the firm's production policy will continue until $\Sigma_i \Delta P^j(i) = 0$. This result implies that the firm is in equilibrium if and only if its market value is maximized. Thus, with the aid of the manager, the equilibrium described by conditions 1 and 2 is indeed consistent with stockholder unanimity (Grossman and Hart, 1979, pp. 300–2). With this issue resolved, Drèze has not only shown that efficient production decisions of the firm reflect unanimously the preferences of all its shareholders, but has also provided credibility for the method of using the weighted average of all shareholders' implicit contingent claims prices as the firm-specific contingent claims prices to compute the market value of the firm.

Portfolio Equilibria for the Stock Market

Denote a stock ownership program by $(\bar{X}, \bar{Y}, \bar{\theta})$, and let all the firms' production be fixed at levels described by $\bar{Y}$. Alternative stock ownership programs can be generated by changing the ownership structure θ through an exchange of shares among the individuals and through concomitant adjustment in the consumer's current consumptions. Associated with the set of attainable stock ownership programs is a pure exchange economy with (a) $J+1$ private goods, that is, the current consumption good and the stocks of the J firms, and (b) I consumers each endowed with a utility function defined on the current consumption and his share of each firm's stock. Exchange of a present consumption good and the shares takes place subject to the constraints that the total demand for the consumption goods cannot exceed its total supply and that the total demand for each firm's shares cannot exceed its total supply. The equilibrium property of such an exchange economy is well known. Given the associated set of consumers' contingent claims prices ρ_s^i, $i = 1, \ldots, I$ and $s = 1, \ldots, S$, there exists a vector of stock prices $(P^1, \ldots, P^J)$ at which the markets clear. If, at equilibrium, individual i holds a positive number of firm j's shares, then i's private evaluation of firm j's worth, that is $\Sigma_s \rho_s^i y_s^j$, must be equal to the stock market value p^j of firm j. However, if at equilibrium, individual i holds no shares in firm j, then this must be because his private evaluation of firm j's worth falls short of the stock market value of firm j, i.e. $\Sigma_s \rho_s^i y^j < \rho^j$. The financial sector is in equilibrium whenever, given the firms' production plans, the allocation of shares in the stock market is Pareto optimal.

Stockholders' Equilibrium

So far we have discussed the equilibria in the production sector and in the financial sector separately. It is natural to postulate that the entire economy is in equilibrium whenever the production sector and the financial sector are simultaneously in equilibrium. This equilibrium occurs whenever there emerge a set of market prices $(P^1, \ldots, P^J)$ in the stock market and a set of shadow prices ρ_s^i, $i = 1, \ldots, I$ and $s = 1, \ldots, S$, satisfying the following conditions.

1   Each and every firm's shares are cleared in the stock market.
2   Each consumer selects current consumption and a stock portfolio which maximizes his utility subject to his budget constraints.
3   Each firm, guided by the firm-specific contingent claims prices, selects a production plan which maximizes its expected profit.

Because the set of stock ownership programs is not convex, the attainment of such an equilibrium is by no means automatic. Drèze proposes a mixed *tâtonnement* and non-*tâtonnement* process which prescribes a sequence of adjustments alternating between exchange of shares and tentative revision of the production plans of firms, that is, alternating between adjustment in the stock market prices P and the shadow prices ρ. The adjustment in the financial sector is non-*tâtonnement* whereas the adjustment in the production sector is *tâtonnement*. The working of this mixed process can best be described in Drèze's own words.

Each "morning" the stock exchange meets, and shares are exchanged until some equilibrium is reached, at which no further trading is forthcoming. Each "afternoon" the firms revise their production plans, according to the preferences of their shareholders, taking into account the ownership fractions generated by the transactions that have actually taken place on the stock exchange in the morning; these plans are announced but not physically carried out until a final equilibrium is reached. The next "morning", new stock exchange transactions take place, on the basis of information about the production plans chosen the previous afternoon. When, on some morning, no transactions take place on the stock exchange, the production plans of the firms are regarded as definitive and are carried out. (Drèze, 1974, p. 152)

Since the set of ownership programs is nonconvex, we cannot be sure that this process will always lead to a Pareto-optimal outcome. Drèze applies the principles of individual rationality and Pareto optimality to insure that every step in the process represents an improvement and thus eliminates the possibility that the process will end up in an allocation worse than the starting point. When the process terminates at a stockholders' equilibrium, given the actions of all other agents, each firm will have no incentive to change its production plan and each consumer will have no incentive to trade his shares. The shareholders of a firm will unanimously endorse the firm's production policy.

We have now completed a survey of Drèze's theory which demonstrates that the market, with the aid of the managers, can be relied upon to provide sufficient information about the shareholder's preference to enable the firm to base its production policy on these preferences. Through a stylistic adjustment process, alternating between the firm's adjustment in production plans and the consumer's trading in shares, the economy will arrive at a shareholders' equilibrium. At this equilibrium, the shareholders of a firm will unanimously endorse its production policy. This demonstration enables us, once again, to reaffirm our confidence in the market's ability to allocate resources even in an incomplete market setting. However, we must not arrive at this conclusion in haste. Before rendering a judgement on the market's capability to allocate resources, we need to discuss some shortcomings of the Drèze model.

Some of the model's shortcomings have been recognized by Drèze himself. They include the myopic nature of the adjustment process and the lack of a market institution to support this process. In Drèze's words, "A major drawback . . . is the implicit assumption that the problem arising at each step will be resolved as if that step were to be the last one; that is, no consideration of advantages to be realized at later steps is recognized" (Drèze, 1974, p. 153). Despite this realization, Drèze went on to justify his work by saying, "the process is thus better viewed as an illustration of the possibilities offered by decentralized, rational, but 'myopic,' decision, rather than as a description of the functioning of the stock exchange" (Drèze, 1974, p. 153). This justification, though reasonable in the context of Drèze's paper, is inadequate in the context of determining whether the market alone (as claimed by the neoclassical economist) is capable of allocating resources in an incomplete market setting. In this context, we must ask what (potential and existing) market institution can be erected in order to insure that the process is carried out. Without the support of such an institution, the theory is detached from reality. This detachment renders the theory meaningless.

In connection with this issue we point out another shortcoming associated with the Drèzean model. This shortcoming stems from the fact that not all the prices needed to guide the agents' decisions are observable. Of all the prices in this system, the stock prices are observable while the consumers' implicit contingent claims prices are not. Since the manager of the firm needs these shadow prices to make efficient production decisions, we need to know how they are obtained. It is not satisfactory to merely assume, as Drèze does, that the manager does know these prices; we need a mechanism to obtain them. Forsythe and Suchanek (1984) dealt with this issue, and we now summarize their results.

Truth-telling Mechanism

We have seen above that stockholders' unanimity can be achieved in an incomplete market setting if the stockholders reveal truthfully to the manager their preferences or their willingness to pay in order to bring about a change in the firm's production plan. To assume that the stockholders will communicate truthfully, however, is not sufficient; there must also exist an incentive for them to tell the truth voluntarily. In an incomplete market setting, such an incentive is clearly lacking. On the basis of the criterion used by the manager to transfer current income from those shareholders who favor the production change to those who oppose it, there clearly exists an incentive for the shareholder to free ride. Suppose that the shareholders have an overall consensus to increase the level of the firm's production. With the Drèze and Grossman–Hart transfer criterion, there exists an incentive for a particular shareholder, say consumer i, to understate his preference. He gains by sending a false signal to the manager indicating that he prefers a low level output. If his fellow shareholders reveal their preferences truthfully, the firm's output will increase. Consumer i now achieves what he wants but has avoided bearing a part of the cost of the increase in the firm's output. Because every shareholder has the opportunity of gaining in the same manner, they will all behave strategically. The end result is that the messages the manager receives are biased toward underproduction. The market thus fails to discipline the shareholders and ends up by producing an equilibrium output falling short of the level preferred by all shareholders.

This free-rider problem, as observed by Grossman and Hart, is caused by the fact that the ownership share serves two functions in incomplete markets. It serves on the one hand as the certificate of claim to the firm's output and on the other hand as a means of reallocating the consumer's risks. When a consumer purchases a given firm's share, it is not possible to tell whether his purpose is to acquire a claim to the firm's output or to reallocate the risk that he faces. The consumer's preferences remain disguised. Only when the motive of his action is made clear will managers be able to ascertain the consumer's preferences accurately. Thus, in order to prevent free riders, a mechanism must be devised to force the consumer to act according to his true preferences. The literature suggests that, since the firm's production problem in the incomplete market resembles the public good problem in a private ownership economy under certainty, the method used to determine the public good production can be adapted to solve the problem at hand. By using the public good theory, we can split the functions performed by the ownership share into two parts – the revenue share and the cost share. The revenue share represents the claim to the firm's output and thus can be thought of as reflecting the shareholder's time preferences, while the cost share can be thought of as reflecting the shareholder's risk preferences. The shareholders' preferences are fully revealed through actions taken by the shareholders regarding their choices on revenue shares and cost shares. On the basis of these revealed preferences, the manager can select an appropriate production plan. Interaction between the consumer and the firm in a competitive market will again bring the economy into a Pareto-optimal equilibrium.

Critical to the public good theory is the selection of a collective mechanism to determine the level of public good in a private ownership economy and the distribution of the cost incurred to the consumers in accordance with their preferences. The strategy used to accomplish this task, which we have alluded to before, involves the selection of an incentive-compatible cost-sharing rule (Groves and Ledyard, 1980) through which the consumer's action truthfully reflects his preferences.

The adaptation of this solution concept in public good production under certainty to private good production under uncertainty naturally involves the selection of a collective mechanism which will help to determine the firm's production level and to distribute its cost of production to the shareholders. The strategy involves separating the shareholder's ownership share from his cost share. The shareholder must now bid for the output level that he desires by committing a certain share of the cost incurred toward its production. This requires a cost-sharing rule. Because a change in the cost-sharing rule induces a change in the consumer's behavior, it must be incentive compatible and determined endogenously. An arbitrarily imposed cost-sharing rule not only induces shareholders to behave opportunistically but may also lead to the nonexistence of a solution to the problem.

In keeping with this spirit, Forsythe and Suchanek choose to adapt the shared-cost mechanism developed by Hurwicz (1979) in public finance to solve the production problem in incomplete markets left unattended by Drèze as well as by Grossman and Hart. Because the execution of the shared-cost mechanism is predicated by a collective action, such an action must also be introduced in the present context. The collective action takes the form of a common production decision mechanism to be followed by all firms in the economy. This mechanism, which is referred to by Forsythe and Suchanek as the managerial decision mechanism, is composed of three parts: a message space, an allocative rule, and a cost-sharing rule. The message space is generated by asking each shareholder to communicate to each manager the amount of inputs he wishes to add to, or subtract from, the aggregate input level requested by the other shareholders. On the basis of the messages collected from all shareholders, the manager uses the allocative rule to select the input level to be employed by the firm and uses the cost-sharing rule to distribute the cost of production to the firm's shareholders. A viable managerial decision mechanism must be one which is consistent with the firm's profit-maximizing goal and involves a cost-sharing rule which is incentive compatible.

Given a managerial decision mechanism, the selection of the firm's production plan becomes a collective activity of the firm's shareholders. In a competitive stock market each shareholder will take the stock market prices and other consumers' messages as given. He will choose his current consumption, stock portfolio, and the messages that he will send to the manager in order to maximize his utility subject to the budget constraints. The manager of the firm will process the messages and will apply the allocative rule in order to determine the firm's input level and the cost-sharing rule in order to distribute the firm's cost to its shareholders. The shareholder is permitted to trade shares in the stock market and the firm is permitted to revise its production plan. These activities take place in the manner described by Drèze until an overall equilibrium is reached in the economy. Forsythe and Suchanek call such an equilibrium the participation equilibrium.

The existence of a participation equilibrium means that there exists a set of stock market prices $(P^1, \ldots, P^J)$ and a set of implicit contingent claims prices ρ_s^i, $i = 1, \ldots, I$ and $s = 1, \ldots, S$, such that the following hold.

1   Each consumer's utility is maximized subject to his budget constraints.
2   Based upon the managerial decision mechanism each firm's cost is distributed to its shareholders and its profit is maximized.
3   Each and every firm's shares are cleared in the stock market.

Given the managerial decision mechanism, the manager now reverts to performing only routine functions. The managerial decision mechanism specifies the rules used to allocate resources; the managers now merely execute these rules. The disappearance of the manager's prerogative does not mean that the market has regained total responsibility in resource allocation. On the contrary the managerial decision mechanism becomes an indispensable part of the resource allocation process. The market ceases to allocate resources by itself and must be aided by an exogenously imposed mechanism. This conclusion is distressing to the economist because it implies that the market can no longer be relied upon to endogenously generate a process of its own to allocate resources. At this juncture, it is pertinent to raise the question of why the shared-cost mechanism is acceptable in public good production but not in private good production. The answer is simple. The shared-cost mechanism is imposed in the public good sector of a private ownership economy for the purpose of restoring production efficiency in the entire economy. Its presence in no way affects the allocative role played by the market in the private good sector. The same cannot be said about the managerial decision mechanism. Since we claim that the managerial decision mechanism must be grafted onto the market in order to improve the efficiency in private good production, this claim is tantamount to the admission that under uncertainty the market alone is no longer capable of allocating resources efficiently. This admission calls into question the basic tenet of the neoclassical theory which asserts that the market alone indeed allocates resources efficiently.

SUMMARIZING REMARKS

In this chapter we have surveyed the literature which calls our attention to the fact that, in the presence of uncertainty, the owner-managed economy fashioned by neoclassical economics breaks down. When markets are incomplete, market prices no longer provide all the information needed for decision-making. The decision-maker's judgement becomes indispensable in the decision process. Because different resource owners generally have different preferences and are endowed with different amounts of resources, based upon their subjective choices, resource owners are seldom able to arrive at a joint production policy by simply exchanging their services through the market. Thus the market fails to coordinate production. Knight resolved this impasse by giving production decision prerogative to the capitalist entrepreneurs. However, shareholders of a firm will still attach different values to a given production plan which is state dependent. Since production will not take place in the owner-managed firm unless all the owners can agree on a single production plan, a lack of unanimity among the owners again causes production to break down. The literature then suggests that this production crisis can be avoided by enlarging the role played by the manager. Traditionally the manager's role encompasses the overseeing of the firm's routine operations. If the manager were entrusted with the task of forecasting the market value of the firm as well as of mediating the shareholders' interest, then a production plan unanimously agreeable to all shareholders may again emerge. However, in order to perform this role, the manager must have access to the shareholders' preferences and must be empowered to shift first-period endowments from one shareholder to another. The literature casts doubt on the possibility that the manager can effectively perform this feat in a decentralized market setting. This is because, in order to exercise his power to tax and subsidize, the manager must know the shareholders' preferences or have the assurance that the shareholders will truthfully disclose their gains or losses resulting from a given change in the firm's production policy. Because the market does not provide a mechanism for supplying this information or for preventing the shareholder from behaving strategically in providing this information, such a mechanism must be imposed from a source outside the market institution. The need to graft such a mechanism onto the market implies that the incomplete markets by themselves are no longer capable of allocating resources. This conclusion indicates that the neoclassical economic theory is not sufficiently robust to be applied to an economy with incomplete markets.

In our judgement, the failure of the neoclassical theory stems from its misidentification of the functional group which controls production and its misspecification of the process by which a unanimously agreeable production policy is achieved. Specifically, the neoclassical theory fails to recognize that in changing from a complete to an incomplete market setting production control shifts from the capitalist owners to the pure entrepreneurs. This shift in the control group fundamentally alters the allocative process from a one-tier market allocation to a two-tier firm–market allocation situation. Unanimity in production policy is no longer achieved through market competition but rather through intrafirm negotiation and bargaining. In this book, we endeavor to present an alternative theory which describes the process taking place in the two-tier incomplete markets. It will be shown that the competitive economy with incomplete markets, unaided by any externally imposed mechanism, is indeed capable of allocating resources in a decentralized manner. However, before doing this, we will summarize the various attempts in the literature to deal with the neoclassical failures.

NOTES

1 The precise nature of this change will be discussed in the next section.
2 The result of this section can be summarized by the following algebraic statement. Let

$$P_j = \sum_s \hat{q}_s y_s^j$$

where $\hat{q}_s$ denotes the estimate of the market contingent claims price in state s. Either $q_s = \rho_s^i$ or $q_s = \Sigma_i \theta_{ij} \rho_s^i$ for $s = 1, \ldots, S$. When the production spanning condition is satisfied, that is, $y_s^j = \sum_h \alpha_h y_s^h$, then

$$P_j = \sum_s \hat{q}_s \sum_h \alpha_h y_s^h = \sum_h \alpha_h P_h$$

for some real numbers α_h. This result is true regardless of which individual's or firm's contingent claims prices are used.

4

Theories of the Entrepreneur and the Firm

Having examined the literature's concern over the failure of the neoclassical economy to gain equilibrium under the conditions of uncertainty, we now take up its concern on two other fronts: the neoclassical economists' failure to acknowledge the entrepreneurial function and profit as a distributive share, and their inaccurate description of firms in the real world. Regarding the latter issue, the literature is particularly critical of the fact that neoclassical economics simply assumes the existence of the firm, ignores its internal organization and its independent decision-making capability, denies the cooperative behavior among agents within the firm, and neglects the presence of non-owner-controlled firms. Critical remarks as well as suggestions for alternative approaches have helped to generate a vast amount of literature. Practical considerations prevent us from surveying this literature in detail. In this chapter we can only review the bare essence of a selected portion, at times merely mentioning topics of interest in passing, in order to show the direction in which the literature has moved and to acknowledge how this literature contributes to our understanding about the way that entrepreneurs and firms supplement the market to allocate resources. The topics included in this brief survey are the role of the entrepreneur, the *raison d'être* of firms, the firm's control structure, internal organization, and decision rules, and the boundary between the firm and the market. The issues concerning income distribution and profits will be postponed until chapter 10.

ENTREPRENEURIAL ROLES

Although the synonyms for entrepreneur – projector or undertaker – were used by French economists as early as the sixteenth century, it was J. B. Say who made the term "entrepreneur" popular at the turn of the nineteenth century (Hoselitz, 1951; Schumpeter, 1965, p. 46). Say's notion of entrepreneurial function, however, was ambiguous. He treated the entrepreneur sometimes as a capitalist and at other times as a laborer. Clearer definitions of the entrepreneur were offered by Cantillon and von Thunen. Cantillon characterized the entrepreneur as an individual who engages in business "without an assurance of the profits he will derive from his enterprise" (Cantillon, 1964, p. 51). Von Thunen described the entrepreneur as a person "who is preoccupied with the fortune of the business"; through trial and tribulation, he deals with daily contingencies (Obrinsky, 1983, pp. 20–1).

Although these are the forerunners of the present-day writers on the entrepreneur and entrepreneurship, the current writings on this topic are, to a large degree, stimulated by the writers' dissatisfaction over the conclusion of neoclassical economics. By assuming ubiquitous knowledge and costless information, the neoclassical economists concluded that the market alone can coordinate production; hence there does not exist a need for entrepreneurs. This conclusion is clearly inadequate under normal market conditions where knowledge is a scarce commodity and information can be acquired only for a price. Moreover, it is not possible to translate knowledge and information automatically to decision-making. For various reasons (to be given below), the market is no longer able to coordinate production by itself; the assistance of specialized decision-makers is needed. However, decision-making requires special talents and these talents are scarce. Those who possess these talents become a distinct factor of production – the entrepreneur.

Even though it is agreed that the entrepreneurial function becomes relevant when production takes place under uncertainty, writers are unable to agree just what constitutes entrepreneurship. This disagreement arises because writers react to the neoclassical model and view uncertainty differently. Consequently, they each select a particular entrepreneurial role as being important. In this section we discuss some major notions of entrepreneurship.

As we have seen in the preceding chapter, Knight criticized neoclassical economics for its failure to distinguish actual from perfect competition. Amidst actual competition, the market fails to coordinate joint production. The Knightian entrepreneur breaks the impasse created by this lack of consistent resource commitment among the resource owners. In Knight's conception, the entrepreneur is a risk-bearing capitalist who is willing and able to bear uncertainties by providing insurance to the other cooperative resource owners. In exchange for his risk-bearing, the capitalist entrepreneur gains the privilege of substituting his own judgement for that of the others and choosing a production plan for the group. In order to hold the entrepreneur responsible for his judgement, the entrepreneur alone bears production consequences by becoming the residual claimant. Knight distinguishes clearly the role of the entrepreneur from that of the manager. The entrepreneur performs the "judgement of the last resort" and bears the ultimate uncertainty associated with it, while the manager only performs "judgement of things" associated with routine business (Knight, 1971, p. 298).

Members of the Austrian School of Economics, who include Ludwig von Mises, Frederick Hayek, and more recently Israel Kirzner, criticize neoclassical economics from a different angle. They believe that the neoclassical economists fail to provide a complete description of the market process because the entrepreneur element has been ignored.

Specifically, the market at any given time is a collection of buying and selling activities conducted by consumers, producers, and resource owners. The neoclassical economists seek to understand the market economy by examining only the structural conditions that are required to make equilibrium possible. To the Austrian economists this approach is inadequate. This is because the presence of market uncertainties places a veil over market opportunities; market participants can no longer perceive all beneficial exchanges. With the imperfection of knowledge about the market and the ignorance of other market participants' decisions, it is inevitable that production and exchange activities at any given moment fail to capture the best of all market opportunities. Widespread ignorance prevents the market from fulfilling its coordinating role and a state of disequilibrium thus emerges. Moreover, while in a state of disequilibrium, the market is incapable of regaining an equilibrium through its own forces.

Under these circumstances we cannot describe the market process by simply examining the maximizing behavior of the resource owners. Because resource owners, who are referred to by the Austrian economists as economizers or maximizers, only respond to exogenously imposed forces, we cannot look to their behavior for explanations of endogenous changes that take place in the market. Instead, we must seek to understand how the market participants interact to generate market forces which bring the market into equilibrium whenever it is out of equilibrium. In the words of Kirzner. "[we need to understand] the market forces which compel changes in prices, in output and in methods of production and the allocation of resources" (Kirzner, 1973, p. 6). The entrepreneurs are identified by the Austrian economists as the agents who generate these market forces. Therefore, in order to understand the market process, we must center our attention on the entrepreneurial element.

The Austrian entrepreneurs are purposeful actors (von Mises, 1962,

p. 34) who, in a state of disequilibrium, explore "hitherto unnoticed opportunities" and interact to generate the market process (Kirzner, 1973, p. 39). In this way, Kirzner views the entrepreneur as the principal player in the market who discovers and disseminates information and sets the market process in motion. While the market is not in equilibrium, production and exchange activities fail to capture the best of all market opportunities. The alert entrepreneur identifies circumstances believed to be relevant to his decision-making and exploits profit opportunities whenever they are present. Since the entrepreneur is alert to hitherto unnoticed opportunities, the existing plans become obsolete as he becomes aware of these profit opportunities. Plans are then modified to reflect the entrepreneur's newly gained knowledge about the market opportunities, and the market is forced to adjust. In this manner, the market process is set in motion. Consequently, it is through the entrepreneurial element that we find explanations for changes that occur in the market. Furthermore, in a market environment where opportunities for arbitrage exist, as the alert entrepreneur uses his newly found information to exploit previously undiscovered market opportunities, his action also reveals these opportunities to other market participants. Competition among entrepreneurs pushes market prices in a direction which gradually limits opportunity for further profit and leads to a gradual fuller awareness of the true levels of market demand and supply. In the end, actions taken by the entrepreneurs to win profit also have the effect of correcting market mistakes and eradicating ignorance. As ignorance and mistakes are eliminated, the market naturally attains a state of equilibrium. In Hayek's view, with the help of the entrepreneur the market is "an efficient mechanism for communicating information" (Hayek, 1945, p. 526). Efficiency, in Hayek's sense, is measured by the speed with which the social institution is able to mobilize information, eliminate ignorance, and bring the market to a socially desirable outcome.

Following this line of reasoning, the Austrian economists identify the entrepreneur as the prime mover of the market process. Since they have already taken the view that the entrepreneur is not a maximizer and that only resource owners are maximizers, they naturally conclude that the entrepreneur is not a capitalist. Further, the Austrian economists also arrive at the conclusion that the entrepreneur is not a risk-bearer. The reason is simple: since the propertyless entrepreneur only acts to take advantage of the market opportunities, what risk is there for him to bear?

Schumpeter criticizes neoclassical economics from yet another perspective: he chides neoclassical economics for its failure to acknowledge the fact that the capitalistic economy is inherently dynamic. In Schumpeter's words, the capitalist economy "incessantly revolutionizes the economic structure from within, incessantly destroying the old one, incessantly creating a new one. This process of Creative Destruction is the essential fact about capitalism" (Schumpeter, 1942, p. 83).

Schumpeter identifies the cause of the revolutionary changes as economic development, which is defined as "carrying out of new combinations" (Schumpeter, 1934, p. 66). However, economic development cannot take place automatically; a motivating force is required. Schumpeter identifies the innovator–entrepreneur as the motivating factor. Recall that no profit exists in an equilibrium situation. However, profit can be obtained by carrying out new combinations, e.g. by introducing an improved method of production or a new product. The entrepreneur, lured by the profits associated with innovation, carries out the act of economic development. Profit emerges with a new method of production which reduces the production costs. Since the market price of the product is relatively stable, reduction in the cost of production necessarily implies profit. Profit can also result from a new product. If it is assumed that the consumer prefers the new product to the old, he will be willing to pay a higher price for the new product. Since the prices of the inputs are determined in accordance with their traditional employment, the cost of producing the new good would necessarily lag behind the revenue. Profits thus emerge. Lured by these profits, the entrepreneur deliberately disturbs the existing market equilibrium by introducing a new combination.

Profit derived from economic development, however, is short lived. Economic development as viewed by Schumpeter involves three stages: invention, innovation, and imitation. Invention is the technical discovery of the new combination. Innovation is the successful commercialization of the new combination. Imitation is the market process which widens the adoption of a new product or process. This market process ultimately has the effect of bringing the market into a new state of "remainderless equilibrium." This post-innovation equilibrium is superior to the previous equilibrium in that society reaches a higher level of satisfaction. From the consumer's point of view this new equilibrium is preferred for two reasons. First, innovation has provided the consumer with a new or improved product. Second, through imitation, the consumer also reaps the benefits of a lower price. From the resource owner's point of view, the post-innovation equilibrium is also preferred. The innovation increases the marginal productivity of factors of production. In the state of a new equilibrium, the price of each factor of production now exceeds the previous level. This implies that innovation raises the income earned by the owners of the factors of production.

Based upon this process of economic development, Schumpeter characterizes the entrepreneur in the following way. The entrepreneur is foremost an innovator. Because it is inevitable that by carrying out economic development the innovator must inflict uncertainty on himself, the entrepreneur is also an individual who has great confidence in his judgement and is not intimidated by uncertainties associated with economic development. In addition, the entrepreneur persistently seeks to carry out economic development despite the fact that profit derived from innovation is short lived; he is also an optimist. Finally, Schumpeter asserts that the entrepreneur is neither a capitalist nor a manager. This does not mean that an individual cannot simultaneously perform the functions of a capitalist, a manager, and an entrepreneur; it simply means that the entrepreneurial function is not identical with the functions performed by either a capitalist or a manager. Since the entrepreneur is not a capitalist, he is not a risk-bearer. Bearing risk is the function of the capitalist. Since the entrepreneur is not a manager, he is not identified by the position he holds. He is only identified by the function he performs. This function is innovation. As soon as he ceases to be innovative, profit vanishes and with it the entrepreneurial role.

From this brief survey of the literature on entrepreneurship, it is apparent that the authors agree only on the point that the entrepreneurial role is relevant whenever uncertainty exists in the market and the market is in a state of disequilibrium. There is no agreement on either the entrepreneurial role or how the entrepreneur as a factor of production can be identified. According to Knight, the entrepreneur breaks the impasses created by a lack of consistent resource commitment among the resource owners and bears the market uncertainties; according to the Austrian economists, the entrepreneur taps the unexploited market opportunities and activates the market process; according to Schumpeter, the entrepreneur is an innovator. These disagreements, as we will see shortly, lead to different perceptions in the literature concerning the nature of the firm, the nature of profits, and the way that resources are allocated.

RAISON D'ETRE OF FIRMS

Generally, in order to posit the firm in the midst of the market, it is implicitly assumed that, in coordinating several production activities, it is necessary to substitute the firm for the market. The neoclassical economists take for granted that the firm exists on technical grounds alone, that is, it enjoys the advantage derived from economies of scale in joint production. Their critics argue that such a firm does not perform an intrinsic allocative role and suggest that the existence of the firm reflects the influence of market uncertainties.

It is commonly agreed that incentives to organize the firm are greatly enhanced under market uncertainties because the market no longer identifies profit opportunities or provides all the information necessary for making production decisions. These market failures provide entrepreneurs with opportunities for gain. The entrepreneurs carry out their activities with the firm as a vehicle. Four basic causes for the firm to emerge are identified in the literature: the firm is formed in order (a) to provide the means of breaking the impasse created by a lack of consistent resource commitment among the resource owners, (b) to gain the advantage of risk-sharing, (c) to avoid the high cost of using the market, and (d) to reduce shirking when output is jointly produced. These themes originated with Knight, the Portfolio Theorists, Coase, and Alchian and Demsetz respectively. In addition, firms are also organized in labor-managed economies and may be controlled by managers. In this section, in addition to presenting the work of the above-mentioned authors, we also summarize Ichiishi's explanation for the *raison d'être* of labor-managed firms and the explanation put forward by Berle and Means for the emergence of manager-managed firms.

Knight has left indelible imprints on the literature of the theory of the firm. His *raison d'être* for the firm ties in intimately with his concept of the entrepreneur. As we have seen earlier, the Knightian entrepreneur is a capitalist who seeks profit from ever-changing market environments and is not afraid to make decisions and bear risks. The Knightian entrepreneur does this by simply accepting all market uncertainties and making other resource owners his employees. The firm emerges as a consequence.

Although entrepreneurs are risk-bearers, it does not mean that they are not interested in finding ways of lightening their burdens. One way of accomplishing this is through risk-sharing. In recent years, based upon the portfolio theory, economists have established risk-sharing as the *raison d'être* of firms. At first, risk-sharing was used to justify vertical integration (Blair and Kaserman, 1978) and the formation of conglomerate firms (Azzi, 1978). More recently, it has been employed directly to explain the existence of the firm (Gilson and Mnookin, 1985).

According to the portfolio theory, all risk-averse investors prefer diversification and risk-sharing. It suggests that there are two ways for entrepreneurs to share their risks: by trading income shares among the entrepreneurs, or by forming a coalition. Trading of entrepreneurial income shares is, in general, ineffectual. Risk-sharing through coalition formation of entrepreneurs is more promising. Risk-sharing becomes a *raison d'être* of the firm. We will develop this point more fully in chapter 5.

Coase rejects Knight's explanation for the firm's existence as well as his characterization of the firm (Coase, 1937). He cites transaction costs as a fresh reason for the firm to exist. In order to make the commitment for production in an uncertain market environment, resource owners must incur a cost for information which the perfect market normally provides. In addition, it is also costly to negotiate and enforce contracts. The magnitude of these uncertainty-related transaction costs will decrease if a firm is created to coordinate production, thus allowing these activities to bypass the market. This view is widely endorsed in the literature (Arrow, 1974b; Williamson, 1981).

Coase suggests that "The most obvious cost of 'organizing' production through the price mechanism is that of discovering what the relevant prices are" (Coase, 1937, p. 390). Determining relevant prices for all inputs and outputs in all states of nature and negotiating contracts for production by all owners is deemed to be a costly endeavor. A Coasean entrepreneur is one who steps forward to relieve factor owners of the burden of negotiating all the bilateral contracts necessary for production. He takes it upon himself to sign contracts with each resource owner "whereby ... for a certain remuneration (which may be fixed or fluctuating), [he] agrees to obey the directions of an entrepreneur within certain limits" (Coase, 1937, p. 391). This leads to the emergence of the firm.

While Knight and Coase postulate that the firm owes its existence to the presence of price uncertainty, Alchian and Demsetz (1972) advance a theory for the existence of the firm based on joint production and production uncertainty. Modern technology accords great advantages to the division of labor and large-scale production. Resource owners can often reap a gain by abandoning individual-based production and embracing team production. However, the decision to switch from individual-based production to team production cannot be made on technical grounds alone; an incentive problem exists. The incentive problem arises whenever the team members' efforts are not costlessly observable and the division of the team's income to its members does not reflect each member's true contribution. If a team member can reduce his efforts without suffering a reduction in income equal to the loss in the team's income caused by his action, the "private cost" of his action is less than its "true cost." This discrepancy in costs will encourage the team members to shirk, thus adversely affecting the team's production. The tendency to shirk becomes particularly strong when both leisure and income enter into a person's utility function. In this case shirking reduces the price of leisure and therefore encourages its consumption. Conversely, if a team member cannot fully capture the increase in the team's income caused by his own efforts, such efforts will not be forthcoming. In both ways, the presence of the incentive problem prevents team production from reaching its potential.

The incentive problem is particularly serious whenever there exists uncertainty in production. The owner of an input can now claim that a reduction in the team's output is not due to his evasion of responsibility but rather to bad luck. Uncertainty in production compounds the problems caused by the inability to observe input efforts and thus contributes to the prevalence of shirking. Whenever shirking of efforts causes a reduction in the team's output and this reduction in output in turn causes an individual resource owner's income to fall below what he can earn by his own efforts, a team involving this resource owner will not be formed. No team will be formed at all if shirking causes every potential team member's income to fall below what each can earn by working alone.

Having established the proposition on shirking, Alchian and Demsetz proceed to describe how a viable team is organized. Their argument is based crucially upon the assumption that "clues to each input's productivity can be secured by observing behavior of individual inputs" (Alchian and Demsetz, 1972, p. 780). Thus monitoring and metering is looked upon as the foundation of team production. However, monitoring activities are costly endeavors. In order for team production to be viable, the team with monitoring must yield a net return to every team member greater than the amount that each can receive under individual-based production.

When production uncertainty is present and the monitoring cost is high, team production cannot be coordinated economically by the market. Production uncertainty makes it difficult for everyone to ascertain marginal productivities of the team members. Owing to the fact that input productivity must be assessed by observing input behavior, the market is particularly ill-suited to coordinate production. Market monitoring is costly because market monitoring is conducted by potential team members who must incur greater cost than the present team members in order to secure information about "where and to what extent shirking has taken place." In addition, it is also ineffectual because the incentive to shirk for the new team member would still be "at least as great as" that for the displaced team member. Consequently, market monitoring does not discourage shirking. Firm monitoring yields better results. Let the firm be defined as a team with a central monitor who is also the central contractor. Alchian and Demsetz argue that the firm can perform the monitoring role more economically since it can resolve the shirking-information problem better than the noncentralized contractual arrangement can.

It is the saving on the monitoring cost that calls forth the firm (Alchian and Demsetz, 1972, p. 780).

Stimulated by Ward's seminal contribution (Ward, 1958), a body of literature has been generated to study the labor-managed firm and the labor-managed economy (Vanek, 1970; Drèze, 1976; Ichiishi, 1977, 1982, 1985). We will present the essence of a model developed by Ichiishi who uses a more general concept of "social coalition equilibrium" to describe the labor-managed economy and provides a reason for the existence of labor-managed firms. This model is particularly relevant to us because the technique introduced by Ichiishi is useful in analyzing the economy which we will present in the later part of this book.

The Ichiishi model contains a fixed number of symmetric agents. Each agent is at the same time a consumer, a laborer, and a capitalist stockholder. There is no market for labor services in the economy although all other commodity markets do exist and are perfectly competitive. However, laborers can channel their services into production through coalition formation (organizing a firm) and derive their income through bargaining. Ichiishi uses a two-period temporary equilibrium model to describe (a) the decision problem of the agent in three roles – as a consumer, a capitalist, and a laborer who not only renders labor services for production but also participates in organizing the firm – and (b) the mechanism which leads to the formation of the firm and the attainment of equilibrium in the economy.

The consumer is endowed with a certain amount of initial wealth and a von Neumann–Morgenstern utility function with goods consumed in the two periods as arguments. He takes the market prices as given and chooses a stock portfolio and commodity bundles, one for each period, in order to maximize his expected utility subject to his budget constraints. Because the individual's budget in the second period now depends on his labor income which, in turn, depends on his activities in the coalition formation, the consumer must also make his labor participation decisions in the first period.

A firm is a coalition of laborers. The formation of a coalition signifies that the workers have entered into agreement with each other concerning (a) the joint production policy and (b) the rule which governs the distribution of the residual. The formation of the firm is conditional on whether the coalition can secure sufficient funds from the stock market to finance production. Limitations on financing imply that not all potential coalitions can become firms. The firm organized in this manner will also have a two-period decision horizon. It issues stocks in the first period to raise funds to finance production; it also hires nonlabor inputs and commences production. The firm sells its outputs in the second period and distributes the residual to the shareholders as dividends and to the laborers as wages.

In this economy each agent will pursue individual interests as a consumer, capitalist, and laborer in order to maximize his expected utility. Assume that each agent is a price taker. Let the commodity and stock prices be given. Each agent as a consumer chooses noncooperatively consumption bundles and a stock portfolio, and each agent as a laborer chooses cooperatively via coalition formation with other laborers a joint strategy regarding inputs, employment, and a residual sharing rule. The feasible strategy is limited by the firm's ability to collect funds to finance its production. The consumer and the firm together generate market activities. The firms are the demanders of resources and suppliers of goods. The consumers are the demanders of goods and suppliers of marketable resources, including capital. Thus demand and supply interact to determine market prices. The economy reaches an equilibrium whenever the prices of the commodities and the stocks satisfy the following conditions: (a) each consumer's consumption and stock purchase fall within his budget constraint; (b) each firm's outlay on inputs does not exceed the available funds collected from its stock sales; (c) each firm's labor input does not exceed the amount that is available in the coalition; (d) all markets are cleared. This equilibrium is stable if no laborer can improve his lot by forming a new coalition.

The Ichiishi model of the labor-managed economy gives a clear reason for the existence of firms in an economy where the labor market is absent and offers a process through which firms are organized. Because of the absence of the labor market, wages and the formation of the firm are determined simultaneously through bargaining and the playing of a society-wide cooperative game.

The discussion of the *raison d'être* of firms is incomplete unless we take manager-managed firms into consideration. Economists generally explain the existence of this type of firm from the historical perspective. Initially, the firms were predominantly proprietorships and partnerships. Over time, the partnerships gave way to corporations. Corporations underwent additional changes. The nature of these changes is elaborated further in chapters 8 and 9. For the present purpose we need only summarize the literature which describes how owner-managed corporations may evolve into the manager-managed type.

As the market expands, the firm must increase its size and complexity in order to gain efficiency in production and distribution. Whenever expansion is financed by cash flow generated from the increased scale of production and distribution, the control of the corporation remains in the hands of the capitalist owners. However, if these expansions are financed through the equity market, the capitalist owners may lose control over the corporation. In principle, the control of the corporation ultimately rests in the hands of the board of directors. Since majority rule prevails within the board, the effective control of the corporation lodges in the hands of those individuals who can elect a majority to the board.

When corporations are small and the capital structures are simple, shareholders participate more intimately in the direction of corporate affairs through a controlled management. The board is generally under majority control. As the corporation attains greater size, the search for capital scatters the ownership. Knowledge of the corporation's affairs becomes more costly to acquire. Many of the shareholders are either unable or unwilling to take an active role in managing the corporate affairs; they become docile and indifferent. Their voting power is either not represented at shareholders' meetings or has lost its significance. When the ownership shares are sufficiently dispersed, an individual who controls a small fraction of the voting shares can gain effective control of the board and thus the corporation. Minority control thus emerges. Further dispersion of ownership shares means that no individual or small group of owners has the capability of exercising effective control. Because the managers hold a strategic position, they are able to gain control of the proxy process and hence the board of directors. The control shifts to the managers. The manager-managed firm emerges as a consequence.

We have now seen the reasons given in the literature for the existence of the various types of firm. Because the literature suggests that both the control structure and the internal organization of the firm affect the firm's choice of its decision rules, we must examine explanations of the firm's internal organization before reviewing the literature on how firms allocate resources in an intrinsic way.

THE FIRM'S INTERNAL ORGANIZATION

Traditionally, economists use the monopoly power possessed by the firm to explain its internal organization. It is well known that a monopolistic firm can reap an excess profit by defying the market and setting prices and output different from those selected by firms in a competitive market. A monopolistic firm, in an attempt to extend its monopoly power from one segment of the market to another, will integrate horizontally and vertically, thus leading to a specific internal organization for the firm based upon product lines. Recently, discussions of the firm's internal organization have extended to include functional lines. These discussions generally follow two approaches: the historical approach or the cost approach.

The Historical Approach

Chandler (Chandler, 1977, chapter 13; Williamson, 1971a) advanced his views from a historical perspective. He observed that the firm, in its early stage of development, produces a single product line and performs a single function in production. All decisions concentrate in the hands of the owner–managers. As the firm expands, it integrates backward to raw material production and forward to sales and distribution, and may also add lines of production. The production and distribution functions now become distinct. Gradually the firm's activities need to be financed through the market; a separate financing function also emerges. As the firm's geographical market enlarges, transportation and communication also become distinct functions. A separate middle management is then needed to administer and coordinate the various functions. Chandler called the firm organized in this functional manner a unitary structured firm.

As the firm continues to expand, coordination among the functions becomes more complex. Managers are needed to coordinate and evaluate the performance of the middle managers. The top executive is needed to devise general strategies and plans for the firm, to reconcile functional disputes, and to allocate resources for the enterprise as a whole. The unitary structure of the firm becomes inadequate.

To remedy this shortcoming, the multidivisional structure emerged in the 1920s. A general office entrusted with the responsibilities for strategic decision-making and control is created in order to separate the strategic decisions from the operating decisions. Chandler called the firm organized in this fashion a multidivisional structured or M-form firm. In his words, "[The] new structure left the broad strategic decisions as to the allocation of existing resources and the acquisition of new ones in the hands of the top team of generalists. Relieved of operating duties and tactical decisions, a general executive was less likely to reflect the position of just one part of the whole" (Chandler, 1962, p. 383). Hierarchically organized managers now jointly share the management of the corporate affairs. The M-form firm not only is efficient but also has the effect of preventing the managers from pursuing their self-interests.

The Cost Approach

Some economists examine the organization problem from the cost point of view. This approach is based upon the belief that a special organizational structure emerges because it reduces the cost and increases the efficiency of governing the firm's operations. A general consensus on what exactly constitutes the governance cost does not yet exist. There are several candidates which include the transaction cost, the monitoring cost, and the agency cost. Among these alternatives, agency cost theory has received the most attention.

The agency cost theory of the firm, principally associated with Jensen, Meckling, and Fama, is constructed to reflect the belief that the firm represents a nexus of contracts written among shareholders, workers, managers, material suppliers, and customers (Jensen and Meckling, 1976, 1979). These contracts specify the internal rules of the game, the rights and obligations of the agents, and the payoff functions which the agents face. Payoffs are divided into two categories – those tied to specific measures of performances determined *ex ante* and those belonging to the residual claimants determined *ex post*. The set of contracts defines the character of a firm and distinguishes one organization from another (Fama and Jensen, 1983, p. 302).

Because contracts cannot be written and enforced costlessly, agents are encouraged to behave opportunistically. The behavior of the agents crucially affects the firm's performance and the payoff that each agent will receive. Because some payoffs are determined *ex ante* and others *ex post*, the residual claimants who receive their rewards *ex post* are particularly vulnerable to agents' opportunistic behavior and contractual abuses. This gives rise to the agency problem.

In particular, the agency theorists note that the agency problem arises because there exist advantages in separating the risk-bearing and decision-making roles. Risk-bearing can be made more efficient by spreading risks that the firm faces among a larger number of shareholders. The attempt to share risks inevitably brings advantages to the specialization of decision-making, by delegating decision-making power to a small number of agents – the board of directors. This gives rise to separation of ownership and control. Separation of ownership and control is deemed to be the major source of the agency problem.

The agency theorists advocate that the integrity of the contracts can be maintained and the interest of the residual claimant safeguarded by appropriately structuring the firm's internal organization. When the agency problem is created by the separation of ownership and control, it can be shown that the problem can be mitigated by a change in the firm's internal structure. Recall that the firm's decision process comprises two parts: operating management and strategic control. The agency theorists contend that the delegation of the operating management and strategic control functions to different managers will have the effect of providing checks and balances among them. These checks and balances serve to decrease the agents' opportunistic behavior and thus contribute to a reduction in agency cost.

The separation of operating management and strategic control does not necessarily lead the firm to adopt the multidivisional internal structure. The M-form firm emerges if the fact that the ability to delegate authority differs markedly in the areas of operating management and strategic control is taken into account. If we follow the organization theorists and treat delegation of authority as a decomposition of tasks, it becomes apparent that the decomposition of operating tasks can be carried out to a much greater degree than the decomposition of strategic control tasks. Suppose that the strategic control tasks can be decomposed into only two vertical levels and are shared by a small number of agents, whereas the operating tasks can be decomposed into several vertical levels and are shared by a large number of agents. In this case it is natural that the large number of operating units will cluster around each strategic control unit and unite to form a subunit or a division. This propensity for bunching thus leads to the formation of the M-form firm. In this way it can be said that the attempt to reduce the agency cost ultimately brings multidivisional firms into existence.

THE FIRM'S DECISION RULE

The discussions of the *raison d'être* and internal organization of the firm pave the way for us to examine the literature's treatment of the crucial issue: how the firm allocates resources, and how a difference in the control structure and internal organization of a firm affect the allocative consequence. The literature's treatment of this issue is again diverse and sometimes imprecise. The various approaches can be classified into two basic categories depending upon whether or not the firm is considered as a maximizer. In this section we briefly review these ideas.

The Firm as Maximizer

Traditionally a firm is assumed to maximize a well-defined objective function. The nature of this function depends crucially upon the firm's control structure. Under this premise, the firm's behavior can be deduced by manipulating its objective function subject to some appropriate constraints. This leads to the conclusion that the control structure of a firm predetermines not only its behavior but also its allocative efficiency. Because the firm's behavior and allocative outcome are determined by its objective, they are not affected markedly by its internal organization structure.

It is commonly assumed that an owner-managed firm will pursue a policy of maximizing profit. This traditional view is considered unacceptable by Scitovsky (1943), who believes that the owner–manager must expend time and effort in order to carry out his business activities. Once efforts become an input and leisure enters into consideration, it is more reasonable for an owner–manager to maximize a utility function which contains profit and leisure.

Scitovsky's reservation on profit maximization is echoed by others who are concerned with the presence of market uncertainty. Economists postulate that under uncertainty the owner–manager needs to formulate some expectation about future events and is forced to maximize expected utility of profits rather than just simple profit. When decisions are made in this manner the owner–manager's attitude toward risk becomes a major determinant of the firm's production policy (Baron, 1970; Sandmo, 1971). Profit alone is no longer sufficient to determine the owner–manager's choice of a production policy. The firm's production policy now reflects the decision-maker's subjective considerations. Since decision-maker's preferences are not observable, it becomes more complicated to ascertain how the firm's production policy is determined and more difficult to assess its consequences. These difficulties multiply when a firm is managed by many owners, leading to the unanimity problem discussed in the previous chapter. If the achievement of unanimity among shareholders is not possible, then it is not clear just what objective the firm should pursue.

The proliferation of ownership shares not only destroys shareholder unanimity in formulating the firm's production policy but also creates concern over whether the owners can even retain effective control over the firm's policy. Many economists prefer the view of Berle and Means (1932) who advocate that proliferation of ownership shares not only causes the control of the corporation to pass from the hands of the owners to the hands of the managers but also alters the firm's objectives. They begin by assuming that the manager possesses a well-defined objective function. The contributors to this literature, however, cannot agree on what constitutes this objective function. Each therefore proposes a specific objective function that the manager will maximize. Williamson (1963b) suggests that when a manager enjoys significant discretion in selecting the firm's policies his utility function includes not only profits but also variables such as the number of staff and managerial emoluments. Baumol (1967), however, claims that the manager's interests can best be served by maximizing the firm's sales subject to the constraint of a certain level of minimum profit. The minimum profit is selected to provide a sufficient rate of return to the shareholders in the short run and to insure the maintenance of an acceptable growth rate in the long run. In contrast, Marris (1963) believes that managerial welfare depends solely on the growth rate of the firm. He therefore finds it plausible to assert that the manager's objective is to maximize the firm's growth rate.

Not only owner- and manager-managed firms possess a well-defined objective; so does the labor-managed firm.[1] Assuming that all workers are identical, most authors, following the lead of Ward (1958), claim that the labor-managed firm strives to maximize the income per worker.

According to those who believe that firms are maximizers, firms with different objectives will allocate resources differently. In particular, compared with the firm which seeks to maximize profits, the Williamson firm will choose a larger staff input, the Baumol and labor-managed firms will choose a larger quantity of output, and the Marris firm will choose a higher rate of growth; all these firms will yield a lower profit. Because the conventional wisdom holds that the production policy of the owner-managed firm is consistent with efficient allocation of resources and since firms under other control structures lead to different production policies, the literature generally concludes that these policies are not socially efficient. In other words, firms controlled by anyone other than the owners are organizationally inefficient.

Of course, the validity of this conclusion depends crucially on the assumption that the firm indeed possesses a well-defined objective function. This position has been widely criticized, and the implications of the various theories have been challenged (Scherer, 1980, pp. 29–40). We have seen that it is implausible to believe that a host of shareholders with different preferences, endowments, and expectations about future events can unanimously adopt a single production policy. Similar statements can be made for manager- and labor-managed firms. In the case of the former, the authority over the firm is shared by a number of managers who have different interests and concerns; the management is hardly monolithic. The same is true for the latter since it is unreasonable to assume that workers with different abilities, tasks, preferences, and wealth will subscribe to a single production policy. The manager- and labor-managed firms must also address the unanimity issue. Dissatisfied with the arbitrariness of the firm's objective functions and frustrated by the lack of agreement on the implications of the various theories, many economists opt to investigate theories of the firm based upon nonmaximization principles. We now attend to this branch of the literature.

The Nonmaximizing Firm

Many economists disagree fundamentally with the premise that the firm is a maximizer. They do so on the grounds that either the firm is incapable of pursuing a maximizing goal or it is not organized to pursue such a goal. Although there are some overlapping positions, the former belief typically underlies the behavior theories of the firm and the latter underlies the bargaining theories of the firm. As the firm is denied an objective function, its internal organization becomes the crucial determinant of the firm's behavior.

Behavioral Theories of the Firm   We include in this category organizational, behavioral, and evolutionary theories of the firm. The economists advocating these theories believe that the firm has a limited knowledge of all available opportunities and cannot decipher all the associated consequences. This limitation in the individual's perception of a given situation is referred to by Simon (1959) as "bounded rationality." Simon believes that the economic environment changes rapidly and is too complex to be comprehended fully by the decision-maker. Thus the firm cannot take into account all information in order to perform maximization calculations over the set of all possible alternatives. It is therefore unlikely to pursue a maximization policy. Instead, Simon advocates the view that the firm does not maximize, it merely "satisfices."

The ability of the firm to pursue a maximization goal is further hampered by the complexity of its internal organization. A modern firm is a network of vertical chains of command and horizontal links among functionary groups. Decisions are made at various hierarchical levels and by different functionaries. Conflicts among these parties are bound to arise. In a given market environment the firm is simply inept at selecting a policy which attains global maximization and, once a policy has been selected, the firm is unable to enforce it by fiat authority. Instead, the firm must arrive at a decision through bargaining among the relevant groups and settle for a mere satisfactory outcome. What is considered to be satisfactory depends upon the aspiration level that these groups set for themselves. "Rules of thumb" and procedures are devised to assure the attainment of these aspiration levels. Assume that these rules and procedures for any given time span attain a certain degree of regularity (Cyert and March, 1963) and that changes in them are governed by certain well-defined routines (Nelson and Winter, 1982). The organizational behavior and evolutionary theorists view the firm as an organism with an internal structure and hold it as a living manifestation of a set of rules and procedures. They concentrate their efforts on conducting empirical analyses of the decision processes of the individual firm and deduce from them the decision rules used by the firm.

Bargaining Theories   In this branch of the literature, the firm is viewed as a coalition of many agents with different endowments, tastes, and interests. Those agents who cooperate with each other use the firm as a vehicle not to strive for a common goal but to pursue their own self-interest. They each do so by influencing the firm's policies in their own favor through bargaining. Since the firm's policies are determined through bargaining, the governing structure and the behavior of the firm depend crucially upon the parties that participate in the bargaining process. Several types of model are considered in the literature: a coalition of laborers (Ichiishi, 1977, 1982, 1985), a coalition of employees and shareholders (Aoki, 1980), a coalition of managers (Cyert and March, 1963), and a coalition of all parties who have anything to do with the firm (Jensen and Meckling, 1976).

Ichiishi assumes that the labor market is entirely absent and characterizes the firm as a coalition of laborers. The firm's policy is determined through bargaining by the cooperative workers. Aoki assumes that workers possess firm-specific knowledge and skill; therefore an organizational rent can be generated by a group of workers belonging to a quasi-permanent firm. The firm can be interpreted as a coalition of workers and stockholders who bargain to determine the firm's policy. Cyert and March view the firm as a coalition of managers. Bargaining among managerial groups takes place continuously, leading to the firm's policy. Finally, Jensen and Meckling treat the firm as a nexus of contracts among workers, shareholders, managers, suppliers, and customers. As such the firm operates by a set of contractual arrangements. Although Jensen and Meckling did not clearly describe the process by which these contracts are formulated, we presume that they are determined through bargaining. In this spirit, the firm becomes a coalition of all parties who have anything to do with the firm.

In this literature, not only does there not exist a consensus on the appropriate composition of the bargaining groups, but the bargaining theorists do not yet have a clear conception of what constitutes the determining factors of the decision rules and how a set of decision rules emerges from the bargaining process. Many factors have been suggested as possible contributors to the determination of the firm's decision rules. In addition to the composition of the bargaining group, these factors include the distribution of information among the members in the bargaining group, the reaction pattern of the bargainers, and the internal organization of the firm. To date no causal relationship between these factors and the decision rules has been established.

BOUNDARY BETWEEN THE FIRM AND THE MARKET

We have now examined the various approaches concerning the firm's internal allocative rule. To assert that there exists a distinct allocative rule for the firm implies that the firm and the market become two alternative modes of resource allocation and that they must share this responsibility. In order to discover how the literature struggles to understand the mechanism of resource allocation in a market economy, we need to investigate its perception of how the firm and the market divide the allocative tasks. In this section, we survey the ideas offered in the literature concerning where the firm ends and the market begins. Since the literature offers a variety of internal decision rules, it is not surprising that it also fails to identify a clear boundary between the firm and the market.

The literature suggests that the market and the firm are set apart by the way in which they allocate resources. The market allocates resources objectively with its members acting autonomously and behaving competitively against each other, whereas the firm allocates resources authoritatively with its members acting obediently to the directives of the entrepreneur or the manager and behaving cooperatively with each other. The firm, in the market context, acts in a dual manner. It buys and sells goods and services in the market based upon market rules but is organized internally under the control of the authoritative entrepreneur or manager. Therefore the boundary between the firm and the market is naturally defined by the behavior of the agents.

As we have seen in the preceding sections, many authors claim that entrepreneurial or managerial allocation as well as cooperation among agents within the firm afford significant advantages. If the firm enjoys advantages over the market in the allocation of resources, it is natural to ask what prevents the firm from expanding indefinitely and why there are market transactions at all. The answer to this question, in general, is that there are also limitations to the advantage of authority and cooperation that the firms enjoy. Coase deals with this question explicitly. Analyzing the firm's behavior from the transactions cost point of view, he asserts that there is not only a cost of using the market but also a cost of using the firm. Specifically, there exists a diminishing return to the entrepreneurs because of (a) a decreasing return to the entrepreneurial function, that is, the increased cost of organizing an additional transaction, and (b) the fact that, as the number of internal transactions increases, the probability of failure by the entrepreneur to make the best use of the factors of production will increase. In the words of Arrow, it is the overloading of the information and decision-making capacity of the authority that brings the firm to its limit. In general, Arrow contends that every organization serves a limited scope and that competition sets limits on authority (Arrow, 1974b, p. 76).

Because there is a cost of either using the firm or the market, neither the firm nor the market can operate exclusively without the other. Since the costs of using the market and using the firm are distinct, "the principle of marginalism works smoothly" in such a way that "a firm will tend to expand until the cost of organizing an extra transaction within the firm becomes equal to the cost of carrying out the same transaction by means of exchange on the open market or the cost of organizing another firm" (Coase, 1937, p. 293). By substituting at the margin, Coase not only resolves the boundary problem between the firm and the market but also finds the optimal size of the firm and the optimal number of firms in the market.[2]

Not all authors subscribe to the view that there is a sharp contrast between the behavior of agents in the firm and in the market. Some believe that the boundary between the firm and the market is never sharply defined. This belief is based upon the observation that the activities within the firm are not always governed by authority and that the agents do not always behave anonymously in the market and cooperatively within the firm. Specifically, the firm is not always organized in a hierarchical structure with agents performing tasks under the supervision of a superior and with the final authority resting in the hands of the entrepreneur. Instead, it represents a system with a built-in incentive structure which uses resources internal to the firm to generate the relevant internal rewards. In this context, Alchian and Demsetz characterize the relationship between employer and employee in a firm as an ordinary contractual relationship and insist that the firm has "no power of fiat, no authority, no discipline action any different in the slightest degree from ordinary market contracts between any two people" (Alchian and Demsetz, 1972, p. 777). Directing and assigning workers to the various tasks involves only the renegotiation of contracts on terms acceptable to both parties.

Some authors also hold the view that market relationships are not always short term and that agents do not always behave anonymously in the market. Frequently, market transactions are also governed by long-term contracts. Since market contracts can be long term in nature, the relationship between buyers and sellers may also be personal and require cooperation. Cooperation among market participants could yield benefits to the contractual parties just as surely as cooperation among the members of the firm. Consequently, long-term contracts and cooperation need not always lead to the formation of a firm. In this spirit, Alchian and Demsetz, although viewing the contractual relation as the essence of the firm, explicitly deny long-term contracts between employer and employee as the defining characteristic of the firm. They insist that "it is the centralized contractual agent in a team production process that. . .introduces the contractual form. . .called a firm" (Alchian and Demsetz, 1972, p. 778).

The mixing of behavior by agents in the firm and in the market blurs the boundary between the firm and the market. This blurred boundary is further made evident by Jensen and Meckling who extend the scope of the firm to include not only centralized contractual arrangements made between employer and employees but also centralized contracts signed with suppliers and customers. Jensen and Meckling thus characterize the firm broadly as a nexus of complex contractual relationships between the legal fiction – the firm – and the owners of labor, raw material, capital inputs, and the customers of outputs. The firm is perceived as a collection of agents, each of whom maintains his autonomy in choosing actions regarding the quantity and quality of the efforts supplied and the amount of information transmitted to others, and each of whom responds rationally to opportunities and incentives that are available to him both from within a firm and in the market at large. The distinction between the firm and the market and the demarcation between intrafirm and interfirm contracts thus vanish altogether.

CONCLUDING REMARKS

Critics of the neoclassical economic theory argue that the presence of uncertainty destroys the ability of the market to independently allocate resources. Entrepreneurial services are needed to restore production activities and the firm must adopt nonmarket rules to guide internal resource allocation. Under uncertainty, the firm and the market together make up the allocative chain. In order to understand how the firm and the market co-allocate resources, writers strive to understand (a) how the firm's allocative rules differ from the price mechanism and (b) how to delineate the boundary between the firm and the market. These activities help to generate a large body of literature.

Although our survey of this literature is too brief to include a critical evaluation of the strength and weakness of the various contributions, it does serve the intended purpose. The survey shows that, the merits of individual theories notwithstanding, the literature collectively has failed to illuminate how the two-tier allocative process works. This failure stems from the fact that entrepreneurs are studied independent of the firm, theories of the firm are constructed with only casual reference to entrepreneurs, and sometimes analyses of equilibrium are conducted without examining the role played by the entrepreneur. Each analysis is carried out from a specific perspective leading to a specialized theory of a limited scope. As the theories proliferate, controversies among them obscure the fundamental issue which is how the firm and the market co-allocate resources.

Specifically, studies of the entrepreneur center mainly on the issues of why the entrepreneur services are needed. They pay little attention to the rules used by the entrepreneurs to allocate resources. This concern has been thought to be unnecessary since the entrepreneur and the firm are assumed to allocate resources conjointly. The literature centers its attention on identifying decision rules of the firm.

The earlier attempt to identify the firm's decision rule is based upon the belief that the firm is organized to pursue a definite objective. Given the firm's objective function, its decision rule can be derived. Further, it is believed that the objective pursued by the firm depends crucially upon the control structure of the firm. Therefore firms controlled by agents belonging to different social groups will adopt different decision rules and thus will allocate resources differently. Recently, the literature has turned its attention to considering different alternatives. Some authors advocate the use of empirical method, that is, the observation of the firm's behavior in order to determine its decision rules; others attempt to uncover the firm's decision rules by studying the bargaining process among relevant agents within the firm.

Because investigations of the firm are made under different assumed conditions, specialized theories and different decision rules are proposed in the literature. Since the issues concerning the firm's decision rules are unsettled, the questions of the boundary between the firm and the market and the nature of the two-tier allocative process naturally cannot be answered. With these unsettled questions, the reader is left with the feeling that the literature is in a state of disarray and is hopelessly confused.

This outcome is not surprising. Since we have seen that a host of specialized theories on value and distribution offered by the classical economists have served to obscure the understanding of the general principles underlying production, value, and distribution, there is no reason to believe that specialized theories of the entrepreneur and the firm will lead to a clear understanding of how the allocation of resources is shared between the firm and the market.

However, decades of intellectual efforts have not been spent in vain. Like the three blind men and the elephant, even though each individual's description of the entrepreneur, the firm, and the firm – market allocation process appears to contradict those of the others, collectively the descriptions begin to produce an image with a definite shape. In the remainder of this book we synthesize the knowledge gained from the literature, add some insight of our own, and present a unified theory which provides a more faithful description of a capitalistic economy with a two-tier (firm–market) allocative process.

In our judgement, the current difficulties arise because entrepreneurs, firms, and profits are brought into formal analysis in a piecemeal manner. In order to build a unified theory of the capitalistic economy, a common thread must be found to integrate theories of the entrepreneur, the firm, and profits. Our strategy is to use the entrepreneur as the common thread in analyzing all problems in a capitalistic economy.

We begin by observing that there is no market for entrepreneurial services. This observation is crucial to understanding the nature of entrepreneurship and the role in the production and allocation process played by entrepreneurs. In order to understand how entrepreneurial activities alter the neoclassical theory on market allocation of resources, we must first resolve the following issues. What makes entrepreneurs behave the way they do? What goals do entrepreneurs pursue? Why must entrepreneurs pursue these goals by forming a firm? For this purpose it is not enough to know only what entrepreneurs do, we must also understand the mechanism by which the services of entrepreneurs are channeled into production. Given the observation that entrepreneurial services are not tradeable but are essential for production, it becomes apparent that these services must be self-mobilized; that is, the entrepreneur must initiate his own employment and take the initiative to organize the factors needed for joint production. Thus the entrepreneur differs from other factors of production in that he is self-mobilizing, self-driven, and self-employing. Whenever a single entrepreneur's effort is not sufficient to make production possible, entrepreneurs must coalesce to make production a common task by forming a firm.

In this book we postulate that entrepreneurs coalesce into firms to pursue either pecuniary or nonpecuniary objectives and present a process through which entrepreneurial coalitions are formed. The formation of a firm signifies that the cooperating entrepreneurs have entered into an agreement concerning a joint production-financing policy, a method of distributing authority and responsibility, a profit-sharing rule for the for-profit firm, and a salary structure for the nonprofit firm. The composition of the entrepreneurs in a firm, the relationship among them, and the control apparatus erected to insure the integrity of agreements give the firm a distinct internal organization and character. Based upon the jointly determined production policy and the control mechanism, the firm converts inputs into outputs. The entrepreneur-centered firm then interacts with the markets to allocate resources. Through this two-tier allocation process, the economy arrives at an equilibrium and each entrepreneur receives a reward (in utility) for his contribution to production. Since entrepreneurs make both production and equilibrium possible, in order to induce the entrepreneurs to participate in production in the profit sector, profits at equilibrium in this sector must be positive. In this way, theories of the entrepreneur, the firm, and profits are formally integrated into a theory of the capitalistic economy.

NOTES

1 The nonprofit firms are also assumed to have specific objectives. We will discuss these objectives in chapter 11.
2 This line of argument is, in fact, inconsistent with the assertion that the entrepreneur and the market use different allocative rules. Allowing substitution at the margin between transactions in the firm and transactions in the market implies that the marginal productivity of the entrepreneur can be established. Once the marginal productivity of the entrepreneur is known, his services become tradeable and therefore command a price. Price mechanism again reigns supreme. The distinction between entrepreneurial and market allocation disappears.

5

Entrepreneurs and Entrepreneurship

Despite the enormous efforts devoted to understanding him, the entrepreneur is still an elusive character in the minds of economists. Commonly, he is acclaimed as the one who stands at the helm of any business endeavor. He supposedly seeks, discovers, and evaluates information and economic opportunities, charts the course for action, leads and even inspires others to get things done, copes with contingencies, trades and diffuses uncertainties whenever possible, and ultimately bears the residual uncertainties heroically by himself. In short, he is viewed as a charismatic leader who, despite the threat of failure, makes things happen; without him the other factors of production would lie impotently idle. He is the very soul of the business enterprise.

Curiously, such a personage seldom finds his way into the formal economic writings and never assumes his rightful place in the literature concerning the theory of the firm (Baumol, 1968, p. 65). Textbook writers portray him merely as a shadowy figure who makes equilibrium possible. In the earlier writings, he is a factor of production who stubbornly refuses to be divisible and thus guarantees the much desired U-shaped cost curves (Robinson, 1950, p. 124). More recently, the entrepreneur no longer enters the production function; he has become a mere catalyst to the other factors of production and a calculator of profit. Because he is a risk-averse calculator of profit and loss, equilibrium becomes possible even if production technology exhibits the troublesome nonconvexity property (Sandmo, 1971). Because the formal (theory of the firm) models stress equilibrium, with the entrepreneur removed from the production function, these models have, in fact, taken him out of the production and market processes. It is not surprising that, even though in name the entrepreneur is the residual claimant, competition invariably leaves nothing for him to claim.

101

Fortunately, as we have seen in chapter 4, the Austrian economists, Knight, Schumpeter, and others have brought the entrepreneur back to life by insisting that he does engage in important activities worthy of acknowledgement. Although these authors agree that entrepreneurs emerge only in disequilibrium market situations where uncertainties and market imperfections prevail, their views of the entrepreneurial role are markedly different. The Austrians assert that the entrepreneur taps unexploited opportunities and ignites the market process; as such he must not be a resource owner. Knight believes that the entrepreneur breaks the impasse created by a lack of consistent resource commitment among the resource owners; as such he is a capitalist risk-bearer. Schumpeter insists that the entrepreneur is an innovator, and not a risk-bearer.

Therefore it is apparent that there is no general consensus on what an entrepreneur is or how he should be identified; an intellectual impasse has been reached. On the one hand, we cannot deny the importance of the contributions made by each of the above-mentioned authors and, more importantly, we are unwilling to abandon the hope that each of these insightful paths may ultimately lead us to a true understanding of the entrepreneur. On the other hand, the three views are conflicting; the acceptance of one viewpoint requires a denial of the others. Some authors, in an attempt to minimize the conflicting nature of the controversy, choose to enumerate all the tasks that an entrepreneur may perform in the hope that this will provide us with a better understanding of entrepreneurship.[1]

Unfortunately, eclecticism helps little in reconciling the controversy; it may even add to its intensity. When confronting the list of entrepreneurial attributes, we obviously need to ask whether an individual must possess all the listed qualities before he is qualified as an entrepreneur or whether a minimum qualification exists. To be specific, must all entrepreneurs bear risks? Suppose he cleverly transfers the risk to other agents, must he become a lesser entrepreneur? Likewise, must entrepreneurship be associated only with successful innovation? Is it not just as entrepreneurial if an individual should succeed in making the producer's environment sufficiently stable to render production and exchange less hazardous? Finally, must an entrepreneur be an owner–manager? When an owner hires a manager, must he relinquish his entrepreneurial role?

By now it seems obvious that defining an entrepreneur by what he does is hopeless. This is particularly true when the tasks performed by an entrepreneur differ according to the occasion under which his services are required and according to the market environment in which his services are performed. In our view, a more fruitful approach to characterizing the entrepreneur is by identifying the common characteristic of all the services that he may perform. In this respect we observe that all the services provided by entrepreneur are nontradeable. It is the inability to trade entrepreneurial services that crucially affects the nature of the production organization and the allocative process.

The purpose of this chapter is threefold. In the first section we examine the source of demand for entrepreneurial services and establish the proposition that entrepreneurial services are not tradeable. Since benefits are often accrued to division of labor and pooling of risks among the entrepreneurs, in the second section we establish the proposition that the modern firm is a coalition of entrepreneurs. Finally, it will become evident that what constitutes entrepreneurial service depends on the market environment within which production takes place. Accordingly, in the third section we develop the proposition that imperfections in different factor markets induce a different set of entrepreneurial activities. This means that the scope of entrepreneurial activities is affected by the factor market environment. We will have more to say about this point in a historical setting. Since the historical development of factor markets has followed a specific time path, in chapter 9 we will see that the services entrepreneurs perform also evolved in a predictable pattern.

UNCERTAINTY AND ENTREPRENEURSHIP

We have learned from the literature that entrepreneurial services are not needed when *de facto* certainty prevails, that is, when the market is complete as described in chapter 2. Entrepreneurial services become indispensable only under uncertainty. In this section we endeavor to establish this proposition. Briefly, uncertainties induce the need for risk-trading markets. However, many forces prevent the establishment of the complete set of contingent claims markets needed to nullify all the adverse effects of uncertainties. The lack of complete markets implies that joint production among individual resource owners cannot be achieved automatically through the market; entrepreneurial services are needed to fill the gap. Entrepreneurs emerge as a consequence. Paradoxically, the presence of the same uncertainties also prevents the need for entrepreneurial services to be translated into effective demand for them and hence blocks the creation of markets for these services. We will analyze the nature of entrepreneurship in this context. In order to begin the analysis, we briefly summarize the argument that entrepreneurial service is not needed under conditions of *de facto* certainty.

Absence of Entrepreneurial Services under de Facto Certainty

In this section we recapitulate the idea that no entrepreneurial service is needed in a market where *de facto* certainty prevails. This analysis is carried out in a multiperiod decision setting. In a *de facto* certainty market environment, rational agents who are faced with a multiperiod decision horizon will want to make commitments now for future delivery of goods and services in each state of nature. Contingent claims markets which open in the current period will take the place of the spot markets which would be opened later. Arrow and Debreu have shown that a set of equilibrium prices exists in the contingent claims market system. Purchases and sales are all contracted and paid for in the current period on the basis of the futures prices. As time elapses and events become known, deliveries are made in accordance with the contractual arrangement; no further use of money is necessary.

When the market is assumed to convene costlessly and clear instantaneously, the market outcome is perceived by all participants. Because all contingent claims markets are present and competitive, as we have seen in chapter 2, competition ensures that the quantity of each factor employed, each product produced, and the optimal size of each production unit are determined impersonally by market forces. The market outcome reflects consumer tastes, the prevailing production technology, and resource endowments in the economy. Operating in this competitive market environment, the individual resource owner will take the contingent claims prices as given and trade away all his risks; he will also take the expected factor prices as given and choose to specialize as an input provider in order to reap the full benefit from division of labor. Since the marginal value product of a given factor is the same across different employments when the economy is at equilibrium, the reward that the factor receives is not tied specifically to the product that it helps to produce; rather it reflects the factor's social value. Because the social value of a factor also reflects the production technology employed in the economy, the reward to the factor also includes the benefit derived from the economies of scale associated with the prevailing production technology. Consequently, through trading in the markets, resource owners are able to join together in production and reap the full benefit from risk-sharing, division of labor, and economies of scale in production. Because each agent must take the market prices as given and cannot through his own action alter the market outcome, the market alone allocates resources.[2] A role for the entrepreneur simply does not exist.

Uncertainty-induced Markets

Uncertainty places a veil over both futures markets open in the current period and spot markets to be opened on future dates. Under uncertainty, resource owners who plan to buy or sell in the future may, for several reasons, shy away from the futures markets. First, information which is not available now may become available with the passage of time. Agents who wish to take advantage of this information may be unwilling to bind themselves by entering into futures contracts. In addition, because there are uncertainties about the future, no one can anticipate all possible contingencies. As a consequence, futures contracts are necessarily incomplete (Williamson, 1971b). Contract incompleteness implies that the costs of arranging and enforcing futures contracts are high. Thus, under uncertainty, some resource owners will tend to avoid futures markets and will instead use the spot markets to be opened later to carry their intertemporal optimization activities.

Uncertainty also places a veil over spot markets to be opened in the future. In order to use spot markets to carry out intertemporal optimization decisions, a resource owner must form some expectations about the quantities that he will produce and the prices that will prevail in the distant spot markets. Since expectations are never accurate and events may not evolve as hoped, errors between the expected prices (quantities) and the realized prices (quantities) will result. Risk-averse individuals who face undesirable contingencies will take steps to reduce risks (Arrow, 1974a, p. 6).

Assume that each resource owner is an independent producer. The independent producer who faces the risks caused by both price and production uncertainties can reduce the impact of these uncertainties through a combination of internal and market means.

Internal Methods   The most commonly employed internal risk reduction method is diversification. The independent producer can lower the impact of price (output) uncertainty by producing an assortment of products. As the number of products increases, the variation in the independent producer's overall profits decreases. Moreover, the independent producer can also reduce the impact of price (quantity) uncertainty by employing an assortment of production techniques. For example, a farmer's output depends upon the amount of rainfall. Suppose that there are two states of nature – too much or too little rainfall – and that there are two corresponding production techniques – plow deep and plow shallow. Let the farmer's subjective probability for each state be a half. A risk-averse farmer can reduce the impact of the risk by plowing half his land deep and half shallow. In this way, regardless of the amount of rainfall, the farmer's expected utility of his production activity is maximized.

Internal diversification of products and technologies is neither always feasible nor always desirable. Frequently, the independent producer cannot depend on the selection of a technological portfolio to eliminate the impact of the output uncertainty becaue there does not exist a complete set of production techniques where each is perfectly suited to one possible state of nature. For example, in addition to the uncertainty associated with rainfall, there is also a chance of hail. Because the farmer does not have a production method to protect his crops from hail damage, a complete set of production technologies now ceases to exist. The farmer is no longer able to arrange for a planting portfolio to cope with the production contingencies he faces. Even if diversification in products and production technologies is feasible, it may not be desirable. Because diversification reduces the advantages associated with production economies of scale, it increases the production cost. Other methods of reducing uncertainty must be found.

Market Means The independent producer not only can mitigate the impact of uncertainties through internal means but also can accomplish it by trading uncertainties in markets specially established for this purpose. Many financial markets have been developed to trade risks; they include the stock, insurance, and commodities markets.

A stock market provides a mechanism for sharing the financial incidence of an uncertain venture. When the uncertainty associated with a future market value or profit stream of a productive asset is so large that no single investor is willing to assume the full burden of this contingency, production will not take place. The stock market provides a mechanism for sharing the financial incidence by dividing a large uncertainty into small shares (e.g. common stocks) or by offering shares with different uncertainty features (e.g. common stocks, preferred stocks, and bonds). Each investor then assumes part of the financial burden by choosing his own scale of incidence according to his attitude toward risk and resource endowment. Whenever the investors are able to collectively finance the venture, production will take place. In addition to providing a mechanism to share production risks, the stock market also enables producers to reap the benefit of production specialization. In the case of the farmer, there is no need for him to incur the high cost of diversification by plowing half the land deep and the other half shallow. Each farmer can obtain the same portfolio effect by exchanging half his ownership shares with an appropriate number of ownership shares issued by another farmer who uses the complementary production technique. In this way, each farmer gains the advantage associated with both production specialization and risk-sharing.

An insurance market, in contrast, pools resources from a class of unwelcome contingencies that have common uncertain characteristics. If the random realization of an event is thought to be governed reliably by a stochastic law, the individuals who are subject to the same contingency may pool insurance premiums *ex ante* in order to spread the impact of an unfortunate realization *ex post*. That is, each uncertainty bearer would pay a small known premium in order to mitigate the possible impact of a substantially larger uncertain loss. In the case of the farmer, even though a production technology to cope with hail damage does not exist, as long as all farmers do not suffer this damage simultaneously, each farmer can avoid the incidence of hail by purchasing hail insurance.

Finally, a commodity market enables the producers, through hedging activities, to shift an optimal amount of uncertainty associated with production and with variations of both factor and product prices to the speculators. Hedging is a double transaction conducted by the producer who sells short in the futures market and buys long in the spot market, or vice versa.[3] Simply put, when the prices of the spot and the futures markets are correlated positively, a windfall gain in one market is offset by a windfall loss in the other. Thus uncertainties faced by the producer are transferred to the speculator.[4]

Despite the availability of these risk-trading markets, the adverse impact of uncertainties cannot be totally eradicated. Two major reasons contribute to this failure. First, there are still too few risk-trading markets. Second, of the existing risk-trading markets, some are imperfect (Ledyard, 1987). By imperfection we mean that the market is either competitive but fails to attain a stable equilibrium or is noncompetitive.

Since a variety of risk-trading markets does exist, it is imperative to define what is meant by having too few such markets. For this purpose, Arrow proposed a set of abstract markets referred to as the contingent claims markets. The contingent claims markets trade uncertainties by buying and selling commitments to be carried out only when a given state of nature has occurred (Arrow, 1971c, chapter 4). As we have seen earlier, this market is based on the notion that goods are distinguished from each other not only by their physical properties and location in time and space but also by the state of nature in which they are delivered. Trading of each good under this circumstance is equivalent to the trading of a contingent claim contract associated with the occurrence of a given state of nature.

After defining this set of hypothetical markets, Arrow further states that contingent claim contracts are the most elementary of all financial contingent instruments. Insurance contracts, common stocks, and futures contracts can each be expressed as a bundle of contingent claim contracts (Arrow, 1981, p. 113). We can easily see that an insurance contract is a bundle of contingent claim contracts since it is usually defined on states of nature partitioned more coarsely than the elementary contingent claims contracts. Common stock and futures contracts are also bundles of the elementary contingent claim contracts because the former guarantees the stockholder a fixed proportion of the firm's profit in each and every state of nature, and the latter gives the contract holder the right to buy and sell a given dated commodity at a particular price level regardless of which state of nature has occurred.

Given that insurance contracts, common stocks, and futures contracts are bundles of elementary contingent claim contracts, if we can characterize what constitutes an incomplete set of contingent claims markets, it becomes possible to assert just what is meant by too few risk-trading markets. In the next two subsections, we first provide a definition for incomplete contingent claims markets and examine the factors contributing to this lack of completeness, and we then establish the theme that it is the incompleteness of these markets that induces the emergence of entrepreneurial activities.

Incomplete Contingent Claims Markets

The contingent claims markets are said to be incomplete if the number of independent contingent claim contracts is outnumbered by the states of nature. Many factors prevent the trading of some contingent claim contracts (Arrow, 1971a, chapters 5, 8, and 9), thus contributing to the incompleteness of these markets.

In general, there is a cost for using these markets. When the cost of administering some contingency contracts is too high compared with the advantage that they may bring, such contracts will not be traded. High brokerage fees in stock and commodity tradings and high loading charges in insurance are cases in point.

Frequently, a market will simply not form unless its base is sufficiently large. For example, an insurance premium generally varies inversely with the size of the insurance base, and the demand for insurance varies inversely with the premium. A small insurance base will require a premium which is too high to make it worthwhile to the insured. Therefore, when the insurance base of a given risk is small, demand for the insurance is low; no insurance company will find it profitable to offer the needed service. Similarly, if a particular stock (futures contract) is traded in a very thin market, a change in the market demand for or supply of this stock (futures contract) will cause its market price to fluctuate widely. Large fluctuations in the price of a financial instrument reduce its liquidity and discourage its use.

Tradings in contingency commodities are not only discouraged by wide price fluctuations but also by the fact that prices may vary in an arbitrary fashion. In markets where traders or potential traders possess monopoly power, prices cease to change randomly; traders with market power can deliberately cause a price change in order to increase their profit. The unfair advantage accorded to the privileged traders discourages the independent users from trading in these markets, and in some cases causes the market to disappear altogether.

Finally, an important cause of failure in contingency dealings is the existence of information asymmetry between buyers and sellers (Radner, 1968). Information asymmetry, as observed by Arrow, gives rise to possible abuse on one side and suspicion on the other side, causing the market to fail. There are two classes of information asymmetry which contribute to market failure. The first is known as moral hazard and the second as adverse selection.

Moral Hazard The precondition for moral hazard is the nonobservability of agents' actions. According to Arrow (1971a, chapters 8 and 9), moral hazard takes place in situations where the occurrence of an event is subject to the behavioral influence of the contractual parties and the contract, by its very existence, alters the incentive, the action, and hence the probability distribution of the event. The most commonly used example for moral hazard is related to insurance. After purchasing a fire insurance policy, the insured becomes careless about smoking cigarettes. This carelessness increases fire incidents and the cost to the insurer. This added cost, if sufficiently large, will discourage the offering of such insurance. Perhaps the potential moral hazard is the greatest in cases where human effort is the subject of a contractual arrangement (Balch and Wu, 1974). Since human indenture by contract is illegal, whenever payments for human effort are made *ex ante*, an opportunity for irresponsible behavior and shirking exists. Services that are promised may not be delivered or at least not rendered to the best of the individual's ability. As a result, these personal services will be discouraged from trading in the market place.

Breach of contractual obligations need not be limited to cases where payment is made *ex ante*. It may also take place when payments are made *ex post*. For example, the options available to the contractual parties frequently differ before and after the signing of a contract. This change in options after contract signing will afford opportunities for gain to the party whose range of options has increased (Klein et al., 1978). The opportunistic behavior of the advantaged party causes the distribution of the actual outcome to shift in his favor. This shift may be so great that it will keep the disadvantaged party from entering into such a contractual agreement. Even though *ex post* distribution does not shift to favor a particular party, moral hazard may still take place. In the case of the farmer, for example, after risk-sharing arrangements have been made, each farmer finds that his *ex post* opportunity is now different. Although shirking affects his income adversely, it also adds to his leisure. Because the adverse effect on income is shared by others while the benefit on lesure is accrued entirely to the shirking farmer, shirking will take place. Shirking by all farmers may render the risk-sharing arrangement useless. Finally, if the settlement of a contract is contingent on the occurrence of an event, payment is dependent upon whether the event has occurred. Frequently the information on the event is readily known to one of the contractual parties but becomes known to the others only by the incurrence of a verification cost. When the verification cost is high, the threat of opportunistic behavior by the informed party will discourage the contractual arrangement (Arrow, 1974a, pp. 9–10; Townsend, 1979).

Adverse Selection　　Adverse selection occurs whenever the buyer does not know the quality of the product or the seller does not know the true cost of providing the service; this occurs even though the actions taken by the buyer and the seller are perfectly observable. One of the earliest contributors to this literature was Akerlof (1970). He studied the "market for lemons," where the market exchanges a product, say used cars, whose quality varies widely and whose seller stands to gain through false disclosure. Since the quality of used cars is not readily identifiable to the buyer, the market price of a used car does not reflect its true quality, causing the owners of high quality used cars to withdraw from the market. The propensity to withdraw high quality used cars from the market also causes potential buyers to suspect that any used car offered in the market is "a lemon." This suspicion leads to a reduction in the demand for used cars. Because the owners of high quality used cars are unable to credibly identify the quality of their products and the buyers are suspicious and fearful of the untruthfulness of the sellers, in the end only lemons are sold in such a used car market.

Rothschild and Stiglitz (1976) demonstrate how adverse selection causes an accident insurance market to fail. Let the consumer suffer an income loss whenever an accident befalls him. He purchases accident insurance for the purpose of shifting income from the no-accident state to the state with an accident in order to equalize his marginal utility of income in the two states. Since only the individual knows his own accident probability, the insurance company cannot prevent the high risk customers from purchasing the low risk contract. This will lead to a greater indemnity payment than expected and will cause a loss to the insurance company. Suspicion and fear on the part of the insurance company will cause it to withdraw from the market altogether or at least reduce the attractiveness of the terms to the low risk individuals. In the latter case, the low risk individual is deprived of an opportunity to purchase full insurance. Whether the firm exits the market or only offers incomplete insurance to the low risk customers, the result is the same; the competitive insurance market fails to provide full coverage to all the potential contingencies, and thus causes the contingent claims markets to be incomplete.

The above examples show that moral hazard and adverse selection prevent the trading of some financial instruments designed to perform risk-sharing functions, and the trading of some commodities whose intrinsic value is subject to uncertainty. When these failures occur, gainful exchanges are prevented from taking place; markets become incomplete. In particular, because financial instruments, such as insurance policies, stocks, options and futures contracts, are bundles of the elementary contingent claims, whenever some of these financial instruments are discouraged from trading in the markets, in theory certain underlying elementary contingent claims become absent. The latter result implies that the number of independent contingent claims falls short of the number of states of nature; the contingent claims markets become incomplete.

Emergence of Entrepreneurs

In an uncertain market environment where the contingent claims markets are incomplete, the decision-maker can no longer avoid uncertainty entirely; decision-making becomes hazardous. In addition, as we have seen in chapter 3, in an incomplete contingent market setting, the individual resource owner must use his own subjective contingent claims prices to evaluate a given production project. Because resource owners have different preferences and endowments, they will not arrive at a consistent decision for joint production. Despite the potential benefits associated with joint production, the agreement will not take place through market arrangements.

Although the existence of uncertainty-related hazards may prevent some resource owners from taking joint actions, it also, as observed by Knight, provides opportunities for gain to those who are willing and able to shoulder the responsibilities with joint production. Thus incompleteness of the contingent claims markets spurs entrepreneurs into action.

However, market uncertainties do place a veil over all economic opportunities. Individuals who are interested in seeking profits must invest some time and effort in order to discover or even recognize profit opportunities. These efforts include the acquisition of basic information concerning production technology and the design of marketing and financing strategies. Despite these efforts, not all market opportunities can be seen. Some opportunities may appear unexpectedly and others may never be detected even by the most persistent profit seekers. Consequently, each market potential is seen by some but not by others, and each individual sees only a subset of all market opportunities. Moreover, the individual may be unable to exploit all the opportunities he may have discovered because he either lacks the knowledge and expertise in production and marketing or fails to gain access to the resources needed to profitably exploit these opportunities. As a result, only a subset of all perceived opportunities is feasible to the individual. It is from this feasible set, if it is not empty, that an entrepreneur must make his choices.

Decision-making under uncertainty requires that the choice be made *ex ante* and that the chosen option be implemented before the precise outcome becomes known. For example, because production takes several periods to complete, a manufacturer must commit resources to production before the exact amount of profit is known. Likewise, an investment decision must be executed before the future market conditions are revealed and the profitability becomes known. Similarly, whether a given innovative activity is worthwhile cannot be ascertained until research and development efforts have been carried out. Despite the differences in each of these production problems, they have one thing in common: associated with every business opportunity is the possibility for losses as well as profit.

Economic opportunities may occur sporadically and vanish rapidly; disasters, once visited, will inflict a debilitating impact which will be felt for some time to come. Therefore the role of the entrepreneur is to choose whether to face a given contingency or to avoid its incidence. Whether he chooses one or the other is dependent upon how he believes the decision-related events will ultimately unfold and upon his attitude toward risk-bearing.

The entrepreneur's belief reflects his knowledge and perception of a given situation and his judgement on the likelihood of the eventual resolution of decision-related events (Balch and Wu, 1974). Sometimes the probability law governing these events is known. In this case a decision is still made with full information and the entrepreneur's judgement is not required. Different decision-makers may choose different options which reflect only the decision-maker's attitudes toward risk. The judgement of the entrepreneur becomes essential when there is a common ignorance about a given situation such that the relative likelihood of the events cannot be described by an objectively determined probability law. Under these circumstances the basis for a universal agreement disappears. An individual's approach to a given context and his judgement become essential to choice-making. Two entrepreneurs may face ostensibly the same situation but still have different judgements as to how the uncertainty is likely to resolve; in this case they will make different choices.

Ignorance about one's own environment can sometimes be reduced by acquiring meaningful information. However, what constitutes meaningful information may also depend upon the individual's knowledge and perception of the situation. Information is colored not only by the individual's own perception about the present but also by his experience and understanding of the past. Thus even the information-acquisition activity must be tempered with judgement. In the end an entrepreneur may take a certain action because he believes that his judgement is more accurate than others and because he trusts his own wisdom accumulated from past experience and his ability to gather information.

In an uncertain market environment where events unfold over time, the decision-maker can no longer make all his decisions at once. Because information becomes available sequentially, production-related decisions of various types, e.g. purchasing of inputs, production of outputs, and sales and pricing decisions, must also be made sequentially. However, the relationship between the time pattern of decision-making and that of information revelation is by no means fixed. In fact, gains can be made by realigning the former against the latter. For example, the decision on the purchase of a variable factor can be determined either *ex ante* or *ex post* (Horen and Wu, 1988). The same is true for the determination of product prices (Wu, 1979). Under these circumstances, the plans associated with various realignments must be devised and compared. A choice must be made among the alternatives, some of which exhibit a greater promise of profits yet are risky or rigid, while others may seem less promising yet are safe or flexible. This choice is made on the basis of the entrepreneur's judgement.

Under uncertainty, the discrepancy between expectation and realization becomes a routine business affair. Regardless of whether the decision-maker is adventurous or timid, he must devise strategies in order to cope with these discrepancies. Because opportunities may present themselves unexpectedly and disaster may descend at the least opportune time, the entrepreneur must be in full control of the moment and act decisively either to take advantage of the opportunity before it vanishes or to cut the loss before it becomes unbearable. Again, whether to act one way or another is dependent upon the entrepreneur's judgement.

Generally, profits are possible if one is able to provide sound judgement to manage production and uncertainties, to discover market opportunities that others do not see, to find new ways of producing existing products, or to invent new products to satisfy existing or emerging wants. Thus entrepreneurs are individuals who believe that they have the talent to see market opportunities not seen by others (Kirzner, 1973, p.67), are capable of devising plans and strategies to exploit these opportunities, and can find solutions to cope with contingencies; in short, they are in control of the situation (Knight, 1971, p. 271). To put it differently, the entrepreneur in an uncertain market environment performs a creative act in the same way that an artist, essayist, or scientist does in his respective field. The entrepreneur believes that he is a creative person who efficiently converts inputs into outputs or who produces outputs which he thinks will give greater satisfaction to the consumer. Since the consumer's tastes are subject to change and the outcome of any productive activity is uncertain, the entrepreneur's task is not routine. He must use his judgement to make production decisions and take the associated risks. Thus the entrepreneur must be a person who has confidence in his judgement and believes that he possesses the ingenuity to solve problems; he must also be a person with the spirit of adventure and the capacity to endure and persevere. He must have the desire to accumulate wealth or to act altruistically, to see that progress is made, and to do things that are different and novel. Above all, he is a person who is driven by the freedom to do things his own way and to set and achieve his own goals. Owing to the very nature of what entrepreneurs do, there does not exist in the market a way of evaluating *ex ante* the entrepreneur's worth on the basis of his marginal productivity. There are three causes for this market failure. First, as observed by Kirzner, ". . . entrepreneurship reveals to the market what the market did not realize was available, or indeed, needed at all" (Kirzner, 1979, p. 181). Second, because the entrepreneur often tampers with market forces by choosing a time pattern of decision-making different from that of information revelation in the belief that his methods are superior to those of the market, evaluations of these claims must be postponed until all the contingencies have been resolved. Finally, there is a threat of adverse selection and moral hazard in connection with the entrepreneur's services. Since entrepreneurs are not owners of resources used for production, they may either exaggerate their entrepreneurial ability or shirk their commitments and thus cause the project to fail. For all these reasons, the market fails to evaluate the entrepreneur's marginal productivity and cannot formulate a demand for his services *ex ante* (Kirzner, 1979, p. 174). Consequently, a market for entrepreneurial services does not exist, and the entrepreneur must wait to claim the reward for his services *ex post* as a residual.

Because entrepreneurial services are not tradeable, they cannot be acquired. The entrepreneur must fashion a production plan on the basis of his judgement and take the initiative to organize joint production through nonmarket means. The entrepreneur-centered firm emerges as a consequence. Subject to the market forces, the entrepreneur, by securing funds from the capital market,[5] purchases inputs in the factor markets and sells outputs in the product markets. In this way the entrepreneur and the market form a two-tier allocative chain.

COALITION OF ENTREPRENEURS

We have now established the proposition that the entrepreneur must take the initiative in hiring resources and organizing production. In managing production, the entrepreneur faces a dilemma created by his desire to gain advantages associated with both specialization and diversification. First, the entrepreneur needs to specialize in order to use his limited skill and knowledge efficiently and to attain minimal economies of scale in production. Second, he also desires to reduce risks through diversification and risk-sharing. Unfortunately these objectives are often incompatible. Specialization in production leads to a greater need for coordination. The production of raw materials and semifinished products must be coordinated with the production of the finished product, and the supply of the various complementary and substitutable products must be synchronized with the market demand for them. Because of the prevalence of market uncertainties and the existence of production lags, market coordination of these activities becomes ineffectual. Unpredictable changes in the demand for the products, supply of factors, and production technology cause the demand and supply of the products and the factors to fluctuate unevenly. Both shortages and surpluses become common occurrences, contributing to the loss of profits. Consequently, specialization leads to a greater uncertainty associated with production and profits. Conversely, the entrepreneur's attempt to control risks also clashes with his desire to gain efficiency through specialization. As in the case of the independent resource owner, the entrepreneur attempts to control the risks of his business by producing different products and using different technologies to produce them. However, this strategy also leads to a reduction in specialization, a sacrifice in scale economies, and an increase in production cost. This discussion implies that a conflict exists between specialization and diversification. In order to succeed in business, the entrepreneur must find ways to reconcile this conflict. This reconciliation is particularly important because the entrepreneur is not a capitalist. His ability to secure financing from the capital market hinges on his ability to reduce the cost of production and the riskiness of his business venture.

There are two ways which make it possible for entrepreneurs to attain simultaneously benefits associated with specialization and diversification: they can trade ownership shares with each other or they can form coalitions among themselves.

Trading Ownership Shares

From the income point of view, the trading of ownership shares among entrepreneurs enables each of them to assemble an optimal portfolio of investments with an optimal level of risk. From the production point of view, trading of ownership shares permits each entrepreneur to specialize in production. Specialization in production enables each entrepreneur to utilize his special skill and knowledge more fully and to tap the benefits associated with economies of scale in production. Thus, through trading of ownership shares, the entrepreneur reaps the benefit of both specialization and diversification.

Unfortunately, this scheme is unreliable. Just as entrepreneurial services are not tradeable, for the same reasons the income shares of entrepreneurial ventures are also not tradeable. Owing to the existence of production uncertainties and to the fact that entrepreneurial efforts cannot be observed costlessly, it is possible for entrepreneurs to benefit from free rides by shirking in their efforts. In addition, the occurrence of market events is not costlessly observable by all trading partners. Information asymmetry gives those who possess the privileged information a chance to misrepresent the true state of nature and thus cheat other trading partners out of their rightful income. Finally, by the nature of the market arrangement, the distribution of income is vested in the hands of the individual entrepreneur. After a particular state of nature has been revealed, the lucky entrepreneur must now distribute income received in that state to the other share owners. Opportunism may lead him to repudiate the agreement altogether, thereby inflicting a loss on his trading partners. This loss is particularly severe for any trading partner who had incurred an investment in order to gain efficiency associated with specialization. The threat of the above-mentioned opportunistic behavior causes suspicion of the income-sharing arrangements, and thus prevents *ex ante* trading of ownership shares from taking place among entrepreneurs.

The above discussion leads to the conclusion that the use of the market to reconcile the conflict created by specialization and diversification is itself a risky undertaking. Because the simultaneous derivation of benefits from specialization and diversification requires the act of cooperation, this conclusion also implies that the desired cooperative outcome cannot be obtained by noncooperative means, that is, through the market. Specifically, because the market is incapable of transmitting specialized information, monitoring performance, and enforcing contracts, opportunism and strategic consideration invariably lead it to the prisoner's dilemma outcome. Game-theoretic forces inevitably lead to the universally disliked noncooperative equilibrium, despite the fact that all entrepreneurs desire the superior cooperative outcome.

Coalition of Entrepreneurs

The alternative method available to the entrepreneurs is to act cooperatively by forming a coalition. A coalition provides opportunities for entrepreneurs to carry out division of labor and thus reap the benefit of specialization in tasks. Through internal organization and coordination, division of labor among entrepreneurs also enables the firm to benefit from economies of scale associated with modern technology. This expansion in the productive capacity, in turn, permits the firm to carry out diversification in production. Consequently, the formation of a coalition by entrepreneurs serves to reconcile the conflict created by specialization and diversification, a feat that the single entrepreneur failed to accomplish.

Benefits notwithstanding, some obstacles do stand in the way of coalition formation. First, because entrepreneurs are endowed with different abilities, information, resources, and preferences, conflicts of interest naturally exist among them. In order to form a coalition, the entrepreneurs must find a mechanism which is capable of reconciling these differences and generating a common policy. The mechanism we adopt in this book is an economy-wide coalitional game. A detailed description of this game will be given in chapter 6 (and in the mathematical appendix). Here we only wish to state that, by playing the coalitional game, the cooperative entrepreneurs reach agreements which are necessary to bring the firms into existence. These agreements include a joint production policy, an internal organizational structure which delineates authority and responsibility, and a sharing rule which governs the distribution of profits among the cooperative entrepreneurs. In addition, because entrepreneurs are not capitalists, the agreements must also include a financing policy stipulating how much capital the firm must raise from the capital market and how this sum is divided between equity and debt financing. Only after these agreements have been reached will the firm be formed.

The existence of such a mechanism still does not mean that the firm is, in fact, a viable production institution. The presence of uncertainty and its attendant lack of information continue to prevent an objective assessment of each entrepreneur's performance, thus encouraging entrepreneurs to behave opportunistically. In order to be a viable production institution, the firm must accomplish what the market has failed to do, that is, safeguard the integrity of the agreements made by the entrepreneurs. As we will demonstrate in chapter 7, this can indeed be accomplished by the firm. Once the entrepreneurs agree to form a firm, the firm gains the control of its income in all states of nature. This collective control over the income makes it impossible for any entrepreneur to repudiate unilaterally his contractual obligation *ex post*. In addition, the firm can also create an internal organization and a set of rules to encourage the compliance of agreements and discourage wrongdoing. In short, the firm has the capability of curbing opportunism, thus enabling the entrepreneurs to attain a superior cooperative outcome which the market fails to provide. Consequently, the multi-entrepreneur firm emerges as a viable industrial organization.

SCOPE OF ENTREPRENEURIAL ACTIVITIES

Because entrepreneurs perform services that the market fails to provide, it is natural to assume that the range of entrepreneurial activities depends not only upon the products that the firm produces but also upon the market environment within which the entrepreneurs operate. In this section we first examine the scope of entrepreneurial activities when all tradeable factor markets exist and are competitive.[6] We then investigate how monopoly elements in these factor markets modify the functions that entrepreneurs perform. In general, the scope of entrepreneurial activities expands with an increase in the degree of imperfection in the factor markets.

Entrepreneurial Activities with Competitive Factor Markets

If all tradeable factor markets are available and are competitive, the entrepreneurs will purchase all inputs needed for production from these markets. In this situation there will be a complete functional specialization among all factors of production.

In an environment where all tradeable factor markets are competitive, the owners of labor, natural resources, and manmade capital will opt to sell their services through the factor markets. This is true since competition will guarantee that each factor owner will receive a return to the factor *ex ante* equal to the expected marginal value product of the factor. There is no benefit for the factor owner to become a residual claimant and wait for payment until the product is produced. From the entrepreneurs' point of view it is advantageous for them to purchase services in the factor markets *ex ante*. The entrepreneurs have no better alternative since it is not possible to pay a lower price and is not profitable to pay a price higher than the prevailing market price. This principle is valid despite the fact that each coalition of entrepreneurs chooses production policies subjectively and different firms may hire a different amount of inputs even when they produce the same product and use the same production technology. The entrepreneurs will take the market prices of the factors as given and employ an amount of each factor to the point where its price is equal to the value of its expected marginal product.[7] Because each factor is paid in accordance with its expected marginal productivity, its role is distinct and separable; therefore functional specialization among factors is complete in this market setting.

So far, we have excluded capital funds and the capitalist from our general discussion of input employment. Because the role of the capitalist undergoes a change when the market environment switches from certainty to uncertainty, employment of capital requires special attention. Despite this change we wish to emphasize that the entrepreneur will still hire capital funds in the capital market and the function that capitalists play will still be specialized.

Because entrepreneurs are not capitalists there remains the question of how the entrepreneur could gain sufficient funds to acquire the needed factors of production. When uncertainty is absent a problem does not exist in hiring capital. The funds needed can always be acquired through the capital market by borrowing. The absence of uncertainty implies that both the borrower and the lender will have an identical evaluation of the firm's future profit stream. As long as the present value of the firm's profit stream is larger than the interest cost the lender will not hesitate to finance the firm's production. In this case the firm can hire the capital it needs and thus faces no budget constraint.

The situation is different under uncertainty. The present value of the firm's profit stream can no longer be objectively determined; the lender and the borrower will generally have different perceptions about the profitability of a given productive venture. Moreover, the attitudes of lenders and borrowers to risk are also different. Since bankers and other lending agents are generally conservative, only a portion of the required funds can be secured through borrowing. The firm must acquire the balance in an alternative way.

A well-organized capital market offers capital funds not only through debt financing but also through equity financing. Equity financing through the sale of stocks differs from borrowing through the sale of bonds in that the rate of return to stocks is not determined *ex ante* but as a share of the prospective residual. An investor capitalizes the expected future profit stream of a firm and assigns to it a present value. Based upon this capitalized value, the investor makes his investment decision on the firm's stock. This enables the firm to convert a part of its present value into present wealth and to use the proceeds to finance current production. The buyers of this future claim become the firm's shareholders and gain the right to claim a portion of the firm's future returns.

In this setting, the firm should be seen differently from the traditional view. The firm is not merely a producer of commodities; rather, it is an entity that sells not only a set of goods and services but also a menu of financial instruments. The success of the firm depends not only upon the profitability of the goods and services it sells but also upon the attractiveness of its financial instruments. It is the sales of these financial instruments that enable the firm to acquire the funds necessary for production.[8]

From the capitalist's point of view the equity market is another outlet for investment. The stock certificates for a given firm are standard contracts with detailed terms; therefore all shares in a given company are homogeneous. The market value of a given stock reflects the (subjectively expected) probability distribution of returns generated by the firm. In the capital market, stocks in different companies can be compared and grouped into various classes based on the probability distributions of their returns. Even though the stocks of different companies are distinct commodities, in the minds of investors they are equivalent as long as the probability distributions of the returns to these stocks are identical. Therefore the capital market serves to erase the identity of individual stocks and makes classes of them homogeneous. Consequently, in a modern capital market the investors face many classes of homogeneous investment opportunities ranging from relatively low risk bonds (fixed rate of return) to stocks with varying degrees of risk and expected return. With this assortment of liquid investment opportunities the investor, through portfolio selection and diversification, can insure a satisfactory rate of return for his investment.

Thus, with the development of an efficient capital market, capitalists gain a new option for making investments. Traditionally, within an imperfect capital market, the capitalist had to rely on the control of the firm's production process to insure a satisfactory rate of return. As capital markets become more efficient, the investor, although nominally a legal owner of the firm, no longer needs to exercise control over the firm's operation; he now has the option of securing a satisfactory rate of return by arranging an optimal portfolio. Whether an investor will choose to invest his money by the traditional method of gaining direct control of the firm or by selecting a stock portfolio obviously depends on the information and operating costs associated with each type of investment.

The types of information needed to guarantee a satisfactory rate of return from direct control over the production process and the portfolio arrangement are very different. The former requires the investors to gain access to often confidential company-specific information; the latter requires only market information which the companies have a clear incentive to supply. Although costs of gathering both types of information exist, in a modern capital market the cost of acquiring market information is substantially lower. Thus the investor prefers investment via portfolio arrangement. An investor's preference for a portfolio is reinforced by the high cost of gaining direct control over a company's production process when stock ownership of a firm is highly dispersed. A stock owner who wishes to gain control of the firm must first become the owner of a substantial portion of the firm's outstanding stock. This undertaking is often beyond the financial capability of the individual. Even if the individual's wealth is sufficiently large to permit him to take this course of action, putting a large portion of his wealth in a specific business enterprise robs him of the portfolio diversification advantage. For all these reasons, capitalists will shy away from entrepreneurial activities and will specialize in the risk-bearing role.

It is now clear that even though entrepreneurs do not have a market to sell their services, if all other factor markets exist and are competitive, functional specialization among the factors will prevail. For those factors which are traded in the marketplace, competition will force each owner to act individualistically. Through the market each owner of a tradeable factor can guarantee a satisfactory return. His fate is not tied to the performance of a specific firm. Entrepreneurs are different. They must earn their incomes cooperatively through control of the firm's production process. Therefore the entrepreneurs' fates are tied solely to performance of productive ventures. Let us call the entrepreneurs who operate under complete functional specialization pure entrepreneurs. Pure entrepreneurs are characterized as follows.

> Individuals who see market opportunities others do not see, possess plans and strategies to exploit these opportunities and are committed to deal with contingencies; they control what to

produce and how to produce it. Pure entrepreneurs, through the markets, gain command over resources in order to carry out their product plan. Since the outcome of the plan is uncertain, they cannot claim the rewards for their services *ex ante*, and must become residual claimants. The entrepreneurial functions cannot be prescribed in detail; they are all but routine. However, one thing is certain: entrepreneurs only perform services that cannot be procured in the factor markets.

Entrepreneurial Activities with Monopolistic Factor Markets

Earlier we postponed the discussion of entrepreneurial behavior in factor markets where monopoly elements are present. We now return to this topic. The presence of monopsony power in a factor market harms the owners of the factor because the buyers of the factor can refuse to pay in accordance with its marginal productivity. The market price of the factor represents an unfair evaluation of the factor's true worth. The owners of this factor may withdraw it from the market and engage in production by forming a coalition with other like-minded resource owners, thus bypassing the factor market and taking up the entrepreneurial role. In doing so, they must give up their claim to the *ex ante* return for their services and must claim their reward as a share of the residual.

When a factor owner bypasses the market to seek income, he must also take up the entrepreneurial role. Functional specialization is destroyed. For example, when the labor market is noncompetitive the laborers may play the cooperative game with the pure entrepreneurs by forming a labor-managed firm. In this case, the role the laborer plays is no longer confined to the one usually attributed to him. He is now both laborer and entrepreneur. Likewise, when the capital market is noncompetitive, capitalists cooperate with the entrepreneur to form an owner-managed firm. The capitalist can no longer secure a return on investment without gaining control over the firm's production process. Finally, when all factor markets are noncompetitive, the roles of entrepreneur, landowner, laborer, and capitalist all merge. These examples clearly show that factor market imperfections destroy functional specialization and enlarge the scope of entrepreneurial activities. We call entrepreneurs who operate under functional nonspecialization "adjunct entrepreneurs," and characterize them as follows.

Individuals who have greater confidence in themselves than the market has in them. They are not satisfied with the return that their services command in the marketplace. Instead, they bet against the market by organizing production in accordance with their own device, and opt to claim their rewards by sharing the residual. They are factor owners who also take on the entrepreneurial role. Similar to the pure entrepreneurs, the adjunct entrepreneur's services are not traded in the market.

Entrepreneurial and Market Allocations Differ

There are many reasons for believing that the entrepreneur and the market allocate resources differently. We will provide a more elaborate discussion of this point in chapter 8. Here we briefly offer two points. First, the entrepreneurs allocate their own services by a rule which is different from the market rule. Because the entrepreneurs must engage in production by forming a coalition, they allocate their services and their rewards through bargaining. Because the entrepreneurs' services are not channeled through the market and their returns are not determined by market forces, the marginal productivity of the individual entrepreneurs is no longer the only relevant criterion for determining their returns. Two entrepreneurs who contribute identical types and equal amounts of a given service may receive a different share of the residual. This difference reflects disparity in their bargaining power. While their value inside the current coalition is identical, their potential contributions to different coalitions are different. The entrepreneur with the greater opportunities elsewhere will command greater bargaining power in the current coalition and will thus receive a higher reward. Second, entrepreneurs' allocation of other services also differs from the market allocation. The reason for this difference stems from the fact that each entrepreneur makes production decisions on the basis of his own subjective judgement of market situations. Since the subjectivity of judgement implies diversity, a coalition of entrepreneurs will select inputs different from that of another coalition even if they operate in the same market. In contrast, the market allocation implies that all decision-makers employ the same decision rule to determine the production policy. Therefore the two allocative mechanisms will, in general, yield different allocation results. Thus the entrepreneurial decisions will result in employment of production factors different from the market allocation.

CONCLUSION

Our characterization of the entrepreneur affords many advantages. First, because conflicts of interest among entrepreneurs are resolved through bargaining, the following implications emerge.

1   Entrepreneurs achieve unanimity on the production policy through the bargaining process. Because this agreement is obtained through bargaining, the entrepreneurs of a given coalition do not surrender their individual objectives to those of the firm. Instead, through the firm the entrepreneurs endeavor to pursue each of their individual objectives.

2   Since the bargaining solution does not depend solely upon the marginal productivity of each entrepreneur, the resultant production policy and distribution rule will yield an allocation of resources different from that determined by the neoclassical market allocation.

These implications help to shed light on the long-standing controversies concerning the nature of the firm, the objective of the firm, and stockholders' unanimity on the firm's production policy. Now, we can state unequivocally that, according to the entrepreneur-centered theory, the firm, unlike that in the Arrow-Debreu model, does play a nontrivial allocative role in the market economy and that the literature's insistence on reconciling the shareholders' interests with that of the firm is unnecessary. The issue of reconciliation, as will be shown in chapter 8, is moot.

Second, our characterization of the entrepreneur enables us to reconcile the many controveries about him in the literature. As readers may recall, controversies arose because the entrepreneur is commonly viewed as a personification of the firm. Since the romantic larger-than-life individual referred to as the entrepreneur at the beginning of this chapter is clearly an idealization of such a personage and rarely exists in real life, a gap exists between what the entrepreneur ought to be and what he really is. This discrepancy had led different authors to select different identifying characteristics of the entrepreneur – hence the disagreements.

In our view, this controversy is unnecessary and unproductive. The entrepreneur is not an individual who provides a unique service and can single-handedly lead the firm in production. Instead, the term entrepreneur is a generic name for owners of all services which cannot be procured in the marketplace but are needed in production, the mobilization of which is left in the hands of the resource owners themselves. Just as different types of labor are needed for production and specialization among laborers is necessary to enhance production efficiency, different entrepreneurs are needed to organize and direct production and a division of labor among the entrepreneurs also helps to improve production efficiency. Thus entrepreneurs do not perform identical functions; they jointly supply all entrepreneurial services needed for production.

By characterizing entrepreneurs in this manner, the controversy surrounding the entrepreneur in the literature is diffused. Because entrepreneurs perform a whole spectrum of services that cannot be procured in the markets, it is not surprising that they will, as the occasion warrants, perform the services championed by Coase, Alchian and Demsetz, Knight, Schumpeter, and others. Some cooperative entrepreneurs in a coalition must find production opportunities and devise production plans. Other members of the coalition must make a contractual arrangement with factor owners and customers. Although all entrepreneurs must bear some risk as a residual claimant because their activities are subject to moral hazard and adverse selection, they share this risk-bearing role with professional risk-bearers – stockholders. Finally, whenever innovative activities are needed and are profitable, some members of the coalition must provide the leadership for this innovation. In short, our characterization of the entrepreneur is all-encompassing and reconciles all controversy about entrepreneurs.

The important point we wish to emphasize is that there must a variety of talents among the entrepreneurs in a firm. Together these entrepreneurs provide the vital leadership for the firm. Despite the multitude of talents required, a precise list of tasks which the entrepreneurs must perform does not exist. In fact, by the very nature of entrepreneurship the entrepreneurial tasks are not prescribable and cannot be made to order. If they are prescribable, the quality of these services could be standardized and measured. Once entrepreneurial activities are standardized, they can be procured in the marketplace and their entrepreneurial quality vanishes.

Third and finally, entrepreneurial activities do not always contribute to the social good. Because the entrepreneur's services are not prescribable, each entrepreneur must be unique. Uniqueness confers on each entrepreneur some monopolistic power over the services he performs. Because the entrepreneur organizes and controls production, as a monopolist he not only can exert monopoly influence over the supply of his own services but also has the tendency to extend this monopoly influence to the product and factor markets. If the entrepreneurs gain the upper hand in the marketplace, monopoly flourishes. It is well known that a monopoly market will lead to under-utilization of social resources and the loss of social welfare. Thus stated, the functioning of the market now depends upon entrepreneurial behavior. We will have more to say about how entrepreneurs' behavior affects the market outcome and social welfare in chapters 7, 9, and 11. Here, we only wish to mention that social good cannot automatically be achieved through the market alone; its achievement depends on conscious human effort and the aid of appropriate social institutions.

NOTES

1 For such a view, see Casson (1982).
2 Uncertainty is not the only cause of market failure. It is well known that the presence of externality and public good also cause the market to fail. Because the purpose of this section is to develop the theme that uncertainties induce entrepreneurial activities in a market economy, we will not concern ourselves here with other causes of market failure.
3 Hedging can also take place in the options market.
4 Recent development in the literature relaxes the condition required for perfect hedging. According to Cox et al. (1981), as long as the futures price coincides with the spot price at the delivery date, a perfect hedge can take place regardless of the nature of the correlation between the spot and futures prices.
5 We will see the financing aspect of the entrepreneur-centered firm in chapter 10.
6 Since the entrepreneur market does not exist, references to the factor markets will henceforth automatically exclude it.
7 Because the firm is a coalition of many entrepreneurs, there is a question concerning whose expectation will determine the factor employment. This issue will be made clear in chapter 7.
8 Only a portion of the future profit stream can be sold in the present as stocks because entrepreneurial behavior is subject to moral hazards. Since entrepreneurial efforts influence profit outcome, the entrepreneurs can never dissociate themselves from the firm's decision process and thus are never detached from the residual.

6

Firms as Coalitions of Entrepreneurs

As we stated in chapter 4, firms are organized for two fundamental reasons: the first is technical in nature and the second is environmental. The technical reason reflects the advantage of joint production and economies of scale, and the environmental reason reflects the presence of market uncertainties and imperfections. The purpose of this chapter is to examine the nature of the firm organized under environmental considerations. This includes (a) a statement on the *raison d'être* of firms in markets where uncertainties prevail, (b) a description of the mechanism by which the firms are organized, and (c) an explanation for the simultaneous existence of all types of firms, that is, firms that are managed by entrepreneurs, capitalists (customarily referred to as owners), laborers, and managers.

The *raison d'être* of firms has, in essence, been dealt with in the preceding chapter. Here we need only recapitulate the argument. Recall that in a market environment beset by uncertainty, entrepreneurs are necessary to organize joint production. Since entrepreneurial services cannot be acquired through the market, the entrepreneurs themselves must take the initiative to organize production through nonmarket means. They do so through the formation of a firm and then act cooperatively with each other in production. A firm is organized whenever the following sets of conditions are satisfied: (a) the cooperative entrepreneurs through bargaining arrive at a mutually agreed production policy, an organizational structure which assigns authority and delineates responsibility, and a rule which governs the distribution of the residual; (b) the coalition can secure sufficient funds in the capital market to finance the intended production.

Having resolved the question of the *raison d'être*, in the balance of this chapter we need only concentrate on the remaining issues. The

127

organization of this chapter is guided by the following three observations: first, the presence of market uncertainties forces the entrepreneurs to act cooperatively with each other; second, the presence of
factor-market imperfections determines the composition of the entrepreneurs in a firm; third, the appearance of the manager-managed firm
follows a distinct path. Accordingly, this chapter is divided into three
sections. In the first section, we assume that all factor markets are
competitive so that we can concentrate our efforts on describing the
process of coalition formation. The issues associated with the type of
firms are taken up in the second section where the factor markets are
allowed to be imperfect. Manager-managed firms are dealt with in the
third section.

THE FORMATION OF FIRMS

The purpose of this section is to examine the process by which firms
are organized in a market environment where all factor markets exist
and are competitive. We choose such a market setting in order to study
the process of coalition formation among the pure entrepreneurs,
unencumbered by issues associated with the organization of different
types of firms.

Just as sound production decisions cannot be devised by ignoring
conditions relevant to exchange, it is not possible for us to comprehend entrepreneurial behaviour without knowing the activities of
all economic agents. In order to set the stage for discussing coalition
formation of the entrepreneurs, we must first identify all the relevant
agents and the roles that they play.

The Agents

There are many agents in a market economy. Each agent plays a dual
role: he is simultaneously a consumer and a resource owner. In order
to sustain consumption, an agent must convert his resources into
income. He does so by participating in production. Since participation
in production requires effort and exertion of effort is disagreeable, the
consumer–resource owner will expend effort as long as the marginal
disutility stemming from this effort is outweighed by the marginal
utility of income derived from it.

Although agents own resources, the resources owned by each agent
may differ. These resources can be classified broadly as land, labor,
capital, and entrepreneurship. Since we have assumed that markets
exist for land, labor, and capital, owners of these resources are able to
convert their resources into income by selling them in the market-

place. As the worth of each unit of service is determined in the market, identical services command identical value. Moreover, the value of the services is not tied to a specific productive venture. The owners of these services can and will act individualistically in pursuing their objectives. Entrepreneurs, in contrast, do not have a market for their services; they convert their resources into income via cooperative action. They must organize and coordinate production activities, purchase the services required from the marketplace, and accept the reward in the form of a residual. More importantly, these returns are tied solely to the performance of a productive venture. In order to guarantee that this residual does not vanish, the entrepreneurs must be in firm control of the production process.

Thus we see that each resource owner participates in production in one capacity or another. As we have seen in the last chapter, whenever markets for land, labor, and capital exist and are competitive, functional specialization of factors will prevail. Production decision-making is also a specialized function. The issue now becomes how functionally specialized agents with different behavioral traits, objectives, and responsibilities can channel their resources into production in a consistent manner. Since resources are channeled into production through the firms, it is central to recognize that the determination of the efforts of the consumer–resource owners, the formation of firms, and the exchange of goods and services belong to an integral part of the economic process; they must be determined simultaneously. Thus the issue associated with the formation of firms is embedded in a general equilibrium problem of resource allocation. As the activities of the consumer–resources owners lead to a state of equilibrium, the firms are also organized as an integral part of the market process. In order to describe this process, we propose the following general equilibrium model.

The Model

In this model[1], the consumer-resource owner occupies center stage; the firm's existence is not taken for granted. The firm emerges only as a means for the entrepreneurs to channel their talents into production. The model describes all agents' decisions both as a consumer and as a resource owner. Specifically, it shows (a) how the agent behaves as a consumer, a laborer, a landlord, a capitalist, or an entrepreneur, and (b) how the consumption and production activities of the agents interact in the marketplace leading not only to the emergence of firms but also to a state of equilibrium for the economy. In order to make a clear presentation of our ideas, we use a simple model based upon the Hicksian solution concept referred to as the temporary equilibrium

(Hicks, 1946, p, 123). It assumes that all agents face a two-period decision horizon – the present and the future. Because markets for the future commodities do not exist in the present, prices of the commodities for the second period are not known. The second-period variables must be chosen in the first period on the basis of the decision-maker's expectations. The nature of these expectations differs qualitatively between the entrepreneurs and the nonentrepreneurs. The latter take the coalition structure of the economy as given when formulating their expectations on prices and income. Because the entrepreneurs can affect the coalition structure of the economy, each entrepreneur's expectations about the future prices and income are conditional on his own activities, that is, on his choice of whether to participate in the formation of a new coalition. Given these expectations, equilibrium in the first-period market can be determined. Since firms must be organized in the first period, the emergence of the firm is examined in the context of this equilibrium situation. In order to present the desired equilibrium, we first describe the activities of the agents.

The Consumer   The consumer is assumed to possess a von Neumann-Morgenstern utility function with goods and services consumed in the two periods as arguments. He chooses a stock and bond portfolio in the first period and a commodity bundle in each period so as to maximize his utility subject to his budget constraints. An individual's budget constraints, one in each period, are now dependent upon the roles that he plays in production as a resource owner. The precise nature of these constraints will be discussed later. Since our present interest is to investigate the mechanism used by the consumer to make his consumption and effort choices, it suffices to acknowledge the existence of these constraints and to proceed forward.

Because we have assumed that futures markets do not exist (markets are incomplete), commodities for the second period cannot be traded in the first period. The consumer makes his choices on consumption and resource committments on the basis of some subjective expectations about the second-period prices and income. Given these expectations, we can use the temporary equilibrium solution technique to solve the consumer's maximization problem. This is carried out in two stages. For any given choice of consumption–investment bundle made in the first period, the consumer takes the second-period prices and income as given and chooses the second-period consumption bundle to maximize his utility subject to the budget constraint of that period. Substituting the second-period optimal values (which are now functions of the first-period variables) into the utility function and taking the expectations with respect to the second-period prices and income, we obtain the consumer's derived utility function for the first period. The derived utility function is now a function of the first period's consumption and investment. The derived utility is then maximized with respect to its arguments, subject to the budget constraint in the first period. The outcome of this maximization problem represents the consumer's equilibrium in the current period.

Since the solution of the consumer's problem depends on the budget constraints that he faces and these constraints, in turn, depend on the resources that the agent contributes to production, it is now necessary for us to make clear the nature of these constraints.

Budget Constraints Because consumers have different preferences and own different types of resources, each agent necessarily plays a different role in production and thus receives a different type of income. Income differences, in turn, lead to different budget constraints. Qualitatively, there are three types of budget constraints: those faced by laborers and by the owners of natural resources and manmade capital goods, those faced by capitalists, and those faced by entrepreneurs. Of course, it is possible for an agent to own several resources and hence to play several roles in production and receive several types of income. In this case, the consumer's budget constraints become a composite of those mentioned above. Because the inclusion of these types of agents does not contribute to the understanding of coalition formation, we will ignore the existence of multiresource-owning agents here and will instead include them in the next section.

Because labor services, natural resources, and manmade capital goods are traded in the marketplace and their prices are determined *ex ante*, a consumer who owns one of these resources knows his income *ex ante* and thus faces budget constraints that involve no random income. Note that with a one-period production lag, resource owners can be paid either in one lump sum in the first period or in two equal installments, one in each period. Because the method of payment does not lead to different substantive consequences, we will simply assume that these resource owners are paid in two equal installments.

In general, over the two-period decision horizon a consumer's endowments and incomes are seldom consistent with his optimal pattern of consumption; that is, given the incomes and endowment in the two periods, the consumer's marginal utilities of income in the two periods are seldom equal. The consumer can increase his total level of satisfaction by shifting income from one period to the other. Assume that this is accomplished by borrowing and lending. On the basis of this assumption, we can conclude that the consumer, who is a laborer or an owner of natural resources or manmade capital goods, faces the following pair of budget constraints. In the first period, his consumption plus savings must not exceed the amount equal to the sum of his first-period endowment and income. In the second period, his consumption must not exceed an amount equal to the sum of his endowment, his income in the second period, and his savings and interest earnings. Note that because savings can be either positive or negative, the agent who saves a positive amount in the first period is a lender and the agent who saves a negative amount in the first period is a borrower.

A capitalist is an individual who either has a high first-period endowment or assigns a greater utility to his future consumption compared with his present consumption. He strives to shift resources from the present to the future. He does so by purchasing debt and equity instruments. Debt instruments (bonds) can be issued either by a consumer or by a producer; they provide the lender with a fixed rate of return for his investment. The equity instruments (stocks) are issued by the producers; they permit the investor to share the uncertain residual with the producer. When a risk-averse capitalist faces a spectrum of investment opportunities involving different risks, he can usually increase his expected return by diversifying his investments as long as returns to the securities are not correlated perfectly and positively. Consequently, the capitalist will select an optimal portfolio of stocks and bonds as his investment.

Because the capitalist shifts his resources from the first to the second period by investing in stocks and bonds, he receives no income in the first period. Furthermore, because returns to stocks are stochastic, his income in the second period is uncertain. The capitalist thus faces a pair of budget constraints different from the case examined above. In the first period his consumption plus investment must not exceed his first-period endowment. In the second period, his non-product-specific investments come to fruition; his consumption is limited to an amount equal to the sum of his second-period endowment, his savings plus interest earnings, and his original stock investment plus the realized dividend income.

The entrepreneur's budget constraints are, in some ways, similar to those of the capitalist. He receives no income in the first period and his income in the second period is uncertain. His budget constraints, however, are different from those of the capitalist in a fundamental way. Because the entrepreneur is assumed to be a person with limited endowments and his income can only be realized in the second period, he must borrow from the others in order to finance his first-period consumption. Thus, in the first period, his consumption cannot exceed his small endowment plus the amount that he is able to borrow. In the second period, his product-specific entrepreneurial efforts come to fruition. His consumption in the second period must not exceed the sum of his second-period endowment and his share of the profit less the repayment of his loan with interest.

Having described the consumers' choice problems and their budget constraints, we now describe the character of the firm.

Firms as Coalitions of Entrepreneurs A firm, which is the basic production entity in a modern economy, is a coalition of entrepreneurs. The formation of the coalition signifies that a group of entrepreneurs have entered into agreement with each other concerning (a) a joint production policy, (b) an organizational structure which delineates authority and responsibility, and (c) a rule which governs the distribution of the residual. The formation of the firm is also conditional upon the fact that the coalition can secure sufficient funds to finance the intended production. Because the determination of the firm's internal organization is exceedingly complex, we will devote the next chapter to this purpose. In this chapter we will not describe in detail how the firm's internal organization is determined, but simply assume that when the coalitions are formed the firm's internal organization is also determined.

Let there be N agents in the economy. Owing to differences in preferences and in the endowment of abilities, not all these agents are able or willing to assume the entrepreneurial role. Denote by n, where $n < N$, the number of agents who want to be entrepreneurs. There are then $2^n - 1$ potential firms. However, not all these potential firms are viable. Some firms will not form simply because the collection of entrepreneurs does not possess the technology and know-how to produce products at a sufficiently low cost or to produce products which attract sufficient demand to be profitable. Other firms may not form because the coalition of entrepreneurs fails to secure sufficient funds to acquire the necessary inputs for production. The firm's ability to acquire funds depends not only upon its capability to produce desirable products but also upon the willingness of the entrepreneurs to share the fruit of their surplus with the shareholders. Thus, if the firm is to be viable, it must offer an attractive menu of financial instruments as well as products to the market. Finally, the firm may not form because of bargaining failures; that is, entrepreneurs of a firm may fail to agree upon an internal organization, a joint production policy, and a sharing rule for the profit. There are two sources of bargaining failures. The first stems from the fact that bargaining among multiple agents often leads to cycling. The threat by one party to leave a current coalition in favor of another may be made by each party so as to make stable coalitions impossible. Further, even if coalitions can be agreed upon, the fact that the efforts of the entrepreneurs are not observable with certainty implies that shirking from commitments cannot be detected and enforced without incurring substantial costs. If this occurs the cost of enforcement may be so high as to make a joint production undesirable.

The firms that do form are the outcome of an economy-wide cooperative game played by the entrepreneurs with the following as the game strategy: (a) the choice of a production policy and the allocation of the available entrepreneurial services, and (b) the division of the value of the game, first between the entrepreneurs and the shareholders (through the selection of the firm's financial policy to be described in chapter 10) and then among the entrepreneurs. When a group of entrepreneurs come together and agree to adopt a given production policy and a given allocation of the above mentioned items, the firm is formed. The firm organized under the assumed environment will also have a two-period decision horizon. In the first period each firm issues stocks and bonds in order to raise funds from the agents in the economy; with these funds it purchases an input bundle and commences production. In the second period the firm produces an output bundle. It then sells the products in the market-place and distributes the residuals partly to the shareholders as a dividend and party to the entrepreneurs as a bonus.[2] After these activities are accomplished, the firm vanishes.

We have now completed the description of all agents in the economy and are ready to examine the two-tier market and nonmarket processes and the nature of the market equilibrium.

General Equilibrium

Having identified the various agents in the economy and stated each of their objectives, it is now possible to describe how these agents, in the process of pursing their self-interest, lead the economy into a state of equilibrium. The tactics used by the agents to attain each of their objectives are different. As consumers and owners of tradeable resources, agents can best pursue their objectives in the marketplace by acting noncooperatively. As entrepreneurs, agents must act co-operatively since their services can only be channeled into production through the intermediary of a firm. Because the existence of the firm cannot be taken for granted, the formation of the firm becomes a part of the equilibrating process. In order to capture the essence of the nature of equilibrium with the formation of firms as an important part of the system, we need only describe the equilibrium in the current period. In other words we must describe the market and nonmarket mechanisms leading to the determination of (a) the prices of the current commodities including the interest rate, (b) for each agent the consumption bundle, savings, and resources committed for production in the current period (the resources commitment includes labor services, natural or manmade resources, and/or stock–bond portfolios, whichever is relevant), (c) a collection of hierarchical coalitions of entrepreneurs, that is, a set of firms with specific internal organization, (d) an input bundle committed to production by each firm, and (e) a stock-bond portfolio that the firm will issue and a bonus rate set, that is, a profit-sharing rule for the entrepreneurs of each firm realized.

The equilibrium process works as follows. Assume that each agent is a price-taker. First, let the market prices be given. Each agent, as a consumer or as a nonentrepreneurial resource owner, chooses his own strategy so that the resulting consumption and resource commitment maximize his derived utility subject to the appropriate budget constraint. The entrepreneurs, however, through the formation of a firm, jointly choose their strategy regarding their resource commitment and rewards. This strategy consists of a quadruplet: the commodity input bundle, the allocation of entrepreneurial inputs, the financial policy, and the profit-sharing rule. These choices must be made within the constraints set by the availability of the funds as well as the availability of the entrepreneurial services to the firm.

From this description of the equilibrium process we see that as a result of the entrepreneurial activities a dichotomy between demand and supply emerges in the market place. The firm, on the one hand, is the demander for resources and the supplier of goods as well as financial instruments. The resource owner, on the other hand, is a supplier of resources and a demander for goods as well as financial instruments. In this way, the demand and supply of goods and services through imputation and competition interact to determine the commodity prices. The economy reaches an equilibrium when the prices of the current-period commodities are determined, all markets are cleared, and no entry or exit of firms takes place. In this state of equilibrium no nonentrepreneur agent can improve his expected utility by changing his own action, and no entrepreneur can improve his expected utility by forming a new coalition.

ECONOMY WITH DIFFERENT TYPES OF FIRMS

In this section we examine the reasons for the simultaneous existence of different types of firms in an economy and the process by which these firms are organized. This section is divided into two subsections:

in the first we examine the motive for organizing different types of firms, and in the second we examine their formation.

Raison d'être *for Different Types of Firms*

In a real world situation, in addition to the absence of the entrepreneurial market, there are imperfections in the factor markets. We believe that the composition of the agents who will participate in coalition formation is determined in part by the types of market imperfection. Hence different factor-market imperfections give rise to different types of firms. Broadly stated, there are three major sources of imperfection in the factor markets: high information costs, monopoly powers, and monopsony powers. If any of these imperfections are present, the resource owners of the tradeable factors can bypass the market and participate in production by joining with the pure entrepreneurs to organize a firm. We now treat each type of imperfection in turn.

High Information Cost   When the outcome of production is uncertain and the employee's efforts can be observed only by incurring an exorbitant cost, both internal monitoring and market discipline of the factor owners lose their effectiveness.

As we have seen in chapter 4, high information cost prevents the entrepreneurs from ascertaining whether mere bad luck or shirking of responsibility by some factor owners was the cause of either a low level or a low quality of output. This inability to assign responsibility is further complicated in a joint production situation where each worker's marginal contribution to output cannot be ascertained with certainty. The employee can now take advantage of the entrepreneur–employer's inability to assign responsibility by resorting to shirking. The factor owner who shirks can evade responsibility by blaming either the random event or the other cooperative factors for the poor outcome. The temptation to shirk is particularly strong because the prices of the factors are determined *ex ante* in the market and the factor owners do not suffer a consequence of their own misconduct. Thus high information cost and *ex ante* contractual arrangement encourage moral hazards and make it difficult for the entrepreneur–employers to prescribe employes' duties and to supervise their performance.

The inability to identify a factor owner's efforts in a costless manner together with the *ex ante* determination of factor prices also makes the market impotent to discipline factor owners. Note that the market's ability to perform the disciplinary role rests crucially upon the condition that the marginal productivity of the factor is known. When this condition is satisfied, the demand for a factor owned by a specific individual is nil whenever this factor owner demands a price higher than the prevailing market price or performs services with a quality lower than the prevailing standard. This fact implies that the market can prevent the factor owners from deviating either in prices or in the quality of services performed. Failing to assess the marginal productivity of a factor implies that the factor owners who perform services below the prevailing market standard can evade penalty for their misconduct. This evasion may still be possible even if the cheater has been identified by the firm. Since there is no clear mechanism for transmitting information concerning misconduct from the firm to the market, the cheater can simply leave the firm, re-enter the market, and again receive a reward equal to the market price. The market thus ceases to perform the disciplinary role. This market ineptness encourages every resource owner to behave opportunistically and thus brings down the overall productivities of the factors. Further, shirking in effort also adds to output uncertainties faced by the entrepreneur–managed firm and serves to discourage the risk-averse entrepreneurs from undertaking production.

In sum, a high information cost prevents the entrepreneurs from monitoring factor performances and contributes to the ineptness of the market in assisting the entrepreneurs in disciplining the factor owners. These inabilities to enforce contractual obligations decrease the efficiency of the factors and cause a decline in the profitability of the entrepreneur-managed firms. This implies that the pure-entrepreneur-managed firm is simply not an incentive-compatible business organization in a market environment where information concerning factor performance is very high.

The market's inability to discipline the factor owners is particularly evident when a commodity is produced with a labor-intensive production technology and by highly skilled laborers. In order to exploit the advantages of division of labor and economies of scale of production, skilled labor can in theory be brought together in joint production by an entrepreneur-managed firm and be paid with the market-determined wages. Because input services are highly specialized and skill is essential for production, the entrepreneurs cannot prescribe service standards and cannot effectively monitor the production activities. The entrepreneurs must leave the performance of the services to the discretion of the workers. If, in addition, the output quality varies randomly, all prerequisites for shirking are present. Temptation is high. However, in this case the damage caused by shirking is also high. Since quality of the output cannot be guaranteed readily, the reputations of the workers become the basis of the demand for their product. In the joint production situation the quality of the output depends on the collective skill and efforts of the cooperative workers. The high quality of one worker must be supported by the high quality of all his co-workers in order to turn out high quality output. Under these circumstances shirking by one of the workers not only reduces the quantity and quality of the product but also destroys the firm's reputation and with it the livelihood of the cooperative factor owners. Shirking thus becomes extremely harmful. Again, because the market lacks the mechanism for collecting and disseminating information on workers' performance, its performance of the disciplinary role is inept. Therefore, it is expected that the entrepreneur-managed firm will be unable to cope with shirking problems. It is not surprising that services produced by professional people, e.g. physicians and lawyers, are seldom conducted under the auspices of the pure-entrepreneur-managed firms. For these products, the pure-entrepreneur-managed business organization is not incentive compatible.

There are two ways of correcting incentive incompatibility between laborers and their employers. Both are based on the observation that the moral hazards associated with the situation described above stem in part from the fact that the factor prices are determined before the production has taken place and the efforts have been carried out. The factor owners who have shirked do not suffer direct consequences of their own actions. Accordingly, both proposed remedies require that payments to labor be shifted from *ex ante* to *ex post*. The first remedy involves a sharing-contract arrangement and the second the formation of labor-managed firms.

A sharing contract stipulates a rule used to divide the actual fruit of production. When production uncertainties prevail, such a sharing contract provides incentive for a laborer to increase his efforts since he is rewarded by a share of the actual output that he has helped to produce (Cheung, 1969; Stiglitz, 1974). Laborers and employers, through the market, bargain for the sharing rule. Since labor's reward now increases (decreases) with the quantity and quality of the output, there exists the incentive for labor to work harder and shirking may thus be avoided. Note that a sharing contract leaves intact the relationship between employer and employee, thus preserving the functional division of labor.

Another way of dealing with the problem of shirking is to let the party who shirks assume the decision role and bear the consequences that they have helped to create. In the case of skilled laborers this approach involves letting the laborers join the coalition, manage production, and share the residual. In this way, the shirking parties must themselves suffer the consequences of shirking. A change from the pure-entrepreneur-managed firm to the labor-managed firm, however, does not automatically stop shirking. Shirking in one's work, although decreasing the quantity and quality of the output, is shouldered by all cooperative decision-makers. If an increase in the individual's marginal utility derived from a decrease in his efforts exceeds the decrease in the expected utility resulting from a reduction in his remuneration as a result of shirking, then shirking will still take place.

There are reasons to believe that, under special circumstances, labor-managed firms can indeed help to check the temptation of shirking. First, laborers in a labor-managed firm, instead of receiving a market-determined wage, must share the firm's residual as an adjunct entrepreneur. This switch in payment method naturally arouses the cooperative workers' interests in monitoring each other's productivity. Whenever expertise is required to monitor a skilled worker's performance, mutual monitoring by his fellow skilled laborers – entrepreneurs also enables the labor-managed firm to reduce its monitoring cost and thus to discourage shirking. If violations of agreements are discovered, through internal procedures, an appropriate penalty can be applied surely and swiftly. This direct retaliation leaves no chance for the violator to escape punishment, and thus serves as a powerful deterrent to shirking.

Finally, highly skilled laborers of a given type often bind together through a professional organization. If firms are organized by members of a given professional organization, the operational efficiency can be enhanced with the aid of the organization. As we have seen above, shirking by cooperative workers has the propensity of reducing the overall efficiency in production, and therefore reducing the total returns to the group. Consequently shirking is incompatiable with the total welfare of the membership of the profession. The professional organization is therefore interested in reversing this tendency. A reversal can be accomplished by establishing professional ethics and codes of conduct and by adopting appropriate mechanisms to enforce rules and to discipline its members. The effectiveness of the professional discipline often exceeds that of the firm for it poses a greater threat to the violator. This is because professional censorship serves to disseminate information about the violators' conduct and their reputation; this information leads to a decrease in the violators' bargaining power during the time of coalition formation. Consequently, disciplinary action of the professional organization is often sufficient to discourage shirking.

In short, because there are many advantages associated with labor-managed firms under special circumstances, it is not surprising that under appropriate circumstances the labor-managed firms will emerge as a preferred business organization.

Monopoly and Monopsony   There are two ways in which the presence of monopoly power in the factor markets leads the owners of tradeable resources to organize firms. Generally, in the presence of monopolistic input sellers, the pure entrepreneurs will hesitate to organize a firm for fear that they will be at the mercy of these monopolistic suppliers. This hesitation translates into a lack of demand for the monopolistic input which, in turn, leads to an unsatisfactory income for the monopolist. Paradoxically, the attempt to extract income through the exercise of monopoly power may actually lead to a lower income for the monopolist. In order to exploit fully the income potential of their resources, the monopolistic resource owners may be forced to take up the entrepreneurial role and to organize production by themselves. Thus, because the pure entrepreneurs are intimidated by the monopolistic resource owners, the entrepreneurial role may be thrust upon the latter group and thus cause the emergence of firms with a different control structure. In short, when the capitalists possess monopoly power in the capital market, capitalists may be forced to organize and manage firms, thus giving rise to owner-managed firms. Likewise, when labor wields monopoly power, labor-managed firms may also emerge.

When the pure entrepreneurs (buyers of a factor) possess monopsonistic power, the outcome is similar. In this case the owners of the tradeable resources (the sellers) have two options. First, in order to secure a fair deal for their services, the sellers may opt to bind together to form a countervailing power so as to bargain for a better price. The labor union is a prominent example of such a situation. Wages in this case are not determined by the impersonal market but through bargaining in the marketplace – henceforth referred to as external bargaining. Note that external bargaining, though affecting the distribution of income, leaves the functional specialization intact.

The second option of the owners of tradeable resources faced with monopsonistic power is more intimately associated with the occurrence of different types of firms. The owners of the exploited factor may choose to avoid exploitation by channeling the factor services not through the market but through the organization of a firm and hence gaining self-employment. In doing so, the owners of this factor accept the entrepreneurial role as described in chapter 5. If this route is followed, the return to this factor is determined as a share of the residual by internal bargaining. Note that internal bargaining differs from external bargaining in that the former destroys the functional specialization among factors, while the latter does not. This difference has serious implications for the theory of profits. These implications will be examined thoroughly in chapters 8 and 10.

We have now provided an explanation for the existence of firms other than those managed by pure entrepreneurs, but have so far fallen short of our stated goal which is to explain the simultaneous existence of all types of business organizations in an industry and in an economy. Because all producers presumably face the same factor markets, both perfect and imperfect, it seems natural to conclude, on the basis of our discussion so far, that all firms in the economy ought to react uniformly to the same market environment and to adopt an identical business organization. Thus, in order to justify the coexistence of different types of firms, an additional explanation must be given. Our explanation is based upon the observation that a special market environment is needed to support the production and distribution of a given commodity which uses a particular production technology, employs firm-specific inputs, and/or needs special input purchasing and output distributional arrangements. Thus a particular productive venture can be extremely sensitive to one type of market imperfection and yet indifferent to another. As a result, different producers, although faced with the same general market environment, may opt to organize in a different fashion. This explains why different types of firms coexist in the same economy. In the following paragraphs we offer two examples to support our contention.

The first example is concerned with the capital market. We frequently observe that, given the prevailing capital market, some firms find it desirable to raise capital through the market while others opt to bypass it. Generally, independent innovators who wish to raise venture capital find the capital market exceedingly expensive, whereas established firms wishing to secure financing for expansionary purposes find that the same capital market serves their purpose quite well. The reason is that the capital market can handle the information needed to finance capital expansion more efficiently than the information needed for venture activities. Consider an independent inventor who wishes to raise capital in order to finance the production of a new product. Since the inventor does not have a financial track record, information concerning the profitability of the venture must be extracted from the nature of the product and the method by which it is produced. The inventor is typically unwilling to disclose technical information concerning the new product for fear that such disclosure will destroy the value of his property rights associated with the invention. From the investor's point of view, the market has failed to handle the required information in an efficient manner and the risk associated with this type of investment is typically high. Consequently, the cost associated with venture capital is also high. In order to carry on his innovation activities, the inventor frequently acts cooperatively with the capitalists to form a joint venture. In this way, the capitalists gain the necessary information and the inventor gains the required capital; together they carry on the innovation cooperatively and divide the profits according to a rule established through bargaining.

The story is quite different for an established firm with a clear financial track record. The investor is seldom interested in the technical nature of the product; his primary interest is the profit potential on his investment. If a firm with a favorable financial track record wishes to expand its current activities, it only needs to provide this information to its potential investors. The financial market is equipped to handle this type of information and the expanding firm will have little difficulty in raising the required capital.

The implications of this example are clear. Although the producers face the same capital market, because investors need different information from them, the capital market may not be able to serve all the producers in an equally satisfactory manner. The firms which face the high capital cost must organize differently in order to secure the capital required for production. Thus young research and development (R & D) oriented firms must raise capital by nonmarket means and therefore are managed by owner–innovator–entrepreneurs, whereas established firms can raise the required capital through the market and hence can be managed by pure entrepreneurs. As a result, owner-managed firms and entrepreneur-managed firms do coexist under the same capital market environment. Not only is there the tendency for these two types of firms to coexist, there is also the tendency for the firm to evolve from the owner-managed type to the entrepreneur-managed type as it gains maturity. The capital market, as shown above, facilitates this progression. As the firm grows to maturity, the entrepreneur and the capitalist gain independence from each other: the entrepreneur sheds some risk-bearing burden while the capitalist relieves himself of managerial responsibility.

The second example has to do with imperfections in the labor market. Producers often employ job-specific workers. Typically the categories of labor traded in the labor market fall short of the job classifications that existed in the economy. Firms using the standard grade of labor will rely upon the market to satisfy their labor requirement. Wages are determined in the market; in this case the sellers (laborers) and the buyers (entrepreneurs) will behave non-cooperatively, each maximizing his own objectives. The fact that job classification is finer than the market classification of labor implies that many jobs are firm specific. Some of these jobs will require substantial human capital investment. Since these labor services cannot be traded easily in the market, human capital investment is risky. Risk-averse individuals will shun this type of investment. Thus, for example, an R&D firm committed to highly specialized research will be unable to find scientists to conduct the required research, and accounting or law firms with extraordinary job specializations will not be able to find accountants or lawyers to fill these positions. Yet because the success of such ventures requires the services of specialized personnel, owners of these services, instead of selling their services in the labor market, will join in partnership with the entrepreneurs and channel their services directly into production. It is therefore not surprising to find that scientists frequently join R&D firms as entrepreneurs, and accountants and lawyers join each other as partners in production. This example shows that even if all firms in the economy face the same labor market, some will opt to use the market and others to bypass it; non-labor-managed firms and labor-managed firms therefore coexist in the same market environment.

Firms and General Equilibrium

The presence of market imperfection in the factor markets causes a change in the composition of the players who participate in the economy-wide cooperative game. This change, as we have learned from the last section, will affect the nature of the resource owner's budget constraints and the way that he will formulate his expectations of the second-period prices and income. In the remainder of this section, we first describe the resource owner's budget constraints and the structure of his expected utility function, and then present the market and nonmarket processes which lead the economy into a general equilibrium where firms with different organization structures coexist.

Budget Constraints Because agents have different preferences and own different types of resources, each agent generally plays a different role in production and thus receives different types of income. In the last section we examined three types of budget constraints – those faced by labor and the owners of natural resources as well as manmade capital goods, those faced by capitalists, and those faced by entrepreneurs. With a change in the composition of the players who participate in the economy-wide cooperative game, a change in the relevant agents' budget constraints will follow. These agents now play several roles in production, and their income may take on a composite form and thus alter the character of their budget constraints.

Specifically, if a laborer joins the pure entrepreneurs to play the economy-wide cooperative game, his budget constraints will no longer be those stated in the first section. He must now face a pair of budget constraints similar to those faced by the entrepreneurs. In the first period, his consumption is limited to his first-period endowment and the amount he is able to borrow, and in the second period his consumption must not exceed his share of the residual less the repayment of his loan with interest. In this case his share of the residual represents a reward to the mixture of his labor and entrepreneurial services.

Likewise, if a capitalist joins the pure entrepreneurs to play the economy-wide cooperative game, his budget constraints will also change. The change in this case is not in form but rather in interpretation. In the first period the capitalist's consumption plus his investment must not exceed his first-period endowment. In the second period, his consumption must not exceed the sum of his second-period endowment, his savings plus interest earnings, and his share of the residual. His share of the residual differs from his dividend incomes (as stated in the last section) in that the former is a combined return to the capitalist–entrepreneur while the latter is a return to the capital service alone.

In addition, when the owner of a tradeable resource is contemplating whether to join the entrepreneurs in organizing a firm, his expectations about the second-period prices and income will now depend upon this choice. As he changes from an unconditional to a conditional expectation of the second-period prices and income, the form of the resource owner's expected utility function will change accordingly. Consequently, with the possibility of organizing the firm in different business forms, laborers and capitalists who end up playing a dual role in the production process will face a different set of budget constraints and a different form of expected utility function.

The Equilibrating Process Although the presence of factor-market imperfections changes the composition of agents who play the economy-wide cooperative game, this change need not affect the market process as described in the previous section. The effect of market imperfection on the market process depends, to some extent, upon whether these imperfections have affected the agent's price-taking behavior. As long as the agent's price-taking behavior is preserved, nothing will change; that is, the presence of market imperfections in the factor markets does not affect the structure of the general equilibrium model and the solution concept of the associated mathematical problem. Suppose, however, that the price-taking behavior is violated by the presence of imperfections in the factor markets. We, of course, know that the structure of the general equilibrium model will be different and that there does not yet exist a satisfactory solution concept for solving the mathematical problem associated with this model. Nonetheless, we believe that the basic market process will still be unaltered. In other words, although some resource owners now join the pure entrepreneurs to play the cooperative game through the formation of the firm, the cooperative and noncooperative forces will again interact in the market in a manner similar to that described in the last section; that is, through the formation of firms the cooperative factors interact with the noncooperative factors to form the demand and supply side of the input and output markets, and through competition the economy reaches a state of equilibrium. Consequently, the firm, as well as other endogenous variables, will again be determined in the equilibrium process. The only difference is that, in the present market environment, at equilibrium the firms will be organized by someone in addition to the pure entrepreneurs. Specifically, if only the capital market is imperfect, at equilibrium there will be entrepreneurs and owner-managed firms, if only the labor market is imperfect, at equilibrium there will be entrepreneurs and labor-managed firms, and if both markets are imperfect, at equilibrium entrepreneur-managed, owner-managed, and labor-managed firms may coexist with firms jointly managed by capitalists, labor, and entrepreneurs.

MANAGER-MANAGED FIRMS

Up to this point, we have not included the ubiquitous manager-managed firms in our discussion. This chapter cannot be viewed as complete unless we provide an explanation for their existence. We now turn our attention to this problem.

Since our concern has been the birth process of the firms, it is not accidental that manager-managed firms have escaped our attention. This is because the threat of moral hazards and adverse selection prevents managers from participating in coalition formation. The firms emerging from this process naturally do not include the manager-managed type. To be specific, in organizing a firm for production the organizer must seek capital from the capital market. In soliciting the required capital, as the reader may recall, the entrepreneurs must first develop a business plan which includes a specification of the product, identification of the relevant market, a description of the business strategies, and a projection of the income stream. In addition, the entrepreneurs must also show their commitment to safeguarding the capitalist's investment. They do so by accepting the role of hostages to the capitalists and becoming residual claimants, thereby sharing the business risk with the capitalists. Although the managers can also devise business plans, they receive salaries which are determined *ex ante*. Since managers are not residual claimants, the threat of moral hazards and adverse selection will cause capitalists to treat potential manager-managed firms with great suspicion. Consequently, this type of firm will be unable to raise sufficient capital and will fail to carry out its plan for production. It is therefore not surprising to find that manager-managed firms are not among the firms organized during coalition formation.

Since managers cannot participate in the coalition formation of firms, the emergence of the manager-managed firm must follow a different path. If we refer to the coalition formation of firms as a process of creation, then in contrast the emergence of the manager-managed firm apparently follows a process of evolution. The entrepreneur-, owner-, and labor-managed firms, through time, may be transformed into the manager-managed type. Because it takes time for a firm to evolve into the manager-managed type, we need the aid of a multiperiod model to describe this process. In this section, we present such a model and use it to describe how the entrepreneurs and self-employed resource owners organize the firms at the beginning of a multiperiod planning horizon and then illustrate how a firm so created can change its character over time and be transformed into the manager-managed type.

Coalition Formation in a Multiperiod Setting

Let the consumer hold a T-period planning horizon and possess an additive separable von Neumann–Morgenstern utility function of the form

$$U = \sum_{t=1}^{T} \rho^{t-1} u\,(.)$$

where ρ represents the discount factor and the arguments in the utility function are goods and services consumed in period t. The consumer seeks an optimal sequence of decisions, that is, a policy, so as to maximize his total expected utility subject to the budget constraints. His budget constraints, as in the two-period model, depend on the role that he plays as a resource owner. By assuming that the consumer maximizes his expected utility in period t, $0 < t < T$, conditional on the fact that his decisions from period t onward are made optimally, the multiperiod choice problem can be reduced to a sequence of interrelated subproblems, one for each period in the planning horizon. In this manner, the consumer can again obtain the derived utility function for the first period of his planning horizon. He again selects the consumption bundle and resource commitments in the first period so as to maximize his derived expected utility subject to the budget constraint of that period. The outcome of this maximization problem again represents the consumer's first-period equilibrium.

Regarding the formation of the firms, the first period is again the day of the creation. Entrepreneurs, pure and adjunct, play the economy-wide cooperative game. Firms are again organized as part of the equilibrium process of the economy in the manner described in the first section. Each entrepreneur is now committed to joining a coalition for the duration of complete T periods.

As time unfolds, information becomes available. A consumer and owner of a market-traded factor will incorporate the current market information and will choose his consumption and resource commitment so as to maximize the derived utility of the current period subject to the budget constraint of that period. The entrepreneur's choice problem is more complex. Since the entrepreneur is committed to a specific coalition at the time of the firm's creation, based upon the currently available information, he must not only make consumption-investment decisions but must also decide whether it is advantageous for him to switch to a new coalition. As the entrepreneurs revise their membership affiliation, both the composition of the entrepreneurs in the firm and the coalition structure of the economy will undergo a change. We can, in principle, state that whenever the composition of entrepreneurs in a coalition changes, a new firm has emerged. This definition of the firm, however, is not practical. If the composition of entrepreneurs in a coalition changes in a merely marginal way, neither the coalition's internal structure nor its production and financial policies will be altered appreciably. It is therefore more practical to consider the life of the firm to be independent of these marginal changes. The life of the firm is, in practice, fairly durable. In this context, a change in the market data between periods produces two sets of responses: first, it may induce a minor modification of the composition of entrepreneurs within the firm; second, it may also induce entrepreneurs to form new firms or dissolve old coalitions. The first response represents the internal adjustment of the existing firms, and the second represents the entry and exit of firms. Thus, in responding to changes in the market data, the economy, through two avenues, moves toward a new equilibrium.

In general, if there is a cost associated with coalition formation, changes in both the composition of entrepreneurs within a firm and the coalition structure of the economy will be marginal. The coalition formation costs include information cost about the utility functions of the cooperative entrepreneurs and the set-up cost associated with the firm's creation. In the presence of these transaction costs, an entrepreneur is apt to retain his affiliation unless the expected gains in utility derived from such a change exceed the marginal disutility associated with these costs. Because the cost associated with coalition formation is nontrivial, we find that between periods the changes in the composition of entrepreneurs within the firms are marginal and the entry and exit of firms in an industry are also kept to a minimum. Consequently, over time the coalition structure of the economy is also relatively stable.[3]

The Emergence of the Manager-managed Firm

Relative stability, both within the firm and within the industry, contributes greatly to the emergence of manager-managed firms. As an industry evolves, the demand for and supply of its product may become relatively stable and may change in a reasonably predictable manner. The firm in this industrial environment may opt to settle on a set of well-established rules to guide its operation regarding ways both to cope with changes in the market data and to deal with interfirm rivalries. Decision-making becomes routinized. Routinization of a firm's operation not only renders the entrepreneurial role redundant but also makes it possible for the market to evaluate the worth of these rules and, with it, the marginal productivities of the executors of these rules, that is, the managers. Knowing the marginal productivities of the managers, the managerial market will emerge. This market will not only determine managerial salaries but will also serve to discipline the managers. If the managers of a firm render substandard services and thus cause the firm's profit to decline, the market value of the firm will decrease. The decrease in the market value of the firm will help to discipline the managers in two ways. First, the loss inflicted on the investor makes it harder for the managers to secure funds in the capital market whenever required and thus hampers the managers' operations and reduces their own market values. Second, the fall in the market value of the firm will also encourage takeover by other entrepreneurs since the firm's potential market value now exceeds its current value. The decrease in the supply of capital funds to the firm passively discourages managerial shirking, while the takeover actively replaces the inefficient managers by efficient entrepreneurs and thereby restores the firm's operational efficiency and, with it, the firm's market worth. In both ways, the market acts to prevent the managers from shirking.

Not only does the stabilization of the market environment encourage the development of the manager-managed firm, the internal dynamics of the firm will also contribute to this end. The success of a business venture depends on many separate but interrelated activities; these activities must be controlled and coordinated efficiently. Efficient management can be achieved by the creation of elaborate and formal administrative networks and bureaucracies. Formal as well as informal rules are created to guide routine affairs. Clear lines of authority and control have to be devised so that people will understand their roles, authority, and responsibilities. Under these circumstances management goals often take precedence over entrepreneurial initiatives. Entrepreneurs thus give way to managers. Business begins to lose its personal tone; personalities and special characteristics of the firm become less important to the credit market. Firms, instead of seeking capital in the specialized capital market, can now obtain capital in the general capital market or through retained earnings. Thus, we see that, even though the managers cannot participate with the entrepreneurs to organize firms through coalition formation, they nonetheless may effectively gain control of the firm via gradual evolution and thereby convert the entrepreneur-managed firm into a manager-managed type.

The manager-managed firms differ from other types of firms in that, at equilibrium, the managers earn salaries determined in the managerial market. Because the rules adopted by the managers of the firm are known to be effective for the given market environment, competition among the firms does not cause profit to vanish but leaves each firm with a normal profit. This profit is distributed to its shareholders as dividend which is equal to the interest rate plus a firm specific-risk premium determined in the capital market.

SUMMARIZING REMARKS

In this chapter we have presented a general equilibrium model with the formation of firms as a part of the equilibrium process. Having understood the process by which the various types of firms come into being, the next logical step is to take up the unresolved issues that we left in chapter 4. These issues include the following:

1   Is it possible for the entrepreneurs of a firm to agree upon a production policy unanimously?
2   What objective or objectives does a firm pursue?
3   Do firms of different types pursue profits with different vigor?
4   Does the composition of the type of firm in the economy change over time?
5   Does this composition affect the course of economic development?

Unfortunately, it is still premature for us to answer all these questions at this time. In general, the firm's behavior not only depends upon its type but also upon its internal structure. Since we have postponed the discussion of the firm's internal structure to the next chapter, we will deal with the first three questions in the next chapter, and the last two questions in chapter 9.

NOTES

1 The precise nature of this model is presented in the mathematical appendix.
2 The division of the residual between the shareholders and the entrepreneurs

is fundamental to the development of a viable profit theory. We will describe this division in greater detail in chapter 10.

3 However, the relative stability of the firm is exaggerated by the prevailing legal–financial institution which treats the firm as a legal entity. Presently, even if the composition of entrepreneurs in a firm has changed drastically, as long as the legal status of the firm remains the same the firm is said to be unaltered. This is contrary to our concept of a firm. We would certainly consider the Chrysler Corporation under the leadership of Lee Iaccoca to be different from the corporation under the leadership of his predecessor.

7

The Internal Organization of the Firm

In this chapter we continue the discussion started in chapter 6 and examine the internal decision processes and the internal organization of the entrepreneur-centered firm. Recall that we employed the general equilibrium approach in chapter 6 to explain how firms come into existence. However, this approach is inadequate for the problem at hand. Just knowing how the firm comes into being will not provide us with an understanding of how it allocates resources internally. In order to gain such an understanding, we must take a partial equilibrium approach and examine how the firm formulates its internal decision rules and how it organizes to implement decisions. It is particularly important to understand the internal workings of the firm in the present context because the firm under consideration does not possess a specific objective and is managed jointly by many entrepreneurs. Without a clear objective, the firm's decision rules cannot be deduced from its objective function; they must be discovered by examining its internal decision processes and the way that decisions are implemented.

As seen in chapter 5, the presence of market uncertainty prevents production decisions from being made instantaneously and objectively; it destroys the market's ability to coordinate production. Information and judgement become important ingredients for decision-making; entrepreneurs emerge to fill the void. Because advantages exist in the entrepreneurial division of labor, information, and risk-sharing, entrepreneurs enter into contract with each other to engage in joint production. However, the achievement of gains from cooperation is not automatic; it is subject to many barriers. First, a conflict of interest exists among potentially cooperative entrepreneurs whose utility functions and initial endowments differ. These conflicting interests must be reconciled by bargaining. If bargaining should fail to establish a mutually acceptable agreement, a coalition will not form. In

151

addition, the presence of uncertainties and the attendant lack of information prevent objective assessments of the quality of each entrepreneur's decisions owing to the difficulty in distinguishing whether a poor entrepreneurial performance is caused by "bad luck" or by a "lack of effort". This inability to objectively assess entrepreneurial performance encourages the entrepreneur to behave opportunistically. Whenever the adverse effect of opportunistic behavior is so great as to offset the gains derived from cooperation, the coalition cannot be sustained even if there is a mechanism through which the cooperative entrepreneurs can arrive at a joint production policy.

After the firm has become a going concern, it must still accomplish what the market has failed to do; that is, it must coordinate information and make decisions efficiently. Because production in a firm is controlled by a coalition of entrepreneurs, each with a specific functional responsibility, decision-making activities are dispersed. The problem of how decisions made by the various cooperative entrepreneurs can be forged into a cohesive policy still exists. The mechanism used to coordinate these decisions depends crucially upon how information is distributed among the cooperative entrepreneurs. If information is accessible to all the entrepreneurs, the firm may opt to coordinate the decisions simultaneously in a collective manner. The rules needed to implement this type of coordination are relatively simple. However, if information is scattered among the entrepreneurs, the various functional decisions are likely to be made in a decentralized manner. The coordination of decisions must be carried out by establishing complex rules. The rules become even more intricate when monitoring and controlling of entrepreneurial performance is also involved.

Because rules do not work by themselves, internal organization among the entrepreneurs must be erected to implement them. There are many ways in which the firm can be organized to implement its rules and policies. As implied by the above statement, the broad nature of the firm's internal organization depends upon whether the firm's decisions are made in a collective or decentralized manner. By internal organization we mean more than just the firm's organizational chart; we mean how the various authorities and responsibilities are distributed and related among the cooperative entrepreneurs. Internal organization describes (a) how decision functions are divided among the entrepreneurs, (b) how authorities and obligations are related among them, (c) how information is distributed and utilized, (d) whose decision will prevail when conflicts arise among the entrepreneurial decisions, and (e) how monitoring and enforcement are carried out to discourage opportunistic behavior.

The purpose of this chapter is to examine the nature of such internal organizations. Broadly speaking, there are two types of internal organizational structure: the hierarchical and the oligarchical. The first two sections of this chapter are devoted to the internal organization needed to support efficient decision-making and to curb opportunistic behavior within a hierarchically organized firm. In the third section we deal with the firm organized in a simple oligarchical structure.

THE HIERARCHICAL INTERNAL DECISION STRUCTURE

In this section, we examine the factors which lead the firm to adopt a hierarchical internal structure and study the firm's decision process under such an organizational environment. By and large the firm organizes in a hierarchical form in order to effectively utilize scattered information, to efficiently coordinate functional decisions made by entrepreneurs who use the firm to achieve personal objectives, and to enforce the contractual obligations of the cooperating entrepreneurs. Clearly, this is a complex task. Fortunately, some of the relevant issues have already been investigated and clarified in a branch of the literature known as team theory. By abstracting from the concern of how a team is founded and by assuming that the utility functions of all the teammates are identical, team theory studies how dispersion of information leads to a decentralization of decision-making. A review of the relevant part of term theory will enable us to share the insights gained on these issues and, at the same time, make it easier for us to present a more complete theory concerning the firm's internal decision process and organization.

Team Theory[1]

A team is assumed to be organized for the purpose of pursuing a common goal. However, the team theorists do not formally consider the process by which the team is organized or how the team's goal is established. They simply take for granted that once the agents have agreed to bind together and form a team they will agree upon a common objective. Each team member will then act as though the team's objective is identical with his own. Because a team operates in an environment with uncertainty, to say that the team members share the same goal requires not only that they have an identical utility function but also that they share the same belief about the environment. In short, the common goal of a team with n members can be expressed by a common expected utility function $\int_\theta u(\mathbf{a},\theta)P(\theta)d\theta$, where u is a von Neumann-Morgenstern utility function, $\mathbf{a} = (a^1,\ldots,a^n)$ denoting the actions taken by the team members $1,\ldots,n$, and θ is a parameter representing the state of nature. The team members will strive to choose actions which maximize the common expected utility.

Normally the quality of the team's decisions can be enhanced by information acquisition. When information is involved, the decision problem shifts from the *ex ante* choice of optimal actions to the *ex ante* choice of optimal decision rules used to govern the choice of action when information becomes available. The selection of such decision rules was first investigated under the rubric of statistical decision theory where only one decision-maker is involved.

Statistical Decision Theory Traditional statistical decision theory deals with a statistical decision problem where a single decision-maker must take actions to maximize his expected utility defined in the form given above. If s carries information about the state of nature θ, then s and θ are jointly distributed with, say, a probability density $p(s,\theta)$. The information value of s on θ is given by the likelihood probability $p(s|\theta)$. The posterior probability can be obtained from the likelihood probability.[2]

Based upon a well-known theorem in Bayesian statistical decision theory, the optimal decision rule must be such that it will maximize the decision-maker's expected utility based upon the posterior probability distribution (DeGroot, 1970). That is, given the information set $s = (s_1, \ldots, s_n)$, the decision-maker will choose a decision rule $\alpha(s) = [\alpha^1(s_1), \ldots, \alpha^n(s_n)]$ which maximizes $\int_\theta u\,[\alpha(s),\theta]p(\theta\,|\,s)d\theta$. This theorem, which ignores the cost of information, thus corroborates the intuition that information always improves the quality of decision and that it is always beneficial to the decision-maker to postpone action until information has become known.

Extension to Team Setting Team theory extends Bayesian statistical decision theory to the situation where there are multiple decision-makers, each of whom receives a unique set of information. Team theory specifically assumes that the information s_i of the ith member is never known to his teammates and that team member i makes his decision solely on the basis of his own information, that is, $a^i = \alpha^i(s_i)$, $i = 1, \ldots, n$. Therefore each team member wants the action functions to maximize the same posterior expected utility function $\int_\theta u\,[\alpha(s), \theta]p(\theta\,|\,s)d\theta$ where $\alpha(s) = [\alpha^1(s_1), \ldots, \alpha^n(s_n)]$ and $s = (s_1, \ldots, s_n)$. This expected utility function obviously depends upon the information structure which the team members adopt.

Information Structure A team member i receives his information from two source – direct observation o_i and messages $m_{ij}(o_j)$ received from teammate j, where $j = 1, \ldots, n$ and $j \neq i$. Let the matrix

$\eta(o) = [m_{ij}(o_j)]$ be called the message matrix. The ith row of $\eta(o)$, denoted by $\eta_i(o)$, depicts team member i's information structure. Let s_i denote the total information received by i; then $s_i = \eta_i(o)$. Naturally, the vector $\eta = (\eta_1(o), \ldots, \eta_n(o))$ can be referred to as the team's information structure. The information received by the team is therefore $s = (s_1, \ldots, s_n)$ where s is clearly determined by the team's information-gathering and internal communication activities. To put it differently, the firm generates a joint probability density function $p(o|\theta)$ and hence a joint probability density function $p(s|\theta)$ from its information-gathering and communication activities. Given $p(s|\theta)$, $p(\theta)$, and $p(s)$, the posterior probability density function $p(\theta|s)$ can be obtained. Because information-gathering and communicaton activities are costly endeavors, these costs must affect the team's choice of the level of these activities; this level of activities, in turn, must affect the team's posterior probability distribution of the environment.

The Decision Problem of the Team Given the available set of information structures $\eta = \{\eta\}$ and the information cost $c(\eta)$, we now examine the team's decision problem. Recall that the statement "acquisition of information about the team's environment will never diminish its gross expected payoff" is made under the assumption that the information cost is zero. Since information is, in fact, costly, the net expected payoff to the team may diminish with the acquisition of additional information. Thus, "it will not, in general, be worthwhile to have every member of the team informed about the same events, and in the same detail" (Marschak and Radner, 1972, p. 129). Therefore advantages exist for the team members to specialize in information in the sense that any information structures η_i and η_j of any two members will be different. Further, specialization in information leads to decentralization of actions.[3] Since there are n team members, the team's information structure and decision rule will consist of n information structures η_i, $i = 1, \ldots, n$, and n decision rules α^i, $i = 1, \ldots, n$, respectively. The main concerns of team theory are (a) the determination of the team's information structure η, that is, given the information cost function, what statistical information will be made available to the various team members, and (b) the team's decision rule α. In the words of Marschak and Radner "the team problem is to choose simultaneously the team's information structure and the team's decision rule that will yield the highest expected utility, taking account of information and decision costs" (Marschak and Radner, 1972, p. 124).

However, finding a solution for this decision problem is not trivial; a well-formulated solution for the general team problem simply does not exist. The difficulty stems from the lack of a natural way of calibrating the measurement units of utility and cost. Since the aim of this section is to survey the structure of the team's decision problem, and not the structure of the solution concept, we will simply assume that a conversion factor between utility and cost does exist, allowing us to sidestep the solution problem.

Having set the difficulty aside, the structure of the team's decision problem can be described as follows. Let $\alpha(s(\eta))$ be the team's decision function corresponding to the information structure η and let $u[\alpha(s(\eta)), \theta]$ be its gross payoff function. Define the team's net payoff function, given $c(\eta)$, as $v[\alpha(s(\eta)), \theta, \eta \mid c(\eta)] \equiv u[\alpha(s(\eta)), \theta] - \mu c(\eta)$, where μ is the conversion factor. The team now chooses an optimal information structure η^* and an optimal decision rule α^* which maximize $E\{v[\alpha(s(\eta)), \theta, \eta] \mid c(\eta)\}$. The pair (η^*, α^*) is found by solving the following simultaneous equation system:

$$E\{v_{\alpha_i}[.] \mid c\} = 0 \qquad i = 1, \ldots, n$$

$$E\{v_{\eta}[.] \mid c\} = 0$$

This solution yields an information structure $\eta_i^*(o)$ and a decision rule $\alpha^{r*}(s_i)$, $i = 1, \ldots, n$, for each team member and thus enables each member to manage his information and decisions in a decentralized manner.

The Internal Organization of the Team   Team theory, by its very nature, is a theory of internal organization. As we have seen in the last section, high information costs lead the team to adopt specialization in information management and decentralization in decision-making. Such specialization and decentralization create the need for coordination. Coordination requires the establishment of an internal organization or network to channel the flow of the various activities toward the attainment of the team's common goal. According to team theorists, a network is defined as "something that transforms incoming messages into outgoing messages in a well-defined, though possibly stochastic, way. Messages coming in from nature are to be interpreted as observations, whereas messages going out to nature are . . . actions" (Marschak and Radner, 1972, p. 268). Based on this definition, a network is simply an organizational manifestation of the team's information and decision structure (η, α) taking into account the information cost. Given the information cost, the selection of the team's optimal information and decision structure from a set of such feasible structures would automatically lead to the adoption of a network which maximizes the net payoff of the team.

However, the team's internal organization is more than just its information–decision structure; it also includes other coordinating apparatus. Recall that the team's optimal information–decision structure (η^*, α^*) is found by solving a set of simultaneous equations. In order to implement this mathematical procedure, a coordinator is needed to make certain that all decision functions (η_i^*, α^{i*}), $i = 1, \ldots, n$, chosen by team members are consistent with each other. This means that the team needs a super-administrative body to oversee this function. The activities of the super-administrative body are, in fact, more than routine. Because the team's optimal information–decision structure is selected *ex ante*, that is (η^*, α^*) is selected before information is known, resolution of *ex ante* conflict among the team members' decision rules does not guarantee *ex post* harmony among their actions. An example given by Marschak and Radner illustrates this point.

Two of a firm's truck drivers ($i = 1, 2$) come to its warehouse from two different departments of the firm, and each driver is instructed to haul away a certain amount a^i of the same commodity. Suppose that

$$a^1 + a^2 > x$$

where x is the stock available in the warehouse. The above inequality is inconsistent with the physical limitation

$$0 \leq a^1 + a^2 \leq x$$

This inconsistency must also be resolved by internal means. It could be resolved by adopting a set of standing rules to guide the member's response to information involving inconsistent messages, or by a court of appeal which arbitrates conflicts, or by adopting a hierarchical system which assigns priorities to the team members. Therefore the super-administrative body must also be organized to handle *ex post* conflict resolutions. Thus the internal organization of the team, in addition to the "network," must also include all the infrastructures which are needed to ensure that all activities are carried out in a consistent and optimal manner.

We have now briefly surveyed the rudiments of team theory and have found that, when a team is faced with high information cost, the strategy chosen to maximize its common objective will involve specialization in information and decision-making. Coordination is needed to synchronize the various activities. To coordinate is to choose an internal organization structure which will enable the team to maximize its net expected utility. Decentralization in decision-making does not imply that each team member can act autonomously. Teammates' *ex ante* decisions and *ex post* actions must still be brought in line with each other by a central authority. However, under certain special conditions, *ex post* autonomy can be achieved automatically. Radner (1962), who takes the information structure of the team as given, has succeeded in finding the sufficient condition for an autonomous system which he called a person-by-person optimization system. A team's decision function is called person-by-person optimal if it cannot be improved by changing the decision function of any one person in the team (Marschak and Radner, 1972, p. 156). Radner found that for person-by-person optimality to imply team optimality, the condition "$E\{u_{\alpha_i}[\alpha(s), \theta]|s_i\} = 0$ for all feasible s_is" must hold for all team members. This condition states that person-by-person optimality is achieved if each team member, assuming his colleagues are using their best decision rules, selects a decision rule which is optimal to himself regardless of what information he might receive.

The Internal Organization of the Entrepreneur-centered Firm

Because team theory is predicated on the assumption that all the team members are willing to subordinate their own preferences and beliefs to the team's common objective, the spirit underlying team theory fundamentally differs from that of the entrepreneur-centered theory presented in chapter 6. In chapter 6, we saw that firms are organized by entrepreneurs through coalition formation, and a firm organized through bargaining does not require the cooperating entrepreneurs to abandon their respective individual preferences and beliefs. In contrast, individuals' interests are served by the firm since it enables the entrepreneurs to reap gains derived from entrepreneurial joint production, division of labor among the entrepreneurs, and risk-sharing. Owing to the fundamental difference in the spirit of the two theories, team theory's prescription for the firm's internal organizaton cannot be applied directly to explain the internal organization of the entrepreneur-centered firm. A considerable modification has to be made.[4]

Since entrepreneurs are lured to join a coalition by the gains derived from division of labor among them, during the process of coalition formation each entrepreneur not only bargains for his share of the residual but also for the functional role that he will play in the firm. The division of the entrepreneurial responsibilities in a firm calls for coordination; hence an internal organization is needed. Moreover, we have learned from team theory that the firm's internal organization is also induced by the dispersion of information among the decision-makers. Since information dispersion among the entrepreneurs is also unavoidable, it is evident that in order to understand the internal organization of the entrepreneur-centered firm the phenomenon of information dispersion among entrepreneurs must also be considered. Accordingly, in this section we will present a theory of internal organization which reflects both the functional division of labor and the uneven distribution of information among entrepreneurs. Normally, in any complex organization, monitoring and control structures must also be erected to ensure faithful execution of entrepreneurial commitments and the firm's policies. However, we will ignore this aspect here and take it up in the next section.

This section is organized in two parts. First, we use bargaining theories to describe how entrepreneurs bargain with each other to form a complex internal organization on the basis of production technology, entrepreneurial talents, and the distribution of information among the cooperative entrepreneurs. It will be shown that the firm's internal organization is a hybrid of those described in chapter 6 and in the previous section. Second, we consider additional factors which lead to a separation of strategic decisions from operating decisions and give the firm a distinct hierarchical internal organization.

Because we rely on bargaining theories to show how a firm's internal organization is determined, before embarking on the main tasks designated for this section it is useful to digress briefly on the relevant bargaining models.

A Digression on Bargaining Models We have observed earlier that the existence of potential gains from cooperation induces the entrepreneurs to engage in joint production through the formation of a coalition. Yet because cooperative entrepreneurs' utilities and endowments are different, conflict of interest arises among them. Cooperation can take place only when these differences are reconciled through bargaining. The resolution of a bargaining game depends upon the rules of the game, that is, the nature of restrictions placed upon the bargainers' behavior. The selection of the rules of the game, in turn, depends upon the nature of the agreements to be obtained. The rules of the game are designed to make the agreements dependable. Generally, there are two types of agreements: collective enforced agreements and individually enforced agreements. Corresponding to the two general types of agreements are the two general types of games – cooperative and noncooperative.

The cooperative game is one which permits preplay communications among players and assumes that it is possible for the players to jointly secure favorable binding agreements. The term noncooperative game is somewhat a misnomer. It does not mean that the players do not engage in joint production; instead, it refers to a solution concept. In a noncooperative game the players are either forbidden to engage in preplay communications or are unsure that the agreements are binding. Under these circumstances the players, in order to engage in joint production, must allow each other to choose an individually optimal strategy conditional on the strategies chosen by the others.

The actual outcome of a game, whether cooperative or noncooperative, depends on the solution concept, that is, the model used to solve the game. This outcome, in turn, contributes to the make-up of the firm's internal organization. Our purpose in this chapter is not to study the specific structure of a firm's internal organization but rather to show how bargaining generally leads to the establishment of certain broad types of internal organization. For our purpose, it suffices to use the simple Nash cooperative game model to obtain collectively enforced agreements and to use the Cournot–Nash model to extract individually enforced agreements.

The Nash cooperative game model (Nash, 1950) is predicated on the assumption that, by acting jointly, the players can achieve greater payoffs than they are able to secure by acting independently. Let each player's potential improvement in utility be defined as the utility received under the cooperative arrangement minus the utility that the player would have received if he were to act outside the said cooperative arrangement.[5] This entire set of potential simultaneous improvements for all the players forms the negotiation set. The Nash cooperative solution concept chooses an agreement which yields from the negotiation set a point which maximizes the product of all players' improvements in utilities subject to the constraints that each player faces.

Because the Nash cooperative solution concept is predicated on binding contracts, it is not appropriate for games where the agreements can be violated unilaterally by any individual player. For these games, the Cournot–Nash solution concept is employed (Nash, 1951). The idea underlying the Cournot–Nash model is that, whenever cooperative arrangements cannot be guaranteed, each player will choose a strategy which represents the best response to the other players' strategies. An equilibrium is reached whenever none of the players can improve his lot by unilaterally changing his own strategy.[6] Thus stated, it is evident that the Cournot–Nash game yields agreements that are incentive compatible and binding. However, by the very nature of the Cournot–Nash model, it yields a solution inferior in utility to that potentially obtainable under the Nash cooperative game model. This loss in utility can be viewed as a cost that the players must pay for behaving strategically.

Having chosen the game models for the subsequent analyses, we return to deal with the main issue designated for this section.

The Determination of Internal Organization through Bargaining As stated earlier, we abandon the general equilibrium approach in this section and analyze the firm's internal organization problem from the partial equilibrium point of view. Partial equilibrium analysis enables us to describe the method determining the firm's internal organization in greater detail.

However, it is important to note that the shift from general to partial equilibrium analyses does not imply that the intrinsic nature of the problem at hand has been altered. The partial equilibrium analysis, suitably constructed, simply represents an extension of the general equilibrium problem. Suppose that a firm with n entrepreneurs is organized as a result of a society-wide cooperative game. As shown in chapter 6, this game can be decomposed into two stages. In the first stage the entrepreneurs bargain to determine the membership and financial structure of the firm, and in the second stage they bargain to determine the internal organization of the firm. Thus the partial equilibrium analyses of the firm's internal organization can be treated as an extension of the second-stage problem.

However, in this chapter the transition from general equilibrium to partial equilibrium analysis is not straightforward; we seek further simplification. Instead of the two-period model adopted in chapter 6, we will switch to a simpler one-period decision model with a slightly modified consumer utility function and use it to describe the entrepreneur's choice problem and to analyze the firm's internal organization.

Let the firm be organized by n entrepreneurs, differentiated by $i = 1,\ldots, n$. Each entrepreneur enters into the cooperative venture with the intention of maximizing his expected utility $\int_\theta u^i(c^i(\theta), A^i, e^i)$ $P^i(\theta)d\theta$ subject to a budget constraint $c^i = b^i(y - \gamma k)$ where $y \in Y^H$, $0 \leq b^i \leq 1, 0 < e^i < \ell_0^i$ and $\Sigma_{i=1}^n b^i = 1$. The entrepreneur's decision problem involves the solution of k, e^i, α^i, b^i, and H (to be explained shortly); it reflects the following assumptions.

1　Entrepreneur i derives utility from consumption c^i and from performing the entrepreneurial function A^i; he incurs a disutility from exerting efforts e^i, where e^i is bounded between 0 and ℓ_0^i.

2　The state of the environment is described by θ. Each entrepreneur i holds his own beliefs about θ, and this belief is represented by the probability density function $P^i(\theta)$.

3　The entrepreneur's income depends upon his share b^i of the firm's profit $(y - \gamma\mathbf{k})$, where γ and $\mathbf{k}$ are respectively vectors of tradeable factor prices and quantities and the output y is an element of the firm's production set Y^H. This notation signifies that the firm's production set Y depends crucially on the firm's internal organization structure H.

Whereas it is self-evident that entrepreneur i's income depends on his share of the firm's net output, the dependence of his income on the firm's internal organization requires explanation. Owing to the advantages associated with joint production, entrepreneurs cooperate with each other by forming a firm in order to reap the benefits derived from entrepreneurial division of labor in tasks and information management and from risk-sharing. Let the n entrepreneurs who make up the firm each perform one of the entrepreneurial functions in $\mathbf{A}$ where $\mathbf{A} = (A^1,\ldots, A^n)$. The firm's entrepreneurial tasks can be distributed among the n entrepreneurs in at most $n!$ ways. In addition, let there be a set of m potentially available information structures denoted by $\mathbf{\eta} = \{\eta^1,\ldots, \eta^m\}$. The selection of the information structure depends crucially on the information cost $c(\mathbf{\eta})$.[7] The firm's technically induced internal organization, denoted by H, can be described by a two-tuple $(\mathbf{A}, \mathbf{\eta})$, that is, a distribution of entrepreneurial tasks and the information structure. Let $\mathbf{H}$ denote the set of all technically induced internal organizations; then $\mathbf{H}$ has $n! \times m$ elements.

Because the entrepreneurs' endowments of knowledge and ability differ, each of them may be suited for handling some, but not all, tasks and managing some, but not all, information. A different distribution of information and tasks among the cooperative entrepreneurs may lead the coalition to face a different production possibility set. Consequently, the firm's production possibility set depends not only on the quantity of the tradeable factors $\mathbf{k}$ employed, the entrepreneurs' efforts $\mathbf{e} = (e^1,\ldots, e^n)$, and the state of nature θ, but also on the information structure $\mathbf{\eta}$ adopted by the firm and on how the entrepreneurial functions are distributed among the cooperative entrepreneurs, that is, the vector $\mathbf{A}$. Again, when information is involved, the quality of the decisions can be improved by acquiring information; the decision problem shifts from the choice of optimal action $\mathbf{a} = (a^1, \ldots, a^n)$ to the choice of decision rules $\mathbf{\alpha} = (\alpha^1(s_1),\ldots, \alpha^n(s_n))$. Consequently, we denote the firm's production set as $Y^H(\mathbf{k},\mathbf{e},\mathbf{\alpha},\theta \mid c(\mathbf{\eta}))$.

Having described the relationship between the firm's internal organization and its production set, we are ready to examine the entrepreneurs' choice problems. Given that each entrepreneur's goal is to choose a cooperative strategy to maximize his own expected utility and that entrepreneurs have different preferences, abilities, and beliefs, the strategies chosen by the cooperating entrepreneurs must be made consistent with each other through bargaining. In this simplified model we have taken the firm's membership and its financial structure as given. The entrepreneurs bargain jointly to select the firm's internal organization, a joint production policy, and a sharing rule. Whereas the determination of the firm's sharing rule is straightforward, the determination of its internal organization and production policy is not. The firm's internal organization and production policy are arrived at indirectly by each entrepreneur bargaining for an assignment of a specific decision function A^i and then selecting a decision rule $\alpha^i(s_i)$ concerning this function. Given the firm's internal organization, its production policy is represented by the triplet $(\mathbf{k}, \mathbf{e}, \alpha)$. Because the entrepreneurs jointly determine both the firm's internal organization and its production policy, the choice of these elements constitutes the entrepreneurs' strategy.

Of course, the precise outcome of this bargaining game depends on the rules adopted. Because our task in this section is to examine the firm's internal organization by ignoring the moral hazard issues, we will assume that all agreements resulting from bargaining are enforceable. According to the convention that we adopted earlier, we will use the Nash cooperative bargaining model to extract a solution for the bargaining problems.

We begin by restating, with minor modifications, the entrepreneur's decision problem. The modification reflects the entrepreneur's desire to take advantage of the information available to him before performing his own actions $a^i(s_i)$. As stated before, the cooperative entrepreneurs, each guided by his desire to make his own posterior expected utility as large as possible, jointly choose the firm's policies. They do so in two stages.

1   Given $\mathbf{e}$, $\alpha(s)$, $\mathbf{b}$, H, and γ, each entrepreneur chooses independently the employment of the tradeable factors $\mathbf{k}$ to

$$\max \int_\theta u^i(c^i(\theta, s_i), A^i, e^i) p^i(\theta \mid s_i) d\theta \tag{7.1}$$

$$\text{subject to} \quad c^i = b^i(y - \gamma \mathbf{k}) \tag{*}$$

$$y \in Y^H(\mathbf{k}, \mathbf{e}, \alpha(s), \theta \mid c(\eta))$$

In this case, the cooperative entrepreneurs will always agree unanimously to choose the $\mathbf{k}$ which maximizes the residual $y - \gamma \mathbf{k}$. At the conclusion of this stage of the problem, $\mathbf{k}$ becomes a function of $(\mathbf{e}, \alpha(s), \mathbf{b}, H, \gamma)$ and can be written as $\mathbf{k}(\mathbf{e}, \alpha(s), \mathbf{b}, H, \gamma)$.

2 The cooperative entrepreneurs collectively determine $(e, \alpha(s), b, H)$ by playing the Nash cooperative game:

$$\max \prod_{i=1}^{n} \{Eu^i(c^i(\theta, s_i), A^i, e^i) - u^{0i}\} \qquad (7.2)$$

subject to (*) in (7.1) for $i = 1, \ldots, n$ and with k substituted by $k(e, \alpha(s), b, H, \gamma)$

$$H \in \mathbf{H}$$

$$0 < e^i \leq \ell_0^i, \ 0 \leq b^i \leq 1, \ \sum_{i=1}^{n} b^i = 1$$

Here u^{0i} denotes entrepreneur i's threat-point utility level. Because the n entrepreneurs have already formed a coalition, the existence of u^{0i} is noncontroversial.[8] In order to see clearly how this bargaining game is resolved, we will divide this stage of the bargaining into two steps. First, let the entrepreneurs' commitments on $(e, \alpha(s), b)$ be given; a particular (e, α, b) is committed under each possible hierarchical organization $H \in \mathbf{H}$. In addition, assume that the information cost function $c(\eta)$ is given exogenously. The cooperative entrepreneurs bargain to determine the firm's hierarchical internal organization. At the conclusion of this step of the Nash cooperative bargaining game, a particular $\bar{H}(A, \eta)$ is chosen. Once $\bar{H}(A, \eta)$ is selected, the relevant $(e, \alpha(s), b)$ is also identified. In the second step of the Nash cooperative bargaining game, the cooperative entrepreneurs bargain to determine $(e, \alpha(s), b)$. Note that the constraint in (7.2) now becomes

$$c^i = b^i [y - \gamma k(e, \alpha(s), b; \bar{H}, \gamma)]$$

$$y \in Y^{\bar{H}} (k(.), e, \alpha(s), \theta \,|\, c(\bar{\eta}))$$

$$\bar{H} \in \mathbf{H}$$

$$0 < e^i \leq \ell_0^i, \ 0 \leq b^i \leq 1, \ \sum_{i=1}^{n} b^i = 1$$

At the conclusion of this stage of the game the firm's policies are determined: (a) the firm has adopted an internal organization $H^*(A^*, \eta^*)$, that is, an information structure η^* and a distribution of tasks to each of its cooperative entrepreneurs A_i^*, $i = 1, \ldots, n$; (b) the cooperative entrepreneurs have agreed upon a joint production policy by committing k^* of tradeable resources and $e^* = (e^{1^*}, \ldots, e^{n^*})$ of

entrepreneurial effort levels and an action policy $\alpha^*(s) = (\alpha^{1*}(s_1),$
$\ldots, \alpha^{n*}(s_n))$; (c) they have also agreed to share the firm's profits
according to the sharing rule $\mathbf{b}^* = (b^{1*}, \ldots, b^{n*})$. Based upon these
agreements, entrepreneur i expects to derive an expected utility of

$$Ev^i(.) = \int_\theta v^i(\alpha^{i*}(s_i), A^{i*}, e^{i*}, \theta \mid H^*) \, P^i(\theta \mid s_i) \, d\theta$$

Now the firm's policies are a collection of mutually consistent
decision rules of all the cooperating entrepreneurs. In particular, they
yield an action rule $\alpha^{i*}(s_i)$, $i = 1, \ldots, n$, for each cooperative entrepreneur i. The entrepreneur i will take the appropriate level of action
$a^{i*} = \alpha^{i*}(\bar{s}_i)$ whenever the information $\bar{s}_i$ is revealed.

We have now given a brief description of the process by which the
firm makes its various decisions. These decisions include the selection
of its information structure, the assignment of its entrepreneurial tasks
to the various cooperating entrepreneurs, the employment of inputs,
the determination of its sharing rule, and the selection of each
entrepreneur's decision rule and action. Because decisions can be
carried out only with the support of an internal organization, the
description of the decision processes also simultaneously provides a
description of the firm's internal organization.

Hierarchical Internal Organization   In an uncertain market environment where events unfold over time, the way that entrepreneurs make
their decisions undergoes a fundamental change. The firm now faces a
multiperiod decision horizon, and the entrepreneurs can no longer
make all their decisions at the same time. Because the firm receives its
information in a sequential manner, the corresponding decisions must
be made sequentially. Under these circumstances, the entrepreneur
who has the opportunity to make a decision first can exert a greater
influence than his successors on the firm's outcome. This follows
because the entrepreneur who holds the first-move privilege can
preempt his successors by choosing some options that would have
been available to them had they possessed the first-move privilege. By
the same token, the second mover can preempt opportunities that
would have been available to his successors etc. The earlier-moving
privilege thus gives the privileged entrepreneur a certain degree of
authority over his successors. This authority relationship among the
cooperative entrepreneurs naturally forms a basis for the firm's
hierarchical internal organization.[9]

The natural time pattern of information revelation may not always
lead to decisions which give the firm its most desirable outcome.
Fortunately, the relationship between the time patterns of decision-

making and of information revelation is by no means fixed. A realignment of the former with respect to the latter may improve the performance of the firm. A simple example will make this point clear. Let the firm in question be a vertically integrated production entity; it produces intermediate goods X for its own use and then produces and sells final products Y for the open market. Three assumptions are needed to make our point. First, the entrepreneur in charge of X only has access to information concerning the cost parameters underlying the production of X while the entrepreneur in charge of Y only has access to information concerning the parameters underlying the market demand for Y. Second, there are costs involved in adjusting the composition and the rate of producing X and Y; the adjustment cost of X is assumed to be less than that of Y. Finally, the firm receives the cost information about X before the demand information about Y. Since the firm receives the cost information first, following the natural pattern of information revelation the entrepreneur in charge of X makes his decision first. This decision now poses an additional constraint to the decision problem concerning Y. This added constraint, *ceteris paribus*, may force a greater change in the rate of production of Y. Suppose that the entrepreneur in charge of Y is given the first-move privilege. To be sure, the forecasting error on the demand for Y is now greater since the entrepreneur must make a forecast for events in a more distant future, and this increase in the forecasting error may inflict a loss on the firm. However, this loss may be offset by the savings resulting from more optimal adjustment in the production of Y. Of course the entrepreneur in charge of X must take the output decision for Y as given and thus bear a greater burden for adjustment. Since the adjustment cost associated with X is less than that associated with Y, shifting the burden of adjustment to X from Y may reduce the overall cost of adjustment and thus yield a greater residual for the firm.

Based upon this example, it is evident that a realignment in tne time pattern of decision-making relative to that of information revelation may improve the performance of the firm. However, such a realignment alters the authority structure among the entrepreneurs and hence requires the firm to erect an internal administrative hierarchy to enforce the chosen decision procedure.

The need to establish a hierarchical control within the firm becomes even more crucial when we consider that the overall performance of the firm reflects actions taken by all the cooperative entrepreneurs and that in a multiperiod planning horizon some decisions exert a greater impact than others on the firm's performance. Frequently, decisions which take a longer period to execute and are in force for a longer period of time will create a greater impact on the firm's performance. Thus the firm's overall performance can be improved if the entrepreneurs who are in charge of the decisions with greater impact have a greater freedom to make their decisions, that is, are given the first-mover status.[10] For example, investment decisions generally exert a greater and longer impact than production decisions on the firm's performance, and production decisions, in turn, exert a greater and longer impact than inventory decisions on the firm's performance. It is therefore not suprising to find that in practice investment decisions are given priority over production decisions, which in turn are given priority over inventory decisions. As mentioned earlier, the establishment of the priority of moves among the entrepreneurs naturally creates a hierarchical authority structure within the firm.

The prioritization of moving privileges not only endows the first mover with the opportunity of selecting an optimal decision relative to his own functional responsibility, but it may also grant him the authority to actively shape the firm's overall performance. Specifically, the first mover, through his ability to influence his successors' choice of options, could make his own decisions in such a way as to prevent the successors from taking actions which might be detrimental to the firm's overall performance. The first mover now takes up the control role. When this happens, the decisions, as observed by Chandler and others, are divided into two categories – strategic decisions and operating decisions. The strategic decision-makers are given the priority moving privileges and are allowed to occupy a higher rung in the firm's hierarchy. The hierarchical authority structure is further solidified whenever the first mover is also given the authority to veto his successors' decisions.

THE INTERNAL CONTROL STRUCTURE

In the presence of uncertainty the benefits of joint production can nonetheless be obtained by employing nonmarket means of coordination. Consciously designed rules made collectively by the cooperating entrepreneurs are now needed to render decisions and actions taken by the individual entrepreneurs consistent with each other. Joint production thus requires joint decision-making. In chapter 6 and in the preceding section of this chapter, we used a bargaining procedure to achieve a jointly determined production policy and the associated internal organization for the firm. The emergence of the firm's production policy signifies that the cooperative entrepreneurs have found a mechanism to coordinate their decisons and to achieve a mutually desirable outcome. The existence of such a mechanism is by no means sufficient to guarantee that the firm is a viable production institution. The temptation for the agents to behave opportunistically undermines the firm's survival. Recall that the entrepreneurs jointly determine the assignment of decision authority and responsibility, the entrepreneurial efforts committed to production, the employment of the tradeable factors, and the sharing rule. Fundamental distinctions exist on how these agreements are executed. The entrepreneurial effort and action commitments are executed by the individual entrepreneurs, whereas the remaining policies are executed by the entrepreneurs collectively. Because the individual entrepreneur cannot alter the collectively executed agreements by means of his own action, it is only with respect to his effort and action commitments that the opportunistic behavior of the entrepreneurs can manifest itself and pose a threat to the firm's survival.

Opportunistic behavior by the entrepreneurs is made possible by two conditions: (a) for any input level, the production outcome is uncertain, and (b) the entrepreneurial inputs (effort levels) are not perfectly observable. In a real world situation production uncertainty exists; the yield of a joint production endeavor depends not only on the level of inputs but also on a random parameter controlled by nature. It is reasonable to assume that a decrease in the level of entrepreneurial services, *ceteris paribus*, decreases the yeild to the firm and a realization of an unfavorable environmental condition, *ceteris paribus*, also decreases the firm's yield. Owing to the nonobservability of both the entrepreneurial efforts and the underlying environment parameter, as in the Alchian–Demsetz case (Alchian and Demsetz, 1972), the true cause of a reduction in the firm's output cannot be pinpointed. Since the execution of the individual entrepreneur's commitment to efforts and action is controlled individually, the opportunistic entrepreneur can now claim that the poor performance of the firm is due to the occurrence of an unfavorable market event even though it is caused by his shirking of responsibility. Further, because the exertion of an entrepreneur's effort level is not observable, the reduction in the firm's profits caused by the reduction in an entrepreneur's efforts is shared by all the cooperating entrepreneurs. If the increase in utility due to leisure exceeds the decrease in utility due to income reduction following shirking, it will be beneficial for the entrepreneur to shirk. The cooperative outcome described in the preceding section becomes unattainable. In other words, the firm organized to carry out decisions in the manner described in the above section is not incentive compatible; it cannot be sustained. In order to make the firm's internal allocation incentive compatible, we need to modify its decision procedure and internal organization.

When the opportunistic behavior of the cooperative entrepreneurs is brought into consideration, the entrepreneurs' decision problems undergo a fundamental change. The entrepreneurs are concerned not only with securing agreements for joint production but also with safeguarding against abuses stemming from the opportunistic behavior of cooperative entrepreneurs; these abuses erode potential gains derivable from cooperation. Consequently, the objective of this section is twofold: first, we make clear how the presence of opportunistic behavior affects the structure of the entrepreneur's decision problems, and then we demonstrate how, through bargaining, the entrepreneurs can arrive at incentive-compatible agreements and the internal organization needed to implement these agreements.

Nature of Decision Problems

As we have observed earlier, with the threat of opportunistic behavior, the entrepreneurs not only are interested in obtaining agreements needed for joint production but are also interested in finding ways to safeguard the integrity of these agreements. This added concern alters the entrepreneurs' decision problems. The entrepreneurs must now adopt different means to extract agreements from each other and must devise means to monitor entrepreneurial performances and mete out rewards. This change in the decision problem is reflected by a change in the arguments of the entrepreneur's utility function and the firm's production possibility set.

Method Used to Achieve Agreements   Because entrepreneurs have the propensity of behaving opportunistically, some of the cooperative agreements may become unattainable. In order to ensure that all agreements are incentive compatible, the game played by the entrepreneurs now depends on the nature of the agreements they expect to extract from each other. As we have noted earlier, the entrepreneurs play the Nash cooperative game to secure jointly enforced agreements and play the Cournot–Nash noncooperative game to determine individually enforced agreements. In the present context, the agreements concerning the firm's internal organization, the employment of the tradeable factors, and the sharing rule are jointly enforced, while the agreements on entrepreneurial actions and efforts, for both production and monitoring, are individually enforced. Consequently, the cooperative entrepreneurs use a mixture of the above-mentioned bargaining models to secure the needed agreements.

As is well known, the outcome of the Nash cooperative game is Pareto optimal whereas the outcome of the Cournot–Nash noncooperative game is not (Shubik, 1959, chapter 4). Thus it is evident that by playing a mixture of the above-mentioned games the entrepreneurs can only expect an inferior payoff compared with that achieved by playing the pure cooperative game. However, the firm as a going concern offers entrepreneurs opportunities to design firm-specific incentive schemes and control mechanisms to upgrade the firm's performance. It is hoped that, by combining incentive and control, the cooperative outcome among the entrepreneurs can reach the second-best level.

The Nature of Incentive and Control   The firm's incentive and control apparatus comprises two parts: monitoring performances and dispensing rewards and punishments. Because each entrepreneur's efforts are not perfectly observable, in order to assess his performances monitoring efforts and costs must be incurred. There are two types of monitoring methods: mutual monitoring and specialized monitoring. In the mutual monitoring system, the entrepreneurs monitor each others' activities in conjunction with their other entrepreneurial duties. Let m_j^i denote the efforts entrepreneur i spends in monitoring entrepreneur j's activities. Then the vector $\mathbf{m}^i = (m_1^i, \ldots, m_n^i)$ represents the monitoring efforts supplied by entrepreneur i and $\mathbf{m} = (m^1, \ldots, m^n)$ represents the firm's monitoring system. In the specialized monitoring system a particular entrepreneur or employee is designated to perform the monitoring duty. In this case the firm's monitoring system is denoted by $\mathbf{m} = (m_1, \ldots, m_n)$.

Broadly stated, the type of entrepreneurial activities in a coalition, the type of products the firm produces, and the cost of monitoring schemes all contribute to the selection of the monitoring method. In general, the mutual monitoring method is suitable for a situation where the size of the coalition is small and the cooperative entrepreneurs interact frequently with each other. These frequent contacts enable them to observe and evaluate each others' performances at relatively lost cost. In contrast, the specialized monitoring method is suitable for larger coalitions.

The selection of a monitoring system is only the first step toward the establishment of an incentive-compatible control system. Recall that there are two sources of disincentives: the entrepreneur either is not fully rewarded for his efforts or is not made to bear the full consequence of his effort evasion. Monitoring is required to determine either the reward to the conscientious entrepreneur or the penalty against the evader. Therefore it is needed to counter both types of disincentives and is an integral part of the firm's incentive scheme and control mechanism.

Incentive can easily be built into the firm's operation whenever the firm is a going concern. As we have seen in chapter 6, because there is a cost associated with coalition formation, in a multiperiod decision horizon the firm is formed with the expectation that it will operate for a considerable time period. Owing to the presence of coalition formation costs, the cooperating entrepreneurs will not always find it advantageous to seek new partners for a new coalition whenever a slight change in the environment has taken place. A firm, once formed, will tend to perpetuate itself. Thus the firm becomes a going concern and the relationships among the cooperative entrepreneurs become more permanent.

Once a firm functions as a going concern, the entrepreneurs' activities and performance can be observed repeatedly over time. Repeated observation of each entrepreneur's activities in a given setting enables the monitor to assess his performances with greater accuracy. This increased ability to evaluate each entrepreneur's performance would immediately serve as a deterrent to his opportunistic behavior.

In addition, as a going concern, the firm involving the same set of cooperating entrepreneurs need not be tied to the same set of policies, that is, production policy, hierarchical structure, and the sharing rule. As a going concern, the cooperating entrepreneurs can periodically bargain to revise these policies. Thus bargaining becomes an ongoing process. The bargaining outcome is now evaluated not by the result obtained in each bargaining session but rather by the results obtained in a series of bargaining sessions over time. In this long-run view, early information accrued about each entrepreneur's performances can be disseminated to all cooperative entrepreneurs; this information becomes an important factor in determining each entrepreneur's share of the firm's residual. An entrepreneur who is known to have shirked reduces his worth to the coalition and thus his bargaining power. This loss in the bargaining power will lead to a decline of his influence in the firm's hierarchy and a reduction in his share of the firm's future residual. Thus the shirking entrepreneur trades his present gains with future losses. If the cumulative future losses should exceed the current gains, then the entrepreneur will refrain from shirking. In game-theoretic language, if entrepreneurs face each other over a sequence of negotiations, the retaliation possibilities inherent in the repeated game mean that the cooperative agreement can be sustained.

An increase in an entrepreneur's efforts also affects his bargaining power in another way. Although a market to determine the prices of entrepreneurial services does not exist, there may be a clearinghouse to disseminate information about entrepreneurs. For example, professional organizations and trade associations often serve in this capacity. A hardworking entrepreneur will eventually earn a good reputation. With a good reputation, his threat to leave the coalition becomes credible and his bargaining power is enhanced. This increase in bargaining power will enable the entrepreneur to gain greater influence over the firm's policies and a greater share of the firm's overall profits. Under the above-mentioned circumstances not only does the entrepreneur not have the incentive to shirk but, in contrast, he will have the incentive to voluntarily make his good performances known to others in order to raise his bargaining power, future influence, and shares of the firm's residuals.

Finally, shirking not only reduces the cheater's long-run bargaining power, but may also eliminate the chance to bargain altogether. The nonshirking entrepreneurs can now refuse to bargain with the perpetrator, that is, exclude the shirking entrepreneurs from the next stage of the coalition. If it is assumed that the existing coalition generates a firm-specific rent, the explusion deprives the excluded entrepreneur from a piece of this rent. Should his loss of utility associated with this rent exceed the gains in utility derived from shirking, no shirking will take place. Even if such a rent is absent, explusion inflicts a loss to the entrepreneur in another way. Expulsion damages the entrepreneur's reputation and his bargaining power, and hence reduces his effectiveness in playing economy-wide cooperative games in the future. If the threat of this loss of bargaining power is sufficiently great, the entrepreneur will find that it is not to his advantage to behave opportunistically.

All told, as a going concern the firm has the opportunity of creating a general environment to encourage work and discourage evasion of efforts. In a firm-specific culture environment, competition for a larger share of the firm's long-run profit may lead the entrepreneurs to perform toward their maximum capacities. However, this general incentive scheme is by no means sufficient to guarantee Pareto-optimal results. Whenever it fails to bring about the desired result, the firm must erect specific control mechanisms to ensure that shirking of efforts does not pay, thus restoring the firm to an incentive-compatible production institution.

A control mechanism comprises two parts: target levels of production and monitoring efforts, and a penalty rule. It functions in the following manner. As production takes place, the monitor checks the performance level of each entrepreneur against his commitment (target) level. Whenever a discrepancy between the actual and the commitment level is found, a penalty is meted out according to the penalty rule. If the policies adopted by the firm are indeed incentive compatible, the outcome of this control mechanism will yield for each of the cooperative entrepreneurs a result greater than that received under a regime without this control apparatus.

Owing to the existence of the monitoring cost and the presence of the law of diminishing returns in monitoring, it is not cost effective for this control mechanism to eradicate shirking altogether and to reach the highest potential of cooperation. Given the control system, each entrepreneur knows that, if he cheats, there is a certain probability that he will be caught and punished. As a rational entrepreneur he will not only commit an optimal effort level but will also select to cheat at a certain level and frequency. As a consequence, the penalty approach can at best guarantee the attainment of a second-best result from cooperation.

Since neither the general incentive method nor the specific control system is perfect, there arises the question of what mixture of these systems a firm should adopt. This question relates to the design of a firm's optimal control system and is outside the scope of this chapter. Here, our interest is limited to investigating how the introduction of incentive and control affects the firm's internal organization. Even this limited scope is still too broad for us to handle. Accordingly, we further limit our discussions to two extreme cases. In the third section we will investigate how the introduction of a general incentive scheme affects the workings of a firm organized under an oligarchical structure, and in the remainder of this section we will investigate how the introduction of a specific control apparatus into a hierarchically organized firm affects the workings of the firm and its hierarchical structure. However, before doing so, we need to make a simple digression to explain how the injection of the control issue alters the structure of the entrepreneur's decision problem.

Structure of the Entrepreneur's Decision Problem   The introduction of monitoring and control affects the entrepreneur's decision problem. The precise nature of its impact will become clear in the next subsection; here we will only deal with some preliminaries. First, because the entrepreneur derives enjoyment from consumption as well as a specific position in the decision hierarchy and suffers disutility from exerting efforts for both production and monitoring, entrepreneur i's utility function now takes on the form $u^i(c^i(\theta), A^i, e^i, m^i)$. In addition, the introduction of monitoring also affects the firm's production possibility set. This is because the firm's production possibility set depends not only upon the technology that the firm employs but also upon the entrepreneurial capacities that the co-operative entrepreneurs are able to mobilize. In turn, what the entrepreneurs can mobilize depends on how efficiently they are organized. In the presence of opportunistic entrepreneurs, the efficiency of the firm's internal organization is affected not only by (a) the way that the entrepreneurial functions are distributed among the cooperative entrepreneurs and (b) the information structure adopted by the firm, but also by (c) the firm's ability to curb opportunistic behavior among its members. Since the firm's ability to curb opportunistic behavior depends crucially upon the monitoring network adopted, the monitoring activities affect the firm's production possibility set. Consequently, we let $H(\mathbf{A}, \boldsymbol{\eta}, \mathbf{m})$ denote the firm's internal organization and $Y^H(\mathbf{k}, \mathbf{e}, \boldsymbol{\alpha}(\mathbf{s}), \mathbf{m}, \theta \mid c(\boldsymbol{\eta}))$ denote its production possibility set. As in the previous case we write Y^H as a function of $\alpha(\mathbf{s})$ to reflect the fact that each entrepreneur must make a decision before the information is completely revealed to him. There is an advantage in selecting a decision rule $\alpha^i(s_i)$ and postponing the taking of an action a^i from a set of feasible actions available to the entrepreneur i until the information s_i from the firm's information system η becomes known.

Bargaining for Incentive-compatible Internal Organization

Having laid the necessary groundwork, we are now ready to describe how, through bargaining, the cooperative entrepreneurs reach a set of collectively and individually enforced agreements safeguarded by a control mechanism. We do so by extending the entrepreneurs' decision problems outlined in the first section. Let the entrepreneurs bargain not only to determine the distribution of the various entrepreneurial authorities and responsibilities, the employment of tradeable inputs, the supply of production efforts, and the sharing rule, but also to determine the control system which includes the target level of production efforts $\mathbf{e}^0 = (e^{01}, \ldots, e^{0n})$ committed by the entrepreneurs,[11] the level of monitoring efforts $\mathbf{m} = (m^1, \ldots, m^n)$, and the penalty rule λ.[12] In the end, a production policy, a sharing rule, and a hierarchical internal structure which includes a control apparatus emerge for the firm.

We begin by describing the individual entrepreneur's decision problem. In addition to the assumption that the entrepreneurs know each other's utility functions and the threat-point utility levels, we also assume that, given the monitoring efforts supplied by the entrepreneurs $\mathbf{m}$, the probability of being caught cheating is $\bar{p}(e^i < e^{0i} \mid \mathbf{m})$ and whenever an entrepreneur is caught cheating only $\lambda \in (0,1)$ of his allotted share of profits will be awarded to him. With these assumptions in place, entrepreneur i's decision problem is guided by his desire to choose $H(\mathbf{A}, \eta, \mathbf{m})$, $\mathbf{e}^0, \mathbf{b}, \lambda$ jointly with all cooperative entrepreneurs and $\mathbf{k}, e^i, m^i, \alpha^i$ individually in order to make his posterior expected utility as large as possible. The cooperative entrepreneurs' decision problem can be divided into three steps.

1   Given $\mathbf{e}$, $\mathbf{m}$, α, H, $\mathbf{e}^0$, $\mathbf{b}$, λ and γ, each entrepreneur chooses the vector of tradeable factors $\mathbf{k}$ individually to

$$\max \int_\theta u^i(c^i(\theta, s_i), A^i, e^i, m^i) \, p^i(\theta \mid s_i) d\theta \qquad (7.3)$$

subject to

$$c^i = \bar{P}(e^i < e^{0i} | \mathbf{m}) \lambda b^i (y - \gamma \mathbf{k}) + (1 - \bar{P}(e^i < e^{0i} | \mathbf{m})) b^i (y - \gamma \mathbf{k})$$

$$+ (1 - \lambda) b^i \sum_{j=1}^{n} \bar{P}(e^j < e^{j0} | \mathbf{m}) b^j (y - \gamma \mathbf{k}) \qquad (*)$$

$$y \in Y^H (\mathbf{k}, \mathbf{e}, \mathbf{m}, \alpha(\mathbf{s}), \theta \,|\, c(\eta))$$

Because $\mathbf{e}, \mathbf{m}, \alpha, H, \mathbf{e}^0$, $\mathbf{b}$, λ and γ are given, despite the fact that $\mathbf{k}$ is chosen individually the cooperative entrepreneurs will always agree unanimously upon this choice since an increase in the firm's residual $y - \gamma \mathbf{k}$ will always increase each entrepreneur's expected income and hence his expected utility. At the conclusion of the first stage of the entrepreneurs' decision activities, $\mathbf{k}$ becomes a function of $(\mathbf{e}, \mathbf{m}, \alpha, H, \gamma, \mathbf{e}^0, \mathbf{b}, \lambda)$ and can be written as $\mathbf{k}(\mathbf{e}, \mathbf{m}, \alpha, H, \mathbf{e}^0, \mathbf{b}, \lambda, \gamma)$.

2   Let the entrepreneurs' commitments on $(\mathbf{e}, \mathbf{m}, \alpha)$ be given; a particular $(\mathbf{e}, \mathbf{m}, \alpha)$ is committed under each possible hierarchical organization $H \in \mathbf{H}$. The cooperative entrepreneurs jointly determine the collectively enforced policies $(\mathbf{e}^0, \mathbf{b}, \lambda)$ and the hierarchical organizational structure $H(\mathbf{A}, \eta, \mathbf{m})$ by playing the Nash cooperative bargaining game, that is, by choosing the above-mentioned policies to

$$\max \prod_{i=1}^{n} [Eu^i(c^i(\theta, s_i), A^i, e^i, m^i) - u^{0i}] \qquad (7.4)$$

subject to $(*)$ in (7.3) for $i = 1, \ldots, n$ and with $\mathbf{k}$ substituted by
$$\mathbf{k}(\mathbf{e}, \mathbf{m}, \alpha, H, e^0, \mathbf{b}, \lambda, \gamma)$$

$$H \in \mathbf{H}$$

$$\lambda \le 1, 0 \le b^i, \ \sum_{i=1}^{n} b^i = 1$$

where u^{0i} denotes entrepreneur i's threat-point utility level. Because the coalition of the n entrepreneurs has already been formed, the existence of u^{0i} is guaranteed. At the conclusion of this Nash cooperative bargaining game, as a particular hierarchical internal organization $\bar{H}$ is chosen, the relevant $(\mathbf{e}, \mathbf{m}, \alpha)$ is also identified. The chosen policies can now be written as $\bar{\mathbf{k}}(\mathbf{e}, \mathbf{m}, \alpha, H, e^0, \mathbf{b}, \lambda, \gamma)$, $\bar{\mathbf{e}}^0(\mathbf{e}, \mathbf{m}, \alpha)$, $\bar{\mathbf{b}}(\mathbf{e}, \mathbf{m}, \alpha)$, and $\bar{\lambda}(\mathbf{e}, \mathbf{m}, \alpha)$. Based upon these policies and the firm's internal organization, the entrepreneur i, $i = 1, \ldots, n$, receives a net expected utility

$$\mathrm{E}v^i(.) = \int_\theta v^i(\alpha^i(s_i), e^i, A^i, m^i, \theta \mid \bar{H}, \bar{e}^0) p^i(\theta \mid s_i) d\theta$$

3   Given the above expected utility functions the entrepreneurs play the Cournot–Nash noncooperative game in order to determine the individually enforced agreements (e^i, m^i, α^i). Let $\mathbf{e}^*_{-i} = (e^{1*}, \ldots, e^{(i-1)*}, e^{(i+1)*}, \ldots, e^{n*})$, and let $\mathbf{m}^*_{-i}$ and $\mathbf{\alpha}^*_{-i}$ be similarly defined. Then the entrepreneur i, $i = 1, \ldots, n$, will take $\mathbf{e}^*_{-i}, \mathbf{m}^*_{-i}, \mathbf{\alpha}^*_{-i}$ as given and will choose (e^i, m^i, α^i) to

max $\mathrm{E}v^i(.)$ \hfill (7.5)

subject to

$$c^i = [1 - (1 - \bar{\lambda})\bar{P}(.)]\bar{b}^i(y - \gamma\bar{k}) + (1 - \bar{\lambda})\bar{b}^i \sum_{j=1}^n \bar{P}(.)b^j(y - \gamma\bar{k})$$

$$y \in Y^{\bar{H}}(\bar{k}, e^i, m^i, \alpha^i(s_i), \mathbf{e}^*_{-i}, \mathbf{m}^*_{-i}, \mathbf{\alpha}^*_{-i}, \theta \mid \bar{c}(\eta))$$

$$0 < e^i, m^i$$

$$e^i + m^i \leqslant \ell_0^i$$

where

$$\bar{e}^0(.) = \bar{e}^0(e^i, m^i, \alpha^i, \mathbf{e}^*_{-i}, \mathbf{m}^*_{-i}, \mathbf{\alpha}^*_{-i})$$

$$\bar{\lambda}(.) = \bar{\lambda}(e^i, m^i, \alpha^i, \mathbf{e}^*_{-i}, \mathbf{m}^*_{-i}, \mathbf{\alpha}^*_{-i})$$

$$\bar{b}^i(.) = \bar{b}^i(e^i, m^i, \alpha^i, \mathbf{e}^*_{-i}, \mathbf{m}^*_{-i}, \mathbf{\alpha}^*_{-i})$$

$$\bar{k}(.) = \bar{k}(e^i, m^i, \alpha^i, \mathbf{e}^*_{-i}, \mathbf{m}^*_{-i}, \mathbf{\alpha}^*_{-i}, \gamma)$$

The Cournot–Nash solution $\mathbf{e}^* = (e^{1*}, \ldots, e^{n*})$, $\mathbf{m}^* = (m^{1*}, \ldots, m^{n*})$, and $\mathbf{\alpha}^*(s) = (\alpha^{1*}(s_1), \ldots, \alpha^{n*}(s_n))$ yields for the entrepreneur i, $i = 1, \ldots, n$, an expected utility $\mathrm{E}v^i(e^{i*}, m^{i*}, \alpha^{i*})$. In addition, after the emergence of $(\mathbf{e}^*, \mathbf{m}^*, \mathbf{\alpha}^*)$ at the conclusion of the bargaining process the optimal collectively enforced policies are also determined; they are $\mathbf{k}^*(\mathbf{e}^*, \mathbf{m}^*, \mathbf{\alpha}^*, H^*, \mathbf{e}^{0*}, \mathbf{b}^*, \lambda^*, \gamma)$, $\lambda^*(\mathbf{e}^*, \mathbf{m}^*, \mathbf{\alpha}^*)$, $\mathbf{b}^*(\mathbf{e}^*, \mathbf{m}^*, \mathbf{\alpha}^*)$, $\mathbf{e}^{0*}(\mathbf{e}^*, \mathbf{b}^*, \mathbf{\alpha}^*)$, and H^*.

Because policies do not work by themselves, an internal organization must be established to implement them. This internal organization not only mirrors the hierarchical relationship $H(\mathbf{A}^*, \mathbf{\eta}^*, \mathbf{m}^*)$ but also includes a super-administrative body which is erected to insure consistency of policies *ex ante*, to handle conflict of interests *ex post*, to dispense reward and punishment, and to uphold the integrity of the agreements.

With the necessary agreements and the internal organization in place, the firm becomes a going concern. Following the established rules, entrepreneur i, $i = 1, \ldots, n$, supplies the production efforts e^i and monitoring efforts m^i, based upon the information $\bar{s}_i$ revealed to him by the firm's adopted information network η, he takes the action $a^i = \alpha^i(\bar{s}_i)$. Entrepreneur i's monitor then checks e^i against e^{0i}. Whenever a discrepancy is found, a penalty of $(1 - \lambda^*)b^{i^*}(y - \gamma \mathbf{k}^*)$ is levied against i. Otherwise, entrepreneur i receives his alloted share of the firm's profit $b^{i^*}(y - \gamma \mathbf{k}^*)$. If the firm's chosen rules are indeed incentive compatible, the cooperative entrepreneurs will reap the reward for cooperation and joint production.

Note again that, owing to the existence of the monitoring cost and the presence of the law of diminishing returns in monitoring, not to mention noise, it is not possible to eradicate shirking and to reach the highest cooperative potential. Given the control system, each entrepreneur knows that, if he cheats, there is a certain probability that he will be caught and punished. Consequently, he will not only commit an optimal effort level but will also choose to cheat at a certain level and frequency. Thus the penalty approach can at most guarantee the attainment of a certain satisfactory outcome derived from cooperation.

OLIGARCHICAL INTERNAL ORGANIZATION

In the previous sections we have offered an explanation for the existence of firms with a highly complex and tightly structured hierarchical internal organization and described the internal workings of such a firm. Casual observation suggests that a large number of firms with much simpler internal organizations also exist. In this section we turn our attention to dealing with firms organized under a simple oligarchical structure. We first examine the rationale for entrepreneurs to adopt such an internal organization and then describe the procedure used by them to select the firm's decision rules and incentive-control apparatus under such an organizational framework.

Conditions Suitable for Oligarchical Organization

Recall that the hierarchical internal organization is designed to fill the need for coordinating interdependent activities created by technical and managerial division of labor, for synchronizing information acquisition and utilization, and for assisting the detection and prevention of evasion of contractual obligations. Therefore it is natural to postulate that, whenever these needs are not urgently present, the oligarchical internal organization becomes adequate to cope with the firm's decision and control problems.

Specifically, there are times when the technical and managerial division of labor does not require close coordination among the divided entrepreneurial activities. Coordination of activities is not needed whenever benefits derived from division of labor stem solely from the specialization of the activities itself or whenever the coalition of entrepreneurs is mainly motivated by the benefits derived from risk-sharing among the various activities. In these cases, coordination of entrepreneurial activities becomes far less demanding.

In addition, coordination of activities is small whenever the sources of information are not scattered or the cost of information is negligible. In these cases, all entrepreneurs possess the same amount of information. Even though there are advantages in division of labor in production and management, the firm's policies can nonetheless be determined collectively and simultaneously through bargaining. There will be no need to specialize in information and decision-making. The internal organization required to support such cooperative activities is drastically simplified.

Finally, not only is the internal organization needed to support coordination in information and decision-making very much simpler under the situation described above, but the internal organization needed to support incentive and control activities is also less complex. Because entrepreneurs can function more or less independently, each entrepreneur's productivity is not affected appreciably by the efforts of the others. Therefore each entrepreneur's award depends primarily on his own efforts and the benefit of risk-sharing. Under these circumstances there is no need to establish target levels and to rely on penalty to enforce effort commitments. In a going concern where the cooperative entrepreneurs bargain repeatedly, monitoring alone is sufficient to discourage excessive shirking. Moreover, if monitoring is fairly effective and monitoring cost is relatively low, it is reasonably satisfactory for all entrepreneurs to share the monitoring role and to monitor each other. All told, the internal organization needed to support a control system is relatively simple.

In sum, whenever production and managerial activities require little coordination and the information cost is low, the firm is likely to be organized under a relatively simple and democratic oligarchical internal structure. In the next section we briefly describe the procedure used to arrive at the decision and control rules for the firm.

Decision and Control

We again assume that the firm is organized by n entrepreneurs indexed by $i=1,\ldots,n$. Through bargaining these entrepreneurs enter into agreements with each other in order to make each of their expected utilities as large as possible subject to a set of constraints. Specifically, entrepreneur i bargains with the others to choose $(\mathbf{k},\mathbf{b},e^i\,m^i)$ where all symbols can be interpreted exactly as before. This decision problem differs in two major aspects from the one presented in the previous section. First, entrepreneurs operate as equals and monitor each other's activities; there is no hierarchy in decision-making and monitoring. Second, no target level or penalty rule is involved.

Again, the precise nature of the bargaining outcome depends upon the rules of the game. Following the general principle outlined in the first section, the entrepreneurs use the market rule to determine the quantities of the tradeable inputs $\mathbf{k}$ employed, play a Nash cooperative bargaining game to determine the collectively enforced sharing rule $\mathbf{b}$, and play a Cournot–Nash noncooperative game to determine the individually enforced agreements $(\mathbf{e},\mathbf{m})$. Under this general procedure the firm's policies are determined in three steps.

1 Given the sharing rule $\mathbf{b}$, the entrepreneurs' commitments on production and monitoring efforts $(\mathbf{e},\mathbf{m})$, and the market prices of the tradeable inputs γ, the entrepreneur will unanimously choose a vector of these tradeable inputs $\mathbf{k}$ to

$$\max \int_\theta u^i(c^i(\theta),e^i,m^i)p^i(\theta)d\theta \qquad (7.6)$$

subject to

$$c^i = b^i(y - \gamma\mathbf{k})$$

$$y \in Y(\mathbf{k},\mathbf{e},\mathbf{m},\theta)$$

Note again that all cooperative entrepreneurs agree unanimously with the choice of $\mathbf{k}$ which maximizes the firm's residual $y - \gamma\mathbf{k}$. At the conclusion of this stage of the decision problem, $\mathbf{k}$ becomes $\mathbf{k}(\gamma,\mathbf{b},\mathbf{e},\mathbf{m})$.

2   Given the entrepreneurs' commitments on $(\mathbf{e},\mathbf{m})$, they bargain cooperatively to determine the sharing rule by playing a Nash cooperative game. Formally, they collectively choose $\mathbf{b}$ to maximize the Nash product subject to the individual entrepreneurs' constraints, that is, to

$$\max_{<b>} \prod_{i=1}^{n} [Eu^{i}(c^{i}(\theta), e^{i}, m^{i}) - u^{0i}] \qquad (7.7)$$

subject to (*) of (7.6) for all $i = 1, \ldots, n$ and with $\mathbf{k}$ substituted by $\mathbf{k}(\gamma,\mathbf{b},\mathbf{e},\mathbf{m})$

$$0 \le b^{i} \le 1, \quad \sum_{i=1}^{n} b^{i} = 1$$

where u^{0i} is entrepreneur i's threat-point utility level. We obtain the optimal sharing rule $\bar{\mathbf{b}}(\mathbf{e},\mathbf{m})$ from this bargaining problem.

3   Each entrepreneur i, $i = 1, \ldots, n$, selects his own production and monitoring efforts (e^{i}, m^{i}) noncooperatively by playing the Cournot–Nash game; that is, each entrepreneur i chooses (e^{i}, m^{i}) which maximizes his own expected utility subject to his own constraints based upon the assumption that all other entrepreneurs have chosen their respective optimal production and monitoring efforts $(\mathbf{e}^{*}_{-i}, \mathbf{m}^{*}_{-i})$. Formally, assume that $(\mathbf{e}^{*}_{-i}, \mathbf{m}^{*}_{-i})$ is given; each entrepreneur i, $i = 1, \ldots, n$, will

$$\max_{<e^{i}, m^{i}> <\theta>} Eu^{i}(c^{i}(\theta), e^{i}, m^{i}) \qquad (7.8)$$

subject to $c^{i} = \bar{b}^{i}(.) [y(.) - \gamma\bar{\mathbf{k}}(.)]$

$$0 < e^{i}, m^{i}, \quad e^{i} + m^{i} \le \mathcal{l}_{0}^{i}$$

where

$y(.) \in Y(\bar{\mathbf{k}}(.), e^{i}, \mathbf{e}^{*}_{-i}, m^{i}, \mathbf{m}^{*}_{-i}, \theta)$

$\bar{b}^{i}(.) = \bar{b}^{i}(e^{i}, \mathbf{e}^{*}_{-i}, m^{i}, \mathbf{m}^{*}_{-i})$

$\bar{\mathbf{k}}(.) = \mathbf{k}(\bar{\mathbf{b}}(\cdot), e^{i}, \mathbf{e}^{*}_{-i}, m^{i}, \mathbf{m}^{*}_{-i})$

The $(\mathbf{e}^{*}, \mathbf{m}^{*})$ which simultaneously satisfies all the above n problems is the solution for the Cournot–Nash game. Because each entrepreneur selects his own optimal production and monitoring efforts by taking into consideration all other entrepreneurs' reactions, there is no incentive for any entrepreneur to deviate from his efforts commitment *ex post*. The solution $(\mathbf{e}^*, \mathbf{m}^*)$ of the Cournot–Nash game therefore yields an incentive-compatible agreement to all the cooperative entrepreneurs.

Based upon the three-step internal decision procedure described above, the firm, by consulting the market prices of the tradeable inputs, will demand $\mathbf{k}^*(\gamma, \mathbf{e}^*, \mathbf{m}^*, \mathbf{b}^*)$ of inputs, and produce $y^*(\mathbf{k}^*, \mathbf{e}^*, \mathbf{m}^*)$ unit of ouputs. Each entrepreneur i, $i = 1, \ldots, n$, will provide (e^{i*}, m^{i*}) level of production and monitoring efforts and receive an income based upon the bonus rate $b^{i*}(y - \gamma^* \mathbf{k}^*)$. In the end, each cooperative entrepreneur i, $i = 1, \ldots, n$, can expect to reap a reward in utility equal to $Eu^i(c^{i*}, e^{i*}, m^{i*})$.

CONCLUDING REMARKS

Production in a firm typically involves a large number of separate but interrelated activities which are carried out by many cooperative entrepreneurs. In order to be successful, the firm must select an efficient internal organization to assign entrepreneurial authority and responsibility and to coordinate the decisions and activities of the cooperative entrepreneurs. In addition we also observed that, because entrepreneurs are human, they are prone to behaving opportunistically. The firm as a production institution must create rules to deter shirking among its members by the threat of punitive actions and must also cultivate an atmosphere which renders shirking unattractive.

Because the firm's internal organization is a composite of both decision and control functions, the crucial question is how to design an overall internal organization which will make the decision and control activities mesh. It is frequently observed that the interaction between decision and control activities affects incentives and thus the efficiency of the firm's operation. The design of internal organizations thus calls for the selection of a relationship between decision and control activities and the establishment of a procedure used to enforce rules and mediate disputes. In this chapter, we have identified two broad types of internal organizations – oligarchical and hierarchical – and have provided a rudimentary analysis of them.

Our discussion of the firm's internal organization has been primarily static in nature. However, as we remarked in the text, the firm is a going concern. As such, decision and control take on an added dimension. When the firm is a going concern, entrepreneurs within the firm bargain repeatedly. Under these circumstances, not only do rules concerning decision and control affect the incentive of the entrepreneurs and the efficiency of the firm's operations, but the rule concerning the frequency of bargaining among the entrepreneurs also affects these outcomes in an important way. This follows because the greater is the frequency with which the entrepreneurs bargain, the more will the current performances of the cooperative entrepreneurs affect the internal allocative rules. Since cooperative entrepreneurs often join together to exploit benefits of risk-sharing, and since risk-sharing is necessarily a long-run phenomenon, undue emphasis on short-run performance is self-defeating. Emphasis on short-run performance prevents the cooperative entrepreneurs from reaping the entire benefit associated with long-run risk-sharing. Moreover, frequent renegotiation encourages opportunistic entrepreneurs to grab the temporary gains derived from a given coalition and then seek opportunities elsewhere (Gilson and Mnookin, 1985); thus it also causes greater instability to the firm.

Not only is too frequent renegotiation of contracts detrimental to incentives, so is too infrequent renegotiation. Without renegotiation, the firm's allocative and distributive rules are rigidly held for a length of time exceeding what is required to allow the law of large numbers and risk-sharing processes to work out. Because changes in factors underlying the allocative and distributive rules do take place over time, the existing sharing rule no longer reflects the determining factors. This implies that entrepreneurs' productivities may have moved out of line with the reward system. Some entrepreneurs, whose productivities have improved, are not rewarded and others, whose productivities have declined, are rewarded with other people's labor. A free-rider problem thus arises. The sharing rule ceases to be incentive compatible. The presence of the free-rider phenomenon will prevent the coalition from tapping fully the benefit of joint production.

Thus both too frequent and too infrequent renegotiation of contracts damages the firm's incentive structure. The frequency of bargaining constitutes a crucial aspect of the firm's control structure. Depending upon the bargaining costs, the risk-averseness of the cooperative entrepreneurs, and the stochastic nature of the (income) uncertainties faced by the entrepreneurs, each firm must find an optimal frequency for contract renegotiation. The design for an optimal frequency for contract negotiation is essential for the entrepreneurs to tap the maximum benefit derived from cooperation (risk-sharing and joint production).

The above remarks clearly indicate that the theory of internal organization is complex. The results presented in this chapter cannot be viewed as a complete theory of internal organization of the firm. Such a theory must identify the internal organization capable of delivering to the cooperative entrepreneurs the second-best outcome of cooperation and must, at the same time, characterize what constitutes the second-best outcome. The characterization of the second-best outcome is nontrivial because it requires a clear identification of the constraints of the cooperative entrepreneurs' decision problems. Because the internal organization of the firm affects these constraints and, in turn, these constraints affect the firm's internal organization, the problem of identifying the second-best outcome becomes exceedingly complex. In addition, the attainment of the second-best outcome becomes inherently difficult as long as the firm relies on penalty schemes to discipline its members. The reliance on penalty schemes brings out not the best but rather a satisfactory behavior of the cooperative entrepreneurs. Consequently, the firm can only deliver a satisfactory outcome of cooperation to its entrepreneurs. The internal organizations presented in this chapter yield examples of such satisfactory outcomes.

NOTES

1 This section is based primarily on the work of Marschak and Radner (1972).

2 $p(\theta|s) = \dfrac{p(s|\theta)p(\theta)}{p(s)}$ where $p(\theta)$ and $p(s)$ are known as the prior probability and the message probability respectively.

3 Decentralization of action is not due solely to information specialization; it may also be brought about by advantage associated with division of labor in decision-making.

4 Groves (1973) extends team theory to include the case where the general members of the team do not share the preferences of the head of the team. Groves is interested in examining an incentive-compatible reward structure which would induce the general members of the team to behave as if their interests were identical with those of the head of the team. This extension is still not sufficient to serve our needs.

5 This is referred to as the threat-point utility level. The identification of the threat point is not trivial. For our purposes we will assume that the identification of the threat point is noncontroversial.

6 The Cournot–Nash solution represents a generalization of the minimax solution for the two-person zero-sum game (Shubik, 1984, p. 240).

7 Strictly speaking, the firm's information structure also depends on strategic considerations. One entrepreneur who possesses some information may be able to reap a gain by sending untruthful signals to his partners. In this case the firm's internal organization also depends on the

choice of these strategies by the cooperative entrepreneurs and by the control mechanisms used to curb this opportunistic behavior. We will ignore this aspect in this chapter.

8 Because the composition of the firm has already been determined, u^{0i} denotes the utility level that entrepreneur i could obtain by adopting the second-best alternative action.

9 For a simple model used to illustrate this idea, see McAndrews (1985).

10 Frequently, when information is exceedingly scarce, it may be informationally advantageous for one to let others move first and thereby learn from their mistakes. In such a case, the first-move privilege belongs to the one who possesses the option to choose his turn of move.

11 In principle, the entrepreneur should also bargain to determine the target level of monitoring efforts. For simplicity, we will ignore this aspect here.

12 Generally the entrepreneurs will also have the option of selecting a penalty rule from a set of more complex penalty functional forms. However, to adopt a general approach here will draw us away from our main analysis which is to study how bargaining leads to a specific hierarchical internal organization. For a more general treatment of the penalty rule see Kai Ma (1984).

8

On the Nature of Firms

Having presented the entrepreneur-centered theory, we are now in a position to examine its implications. The inclusion of a human factor – the entrepreneur – in economic theory has the potential of altering the perception of a wide variety of theoretical and institutional issues. The functioning and performance of the market now depend on the entrepreneur's quality, vision, and purpose. Social goals cannot be achieved automatically through the competitive market alone; the achievement of these goals now depends on conscious human efforts and the aid of various social and ethical institutions. The solution of economic problems can no longer be sought in isolation from social and ethical considerations. However, investigation of the linkage between economic, social, and ethical systems will take us far away from the central purpose of this book. We need to restrict our attention to the theory's implications for economic issues. Even within the realm of economics we still need to limit the scope of our discussion. Two sets of issues will be dealt with in this book. In the present chapter we examine the theory's implications for the firm's objective, the boundary between the firm and the market, and the firm's behavior and performance. In subsequent chapters we shift our attention to issues outside the firm and examine the theory's implications for the nature of profits, the historical evolution of entrepreneurship, market and other economic institutions, and the nature of nonprofit organizations.

THE FIRM'S OBJECTIVES

As we have seen in chapter 4, one of the most controversial issues associated with the theory of the firm has to do with the objectives that it pursues. The theory proposed in chapter 6 has rendered this controversy inconsequential. Factor owners who can sell their services in the market will resolve their conflicts of interest by trading. Other factor owners whose services either cannot be sold or who do not wish them to be traded in the market will pursue their interests through playing the economy-wide cooperative game, that is, the formation of firms. Because each player's share of this residual is determined through bargaining at the time when the coalition (firm) is formed, at the conclusion of the game each player must, by definition, achieve a utility level which cannot be improved upon by switching to any other strategy. The fact that the firm is a coalition of entrepreneurs thus implies that, despite the divergence in preferences among those who have joined the same coalition, no further mediation among them is necessary. This fact also implies that the firm ceases to have any objective of its own and is no longer an entity organized specifically to resolve conflict among its components.

To say that the firm does not have an objective of its own does not mean that it will never give the appearance of pursuing a set of well-defined goals. This appearance is an equilibrium phenomenon. Since firms are formed as a result of a society-wide cooperative game, when the economy is at an equilibrium, the entrepreneurs of a given firm will have agreed upon a common set of policies even if they do not have identical tastes and beliefs. The pursuance of these policies becomes the goal of the firm. The important point to note here is that firms do not pursue the same set of goals; depending upon the composition of the entrepreneurs, each firm pursues a unique set of policies.

Thus we see that the firm's policies are not derived from the firm's objective function but rather from the desire of entrepreneurs to exploit the advantages associated with joint production and risk-sharing. The proposed theory denies the personification of the firm and the traditional assertion that all its members must defer their self-interest to that of the firm and must work single-mindedly toward the attainment of the firm's goal. Instead, the theory advocates that entrepreneurs organize a firm in order to pursue their own objectives and insists that in a modern economy this self-interest can best be attained through joint production. However, joint production is possible only when the entrepreneurs can agree upon joint policies. The condition required for a joint policy is that the services of the co-operative entrepreneurs are sufficiently complementary to generate results that can best serve each entrepreneur's self-interest.

The message we wish to convey is that uniformity of preferences and beliefs among cooperative entrepreneurs is not a necessary condition for joint policy formation. Of course, this does not mean that we must either deny the fact that a common policy can be found with greater ease if all entrepreneurs of a firm have similar tastes and beliefs, or repudiate the assertion that there is a tendency for entrepreneurs of a similar persuasion to come together and form a coalition. In fact, despite the multitude of objectives that each entrepreneur may pursue, some commonality of interest usually exists among cooperative entrepreneurs. Let the objectives that each entrepreneur pursues be income derived from his share of the profit, degree of autonomy in decision-making, prestige associated with certain enterprise and responsibility, pride associated with success, perks derived from work, etc. It is not hard to find commonality in some of these interests among all cooperative entrepreneurs. It can hardly be denied that all entrepreneurs must, to a varying degree, be interested in profits. Several reasons can be used to support this contention. First, even though each entrepreneur in joining a firm may pursue many objectives, profits must always figure prominently as an important motive. This is simply a matter of necessity. In opting to become an entrepreneur, an agent, forgoes the sure income of a wage earner and instead becomes a residual claimant. Since the entrepreneur may own little of other resources, profit becomes the only major source of his income. Thus, in order to support his consumption, the entrepreneur is forced to devote a fair amount of attention to profits. Second, entrepreneurial income derived from the. residual is not just an income; it also reflects and signals the degree of success due to the entrepreneur's decisions and judgements. Since the entrepreneurs commonly exhibit pride in their ability to make correct decisions and render sound judgements, the size of the residual reflects the quality of the entrepreneurial decisions and the value of their judgements; the entrepreneurs, *ceteris paribus*, would naturally have the incentive to make the residual as large as possible. Finally, the incentive to strive for profit is further bolstered by the entrepreneur's desire to become a capitalist. In this regard, we believe that Knight's observation is in error. In a modern economy, it is not true that only capitalists can assume the entrepreneur's role; on the contrary, a person may opt to become an entrepreneur for the purpose of gaining the chance to make a success and then becoming a capitalist. The lure of the amenities afforded a wealthy capitalist is so strong that it will keep the entrepreneur's attention firmly on profit. All told, we must conclude that, in general, entrepreneurs are profit-conscious people. Since entrepreneurs determine the firm's policies, despite the fact that each entrepreneur may have some private reasons for joining a coalition, all entrepreneurs must have one objective in common – the pursuit of profits. In addition to profit, there undoubtedly exist other common interests among the entrepreneurs. The presence of these common interests, although facilitating cooperation among entrepreneurs, does not change the fact that as long as each entrepreneur seeks self-interest and the entrepreneurs' interests conflict with each other, the firm's policy cannot be derived through the maximization of a common objective function. These policies must be derived in a personalized manner through bargaining. In a society-wide bargaining setting, the entrepreneurs' interests are resolved by finding partners who are willing to accommodate each other for joint production so that by the adoption of a joint policy each party's interest attains its highest potential.

Although the pursuance of profit is a common objective of all entrepreneurs, as long as entrepreneurs also seek other benefits and the firm is formed as a coalition of entrepreneurs through bargaining, it is inevitable that profit cannot be the sole determinant of a firm's policy. At this juncture we naturally postulate that the importance of profit as a determinant of policy must depend upon whether the firm is owner, labor, entrepreneur, or manager managed. Does one type of firm exhibit greater propensity to pursue profit more vigorously than the others?

The traditional view, as presented in chapter 4, has been that the owner-managed firm is most conscientious with respect to profits. Under this type of management structure owners alone receive profit; it is therefore in their self-interest to follow a single-minded profit-maximizing policy. Further, a separation of ownership and control exists in all other types of firms. In these cases, it was believed that the decision-makers do not receive profits. Since the decision-makers have interests of their own, the non-owner-managed firm must divert attention away from profit. They maximize perquisites (Williamson), sales (Baumol), or growth (Marris). In the long run the non-owner-managed firms must earn less profits.

Of course, this traditional view is not consistent with the entrepreneur-centered theory. We disagree with the proposition that "only owners receive profit." In our view, whoever makes the decisions in the firm – whether it is the shareholders, laborers, or pure entrepreneurs – must assume the entrepreneurial role and become a residual claimant. All residual claimants are keenly interested in profits because their livelihood depends upon the size of the residual that is intimately intertwined with profit. A more detailed analysis of this issue will be presented in chapter 10. Here, we only wish to note that there is no a priori reason justifying the proposition that owner-managed firms pursue profits more vigorously than firms controlled by other resource owners.

Empirical studies of owner-controlled versus non-owner-controlled firms corroborate our assessment.[1] These studies suggest that when performances of the non-owner-controlled and owner-controlled firms are placed side by side and compared, no significant difference in profit performance is apparent. In fact these studies, although typically giving primacy to profits, do not present strong evidence to suggest that profit maximization has ever been the sole objective of most businesses. These results echo the sentiment expressed by Gordon (1966, p. 336) that profits and profit expectations continue to guide decision-making in giant as well as small enterprises; few firms will ever go to the extreme of adopting a single-minded profit-maximizing strategy.

The issues associated with the so-called "separation of ownership and control" can be placed in a different perspective under the proposed theoretical framework. Separation of ownership and control, or more precisely of risk-bearing and decision-making, now becomes a natural progression associated with the developmental stage of the economy, the financial market, and the firm. The dominance of the owner-managed firm in the economy is primarily a historical phenomenon. (We will say more about this issue in chapter 9.) Because the capital market was typically not well developed in the earlier stage of economic development, the owner-managed firm was the dominant organizational form during that stage. As the economy develops and the financial markets grow and become efficient, the entrepreneurs can increasingly shift the risk-bearing role to the specialized risk-bearers, that is, the stockholders. At the same time, the capitalist's ability to spread risk via portfolio management will also improve. The stockholders can now, through the capital market, ensure a certain expected rate of return subject to a given degree of risk. This implies that, as the economy matures, there is a tendency toward specialization in the functions of risk-bearing and decision-making. Viewed in this way, the owner-managed firm should not be considered as a normatively superior organizational form, and a firm with separation of ownership and control should not be considered as an anomaly. On the contrary, the appearance of the phenomenon of separation of ownership and control should be taken as a signal reflecting that economic progress is taking place and that the market is moving toward maturity. All told, there is no a priori reason to believe that the owner-managed firms will pursue profits more vigorously than firms organized by other types of entrepreneurs.

NATURE OF FIRM AND MARKET ALLOCATION OF RESOURCES

In order to understand how the market system channels resources into production and consumption in an economy where both the market and the firm allocate resources, it is necessary to gain a clear view of two related issues: first, the difference between the firm's internal allocation rule and the market's price mechanism; second, how the allocative tasks are divided between the firm and the market. In chapter 4, we have seen that the literature's treatment of these problems is confusing and inconclusive. The entrepreneur-centered theory contributes greatly to the clarification of these issues. In this section we describe this theory's implications for the distinction between the ways that the firm and the market allocate resources and shed light on the issues concerning the boundary between the firm and the market.

Rules Governing Firm and Market Allocation

We have seen in chapter 2 that the neoclassical economists believe that the market alone allocates resources; therefore they center their attentions on how resources are allocated by the price mechanism. To recapitulate, in the neoclassical economy there are two sets of primitive agents: the consumers and the firms. Consumers own both resources and firms, supply all inputs required for production, receive all income (wages, rents, interests, and dividends), and consume all final goods. Firms appear simply as production units taking prices as given and converting inputs into outputs. Their existence is taken for granted. It is assumed that markets are complete and all prices are determined competitively within the markets. All agents will take the market prices as given and act to pursue their respective self-interests. Specifically, the consumer converts his resources into income in the market in order to complete his consumption program; he does so by taking the prices as given and chooses an optimal investment–consumption portfolio to maximize his expected utility subject to the budget constraints. The firm, through the complete contingent claims markets, also faces a set of certainty equivalent prices for its inputs and outputs.[2] Based upon these prices, the firm employs each input to the extent where the value for the marginal product of the factor equals its price and produces each output where the marginal cost of production equals its price. Thus the firm uses prices both internally and externally to guide its activities in maximizing expected profits. Because maximizing expected profit for the firm implies maximizing expected income for the consumer, at equilibrium all consumers' utilities are maximized, all owners of the resources (landlords, laborers, and capitalists) agree unanimously with the firm's production plan, and all firms' profits are equalized. The resulting allocation is Pareto optimal.

The entrepreneur-centered theory views the economy differently. The consumers are now the only primitive agents. As in the neoclassical economy, they own all the resources, supply all inputs required for production, receive all income, and consume all final products.

Consumers again need to convert their resources into income in order to complete their consumption program. Because the markets are incomplete, there are now two types of resource owners: those who can trade their resources in the market and those who cannot. The resource owners whose services are tradeable will simply, as in the neoclassical case, convert their resources into income by selling the resources in the factor markets. The resource owners whose services are not tradeable must assume the entrepreneurial role and derive their income by forming a firm and then claiming part of the firm's residual. Because the firms in this economy are organized endogenously, they lose their primitive agent status. Moreover, contrary to the common belief, firms are not organized to pursue any specific objective; they are merely organized as a means of enabling the entrepreneurs to channel their resources into production, to receive incomes, and to complete their consumption programs. Owners of resources, both tradeable and nontradeable, can now base their expectations on the market prices to choose an investment–consumption portfolio which maximizes the individual's expected utility subject to the appropriate budget constraints. The firms, their derived status notwithstanding, interact with the consumers to determine the market prices of all tradeable commodities in the impersonal market environment.

Faced with such an economy, the task at hand is to gain a clear understanding of how the firm allocates resources in the context where the tradeable goods and services are allocated by the price mechanism while the nontradeable entrepreneurial services are allocated through bargaining. We will show that the firm's activities are carried out by using a mixture of these mechanisms.

Nature of Mix Because the firm uses both tradeable and nontradeable resources for production, in order to understand the internal allocative process of the firm we must examine the relationship between the allocation of entrepreneurial services and the allocation of all tradeable services. In this regard, we will treat the allocation of the entrepreneurial services as the nucleus of the firm's allocative activities. This is because the allocation of the entrepreneurial services (through economy-wide bargaining) not only determines the entrepreneurial composition of the firm and the firm's financial structure, but also determines the role each entrepreneur plays in the firm's decision-making hierarchy. The hierarchical position that each entrepreneur assumes crucially affects the firm's production possibility set and its production policy. It is this production policy that eventually interacts with the market to determine the overall allocation of tradeable resources within the firm.

Specifically, the firm's production policy determines its demand for the tradeable factors of production; in turn, this demand interacts with the supply of factors to determine the price and quantity of each factor employed. Thus the entrepreneurs' allocation of their own services indirectly alters the firm's employment of the tradeable factors and makes these employments differ quantitatively from those prescribed by the neoclassical theory. It is important to note that this difference is not caused by the fact that the neoclassical firm and the entrepreneur-centered firm use different rules in employing the tradeable factors; rather, this difference is caused by the fact that the entrepreneurs' allocation of their own activities indirectly affects the firm's production policy. In this context, employment of the factors is now different; this difference affects the supply of the output. Through the interaction of demand and supply in the product markets, the allocation of the entrepreneurial services also indirectly affects the prices of the final products.

Thus we see that the firm's allocation of resources starts from entrepreneurs bargaining to determine how their own services are distributed in order to carry out the firm's productive activities. Because allocation of entrepreneurial services inevitably affects the firm's production policy, the firm's allocation of the entrepreneurial services spills over to affect allocation of all other resources even though the tradeable commodities still operate under the jurisdiction of the price mechanism.

Impact of Market Friction on the Price Mechanism Because the efficiency of the market mechanisms is affected by the presence of transactions costs and market uncertainties, it is helpful to investigate in greater detail the way that tradeable factors are allocated by the price mechanism in the presence of these market frictions. The presence of these frictions often causes the employment of the tradeable factors to exhibit some degree of nonresponsiveness toward a change in the market price even though the employment of the factor is determined by the price mechanism. Suppose that the tradeable factor is labor. Transactions costs in this case may take many forms, e.g. contract costs, enforcement costs, etc. For simplicity, let the transactions cost take the following simple form: when the worker is hired, the employer must incur a training cost; when the worker is dismissed, the employer must incur a severance pay. Under these circumstances a change in the market wages may not affect the employment of labor. Specifically, let the market wage rate decrease (increase). If this decrease (increase) in wage rate is less than the training cost (severance pay), then it is to the benefit of the employer to hold the employment of labor constant. The presence of the transactions cost thus sets the bounds (depending upon the level of the transactions cost) within which changes in the market wages will not affect the amount of labor hired. This principle applies equally well to all tradeable commodities.

To be sure, nonresponsiveness in factor employment toward a change in the factor price will induce a loss of profit for the firm. However, this loss can be mitigated by internal substitution among existing factors whose elasticity of substitution is sufficiently large. Based upon the new factor price ratio, the firm will adjust internal utilization of the existing factors to achieve the desired marginal rate of substitution among these factors. Thus the presence of transaction costs reduces the degree of factor specialization and creates a difference between factor employment and factor utilization. The firm now shifts its response to changes in price from the market adjustment in factor employment to the internal adjustment in factor utilization. This lack of market adjustment creates an impression that the employment of the tradeable factor in the firm is insensitive to changes in the factor price and that the firm no longer uses the price mechanism to allocate the tradeable factor services. This impression is inaccurate for two reasons. First, internal allocation of factor utilization is still responsive to market prices. Second, even the market adjustment in factor employment is not suspended altogether. When changes in the market price exceed the bound set by the level of the transactions cost, the market employment of the factor will again be responsive to the price changes. Consequently, it is erroneous to assert that, in the presence of transactions costs, the employment of tradeable factors within the firm ceases to follow the price mechanism.

The effect of uncertainty on the employment of the tradeable factor is similar. In addition, uncertainties cause both employer and employee to prefer general contractual arrangements. From the firm's point of view, the presence of uncertainty also creates adjustment costs which cause the firm's employment of the factors to be less responsive to both the changes in market demand for the firm's products and the changes in the market supply of factors used by the firm. This lack of response again induces a loss in the firm's profits. As in the preceding case, this loss in profit can be partially offset if the factors of production are less specialized and are made to perform a wide range of tasks. In short, the firm now prefers general employment contracts. Factor owners also find that under uncertainty it is to their advantage to enter into general employment contracts. Market uncertainty induces income uncertainty for the factor owners. The risk-averse factor owner is willing to pay a risk premium in order to insure against this income uncertainty. For example, let the resource owner's utility be a function of two variables: income and the range of work performed. Assume that the resource owner prefers a higher income and dislikes a wider range of work assignments. Then his insurance premium may take the form of being willing to accept a wider range of work assignments. Thus, under uncertainty, both the cost-conscious employer and the risk-averse employee prefer general contractual arrangements. The adoption of this form of employment implies that the factor services are less specialized and the adjustment to changes in market environment will first take place internally by changing the utilization rate of the existing factors. Only when this adjustment is found to be inadequate will the firm change the quantity of the factors employed. This two-stage adjustment tactic gives the impression that during the first stage of adjustment the employer uses "discretion" to direct the activities of the employee within a limit determined by the level of the adjustment costs and the risk-averseness of the employee.

This point can best be made clear by the use of a concrete example. Let the firm be given the option of either hiring typists, filing clerks, and telephone operators, or hiring general secretaries who perform all these functions. As we will demonstrate, the presence of uncertainty favors the employment of the secretary who agrees to type, file, and answer the telephone at the discretion of the employer.

Suppose that there are demand uncertainties associated with the firm's outputs. The derived demand for typing, filing, and answering telephones also becomes uncertain. If the firm's employment of each type of worker reflects changes in these demand schedules, the incomes of the typists, filing clerks, and telephone operators will also become random. Since workers are risk-averse, they are willing to pay a risk premium in order to insure against their income uncertainties. One way of insuring against such uncertainties is by agreeing to serve in different capacities as the *ex post* situation dictates, that is, agreeing to serve at the discretion of the employer as demand information becomes available to him. From the firm's point of view, the random fluctuation in the demand for the firm's products may induce a disproportionate change in the demand for typists, filing clerks, and telephone operators. This disproportionate change calls for the firm to alter the composition of those workers in the work force. However, this is impossible unless the firm is willing to incur an exorbitant cost. Employment of these workers must be made *ex ante*, not *ex post*. Therefore *ex post* realization of the firm's demand offers little opportunity for the firm to make an adjustment of the employment of these workers. Owing to the rigidity in factor employment, the firm will incur a loss in profits. This loss in profit can be lessened by internal adjustment across the workers' categories, that is, by shifting the duties of the typists, filing clerks, and telephone operators. Thus the employer will be willing to pay a premium price for a general secretary who is willing to "grant ownership right to the employer," allowing him to allocate the secretary's time among the various tasks as uncertainty is revealed.

Since the worker is willing to exchange the promise to obey orders for stable employment and the employer is willing to pay a higher wage for the right to adjust the workers' work assignments, the general contractual form of employment is mutually preferred. Therefore this contractual arrangement is widely adopted. It is important to again note that the employer's "discretionary power" under this contractual arrangement does not mean suspension of the price mechanism in the employment of secretaries. The internal utilization of the various factors of production is still guided by the marginal productivities of the factors and their prices. The only exception is that the marginal productivity of a given factor is no longer calculated on the basis of the factor's performance of a narrowly defined task; it is now calculated as a weighted average of the marginal productivities of all tasks performed by the factor. In the case of the secretary, his marginal productivity is the weighted average of the marginal productivities of typing, filing, and answering the telephone.

In sum, there are two ways of allocating the resources in an entrepreneur-centered production economy: (a) the nontradeable entrepreneurial services (both pure and adjunct) are allocated through the playing of an economy-wide cooperative game, and (b) the tradeable goods and services are allocated by the price mechanism. Because the firm's production policy is determined as a consequence of bargaining among the entrepreneurs, the allocation of the entrepreneurial services also indirectly affects the demand for tradeable factors of production and the supply of commodities produced by the firm. This indirect influence does not alter the fundamental fact that the tradeable factors are mainly allocated by the price mechanism, that is, by comparison between the factors' weighted marginal rate of substitution and their price ratio. However, the presence of transactions costs and market uncertainties makes the employment of the tradeable factor less sensitive to changes in the market price and causes the changes in the market demand for the output (supply of the factors) to not always translate into a change in the firm's demand for the factors (supply of the products). The trading partners of factors of production now prefer a general employment contract over a specific-employment contract; factors then become less specialized. This change in the trading partners' preferences enables the firm to shift its response to changes in market conditions from the adjustment in factor employment to the adjustment in factor utilization. This tactical change shifts the burden of adjustment from the market to the firm. We will have more to say about this point in the next section. Here we only wish to note that this shift in the burden of adjustment leads to the internalization of market uncertainties within the firm.

Because internal utilization of the tradeable factors of production is still guided by the market prices, the firm's allocation of these commodities does not represent a suspension of the market mechanism. Thus stated, we see that the firm relies upon both market and nonmarket means of allocating resources. How does this conclusion square with the common understanding that the boundary between the firm and the market also separates the behavior of the agents operating with them? It is to this topic that we turn in the next subsection.

The Boundary Issue

As we have seen in chapter 4, under the assumption that the agents behave differently in the firm and in the market, the literature attempts to delineate the boundary between the firm and the market by the character of the agents' behavior. This issue of the boundary is important because it is believed that the firm's decision rule can be deduced from the behavior of the agents operating within it. Equipped with a knowledge of the firm's decision rule and the location of the boundary between the firm and the market, the economist can assess how the firm and the market divide the allocative responsibilities and gain an understanding of how the two-tier (firm and market) allocative process functions within a capitalistic economy.

This analytical strategy fails to provide the desired result because economists cannot agree upon just how the agents behave within the firm and in the market. As we have seen in chapter 4, economists such as Coase and Simon advocate the authoritative view of the firm. They assert that outside the firm economic activities are coordinated by the price mechanism under voluntary exchange, whereas within the firm voluntary exchange is suspended and entrepreneurial authority replaces the price mechanism for directing the resource allocation. Others, such as Cyert and March, advocate the cooperative view of the firm. They claim that outside the firm agents behave noncooperatively, whereas within the firm they behave cooperatively. Not only do these behaviorial criteria fail to provide a concrete decision rule for the firm and a clear-cut separation of the firm and market, they create considerable controversy and confusion.

According to the authoritative view of the firm, the entrepreneur who purchases inputs in the factor markets will nonetheless turn around to allocate them for various usages in an authoritative manner without taking into account their prices and their marginal productivities. Thus, says Coase, "If a workman moves from department Y to department X, he does not go because of a change in relative prices, but because he is ordered to do so" (Coase, 1937, p. 388). Although Simon (1957a) recognizes that the authoritative relationship between the employer and the employees is not forced upon the employee but is a mutually advantageous arrangement, he nonetheless gives the impression that the employer can give orders to the employee at will, though "within certain limits," without regard to the prices and the marginal productivities of the inputs. For two reasons these assessments are unacceptable. First, the arbitrariness of the entrepreneur's action does not define a clear decision rule; second, why would the entrepreneurs want to allocate an input to a specific employment which yields a suboptimal result? Whenever the entrepreneur does consider the prices and the marginal productivities of the inputs and acts according to some kind of a rule, the employment of the tradeable factors ceases to be arbitrary. As we have seen in the previous section, the inputs are indeed employed under the rubric of the price mechanism albeit with friction created by the presence of transactions costs and uncertainties. This conclusion clearly contradicts the Coasian assumption that the firm and the market always allocate resources in a different manner.

The cooperative view of the firm is different. The boundary between the firm and the market is delineated by the differences in agents' behavior. The agents in the market take cues from the prices and behave anonymously and noncooperatively. They are viewed as responding to personal incentives and seeking to achieve their individual short-term goals. In contrast, the relationship among agents within the firm is long term in nature. This enduring relationship among resource owners is personal. Competition among agents gives way to cooperation. According to Cyert and March, this transformation from individualistic behavior in the market to cooperative behavior in the firm sets the firm and the market apart.

The distinction between the short-term relationship among agents in the market and the long-term relationship among agents within the firm is clearly exaggerated. It is not difficult to find examples of long-term market-oriented contracts between a buyer and a seller. Ask any restaurateur how he arranges for the restaurant's food supplies. It will be found that the fresh produce is delivered daily without haggling over prices. Dependability and mutual trust are crucial to the buyer–seller relationship. Thus, not only do long- and short-term relationships fail to distinguish agents' behavior in the firm and in the market, cooperative behavior and noncooperative behavior fail to do so as well. On certain occasions, buyer and seller bargain jointly to exploit mutually advantageous market opportunities. Clearly, the market relationship can also be cooperative in nature.

Because economists cannot agree as to what constitutes agents' behavior in the firm and in the market, it is not possible to delineate the boundary between the firm and the market and to discover the firm's internal decision rule. As a consequence, we are left without a clear concept of the central issue – just how does the two-tier allocative process operate in a capitalistic economy under the condition of uncertainty?

The entrepreneur-centered theory can shed light on the boundary issue and illuminate the nature of the two-tier allocative process. As we have seen earlier, the firm uses both price and nonprice mechanisms to allocate resources. It allocates the nontradeable entrepreneurial services through economy-wide cooperative bargaining among entrepreneurs and allocates the tradeable factor services by the price mechanism. Because the allocation of entrepreneurial services simultaneously determines the firm's production policy, the firm's internal allocation of them also indirectly determines its demand for the tradeable factors of production and supply of its products. Thus the two-tier allocative process represents the allocation of the nontradeable entrepreneurial services by the firm and the allocation of the tradeable factors of production and output by the market. This theory clearly implies that the behavior of the agents does not determine the boundary between the firm and the market and conversely this boundary does not separate the agents' behavior in the firms and in the market. The boundary has little to do with the determination of the firm's internal decision rule and with the understanding of how the two-tier allocative process operates.

So far, we have described the two-tier allocative process under the assumption that the tradeable factors are exchanged in the market on the basis of the market-determined price. Since we have also observed that both the market and the firm may resort to bargaining either cooperatively or noncooperatively to arrive at either long- or short-term contractual arrangements, the crucial question at hand is whether the two-tier allocative process still functions under these circumstances. The entrepreneur-centered theory implies that the two-tier allocative process is intact; there is still a clear distinction between the firm's internal allocation of nontradeable factors and the market allocation of tradeable factors. This distinction stems from the fact that internal bargaining destroys the division of income along functional lines whereas the market bargain does not. Frequently, laborers and entrepreneurs bargain in the market to determine either short-term or long-term wages, or capitalists and entrepreneurs bargain in the market to determine either long-term or short-term interest rates (or, as we will see in chapter 10, dividend rates), or landlords and entrepreneurs bargain in the market to determine either long-term or short-term rents. The wages, interest rates, and rents determined in this manner, though affecting the relative shares of income among the distributive classes, preserve the functional division of income. In contrast, the internal bargaining among entrepreneurs (pure or adjunct) takes place not as laborers, capitalists, and landlords versus entrepreneurs, but as entrepreneurs versus each other. Specifically, when laborers or capitalists join the pure entrepreneurs to form a labor- or owner-managed firm, they cease to be laborers or capitalists alone; they each become adjunct entrepreneurs and bargain to share the residual of the firm as entrepreneurs. The distribution of income is now determined not along functional lines but on the basis of each entrepreneur's bargaining power, bargaining skill, preferences, and beliefs. Functional distribution of income is destroyed. Thus we see that the crucial distinction between the market and the internal allocation of the firm is that the former takes place along functional lines while the latter does not.

Because the firm allocates resources by both market and nonmarket means, it is important to know how a specific mixture is determined. The proportion of these mechanisms used depends crucially upon the factor-market environments. As we have seen in chapter 6, when a factor market is imperfect, the resource owner may abandon it and opt instead to convert his resources into income by becoming an adjunct entrepreneur. An extreme case can occur whenever all factor markets are imperfect causing all factor owners to become adjunct entrepreneurs. Instead of selling services in the factor markets, each factor owner now derives his income by bargaining for a share of the firm's residual. In this case, the nucleus of the firm is the firm itself. In the opposite spectrum, the nucleus of the firm vanishes altogether. This occurs whenever all entrepreneurs abdicate their responsibilities and allow the firm to adopt well-established routines to guide its operations. As the entrepreneurial activities are reduced to well-known routines, their worth can be established in the marketplace. Entrepreneurs give way to managers. The price mechanisms now operate within and without the firm. The result is the neoclassical Marshallian firm.

The implication of the entrepreneur-centered theory for the boundary issue and the nature of resource allocation is now clear. It suggests that, in order to understand the allocative process, we must pay attention to the hybrid nature of the firm's allocative apparatus: the entrepreneurs must first allocate their own services to the various entrepreneurial tasks and then use market means to allocate tradeable factors and commodities. The important point to note is that the entrepreneur does not allocate all resources through nonmarket means. Rather, it is the unique way that the entrepreneurs allocate their own services that indirectly affects the allocation of other factors and commodities. Thus it is through the allocation of entrepreneurial services that a two-tier allocation of resources takes place in the economy. This insight constitutes the contribution of the entrepreneur-centered theory toward the understanding of how the market system functions under uncertainty.

Having observed that the firm has no objective of its own, we now raise the question regarding the theory's implications for the firm's behavior and its allocative efficiency. These are, of course, large questions, and it is not possible for us to treat them fully at this time. Here, we can only demonstrate that the proposed theory is capable of drawing both positive and normative implications, and that these implications are frequently richer than those of the traditional theory. For this purpose, we will discuss three problems: (a) the firm's response to an increase in the demand for its product, (b) the firm's selection of its size and internal composition, and (c) whether the firm allocates resources efficiently.

Response to Demand

Because a firm is a coalition of entrepreneurs with each entrepreneur using the firm to pursue his own objectives, the reaction of a firm to any external change in market conditions is necessarily more complex than in the case where the firm is assumed to have its own objective. When the market demand for a product increases, the marginal revenue of a firm producing that product will rise. The neoclassical theory of the firm unequivocally implies that the firm, in order to maximize profit, must increase the supply of its output. Under the entrepreneur-centered theory, the answer to this question is no longer simple. An increase in the market demand for a product still increases the marginal revenue of the firm; however, this increase in revenue may not be translated into a greater supply of the product. From an individual entrepreneur's point of view, an increase in the firm's revenue increases the size of the residual and thus his income. Since he seeks to fulfil objectives besides income in connection with his entrepreneurial activities, he may now desire the firm to shift its resources toward some nonpecuniary objectives. If these shifts in resources do not contribute to production, then this entrepreneur will promote policies toward a reduction in the firm's output. Moreover, even if some entrepreneur's response to the increase in the firm's product is to assign greater resources for production, the diversity of responses among the entrepreneurs must be reconciled through bargaining and through internal transfer of income. The net effect of the demand increase on the firm's production depends on this bargaining outcome. The direction of its movement is by no means always the same.

At this juncture, a historical example may be useful. There has been a constant increase in the demand for medical services since the end of the Second World War. This increase in demand has greatly increased the physician's income. In the 1950s, physicians began to form partnerships and organize clinics. The partnership and clinic form of business organization not only enabled physicians to exploit the benefits derived from economies of scale in production- and risk-pooling but also encouraged greater specialization. Physicians were interested not only in income derived from practicing medicine but also in the intellectual satisfaction and prestige associated with being a specialist. As the demand for medical services and the physicians' income increased, physicians with the aid of the clinic form of business organization shifted increasingly toward greater specialization. By the 1960s and 1970s the response to the increase in demand for medical services was a proliferation of specialties and specialists instead of a reduction in the long-standing shortages in medical services. It had left the common diseases unattended.

Not only is internal adjustment of the firm toward changes in market conditions unpredictable, the presence of transactions cost and market uncertainties also breaks the cohesiveness between market and firm adjustments toward any change in market conditions. Generally, the market takes the demand for and the supply of the commodity as given and selects a price which clears the market, whereas the firm takes the market prices as given and selects quantities, that is, the inputs employed and the outputs produced.

In a frictionless neoclassical economy, the firm and the market react to changes in the market conditions in a cohesive and harmonious manner. The market and the firm adjust concomitantly to changes in market conditions. A change in the market price of an output (input) translates immediately into changes in the employment of inputs (the supply of the output). Conversely, a change in the firms' demands for an input (supply of an output) causes a change in the factor (output) price. Thus the factor and the product markets are fully connected. A change in any part of the economy will produce a ripple effect in all parts of the economy; adjustment will take place in the firm, in the market, and in every sector of the economy until a new equilibrium is achieved. Furthermore, in making these adjustments no distinction is made between stock and flow because in a frictionless economic environment the relationship between stock and flow is fixed. The change in the stock of a factor employed in production reflects fully the flow of its services. Thus any change in the market condition instantaneously affects the market demand and supply and hence the market price. Assume that each agent can accurately forecast information available to all other agents by observing only the market prices; then the resultant change in market prices will be rationally anticipated by all agents. The new equilibrium is a rational expectations equilibrium.

The nature of adjustments made by the market and the firm in a friction-laden entrepreneur-centered production economy is quite different. The market and the firm may now react disharmoniously and incohesively to changes in market conditions. Owing to the adjustment costs, the relationship between the stock of a factor and the flow of its services is no longer fixed. Employment of the factor now differs from its utilization. This difference is made possible by accumulating inventories and decreasing specialization of the factors of production which facilitate mutual substitution among factors. With these tactics, the firm develops internal adjustment mechanisms causing the firm and the market to react syncopatically to changes in market conditions. That is, given a change in the market condition, the market price and firm's employment of inputs and production of outputs may not change in concert with each other, or a change in the market condition in one sector of the economy may not affect the market environment in another. Markets become disconnected. The disharmony between the firm and the market prevents market prices from fully revealing all private information. Each agent can no longer accurately forecast information available to all other agents by merely observing the market prices. In addition, the change in market prices caused by a change in the market condition cannot be rationally anticipated by all agents. The rational expectations equilibrium ceases to exist.

Although the rational expectations equilibrium does not exist in an entrepreneur-centered production economy, the presence of adjustment costs leads the economy to a different type of equilibrium. In the presence of adjustment costs, even though the expectations and realizations of an agent on a given outcome are different, as long as this difference falls within the limits set by these adjustment costs the agent will not change his established investment–consumption policy. Whenever all agents in the economy uphold their respective policies, despite the existence of a possibility that agents disagree with each other on the assessment of the market environment, the economy will have reached a state of equilibrium. This equilibrium is a generalized version of the Hicksian temporary equilibrium.

The General Make-up of the Firm

In chapter 6 and 7, we have dealt extensively with the way that the firm is formed and its internal decision structure is determined. However, we have ignored the issues concerning the general make-up of the firm, that is, the size of the firm, its vertical and horizontal structures, and whether it is a conglomeration of many independent functional units. We will now make amends to this negligence and examine the implication of the proposed theory on the general composition of the firm.

Many factors contribute to the physical make-up of a firm. As stated in chapter 2, when market uncertainties are absent, the firm deals primarily with the procurement of inputs, the transformation of inputs into outputs, and the marketing of its products. The internal make-up of the firm is determined primarily by technology and the size of the market. Technology determines the economies of scale in production and distribution. By comparing the extent of these economies with the size of the market, the internal organization of the firm can be objectively determined. This objective determination is possible because it does not matter who makes the decision; the choice of the firm's make-up will be the same.

When market uncertainties are present, the entrepreneurs must deal not only with the procurement of inputs, transformation of inputs into outputs, and marketing the product, but also with the management of uncertainties. In managing uncertainties, the entrepreneurs have a three-pronged strategy available to them. First, they can convert uncertainties into risks through information acquisition. Second, they can diffuse the impact of uncertainties by trading them in markets organized explicitly for these purposes; these markets include insurance, commodities, and security markets. Finally, they can shape the physical and financial make-up of the firm in such a way that it will enable the firm to bear the remaining uncertainties in the least painful way. Thus, under uncertainties the firm's physical and financial make-up is determined by the nature of the product that the firm produces, the production technology that it employs, the nature and extent of the market uncertainties that the entrepreneurs face in conducting the business, and the entrepreneurs' risk attitudes. Since we have dealt with the information issues in chapter 7 and will deal with the risk-trading aspects in chapter 10, we will now limit our attention to discussing how entrepreneurs manage uncertainties through altering the firm's physical make-up.

Managing Uncertainties through the Composition of the Firm   There are three methods by which entrepreneurs can use the firm's physical make-up to alter uncertainties faced by it. First, they can often reduce the firm's uncertainties by increasing its size. To begin with, market information is scattered among the entrepreneurs. A coalition of entrepreneurs allows them to pool private information about market characteristics and thus formulate a more accurate assessment of the market environment (Clarke, 1982, 1983). Moreover, an increase in size also enables the firm to take advantage of the law of large numbers associated with some of its operations. Inventories are customarily accumulated to deal with contingencies stemming from nonsynchronization between random variations in the demand for and the supply of a firm's products, and maintenance teams are organized to combat random failures of the firm's production equipment. Owing to the law of large numbers, the cost of coping with these contingencies does not increase proportionately with the size of the firm's operation. Consequently, the entrepreneurs can reduce the impact of these uncertainties by simply enlarging the size of the firm horizontally and producing more of the same products.

Second, in a multistage production situation, reliance on the market to allocate inputs often exposes the producers to certain types of uncertainties. These uncertainties arise from nonsynchronization in the demand and supply of inputs and outputs. When the supply of an input is not reliable, production is disrupted. This disruption in production not only causes an increase in the cost of production, but also a loss in revenue. Vertical integration facilitates the coordination of input and output flows and hence eliminates the uncertainties associated with nonsynchronization in their demand and supply.

Finally, when the random profit streams derived from the various production units are correlated statistically in an appropriate way, integrating these production units can help to stabilize the overall profits of the combined production entity. This result is in accordance with the well-known portfolio principle. This principle states that a risk-averse investor can increase his expected utility by diversifying his investment. As long as the returns to the securities are not perfectly correlated, the lower (higher) is the positive (negative) interdependence among the returns and the greater is the number of securities over which the investor is able to diversify his portfolio, the more the investor stands to gain from portfolio diversification. In the present case, instead of diversifying over financial securities, the objects of diversification are the productive assets. The entrepreneur, through diversification in production assets, lowers the uncertainties faced by the firm.

We have examined how the firm is formed as a coalition of entrepreneurs and how its internal organization is determined. We are now in position to comment on what constitutes the optimal size of the firm. Recall that, in a neoclassical competitive market, the size of the firm is determined solely by the production technology. In the entrepreneur-centered production economy, however, the size of the firm is determined in a much more complex way. Production technology, the nature of uncertainties, information and monitoring costs, and the entrepreneur's tastes and preferences all contribute to the determination of the firm size. The entrepreneur-centered theory suggests that the entrepreneurs bargain in an economy-wide setting to determine the coalition structure in the economy and the internal organization of each firm. The optimal size of each firm is simultaneously determined at equilibrium. This theory implies that a single rule to determine the optimal size of all firms does not exist and that the optimal size of a firm is coalition specific. The size of a given firm reflects the production technology adopted by the coalition, the nature of uncertainties, information and monitoring costs faced by the coalition, and the tastes, preferences, and bargaining power of the cooperating entrepreneurs.

Is Diversification of Production Assets Essential? Some have argued that even though the total profit derived from the combined unit will vary less than the sum of the profit derived from the individual production units, the total risk faced by investors is not altered by the diversification of the production assets. This is because the superior return derived from the combined firm could have been achieved by the investor's individual efforts independent of the creation of the conglomerate firm. The investor could simply assemble an appropriate portfolio of shares from independent firms and accomplish the same result for his investment. Thus, despite the stabilizing diversification effect, a conglomerate integration of independent production units *per se* does not create opportunities for risk diversification above and beyond what was possible to the investors through the use of the capital market. Consequently, no real benefit is created by a conglomerate integration of production units.

This conclusion is true only when the firm is managed by the owners as postulated in the neoclassical model; it is not valid when the firm is managed by the entrepreneurs as postulated in the proposed model. Since the pure entrepreneurs do not own capital, they cannot diversify their risks through stock portfolio selection; they must diversify by selecting a portfolio of assets through forming a coalition of entrepreneurs. Since portfolio selection in assets also reduces the risk faced by the entrepreneurs of the firm and since the entrepreneurs are risk-averse, the decrease in risk will lead to a greater level of productive activities. Because the level of outputs produced by the firm is different under stock portfolio selection made by the investors and assets portfolio selection made by the entrepreneurs, the profit stream under the two regimes will also be different. Consequently, altering the firm's internal make-up through conglomerate combination of productive assets will also aid the firm to reduce uncertainties faced by the entrepreneurs. We therefore conclude that the entrepreneurs, through a change in the physical make-up of the firm, can reduce the uncertainties faced by them. This reduction in uncertainties enables the combined firm to produce the products at a lower expected cost and to employ resources more efficiently.

So far, we have examined a passive way for the entrepreneur to manage uncertainty by altering the make-up of the firm. This way merely requires the entrepreneur to adapt the make-up of the firm to mitigate the impact of the market uncertainties. Since we have characterized the firm in an uncertain market environment as a business entity which not only offers an array of products to the consumer but also an assortment of securities to the investor, it is evident that we cannot treat the topic of uncertainty management without making reference to the financing aspect. The entrepreneurs must secure sufficient funds to finance the firm's productive activities. The introduction of financing changes the character of uncertainty management; it transforms the manipulation of the firm's composition from a passive to an active way of managing the firm's uncertainty. Generally, a change in the firm's physical make-up changes the random events underlying the distribution of returns to the firm's securities. With the marketing of the firm's securities in mind, the entrepreneurs must take the initiative to shape the physical make-up of the firm in order to present to the capital market a set of securities which is capable of yielding to the firm the desired level of finance. The active nature of uncertainty management is now apparent. The entrepreneurs not only passively adjust the firm's physical make-up in order to shoulder the uncertainties in the least painful way, they also actively shape the physical make-up of the firm in order to achieve a certain configuration of uncertainties for the firm's securities in the capital market.

Although the presence of market uncertainty affects the make-up of all firms, it does not affect them in a uniform way. Under certainty, technology and the size of the market determine the number of firms in the industry as well as the physical make-up of the firms. Because firms employ the same technology, a given physical make-up which is optimal for one firm will be optimal for another. Thus the physical make-up of firms in the same industry tends to be similar. Under uncertainty, the result is different. Because the risk preferences of the entrepreneurs are different, any physical make-up which is optimal for a given coalition of entrepreneurs may not be optimal for another. The physical make-up of firms in an industry will generally be different. This is particularly true when different coalitions of entrepreneurs wish to take a different posture in the capital market. Some, wishing to project a more conservative image, will offer securities which promise lower expected rates of return but are relatively safe, whereas others, wishing to project a more adventurous image, will offer securities which promise higher expected rates of return with greater risk. The internal make-up of the firm corresponding to the former will differ from that corresponding to the latter. Hence, under uncertainty, the physical make-ups of firms in an industry will exhibit greater diversity.

On Efficiency of Business Organizations

No theory is complete unless its implications on resource allocation have been assessed, that is, unless we have assessed whether the economic system that the theory describes is capable of allocating resources efficiently. We must now briefly deal with this question. Whether a system is efficient or not is, of course, dependent upon the definition of efficiency and the conditions under which the efficiency issue is considered. In a society whose members' preferences are often in conflict with each other, economists typically rely upon the concept of Pareto optimality to judge social welfare.

The traditional welfare analysis is conducted in a setting where the consumer and the firm are assumed to be the two independent decision units: they both take the prices as given and pursue their self-interests in a noncooperative manner. The consumer acts to maximize utility subject to a budget constraint and the firm acts to maximize profit. Through a competitive market a state of equilibrium will emerge where the utility-maximizing choices of the consumer and the profit-maximizing choices of the firm are made consistent. Since at equilibrium each agent has achieved his objective as well as he can, the resulting equilibrium allocation is obviously Pareto optimal. Moreover, in this analytical framework the presence of any nonmaximizing agent threatens to destroy Pareto optimality and yields either a wrong mix of outputs or an inefficient allocation of inputs. Thus the traditional welfare analysis holds profit-maximizing behavior as crucial to the realization of a Pareto-optimal outcome. Following this reasoning, the traditional welfare economist concludes that business organizations other than owner-managed firms contribute to inefficient allocation of resources because the non-owner-managed firms do not seek to maximize profits.

Because the neoclassical economic system and the proposed economic system are incongruent in the sense that the former assumes that all agents act noncooperatively and the latter assumes that some agents (the entrepreneurs whether pure or adjunct) act cooperatively, the welfare propositions derived under the neoclassical framework cannot be applied to the proposed system. Specifically, we cannot accept the proposition that only the owner-managed firm is an efficient business organization. The efficiency of the business organizations in the economy must be evaluated using a different criterion.

In the present economic environment, the criterion used to evaluate the efficiency of business organizations is necessarily more complex than the one used in the neoclassical economy. Whether a given business organization is efficient depends not only upon the availability of the various factor markets but also on the prevailing conditions within these markets. Suppose that all factor markets, except the entrepreneurial market, are present and are also competitive. Firms, as we have seen in chapter 6, are managed by pure entrepreneurs. Recall that in this market environment all tradeable resource owners channel their services into production through the market and pure entrepreneurs alone play the society-wide cooperative game. When a social coalitional equilibrium is reached, all exchanges conducted in the market sector lead to Pareto-optimal outcomes.[3] That is, consumers who are owners of tradeable resources will have purchased goods and sold resources in such a way that each of their utilities is maximized. Each of the entrepreneurs who plays the cooperative game has also achieved a level of utility higher than any other alternative available to him. It can thus be said that society as a whole has also achieved a Pareto-optimal level of welfare. Consequently, the entrepreneur-managed firm in this economic environment is an efficient form of business organization.

If a potentially tradeable factor finds that a market does not exist, the owners of this factor will not be able to trade its services through the marketplace. In order to channel this factor's service into production, the owners of the factor must assume the adjunct entrepreneurial role and participate in the playing of the society-wide cooperative game. As long as the remaining factor services are traded in competitive market environments, the conclusion reached in the above paragraph concerning the efficiency of the firm remains valid, except that now the optimal resource allocation is constrained by the absence of the factor market. The firms are not now managed by pure entrepreneurs; they are managed by labor entrepreneurs if the labor market is absent, by capitalist entrepreneurs if the capital market is absent, and by both types of adjunct entrepreneurs if both factor markets are absent. In these assumed market environments, all appropriate forms of business organization are efficient under the constraint that the relevant factor market is absent.

Finally, as shown in the second section of chapter 6, when all factor markets exist but are not competitive, labor-managed firms and owner-managed firms coexist with entrepreneur-managed firms. Whether one type of business organization is more efficient than another depends crucially upon the motive upon which each of these firms is organized. If the formation of a labor-managed (owner-managed) firm is motivated by the laborer's (capitalist's) desire to exploit his monopoly power, the presence of the labor-managed (owner-managed) firms will lead to inefficient allocation of resources. If, however, the function of the labor-managed (owner-managed) firm is motivated by the desire to circumvent the monopsony power wielded by the entrepreneur buyers, the organization of the labor-managed (owner-managed) firms will help to correct the misallocation of resources resulting from the presence of monopsony power in the marketplace and thus improve efficiency. It becomes apparent that, in the proposed economic system, we can no longer state unconditionally whether the labor-managed firm and/or the owner-managed firm and/or the entrepreneur-managed firm are *ipso facto* efficient business organizations. This question can no longer be answered without first knowing the market environment within which the firms conduct their businesses. Although we cannot state a priori whether the existence of an owner- or labor-managed firm causes inefficient allocation of resources, one conclusion is, however, certain – the presence of firms other than the pure-entrepreneur-managed firm implies the presence of certain market imperfections. If these market imperfections are removed, the allocative efficiency will certainly be improved.

NOTES

1 For a summary of this literature, the reader is referred to Scherer (1980, pp. 27–36).
2 Recall that a certainty equivalent price of a commodity is equal to the sum of the market contingent prices of the commodity.
3 This conclusion is valid provided that entrepreneurs do not behave opportunistically.

9

Entrepreneurs and Production Organizations from a Historical Perspective

We have now established the theme that entrepreneurs only perform services that cannot be procured in the marketplace. Thus the functions performed by the entrepreneurs must change with the market environment in which they operate. Although the product markets usually serve as the battleground for determining the entrepreneur's success and failure, in general it is the nature and availability of the factor markets that determine the degree of functional specialization among the factors of production and the scope of entrepreneurial activities. Since the development of the various factor markets followed a specific time path, the functions that the entrepreneurs performed in the past should have evolved in a predictable fashion. In this chapter we provide a brief discussion of the historical development of the various factor markets and examine production organizations and the roles played by the entrepreneurs in each stage. We will show that a historical relation does indeed exist between the market environment and the entrepreneurial functions, and that this relationship is consistent with that described in chapters 5 and 6.

Owing to the brevity of this historical survey, we wish to emphasize at the outset that it is not our intention to give the impression that there is a clear chronological division separating the various market and production institutions. On the contrary, we recognize that each stage of development is intertwined with the others. Stagnation or even regression could occur in the course of economic development, and the pattern of development among regions undoubtedly was different. Our contention is that there does exist a recognizable developmental trend toward which the historical events gravitate. The purpose of this chapter is to make clear that a trend involving the market environment, the production organization, and the functions performed by the entrepreneur does exist in history.

To achieve this objective it is neither possible nor desirable to draw on the totality of historical experience. We must limit the scope of our analysis. In this chapter we will investigate the historical relationship between the emergence of a certain type of market and the appearance of the corresponding production organization as well as the functions performed by the entrepreneurs in the industrial sectors of the economy. For this reason the approximate date to start our inquiry is around 1250 AD when the economic activities in the towns had assumed some importance (van Werveke, 1963, pp. 11–13). The chapter is divided into four sections. We deal with the early entrepreneurs of the infant market economy in the first section, with the capitalistic coordinating entrepreneurs of the putting-out system in the second section, with the innovator–entrepreneurs of the factory system in the third section, and with the pure entrepreneurs of the modern corporations in the fourth section.

THE EARLY ENTREPRENEURS

Although production was still overwhelmingly agrarian in the thirteenth century, there were once again towns where artisans and merchants congregated (de Roover, 1963). The artisans and the merchants were both motivated by profits. Artisans sought profits by converting raw materials into finished products, and merchants by trading raw materials and finished products among a clientele scattered in different marketplaces.

Production by the artisan was labor intensive and skill was essential. Even though there was little division of labor and there existed limited economies of scale in production, business frequently required more than one person. Since the market for a given type of skilled labor was either highly imperfect or did not exist at all, the labor required had to be secured by nonmarket means. The artisan trained his own assistants. In order to guard against the possibility that once trained the worker would abandon his trainer and seek work elsewhere, the trainee was required to become an indentured laborer for a limited period of time. The institution chosen by the artisans to support this arrangement was the guild system (Thrupp, 1963). Under this system, production took place in the hierarchical format of master–journeyman–apprentice.

Masters worked alongside their helpers with little differentiation in tasks. Training and production took place simultaneously – learning by doing. With the blessing of the master the apprentice aspired to become a journeyman and eventually a master. The guild system therefore offered a way for artisans to secure skilled labor services and served to control entry into the product market.[1]

Since the capital market did not exist, the artisans had to own the tools of production. However, the capital requirement was relatively small and tools were frequently made by the workers themselves. In any event, there was no separation between the producer and the means of production. Moreover, the artisans usually sold the product to the customers directly. Production and marketing were thus integrated under a single control. Finally, the artisans sold only finished products and commissioned services, and not their entire labor. In short, within the confines of rules set by the guild, the artisan–entrepreneur had complete control over the means of production, the production process and the distribution of the products.

The merchant, however, did not himself engage in physical production but earned profits through trading. He specialized in the trading of raw materials and finished products among distant markets. Sometimes he also made markets by creating the trade of commodities that had never been traded before. Since markets were islands in the midst of a self-sufficient manorial economy, they were small and highly imperfect. Knowledge of the markets and the ability to transport goods from one place to another were essential for success. Moreover, because transport facilities were primitive, the turnover rate was low; circulating capital was indispensable to the financing of long-distance trades. Since the money market was primitive and credit was expensive, the merchant had to be endowed with the necessary working capital.[2]

Thus stated, we see that the main economic function performed by the artisan and the merchant was different. The former was a skilled laborer and the latter was a knowledgeable marketeer. Nonetheless the artisan and the merchant had one thing in common: each of them was the proprietor of a business and was in control of its operation. Since all factor markets were highly imperfect or even absent, each proprietor not only had to be self-inspiring and self-mobilizing, but also had to provide from his own resources almost everything that was needed for production. In other words, the proprietor in this stage of economic development was not only a pure entrepreneur but also a laborer and capitalist all wrapped into one. He was an entrepreneur of the most inclusive type.

When the proprietor wears many hats it becomes difficult to sort out distinct entrepreneurial roles. At this stage of economic development the functional specialization among the factors of production lacked refinement. An action taken by the proprietor could be interpreted as performed by the laborer or the capitalist or the entrepreneur. For example, consider a silversmith who had designed a tool and used it to make a novel trinket. In doing so the silversmith acted simultaneously as a capitalist, a laborer, and an entrepreneur. He was a capitalist because he owned the tool; he was a laborer because he crafted the trinket; he was an entrepreneur because he alone took the initiative of making the new product and guided its production. The role of the proprietor would become even more complicated if the silversmith had demonstrated to the apprentice how the trinket was made.

It is now clear that we cannot hope to discover the true nature of the entrepreneur by examining him while still in his embryonic state of development. Knowledge of the entrepreneur can, however, be obtained by following his evolution. The remainder of this chapter relates the story of the evolution of the entrepreneur.

THE AGE OF THE CAPITALIST COORDINATOR

In this section we present the history of a long process which ultimately led the coordinating role of the merchant entrepreneur to expand, and eventually resulted in the elimination of labor from participation in the entrepreneural function following the emergence of the industrial labor market. The process was carried out in conjunction with the growth of rural industries under the kauf and putting-out systems.[3]

The expansion of interregional and international trade during the thirteenth and fourteenth centuries uncapped the feudal lords' insatiable appetite for luxury goods, which in turn induced an upward demand for the trading of commodities. As the product market expanded, the transaction cost declined and the merchant's opportunity to make profits grew accordingly. The set of tradeable commodities proliferated to include nonluxury goods. In order to capture these trading opportunities, the merchant must secure a greater quantity of commodities. For two reasons the supply of these commodities was inelastic. First the supply of labor in the towns was limited (Thrupp, 1963, p. 263). Because production was highly labor intensive, the inelastic supply of skilled labor translated naturally into an inelastic supply of the trading commodities. Second, the monopolistic guilds in the towns took advantage of the favorable market situation by forcing up prices (Thrupp, 1963, p. 247). The guilds restricted the artisans' output, controlled prices and quality, opposed the introduction of new techniques, limited access to the market, and so forth. All these practices hampered the merchant's opportunities to make profits (Kriedte et al., 1981, p. 22). The merchant–entrepreneurs sought to circumvent these artificially created shortages in the towns by turning to an alternative source of supply in the countryside. They encouraged industrial production among household producers. For two reasons this strategy was feasible. First, the decline of serfdom ultimately created a pool of labor. As the landlords relied increasingly on the market to satisfy their wants, servile labor rent was commuted to rent in kind or money rent. Monetization of rent not only made land services tradeable but also forced peasants into agriculture labor or petty commodity production (Cohen, 1978, p. 39). Second, production was labor intensive and output could be expanded by a more extensive application of labor.

The Kauf System

In the beginning the merchant performed his customary role of trading by merely interposing himself between the producer and the consumer. The petty commodity producer in the country offered a product to the merchant as an independent seller (Thrupp, 1963, p. 268). The producer controlled both the product and production. He allocated his work on the basis of his preference over income and leisure. His objective was to earn an additional income in order to supplement his agrarian production (Kriedte et al., 1981, pp. 44–5). The merchant was happy with the arrangement because there was an abundant supply of household producers which enabled him to meet the increased demand for the finished products.

However, the equal partnership between the merchant and the household producer was inherently unstable. As the demand for the trading commodities increased further, the supply of the household producer ceased to be perfectly elastic. The merchant could no longer rely upon extensive application of labor to expand his trading activities. Other methods of expansion had to be devised. This was accomplished by taking advantage of a finer division of labor through vertical disintegration in production.

Vertical disintegration in production was made possible because there existed an informational asymmetry between the petty commodity producer and the merchant (Marglin, 1974). The merchant, who had information about the market, saw the relationship between demand and supply. The rural commodity producers, however, did not deal with the customers directly and were ignorant about the markets in faraway places. The information asymmetry gave the initiative for decisions to the merchant.

Thus the merchant, who knew market demand and supply and understood how each stage of production fitted into the whole scheme, began to augment the supply of the finished product by promoting greater division of labor through vertical disintegration in production. Petty commodity producers were encouraged to specialize in the production of a particular semifinished product (Kriedte et al., 1981, pp. 108–9). Specializing in production increased output because it enabled the household producer to gain efficiency in production by repetitive application of a given task. The merchant, who knew how each stage of production fitted into the whole scheme, would then arrange to put the separate parts together into a marketable finished product. The disintegration in production had indeed augmented the merchant's ability to supply the finished goods; however, it was accomplished by depriving the petty commodity producer of his prerogative to make decisions on what to produce and how to produce it. This surrendering of decision-making prerogatives marked the beginning of the decline of the household as an independent unit of production (Marglin, 1974, p. 91).

Now the merchant not only performed his traditional marketing role but had expanded his activities into the realm of coordinating the production. With the expansion of his roles, the merchant's authority in production also increased. Once the merchant gained the upper hand in influencing production decisions, it was natural for him to consolidate his control over production by owning the raw materials as well as the tools of production. This ushered in the putting-out system.

The Putting-out System

Owing to frequent changes in styles and occasional introductions of new products, demand for commodities fluctuated in distant market-places. All advantages accrued to the merchants who could bring the desired products to the market quickly. Because the control of production was in the hands of the petty commodity producer, this meant that a successful merchant must persuade the producer to make goods that were in demand. Often the power of persuasion was enhanced if the merchant could provide the household producer with the raw materials, circulating capital, and new tools needed for producing these products. The putting-out system thus emerged. By assuming the burden of owning the tools and providing the circulating capital, the merchants became capitalists. Increasingly the petty commodity producer worked only on the commission of the putting-out merchant and became more dependent upon the merchant for his livelihood.

After centuries of growth, the economic conditions which fostered the development of the putting-out system had undergone funda-mental change. This change produced profound consequences. It revealed the inherent contradiction that existed between the house-hold and the merchant (Kriedte et al., 1981, pp. 108–9), greatly increased the supervisory cost to the merchant, and accelerated the growth of the industrial labor market.

The contradiction between the household producer and the

merchant arose from a difference in their motives for production. To the average petty commodity producer the goal of production was to achieve a livelihood. He was interested in the use value of the commodities that he could obtain with his product through exchange (Kriedte et al., 1981, p. 41). The principle guiding the allocation of his production activity was his preference for consumption and leisure. As the price of this product rose, the income of the household increased. Since there was an upper limit on the use value of the commodities he consumed, the income effect was negative, translating into a decrease in the supply of labor. The household's supply curve of the commodity frequently bent backward (Kriedte et al., 1981, p. 100).

The merchant's motive for economic activity was entirely different. He was concerned more with maximizing profits. His actions were determined by the exchange value of his product, and not its use value. An increase in the price of the commodity would increase his income, and since the merchant's desire for income was insatiable his response to an increase in the demand for his commodity was to expand his trading activity. His supply for the commodity was therefore price elastic.

Because the merchant's ability to supply the commodity was dependent upon the willingness of the household to produce it, a contradiction arose whenever the supply of the petty commodity producer restricted the merchant. To overcome the lack of co-operation from the household, the merchant ultimately sidestepped it by moving production to a centralized workshop – the factory – and putting workers under direct supervision (Ashton, 1962, p. 109; Marglin, 1974, p. 82).

Although the inherent contradiction between the household producer and the merchant provided the major impetus for the reorganization of the mode of production, there were other factors. As the putting-out system reached maturity households ceased to engage in all stages of production. Even in linen-producing regions, where only local flax and hemp were used, it was exceptional to see cultivation, processing of raw materials into yarn, and weaving all performed in the same household (Kriedte et al., 1981, p. 106). Eventually, specialization by individual laborers became so advanced that it was more economical to secure specialized workers than to rely on a single family to supply the work for all stages of production. In fact, even within a single family unit each individual had begun to specialize in a given task and had become an independent laborer (Kriedte et al., 1981, p. 107).

In turn, this development yielded two important consequences. First, as production became more specialized, supervision cost increased. Supervision cost became particularly high when the various stages of production were scattered in different locations. The costs placed constant pressure on the merchant's profit. The erosion of profits became more acute when the merchants owned the raw materials and tools of production. The domestic producer used them without proper care, and material waste tended to be high. Pilfering was also common. Furthermore, the merchant would want his tools to be used fully at all times. Since the merchant did not have full control over the production process under the putting-out system, full utilization of capital could not be guaranteed. In any case, workers in the backward-bending portion of their supply curve had no interest in running the machinery at full tilt.

Second, specialization of production among members of the household destroyed the household as a production unit. Each working member of the family now became an independent worker. Furthermore, when products became interchangeable the marginal productivity of labor could be measured. Now one standard laborer's work became equivalent to that of another and the market for industrial labor thus emerged. Once an industrial labor market came into existence, it was only a matter of time until the factory system was adopted. The factory system of production enabled the capitalist to curb the worker's freedom (Marglin, 1974, p. 102; Marx, 1967, chapter 13). Thus, it was the emergence of the labor market which dealt the final blow to the putting-out system.

The Coordinating Entrepreneur

As we have said, in the early stages of rural industrial development, the household producer and the merchant were equal partners – both entrepreneurs in their own right. These entrepreneurs, however, were embryonic in character; they performed all necessary tasks. The household producer specialized in the physical creation of the commodities while the merchant specialized in marketing them. Under the putting-out system coordination of production transferred into the hands of the putting-out merchant. Profits now depended heavily on how efficiently the merchant could exploit the advantage of the division of labor in the production of the semifinished products and how cheaply the merchant could assemble the finished product. Thus the coordinating role of the merchant–entrepreneur expanded enormously. The promotion of specialization among the petty commodity producers, however, represented only an initial effort made by the merchant to augment profit. His influence would again increase when he elected to become the owner of both raw materials and tools of production. The putting-out merchant's ability to control the production process, however, was never complete. Only under the factory system had the capitalist's control over production become absolute.

While the merchant expanded his coordinating role, the petty commodity producer's role as entrepreneur underwent a steady decline. These changes hastened the development of the industrial labor market. As we have mentioned earlier, the decline of serfdom not only encouraged petty commodity production but also forced peasants into agricultural labor. Now the expansion of the merchant's role, in turn, caused the petty commodity producers to separate from the means of production and gave them nothing to sell but their labor power. They were now a part of the labor pool. The industrial labor market was further aided by population growth and the enclosure movement. Estates were enclosed and consolidated in England between the mid seventeenth and eighteenth centuries. Some historians believe that many copyholders and small freeholders either lost their claims to the land or sold out. They also became part of the industrial labor force (Ashton, 1962, p. 26; Mingay, 1968; Cohen and Weitzman, 1975).

The development of the labor market inevitably leads toward the functional specialization of labor. As the industrial labor markets emerged in the seventeenth and eighteenth centuries, entrepreneurs preferred to purchase labor services from the market and thus shed the labor role. If the labor market were perfect, then there would be no advantage for labor in retaining the adjunct entrepreneurial status; the specialization of the labor function would have been completed. Unfortunately, because the early labor markets were highly imperfect, we must await the specialization of the labor function until a much later date.

THE AGE OF INNOVATORS

The change from the putting-out system to the factory system was due not so much to the technical superiority of the early factories as to their supervisory efficiency. Because labor could now be procured in the market place it became possible for production to be organized under a single roof. Though workers were now in a centralized place, the different stages of production were still independent of each other. The factory merely performed tasks formerly entrusted to the household producers. Synchronization still needed to be achieved. The entrepreneur was still a coordinator.

Nonsynchronization of productive activities manifested as a bottleneck among the various stages of production. Traditionally synchronization required painful adjustment in the supply of skilled labor. Now, with the development of the industrial labor market, the entrepreneur shed the labor role. Since the entrepreneur ceased to be a laborer, his approach to solving the bottleneck problem created by the shortage of labor took a different turn. He sought through mechanical innovation to substitute the skill of a laborer by the precision of a machine. The entrepreneur now took on the role as innovator.

Ostensibly, the Industrial Revolution was the story of innovation frequently motivated by entrepreneurs' attempt to remove bottlenecks in production. It is usually illustrated by the development of the woolen and cotton textile industry (Mantoux, 1962). In cotton textile production the two basic processes were spinning and weaving. In order to synchronize production in any given period of time the amount of thread spun must correspond to the amount of cloth that can be woven. In 1733, skilled weavers were replaced by John Kay's flying shuttle which increased the speed of weaving and made it possible to weave wider materials, thus greatly increasing the demand for cotton cloth. Better weaving, however, led to great shortages in yarn. Spinners were then replaced by mechanical spinning machines in the 1770s, producing an abundance of yarn. Once again the bottleneck shifted to the weaving stage of production, which eventually led to the power loom. All stages of cotton textile production could now be synchronized by a mere adjustment in the number of machines used at each stage. Similar stories of innovation can be told for many other industries.

Thus said, the factory was not the effect of technical innovation but its cause. Technology developed because the factory system allowed the entrepreneur to shift his attention from exploiting the profit opportunities existing under the natural division of labor to those that could be obtained under an organized division of labor aided by improvement in technology. In addition, the factory system also provided a congenial climate for innovation to take place; it ensured that the innovator would retain the property rights created by innovation and could therefore capture the benefits derived from it (Marglin, 1974, p. 90). All told, the factory system helped to transform the entrepreneur into an innovator.

The substitution of machines for skilled labor not only changed the fundamental process of production but also frequently decreased the average skill of labor required for mass production. The laborer, instead of using tools to help himself create a product, now tended the machine. Unskilled labor's productivity increased enormously. At the turn of the nineteenth century, "Two steam looms operated by a fifteen-year-old boy, could weave three and one half pieces material, while in the same time a skilled weaver, using the flying shuttle, wove only one" (Mantoux, 1962, p. 244).

Mechanization of production also brought economies associated with large-scale production and increased the capital requirement. For example, a spinning factory in 1775 had a capitalization of approximately £5,000 and a machine shop doubling that amount (Beard, 1969). Though it was not uncommon for a single wealthy individual to own several factories, it was also true that such an undertaking frequently involved more than one individual. Joint enterprise became increasingly common.

Since no market existed for inventors and the capital market was far from perfect, in order to succeed in business the partners had to supply the capital and frequently the inventiveness as well as the entrepreneurial talents. The firm ceased to be led by an entrepreneur who was at the same time a capitalist, innovator, etc. It became a coalition of entrepreneurial-minded owners of resources, though every member of the coalition did not need to be a capitalist and an inventor.

To put it differently, in the absence of satisfactory factor markets, to participate in production the capitalist and the inventor must each assume the entrepreneurial role. This, however, does not imply that the entrepreneur must be a capitalist or an inventor. The most illustrious entrepreneur in this era was Richard Arkwright. In the words of Mantoux:

> He (Arkwright) was no inventor. At the most, he arranged, combined and used the invention of others which he never scrupled to appropriate for his own ends.... Arkwright's real claim to fame lies in the fact that he was ... the first who knew how to make something out of other men's inventions, who built them up into an industrial system.... In order to raise the necessary capital for his undertakings, in order to form and dissolve those partnerships which he used successively as instruments with which to make his fortune, he must have displayed remarkable business ability, together with a curious mixture of cleverness, perseverance and daring.... He personifies the new type of the great manufacturers, neither an engineer nor a merchant, but adding to the main characteristics of both qualifications peculiar to himself: Those of a founder of great concern, an organizer of production and a leader of man. (Mantoux, 1962, p. 233)

Thus Arkwright – the champion of the modern factory system, and the entrepreneur par excellence – was neither a capitalist nor an inventor.

THE AGE OF THE PURE ENTREPRENEUR

By the end of the nineteenth century the economy had undergone another marked transformation associated with the emergence of the modern corporation. The entrepreneur had shed the capitalist role and had, at long last, assumed the pure form.

The Corporation

The joint-stock company was the forerunner of the modern corporation. It first appeared in the fourteenth century when several parties would join together in partnership to carry out a specific trading venture. Such a partnership would dissolve at the conclusion of the venture, whether successful or not. In 1599 the British East Indian merchants asked for and received the privilege of engaging in a perpetual succession of trades, giving the joint-stock company a certain degree of permanency. Dissolution would take place only with the resignation of a partner. With the establishment of the Mine Royal Charter of 1625, companies were allowed to issue transferable shares. This meant that the joint-stock company could exist independently of the personalities of its shareholders. Death or resignation of a partner no longer mandated liquidation.

The partners of the joint-stock company were still held responsible for their own debts incurred on behalf of the company's business activities; the company as an entity could not incur debts for its partners. In 1855 incorporation with limited liability became generally available, giving birth to the modern corporation.

Although the modern corporate form of business organization was made legal in England during the 1850s and in the United States at approximately the same time, most resources were under the control of partnerships for decades to follow. In the United States, incorporation was for a long time an elaborate procedure which required the passage of a special act in the legislature (Purdy et al., 1950, chapter 3). Even though some states had adopted general acts of incorporation the term of the law governing incorporation was still not in the corporation's favor. Further, economies of scale in production were still relatively small. The largest textile factory did not require capital beyond the means of a single wealthy individual. Rolling mills could be built for less than $150,000 (Robertson and Walton, 1979 p. 95). In fact, Andrew Carnegie and his partner Edgar Thomson each contributed only $20,000 to form the Carnegie Steel Company (Kirkland, 1961, p. 217). The firms in the petroleum industry were also small: a refinery cost between $10,000 and $50,000 (Kirkland, 1961, p. 217). In 1888, the original capitalization of the Pittsburgh Reduction Company, the forerunner of the Aluminum Company of America (ALCOA), was merely $20,000 (Purdy et al., 1950, p. 203). Under these circumstances there was no great urgency for producers to adopt the corporate form.

All this changed quickly toward the end of the nineteenth century.

The state of New Jersey – the "mother of trusts" – led the liberalization of the incorporation law, introducing a simple procedure for incorporation, assessing low corporate fees and taxes, removing the limitations on the duration of corporate charters, and allowing the corporation to issue different types of stock and to hold stock in other companies. Changes in the incorporation law by the states stimulated a merger movement between 1885 and 1904. More fundamentally, decades of improvement in communications and transportation had broadened the market from the local to the national level. The worldwide recession in 1882 led to excess capacity and cut-throat competition; merger by way of incorporation became a popular solution. By the end of the nineteenth century, a large number of industries were dominated by giant corporations. For example, in 1860 there were more than 300 petroleum refineries, by 1870 there were 150, and by 1879 the Standard Oil Company owned over 90 percent of American refining capacity. The stories are similar in many other industries serving national markets (Scherer, 1980, pp. 119–40).

Although avoidance of destructive competition served as a powerful incentive for incorporation through merger, the innovator also sought to incorporate in order to gain immediate possession of the fruits of his inventive efforts. Under the proprietorship and partnership forms of business, payoffs to innovation can only be realized over time through the sale of the product. Since the present share value of the corporation reflects the expected profit stream that its inventions generate, the incorporated innovator can transfer his future gains to the present. Shares can be sold at once to finance production. The tendency toward incorporation was further strengthened by the later advances in technology. It is fair to say that technical economies of scale were not an important factor in bringing about the giant firms before the turn of the century. Technical economies became a factor only after Henry Ford had made automation a common mode of production. The immense increase in the optimal scale of production during the present century implied that larger and larger amounts of capital were needed. The capitalization of ALCOA in 1907 reached $20 million (Purdy et al. 1950, p. 203). With this kind of capital requirement, it became evident that the financing of production now exceeded the capability of even the wealthiest individuals. Business organizations were generally forced to change from partnerships to corporations. By the turn of the century, corporations were firmly entrenched in business.

Emergence of the Pure Entrepreneur

With the liberalization of incorporation laws, the stock market became a source of capital. This development paved the way for further refinement of the entrepreneurial role and division of labor between the entrepreneur and the capitalist. As we have noted, once a firm is organized it becomes possible to convert a portion of the future stream of profit into present wealth. Only a portion of this stream can be converted into present wealth because under uncertainty the decisions of the firm must be made sequentially. Since these decisions influence profits, entrepreneurs can never dissociate themselves from the firm's process of decision-making. They must remain in control of production and are limited in their return to the size of the residual. However, the ability to realize at least a portion of the future stream of profits implied that a coalition of entrepreneurs could now gain access to capital needed for production by means of the capital market and thus could shed the financing role associated with the pure capitalist.

The stock market also enabled the capitalist to relinquish control of the corporations. From the capitalist investor's point of view, the stock market offered a new outlet for investment and a new way for him to manage his investments. Before the last quarter of the nineteenth century, the investor had only two investment outlets: he could invest his money in the bond market or directly in capital assets which would require him to tie up his money for relatively long periods of time. After the modernization of the stock market, it became possible to trade capital stock; this made shares of equity a relatively liquid form of investment. Since the stock certificate of a given company is a standardized contract with detailed terms, all shares of the same company are homogeneous. The market value of a share reflects the probability distribution of its returns. As we will see in chapter 10, the stocks of different companies can be compared and grouped into various homogeneous classes on the basis of such probability distributions. Thus the investor, through portfolio selection and diversification, can ensure a satisfactory rate of return to his investments.

In the presence of the stock market, control of the production process is no longer a necessary condition for the investor to guarantee a satisfactory rate of return. He now can achieve the same objective through diversification. As we have mentioned in chapter 6, the information requirements to guarantee a satisfactory rate of return directly from production and indirectly from a stock portfolio are very different. The former requires the investor to gain access to specific (and often secret) information about the company. The latter requires only market information, which companies will have a clear incentive to make available to the investors. Costs of gathering both types of information exist but they differ markedly. As the stock market matured the cost of acquiring market financial data of firms decreased sharply. Therefore it is not surprising that since the turn of the century more and more investors have given up making investments which required controlling production and have opted instead for investments in portfolios of securities. The capitalists abandoned the entrepreneurial role and became mere lenders of funds and risk-bearers. They left the control of the production process in the hands of the pure entrepreneurs.

Thus at long last the stock market and the laws governing incorporation became mature and the entrepreneur and the capitalist no longer needed to form a coalition. Since landlord and labor had long ago left the coalition, the long historical evolution toward functional specialization among the factors of production had reached its destination.

CONCLUSION

History fits well with the characterization of the entrepreneur described in chapter 5:

> Entrepreneurs control what to produce and how to produce it. They gain command over resources and control over production in order to carry out their production plan. Since the outcome of the plan is uncertain, the entrepreneurs cannot claim the rewards for their services *ex ante*; they are residual claimants. The entrepreneurial functions cannot be prescribed in detail: they are all things but routine. Moreover, their functions vary with the market environment. One thing is certain, however: entrepreneurs only perform those services that cannot be procured in the factor markets.

In the early stage of entrepreneurial history, when the factor markets were not developed, there were no pure entrepreneurs. In order to produce at all, the entrepreneur had to gain control of all required resources through nonmarket means. Since the size of the production unit was small, the entrepreneur himself often possessed all the resources required for production; he was a self-sufficient composite entrepreneur.

As the market and the production unit expanded the composite entrepreneur often became a coalition of several entrepreneurs who jointly controlled the enterprise and shared the residual. The reward to each member of the partnership was determined through bargaining. As the market continued to expand and the market for industrial labor developed, labor relinquished the entrepreneurial role and the entrepreneurs shed the labor functions. Entrepreneurs now gained control over the laborer's services by purchasing them in the marketplace. Specialization between labor and nonlabor functions in production thus appeared. Later the capital market in manufacturing also developed. The capitalists now relinquished their entrepreneurial role, while the entrepreneurs shed their financing function. Control of the production initiative and the production process was now left entirely in the hands of the pure entrepreneurs. Since the land services market had been developed for a long time, with the development of the labor and capital markets, functional specialization among the factors of production was complete.

The presence of land, labor, and capital markets has provided the opportunity for landlords, laborers, and capitalists to relinquish their entrepreneurial roles. Landlords become suppliers of natural resources; laborers become those who directly engage in the production and marketing of the commodities and routine management; capitalists become those who lend money and bear risks on capital investments. The control of the production process is left entirely to the pure entrepreneur.

Although this principle is well understood by economists, nonetheless there exist seemingly insurmountable controversies on the implications of the growth of factor markets. The followers of Karl Marx view the labor market as a campground for the reserve army of surplus workers, whereas the industrial economists view the development of the modern capital market as detrimental to the interests of capitalists. In either case, the development of a factor market, though a natural progression of economic development, is treated as detrimental to the factor owner in question. These economists insist that the development of factor markets hastens the manifestation of inherent contradictions within the capitalistic system. We disagree with this assessment. In our view, the development of any market does not in the long run lead to any contradiction.

Specifically, the followers of Marx view the development of the labor market as necessary for the creation of surplus, and the creation of surplus as necessary for capital accumulation and economic development. Capitalist industry creates a surplus value because the value of output produced by labor with the assistance of capital exceeds the wage cost of labor. This surplus was used by the capitalist to increase the capital stock so that more labor power could be combined with it to generate even greater surplus. This process eventually leads to a contradiction because of the "law of the falling tendency of the rate of profit." In chapter 2 we noted that the rate of profit defined by Marx is $s/(c + v)$, where s, c, and v are respectively surplus, constant capital, and circulating capital (mainly wage fund). Because surplus can be created only by circulating capital, as the capital stock c increases, the rate of profit falls. At the same time, growth of accumulation also stimulates the demand for labor power and causes wages to increase. Rising wages further depress profit.

Finally, the consumption of the masses is restricted by low wages and mass unemployment; therefore the economy lacks purchasing power. Diminishing rate of profit and underconsumption ultimately lead to a state of overproduction, discourage further accumulation, and precipitate a crisis in the capitalist system. Thus according to the Marxists, the labor market, which was developed to facilitate extraction of surplus and capital accumulation, ultimately contributes to the demise of the capitalist system.

In our view, the development of this labor market is neither a necessary nor a sufficient mechanism for extraction of surplus value from the workers. Laborers were exploited as serfs and slaves long before the labor market came into existence. It is true that laborers are again exploited in labor markets where monopsony power prevails. Exploitation of marketed labor was common when the labor market was young and highly imperfect, but from a long historical perspective the exploitation was transitory. The continuing development of the labor market in fact offers the laborer the best safeguard. Standardization of labor services makes one laborer's services interchangeable with another's and one employer's work equivalent to that of another's, contributing to the mobility of labor and extending the size of the labor market. This extension of the labor market diminishes monopoly power of the employers and ensures that the workers will receive a compensation commensurate with their productivities. Exploitation of labor ceases to take place. The growth in the competitiveness of the labor market therefore offers the laborers the ultimate safeguard against exploitation.

The development of the capital market has been greeted with equal suspicion. The capitalist who was the exploiter of labor is now viewed as the subject of exploitation. The source of this exploitation stems from the growth of the large corporations. The literature, which follows Berle and Means (1932), considers that the corporate form of organization is the cause of the separation of ownership and control which, in turn, leads to a low profit rate, a low growth rate, and a slow rate of innovation.

These claims, as we have seen in chapter 8, are not corroborated by evidence. As in the case of labor, the fact that the capitalist had relinquished control of production did not, in itself, imply that he became a subject of exploitation. To be sure, the capitalist can also be exploited by the monopsonistic entrepreneur, but as the capital market grows and becomes more efficient, the opportunity for exploitation again vanishes.

The expansion of the capital market offers the firm greater opportunities to secure financing and provides the investor with wider investment alternatives. The increase in investment alternatives enhances the investors' bargaining power and diminishes the firm's ability to exercise its monopsonistic control. As the investors gain wider investment opportunities, the firm must compete for their funds and must offer potential investors more favorable terms. As we will see in the next chapter, the demand for a firm's share, *ceteris paribus*, depends on the probability distribution of the firm's residual, the percentage of the residual allocated to the shareholders as dividends, and the price of shares. Specifically, the demand for the firm's shares increases with an improvement in the firm's probability distribution of returns and with an increase in the percentage of residual allocated to the shareholders; it decreases with an increase in the share price. Since the firm issues shares for the purpose of financing its initial production, it must charge a sufficiently high price for its shares in order to obtain the required funds. In order to make this possible the firm must generate a sufficiently attractive distribution of returns and must allocate a sufficiently high percentage of the residual to the shareholders. Consequently, in order to avoid jeopardizing the firm's ability to raise funds in the capital market, the entrepreneurs must protect the value of shares as jealously as the capitalist would and must offer the investors a satisfactory rate of return. Hence if the capital market is efficient, disparity between the entrepreneurs and the capitalists will disappear. In short, entrepreneurs can claim a disproportionate part of the residual only if they possess excess monopsony power. Exploitation of the capitalist by the entrepreneur is again a strict consequence of imperfection in the capital market.

Our analysis suggests that it is the presence of monopsony powers in the factor markets, and not the emergence of these markets themselves, that led to the exploitation of the factor owners. To eradicate exploitation, the proper course of action should not be the removal of the markets but the removal of market imperfections. The market is improved by an infusion of market information, a reduction in transaction cost, and an enlargement of market size. These improvements in market efficiency ultimately serve to ensure that each factor receives a payment commensurate with its productivity and to guarantee that no exploitation will take place.

Even when monopsony power does exist in the factor markets, entrepreneurs' activities also serve to soften its impact. Resource owners who "have greater confidence in themselves than the market has in them" will take up the entrepreneurial role. If monopsony power exists in the labor market, some laborers may prefer to join the ranks of the pure entrepreneurs by forming a coalition in production, instead of selling their labor in the marketplace. This occurs whenever the laborer believes that, by pooling his resources and talent with the pure entrepreneur and by participating in the control of the production process and jointly claiming the residual, he can accomplish more than the market has in store for him. If laborers alone join a coalition, a labor-managed firm results; the residual consists of the wage–profit combination. The same reasoning holds for capitalists. If capitalists alone join a coalition, an owner-managed firm emerges; the residual consists of the dividend–profit combination. Thus, in order to escape exploitation, capitalists and laborers abandon their respective markets by becoming adjunct entrepreneurs. In so doing they avoid the consequence of market imperfection and claim an expected higher return in the form of a residual. Since a residual is a joint return to combined services, it obscures the nature of the return to the entrepreneur and leads to confusion in the literature about the roles of entrepreneurs in production. History makes the distinctions clear.

Although the main purpose of this chapter is to develop the theme that the characteristics of the entrepreneur evolved with the development of the factor markets, this historical study, together with the material presented in chapter 5, also enables us to shed some light on the process of economic development.

There are many competing theories of economic development. The following are some examples in the literature. The classical economists based their theory of economic development on division of labor, capital accumulation, population growth, and technological progress. The Marxists identify dialectical materialism and the struggle over the appropriation of surplus among people in different classes as the driving force of human history. The German National Economic School and the neomercantilists emphasize conscious national policy as the source of economic development. The followers of Schumpeter believe that the process of creative destruction via innovation is the fundamental engine of economic progress.

Our analysis suggests a different theme. Economic development is a process of adaptive evolution involving the entrepreneur and the market. The entrepreneur and the market constantly stimulate each other into changes which reflect the ceaseless struggle between them, each wishing to gain the upper hand in the marketplace.

Despite the fact that there is no market for entrepreneurial services, the entrepreneurs need the market to procure the inputs required and to sell their products. Because the entrepreneurs must use the market to carry out their production activities, these activities necessarily stimulate growth of the market. The merchant stimulated market growth by promoting exchanges and creating new markets, the petty commodity producer did so by converting household consumption goods into cash products, the putting-out merchant did so by reducing the cost of production through improvement in production co-ordination, and later the factory owners did so by introducing new production technology and new products. Thus, in attempting to find unique ways of securing profits, the entrepreneurs create markets that never existed before, undertake risks others found to be intolerable, organize production more efficiently than previously, and produce new goods to satisfy existing or new wants.

The market, in contrast, responds to entrepreneurial stimuli by enlarging its size and expanding its scope. Existing markets become larger and new markets come into being. The profit opportunities created by the entrepreneurs also attract imitation and competition. Competition improves the quality of the market. Moreover, enlargement of existing markets and introduction of new markets also encourage greater division of labor and standardization of products. These developments offer further profit opportunities for the creative entrepreneur. This mutual stimulation between the market and the entrepreneurs goes on endlessly.

The development of a market is by no means instantaneous, as attested to by the earlier description of the growth of land, labor, and capital markets. The early stage of a market is necessarily imperfect. Market imperfections invite the strong trading partner to exploit the weak. However, the ingenious entrepreneurial quality of the oppressed partner will find ways of escaping exploitation and encouraging the development of countervailing power in the market place. The shift in the source of supply from the artisans to the petty commodity producers and the formation of non-entrepreneur-managed firms in the modern economy are cases in point. In the end, the entrepreneurial activities again increase the size and scope of the market and improve its quality.

The lesson we learned from this historical study is that both the nature of the entrepreneur and the character of the market evolve over time as a result of interactions between the entrepreneur and the market. Through these interactions product and factor markets developed and the quality of these markets improved. Moreover, through ceaseless entrepreneurial activities, the market is brought into a constant flux. Different products and technologies are introduced, and different inputs are in demand. Profit opportunities are created. Other entrepreneurs, through the market, attempt to share the profit opportunities by imitation. In this way, entrepreneurs' activities not only benefit themselves but also through imitation and competition enhance the welfare of society.

Beneficial as it can be, the entrepreneurial contribution to society is often at odds with the entrepreneur's self-interest. Economic progress can achieve its maximum potential only when the entrepreneur's ability to exploit advantages derived from past contributions and the market's propensity through competition to diffuse these advantages are delicately balanced. Because entrepreneurial services are not prescribable, it is natural to assume that each entrepreneur is unique, that is, each entrepreneur possesses the monopoly over the services which he performs. Because the entrepreneurs organize and control production, the tendency is for them to extend this monopoly of their own services to the product and factor markets. If the entrepreneur gains the upper hand, the markets become monopolistic. It is well known that the presence of monopoly elements in the market will cause under-utilization of economic resources and loss of social welfare. If the market gains the upper hand, the outcome is equally unsatisfactory. Although competition in the market has the propensity of eradicating monopoly influences, excess competition may also destroy the uniqueness of the entrepreneurs and decrease their worth. Excess competition decreases profit opportunities and incentives for the entrepreneurs to offer their services. Although reduction in entrepreneurial activities does not stop production activities, it does reduce these activities to the routine types and hence leads to economic stagnation. Thus a high rate of economic progress can be sustained only when entrepreneurial advantages and market competition have reached a balance; that is, competition is sufficient to eradicate excess monopoly elements in the market but it is not enough to destroy the uniqueness of entrepreneurs. It is this balance between the entrepreneur's uniqueness and the competitive force in the marketplace which leads to the efficient allocation of resources over time and orderly economic progress. The struggle between the entrepreneur and the market is a tug-of-war. Only when the opposing forces are in balance will society achieve its maximum benefit.

NOTES

1 In addition, the guild also controlled the quality of outputs and limited price competition.
2 This does not mean that capital could not be acquired from nonmarket arrangements. For a description of the development in early money market see Bernard (1971).
3 For an excellent description of these systems, see Kriedte et al. (1981).

10

On the Theory of Profits

The fundamental problems facing the economist have been the determination of values for goods and services, the identification of conditions for efficient utilization of resources, the discovery of laws governing economic development and distribution of products, and the understanding of the principle for combating persistent under-employment of resources. A workable theory of value and the concept of efficient resource allocation emerged with the general equilibrium analysis of the economy. However, the remaining problems are still unsolved. Regarding the issues concerning distribution, the prevailing theories of wages and rent enjoy a general acceptance among economists. The major difficulty for economists has been the lack of a clear understanding concerning the origins of interest income and profits. The key to unraveling these outstanding problems regarding the distribution of income is to find the source of profit. Because interest and profit are intimately intertwined, once the nature of profit is clearly understood the concept of interest will also become clear.

Since profit is widely attributed as a return to the entrepreneur, the confusion surrounding the profit puzzle is related to the lack of a clear understanding of entrepreneurship. Entrepreneurs are regarded as any or all of the following: residual claimant, innovator, risk-bearer, prime mover of the market process, ingenious manager, monopolist, etc. It is not surprising that profit is regarded correspondingly as implicit rent, reward for innovation, reward for risk-bearing, interest and wages, monopoly earnings, and any residual or surplus, as well as exploitation of labor in the Marxist framework. Because there does not exist a consistent and coherent theory of the entrepreneur, we naturally find confusion in profit theory.

Without a clear concept of entrepreneurship, economists traditionally examine profits from two points of view: profit is either a payment to a factor of production or a surplus over costs. When profit is treated as a payment to a factor, it becomes a cost of production. This view posits a direct relationship between the profit income and that factor's contribution to production. When profit is treated as a surplus, it is defined as revenue minus costs. This view denies a functional relationship between the contribution to production made by the factor which receives the profit income and the size of that income.

These two views are inconsistent. Profit as a payment to a factor implies that the marginal productivity of that factor is known. Through competition and imputation, the size of the profit is equalized between all firms in the economy. Through entry and exit of firms, profit vanishes altogether. Therefore, in the end, no surplus exists. This outcome is distressing for several reasons. The promise of profit is commonly believed to serve as the motive for "entrepreneurs" to initiate productive activities. If the payoff for these activities is zero, why would the entrepreneur, who sets out to seek profit, be willing to receive nothing at all? Moreover, in the capitalist economy a permanent profit income exists empirically.[1] Therefore the zero-profit outcome is inconsistent with the evidence.

Profit as a surplus is also difficult to defend. The difficulty arises when deciding what constitutes cost and, more importantly, why the differential between revenue and costs should persist. Without defining precisely what costs are, it is impossible to determine the size of the profits. The controversies generated by the classical economists can be traced precisely to this source. Even if the costs can be determined unambiguously, there still exists the question of why profits persist. The existence of profits must be tied to productive nature of the factor which claims residual as the return to its contribution in production.

Because of this inconsistency, neither view alone can be accepted as a valid explanation of profit. A valid profit theory must simultaneously explain profit as a return to the factor of production – the entrepreneur – and as the lone residual income.

Our theory of the entrepreneur, presented in chapters 5 and 6, suggests a natural resolution of the profit puzzle. Recall that, because entrepreneurial services are highly susceptible to moral hazards, the entrepreneur is the only factor of production for which a market to trade his services will never exist. Hence, entrepreneurial income can never become a contractual income. Yet when market uncertainties prevail, the entrepreneurial function is absolutely indispensable for production to take place. If there is no entrepreneur, there will be no production. Entrepreneurial services can be mobilized only by entrepreneurs themselves. Entrepreneurs must take the initiative to organize production through nonmarket means, that is, by organizing a firm. The entrepreneurs now receive a return for their services by capturing the residual. Because the value of the entrepreneurial services cannot be determined *ex ante* and is determined *ex post*, entrepreneurial return depends upon the quality of the entrepreneur's efforts and on chance. In this sense, it is reasonable for us to claim that profit is, at the same time, a reward and a surplus.

In order to judge the plausibility of the proposed theory of profits we need to summarize the existing literature, take stock of what we have learned from it, and critically examine its shortcomings. In this way we can clearly see the point of departure of the proposed profit theory. Accordingly, this chapter is divided into four sections. The classical profit theories and the profit theories of Knight and Schumpeter are summarized in the first and second sections respectively, the proposed profit theory is presented in the third section, and the implications of this theory are examined in the fourth section.

CLASSICAL PROFIT THEORIES

Adam Smith propounds two profit theories, each rooted in one of the two pillars of classical political economy – the cost theory of value and the surplus theory of distribution. From the cost point of view, Smith states that "wages, profits and rent are the three original sources of all revenue as well as of all exchangeable value" (Smith, 1937, p. 52) and "high or low wages and profits are the cause of high or low prices" (Smith, 1937, p. 146). Thus profit is a return to a distinct factor of production and is a determining factor of price. In contrast, from the distribution point of view, Smith views profits as the difference between "the value which the workmen add to the materials" and "their wages" (Smith, 1937, p. 48). Since the former determines the market worth of the commodity and the latter is determined by the amount required to maintain the workmen's subsistence, profits thus emerge. In this case, profits vary with the price of the commodity. Thus, Smith puts forth two contradicting versions of profits. In the first view profits together with wages and rent determine the price, and in the second view profits are determined by price. Even more remarkable than this inconsistency is the fact that, as observed by Obrinsky (1983, p. 13), he crosses over from one position to the other almost without knowing it.

Even though Adam Smith did not succeed in presenting a satisfactory profit theory, he offered a good deal of insight to the problem. It was Smith who had clearly identified profit as a separate and distinct income and had pointed out its significance as a motivating power for economic activities. Smith also clearly distinguishes profit from interest on capital. He stated that interest is "the compensation which the borrower pays to the lender for the profit which he has an opportunity of making by the use of money" (Smith, 1937, p. 52). More importantly, it was Smith who set the tune and the research agenda on profit, among other things. Classical economists followed his lead to investigate profit either from the cost of production perspective or from the surplus value perspective. A brief summary is given below.

Profit As a Cost of Production

From the point of view of cost of production, the efforts were spent in seeking the "profit factor," that is, in uncovering the productive factor that generates profits. After such a factor is identified, it is hoped that it will become possible to obtain an independent measure of this factor's contribution to output and then include this amount in the cost of production.

To the classical economists the profit factor turned out to be elusive. Profits were frequently confused with wages and interest. Although J. B. Say endeavors to tie profits to the entrepreneur, he treats the entrepreneur sometimes as a capitalist and at other times as a laborer. In doing so, he confounds profits with interest and wages. Say treats entrepreneurs as capitalists by insisting that the entrepreneur "must at least be solvent and have the reputation of intelligence, prudence, probity and regularity" (Say, 1830, p. 285). However, he never clearly distinguished the entrepreneurial role from that of general labor. Since the entrepreneur takes on both capitalist and laborer roles, it is not possible to separate profits from interest and wages.

On the other hand, Senior identifies abstinence from consumption as the profit factor, apparently taking for granted that the party who saves also invests. Senior thus claims that the capitalist should receive the profits. According to Senior it is the capitalist who must abstain from current consumption to make production possible. After the production process is completed, the capitalist "is paid for it by his appropriate remuneration, profit" (Senior, 1965, p. 93). Moreover, this remuneration is dependent upon the "proportion which the value of that produce...bears to the value of his advances, taking into consideration the time for which those advances have been made" (Obrinsky, 1983, p. 19). In this way, profit is identified with returns to the capitalist and is therefore indistinguishable from interest. Because savers and investors are generally different individuals, it is difficult to justify that by merely abstaining from current consumption the capitalist is entitled to receive the reward of profits. Abstinence is strictly a saving phenomenon while profit must be associated with the act of production. To assert profit as a return to abstinence is to reward profit to the wrong factor production.

Only in von Thunen's writings have we seen a glimpse of a profit theory. Von Thunen attempts to tie profits to the entrepreneur. He begins by searching for the entrepreneurial quality. According to von Thunen, the entrepreneur is a person who is preoccupied with the fortune of the business. Through the trials and tribulations, he deals with daily contingencies. The entrepreneur is put in a position and "becomes an inventor and discoverer in his sphere" (von Thunen, 1951, p. 146), and for this the entrepreneur is rewarded with profit. Profit is identified as a residual after all costs, including interests, insurance premiums, and managerial salaries, have been subtracted from the revenue. It is, by its nature, uninsurable. Because entrepreneurs would be reluctant to go into business without it, profit is also inexpendable. Even though von Thunen's profit theory is sketchy and far from complete, his efforts to discover the characteristics of the entrepreneur can be seen as the forerunner of the profit theories of Knight and Schumpeter.

Profit as Surplus

From the surplus point of view, efforts have been devoted to separating property income into three components: rent, interest, and profits. Although the results of this research are no more successful in identifying profit than those described above, research activities in this area have generated a great deal more excitement.

Taking the hint from Adam Smith, Ricardo set out to develop a labor theory of value and a surplus theory of profit. Obrinsky succinctly stated these theories as follows: "the value of the product is determined by the amount of labor embodied within it, the wages of labor are determined by the amount of labor necessary to produce subsistence, and profits arise from the difference" (Obrinsky, 1983, p. 30). Obrinsky also notes, "Profits then are purely the result of the ability of society, in cooperation with nature, to produce a surplus of a product greater than that required to maintain the population" (Obrinsky, 1983, p. 29). Therefore profit is a surplus. Ricardo, however, did not address the question as to why labor does not capture the entire value of the product but only receives enough for subsistence. This issue was left to be dealt with by Marx. Ricardo, as we have seen in chapter 2, devoted his attention to using differential rent theory to decompose the surplus into rent and profit. However, this profit is not yet a pure profit; it includes, as Mills has observed, remuneration for risk, interest on capital, and wages of supervision.

Karl Marx took up the challenge left by Ricardo to resolve the source of the surplus. Marx identifies labor power instead of labor as the relevant commodity. In a capitalist economy there is a separation between production and means of production. Labor must sell the capitalist his labor power. The institution of property has put the laborer in a subordinate position. Workers now depend on the capitalist for wage advances. This dependence gives the capitalist extraordinary bargaining power over labor, and as a result the capitalist is able to pay only a subsistence level of wages to the worker. The value of a commodity is dependent upon the amount of labor embodied within it. Because labor adds more to production than is required to maintain his subsistence, surplus appears. Moreover, according to Marx, surplus is the result of exploitation. Although Marx recognized that surplus is not identical with profit and that profit is the residual minus rents and interest, he was not successful in breaking the residual into its individual components.

As demonstrated by the above summary of the classical economists' contributions on profit theory, it is fair to say that up until 1870 a coherent theory of distribution and theory of profits did not exist.

PROFIT THEORIES OF KNIGHT AND SCHUMPETER

While the classical economists struggled but failed to find the profit factor, as we have seen in chapter 2, the neoclassical economists eliminated the profit factor altogether in their scheme. Fortunately, this position is not taken by all economists. The absence of the profit factor in the neoclassical economic theory stems from its exclusion of the impact of uncertainty from the formal analysis. By including uncertainty in the theoretical reasoning, Knight and Schumpeter not only restore entrepreneurs to the center stage of the economic arena but also lay the foundation for a meaningful theory of profits. However, since Knight and Schumpeter view the nature of uncertainty differently, they assign different roles to the entrepreneur and thus arrive at different theories of profits.

The Knightian Profit Theory

As the reader may recall, Knight distinguishes risk from uncertainty and establishes that uncertainty is the fountain of profit income. The presence of uncertainty prevents the resource owners from agreeing on a joint production policy through the market and thus destroys the market's ability to coordinate production. The entrepreneur emerges to break the impasse. Production now takes place under the direction of a capitalist entrepreneur who uses his own expectations and judgement to set production policy. The capitalist entrepreneur in the factor markets hires the resources needed for production and absolves the factor owners of their responsibility to cope with uncertainty.

The Nature of the Knightian Profit In an uncertainty environment, commitment of resources to production must be made *ex ante* on the basis of the value of the inputs. Observe that the value of any input depends upon its marginal physical productivity as well as on the price of the commodity that it helps to produce. Since both these terms are uncertain, the *ex ante* value of the input must also be uncertain. When the entrepreneur does not know the value of a factor, he must base his bid for its services on the expectations of the factor's contribution to the marginal value production. In general, *ex ante* expectations and *ex post* realizations of each factor's marginal productivity differ; hence payments to the factors do not generally exhaust the total product.

Thus, under uncertainty, the market fails to reward factors of production in accordance with their actual contribution to the total product based on their marginal productivity. Since the demand for an input is based on expectations of a future outcome rather than the future outcome itself, the price established in the factor market may differ from the *ex post* value of the input. The Knightian profit theory is built on this difference (Knight, 1971, p. 198). He defines profit simply as

the difference between the market price of the productive agencies he employs, the amount which the competition of other entrepreneurs forces him to guarantee to them as a condition of securing their services, and the amount which he finally realizes from the disposition of the product, which under his direction, they turn out. (Knight, 1971, p. 217)

Profit is therefore a reward to the entrepreneur; it is the

entrepreneur's income which is associated with the performance of his peculiar twofold function of (a) exercising responsible control and (b) securing the owners of productive services against uncertainty and fluctuation in their incomes. (Knight, 1971, p. 278)

Knight emphasizes that profit should be distinguished from contractual incomes in that the latter are imputed while profit is an unimputable residual whose

occurrence is manifestly due to the fact that men must base their acts on past conditions, or on uncertain inferences as to the future based on past conditions, and not on the actual future conditions to which they really relate. (Knight, 1971, p. 90)

Because there does not exist a market for entrepreneurial services, the residual serves as an enticement for the entrepreneur to provide his services. Moreover, because the entrepreneur is a risk-bearer who insures "the doubtful and timid by guaranteeing to the latter a specified income in return for an assignment of the actual results" (Knight, 1971, pp. 269–70), he must be a person of wealth. Thus Knight states that "it is clear that only the possessor of transferable wealth already produced or of future productive capacity in some form can make guarantees or really bear uncertainty or take risks for other persons. . . . [Thus] control of the enterprise falls in the hands of the owner" (Knight, 1971, p. 299).

In conclusion, Knight attributes profits as returns to the capitalist-entrepreneur for his willingness to bear risk. In the modern parlance of Sandmo,

> the risk neutral firms will set marginal cost equal to expected price, while the risk averse firms in the industry will choose output levels for which marginal cost is less than expected price. In general, the distribution of output and expected profit among firms will vary with their degree of risk aversion. Expected profit will be highest for those firms which come very close to being risk neutral and have the highest output in the industry. This observation confirms a view which has long traditions in economic theory, viz., to profit as a reward to risk bearing. (Sandmo, 1971, p. 72)

Properties of the Knightian Profit Theory First, since the entrepreneur is identified with the capitalist, the residual is not pure profits – it also includes interest. Knight has recognized that there is a difference between interest income and profit income, the former being a contractual income and the latter a residual. Yet because the entrepreneur is confounded with the capitalist, profit is necessarily confounded with interest; they cannot be separated in practice. In Knight's words,

> It is useful, however, to distinguish between the return actually realized by an entrepreneur and the 'competitive' rate of interest on high-class 'gilt edge' securities where the risk and responsibility factor is negligible. . . . [However], it would not be fruitful to attempt an accurate separation of profit from interest. (Knight, 1971, p. 304)

Second, the Knightian profit exists only when entrepreneurs underestimate the value of productive services and/or do not overestimate their own ability to convert inputs into high valued outputs. According to Knight, high profits will result

> in a population combining low ability with high 'courage.' On the other hand, if men generally judge their own abilities well, the

general rate of profit will probably be low, whether ability itself is low or high, but much more variable and fluctuating for a low level of real capacity. The condition for large profits is a narrowly limited supply of high-grade ability with a low general level of initiative as well as ability. (Knight, 1971, p. 284)

High quality entrepreneurs with keener judgement will anticipate the future more accurately; this implies that a lower degree of uncertainty will prevail in the marketplace. Since entrepreneurs are the bearers of uncertainty, the reduction in market uncertainty reduces the worth for the bearer and hence the size of his reward. Thus a lower profit rate will result. Paradoxically, high quality entrepreneurs induce low profits.

Finally, the Knightian profit exists only in disequilibrium market situations. Profit arises only when a previously unanticipated change takes place which causes a discrepancy between *ex ante* evolution and *ex post* realization of a factor's marginal contribution to the product. Errors on the part of the entrepreneur are corrected as he learns to adjust to the new market conditions of supply and demand. Profits are eliminated as entrepreneurs revise their expectations in the light of the information; entrepreneurs bid the price of a factor up or down depending on whether the marginal productivity of the factor is underestimated or overestimated. This revision will continue until the factor price becomes equal to its *ex post* value of marginal product. Thus, as the market returns to equilibrium, the economy returns to a remainderless distribution of total product.

The Schumpeterian Profit Theory

Schumpeter characterizes the entrepreneur differently than Knight; consequently, Schumpeterian profit is different from the Knightian profit. Schumpeter differentiated economic growth from economic development. Economic growth is related to a known pattern, whereas economic development is caused by "the carrying out of a new combination." Economic development causes the existing resources to be employed differently by either producing an existing good with a new method or by producing a new good altogether. Schumpeter calls the carrying out of new combinations the enterprise, and the individual who carries out these enterprises the entrepreneur.

The Schumpeterian entrepreneur exhibits the following traits. First, the entrepreneur does not handle routine business. Instead, he is an innovator who makes and executes strategic decisions. The success of the entrepreneur depends on his judgement, that is, on his capacity to see things *ex ante* that prove to be true *ex post* even though he cannot give an account of the principle by which the decision was made. In this context, the exercise of entrepreneurial judgement is event specific: therefore entrepreneurship cannot be attached permanently to any individual. Accordingly Schumpeter emphasizes that entrepreneurship is not a profession and that entrepreneurs do not form a special class like the landowners, capitalists, or laborers; in addition, the entrepreneurial function cannot be inherited (Schumpeter, 1934, pp. 78–9). Second, the Schumpeterian entrepreneur does not own any other resources. In order to carry out economic development, he must gain control over the required resources. He does so by becoming a debtor. Consequently, the entrepreneur is "never a riskbearer," but the creditor is (Schumpeter, 1934, p. 137). In Schumpeter's words, "risk bearing is in no case an element of entrepreneurial function. Even though he may risk his reputation, the direct economic responsibility of failure never falls on him" (Schumpeter, 1934, p. 137).

Based upon these entrepreneurial traits, Schumpeter develops his profit theory in two steps. He first defines gross profit as surplus over cost which includes all the disbursements the entrepreneur must make in order to carry out innovative activities. Schumpeter then observes that this surplus encompasses two income categories – interest and pure profits. Since interest is a permanent income and profit is not, Schumpeter must find a way of extracting a permanent interest income from the transitory gross profits. After interest income is separated from the surplus, the pure profit emerges. We now describe the Schumpeterian profit theory in greater detail.

Existence of a Surplus   Positive surplus exists because economic development associated with innovation necessarily implies that resources used for the new combination are more efficient than those used for the old. By resources Schumpeter means the two original factors of production – land and labor. In a circular-flow equilibrium, the value of the product must be equal to the cost of production imputed to land and labor (Schumpeter, 1934, p. 160). However, with the advent of economic development, rent and wages are still determined by the old mode of production. Yet the marginal productivities of land and labor are now higher under the new mode of production. They are higher as a result of either an improved method of production or of a new product which commands a higher price than its substitutes. On the basis of this adjustment lag, a surplus appears. However, the existence of such a surplus is transitory. The presence of an innovative profit induces imitation. Imitation will, on the one hand, bid up rent a wages and, on the other hand, drive down the product price of the new combination. Therefore, through imputation and competition, the market reaches a new equilibrium where rent and wages are again equal to their higher value of marginal products; profit will vanish.

Relationship between Profit and Interest In order to initiate economic development, the entrepreneur must gain control of resources. Since the entrepreneur is not a capitalist he must do so by becoming a debtor and by paying a price for the debt incurred. This constitutes the demand side for credit. The capitalist, however, enticed by the promise of interest payments, would be willing to "transfer a definite sum to the entrepreneur by withdrawing it from its customary uses, that is, by restricting his expenditure either in production or in consumption" (Schumpeter, 1934, p. 191). This is the supply side for credit. The price for debt interest is determined in the money markets through the interaction of demand and supply. This price is positive because the transfer of credit at this price diverts the resources from current usage to a more productive application. Therefore Schumpeter asserted that "Present purchasing power must regularly be at a premium over future purchasing power in the money market" (Schumpeter, 1934, p. 188).

Since profit is a transitory income and by all accounts interest income is permanent, Schumpeter needs to explain "how is this permanent stream of interest, flowing always to the same capital, extracted from the transitory, ever changing profit" (Schumpeter, 1934, pp. 175–6). He answered this question by observing that "new businesses are continually arising under the impulse of the alluring profit" (Schumpeter, 1934, p. 131). Even though profits associated with a particular development are temporary, overall economic development activity is never ceasing. Consequently, the demand for credit will be an ongoing phenomenon. Because interest is associated with upcoming development projects, it becomes a permanent income even though its source is the temporary profit. Thus Schumpeter not only provided us with a theory of interest, he has also suggested a way of decomposing surplus into two components: interest income and pure profit. Interest is determined in the money market. Pure profit becomes the lone residual.

Nature of Pure Profit The Schumpeterian pure profit has several distinct characteristics. First, the entrepreneur is the only recipient of pure profit derived from economic development. Because the entrepreneur is not a capitalist, pure profit is not a return to capital; interest is. Furthermore, because each innovation is unique, there is no common denominator with which to compare all innovative activities. Lacking such a common denominator, a tendency toward equalization of profits among all enterprises is absent. Second, profit is not determined according to the marginal productivity of the entrepreneur; it is a residual. The size of this residual, as we have observed before, differs from enterprise to enterprise except that it must be sufficiently large to call forth the entrepreneur's services. In addition, the value of the entrepreneur's services cannot be determined *ex ante*. Because entrepreneurship is not a profession, profit is not a branch of permanent income. According to Schumpeter, "if one counts the regular recurrence of a return as one of the characteristic features of income, once economic activities cease to be innovative and have become routinized, profit vanishes immediately" (Schumpeter, 1934, pp. 153–4).

Comparison of Knightian and Schumpeterian Profits

Knight and Schumpeter disagree on both the source and the intrinsic nature of profits. These disagreements arise because they hold different views concerning the nature of uncertainty faced by the entrepreneurs.

Knight's primary concern is the inhibiting effect of the exogenously given market uncertainty on joint production among resource owners. Accordingly, he characterizes the entrepreneur as a risk-bearing impasse breaker. Because the resource owner who can best cope with uncertainity is a property owner, profit becomes the return to the capitalist – entrepreneur. Since profit is a return to capital and capital is homogeneous, through competition, there is a tendency for the rate of profit derived from all business ventures to equalize. Finally, an increase in the average ability of entrepreneurs decreases judgemental errors and hence reduces the impact of uncertainty. Owing to the assumption that profit is a reward for risk-bearing, a decrease in the impact of uncertainty must imply a decrease in the entrepreneurial reward. Thus, according to Knight, an increase in the quality of the entrepreneurs paradoxically leads to a decrease in profits.

Schumpeter, however, focuses on the endogenous uncertainty created by the entrepreneur's attempt to innovate. Profit is the fruit of innovation. The absence of innovation not only does not give rise to profit, it also does not bring forth uncertainty. Lured by profits, the entrepreneur who opts to innovate is obviously not inhibited by the uncertainty that innovation creates. This is particularly true since the innovator is assumed to borrow all the funds required from the credit market and thus shift risks to the capitalist. In Schumpeter's view, uncertainty does not create an impasse to production and the entrepreneur does not serve as a risk-bearer. Reasoning in this way, Schumpeter gives entrepreneurship a new dimension and profit a new interpretation. Profit is a return to a special function which is not performed by a property owner. Because enterprises are heterogeneous, competition among entrepreneurs does not lead to equalization of the profit rates. Finally, an increase in the average ability of the entrepreneur increases innovation, thus leading to higher profits.

When everything is considered, the Knightian and Schumpeterian profit theories differ widely. The only commonality is their assertion that profit arises only in disequilibrium situations; as soon as the market reaches an equilibrium, price equals cost and profit vanishes. On all other vital issues, their theories are diametrically opposed. The impression is given that the strength of one theory is the weakness of the other.

The strength of the Knightian profit theory is its recognition of the entrepreneurial role in impasse breaking. Its weakness stems from its denial of an independent entrepreneurial role and its insistence on tying entrepreneurship with the capitalist. In so doing, Knight narrowly defines profit as a reward only for risk-bearing.

The strength of the Schumpeterian profit theory is its recognition of entrepreneurship, independent of a property owner. However, it suffers from two major shortcomings. First, Schumpeter ignored exogenous uncertainty. In reality, market uncertainty flows from both endogenous and exogenous sources. By ignoring the exogenous sources Schumpeter gives the impression that entrepreneurs are not inhibited by, and the capital market is not concerned with, the presence of uncertainty. This attitude is incorrect even if uncertainty is solely induced by innovation. Such an endogenously generated uncertainty could still inhibit entrepreneurs from taking action. In reality, it is not hard to find evidence of aspiring entrepreneurs who have abandoned their projects because the uncertainty caused by their own action was too overwhelming. In our view, uncertainties, whether endogenously or exogenously generated, do inhibit entrepreneurial action. Thus the issue raised by Knight should not be readily dismissed. Schumpeter's optimism stems from his definitions of innovation and entrepreneurship. The entrepreneur is an innovator who has successfully gained commercialization of a new combination. This tautological view of innovation (that is, the innovator is the one who successfully innovates) was the cause of his optimism which holds that the entrepreneur is never inhibited by the uncertainty generated by his own action.

Second, Schumpeter is overly optimistic about the ability of the entrepreneur to borrow all the funds required from the credit market. In the presence of uncertainty, as we have seen in chapter 5, the entrepreneur neither can nor wants to do this. Because moral hazards are invariably associated with entrepreneurial activities, the entrepreneur is not permitted to borrow all that he needs. In addition, because the entrepreneur is a risk-averse individual, even if he were allowed to borrow all the funds required from the credit market, he may prefer to borrow only a fraction of that amount and secure the remainder from the equity market. In doing so, the entrepreneur gains the opportunity of sharing the market uncertainties with the capitalist. To state this proposition differently, entrepreneurs cannot shift uncertainties completely to the capitalist; they must bear a portion of this uncertainty and are therefore also risk-bearers.

The irreconcilable differences existing between the two leading profit theories underscore the hopeless state of profit theory. However, the fact that the strength of one theory is exactly the weakness of the other suggests that a viable theory can be found if we seek a way of reconciling the diametrically opposed results of the Knightian and Schumpeterian profit theories under a single framework. It is to this task that we turn in the next section.

PROFIT THEORY: A REFORMULATION

In the last section we observed that the source of controversy on profit theory is that the writers hold different views on the nature of uncertainty faced by the entrepreneur and on the role that the entrepreneurs play in production. This observation suggests that a common view on entrepreneurs must be found before a universally acceptable profit theory can be constructed. In chapter 5 we developed such a view which describes the entrepreneur not by the function he performs but by the fact that his services cannot be traded in the market place. We now present a profit theory based upon this view of the entrepreneur.

We stated in chapter 5 that uncertainty destroyed the market's ability to coordinate production. Entrepreneurs emerged as a factor of production to perform this coordination function. Owing to the inability of the market to evelute the entrepreneur's services *ex ante* and the threat of moral hazard and adverse selection in connection with the performance of these services, the market for entrepreneurial services fails to form. Thus entrepreneurs cannot derive their incomes by selling their services in the market and must do so through nonmarket means. They join their talents together in production by organizing a firm and each claims as income a share of the firm's residual.

In order to commence production, the entrepreneur must gain control of the inputs required. If it is assumed that markets for all tradeable factors of production exist, the entrepreneur can gain control of the factors by purchasing them in the markets. Since entrepreneurs are not capitalists, in the beginning they must rely upon the firm's future earning power to secure capital by selling bonds and stocks in the capital market. Moreover, because entrepreneurs are risk-averse, selling stocks in the capital market also enables them to shift part of their income uncertainty associated with the firm's residual to capitalists. Thus, by sharing risks with entrepreneurs, capitalists join with them to make production possible. However, the roles played by capitalists and entrepreneurs in production are different. The formulation of a viable pofit theory depends crucially upon a clear understanding of this difference.

The Roles of the Entrepreneur and the Capitalist

As observed earlier, the presence of competitive land, labor, and capital markets led to functional specialization among all factors of production including entrepreneurs. In this section we make clear the nature of this specialization between the capitalist and the entrepreneur. This functional specialization takes the form that the capitalist does not make production decisions and the entrepreneur does not finance production.

The Capitalist's Role The presence of the debt and equity markets enables the capitalist to convert his capital resources into income. Based on the firms future earning powers, the capitalist invests his capital by purchasing bonds and stocks. The returns to bonds and stocks take different forms. The interest income is determined *ex ante* and is relatively safe, while the dividend income is determined *ex post* and is relatively risky. As we have seen in chapters 5, 6, and 9, for the purpose of securing a satisfactory return on his investment, the shareholder has two options: first, he could participate in the control of the firm's operation by becoming an adjunct entrepreneur; second, he could arrange for a most desirable portfolio of investments through diversification. With these opportunities available in the modern capital market, control over a firm's decision, as observed by Fama (1980, p. 291), is not the natural province of shareholders.

In the presence of a modern capital market, the value of a firm's shares reflects the probability distribution of the firm's returns to the shareholders. Based upon this probability distribution of returns, stocks of different firms can be compared and grouped into different classes. In a capital market, the investor faces many classes of investment opportunities ranging from relatively low risk bonds to stocks with varying degrees of risk. Based upon the financial information made available through the capital market, the risk-averse investor selects from a wide range of investment opportunities a portfolio which yields a satisfactory rate of return to his investments commensurate with his wealth and risk attitude. Since the investor holds securities of many firms so as to avoid having his wealth dependent upon the fortune of a single firm, an individual investor generally has no special interest in gaining control of the detailed activities of any given firm. This tendency is reinforced by the fact that the capital market does not offer the firm-specific information needed for exercising control over the firm's operation. Consequently, in the presence of a modern capital market, it is no longer necessary and desirable for the investor to gain control of the firm's operation to secure a satisfactory rate of return. Thus the capitalist sheds the control role and becomes a professional lender. Yet whenever he lends his capital through the stock market, he becomes a risk-bearer. The risk-averse capitalist is willing to accept the risk associated with each stock investment because he can soften the impact of this risk through diversification and portfolio selection.

The Entrepreneurial Role   The capital market also serves the interest of the entrepreneur. Once the firm is formed, the entrepreneur, through the capital market, can convert a portion of the firm's future stream of profits into present wealth. This conversion not only enables the coalition of entrepreneurs to gain access to the capital needed for production, but also enables them to shift part of the uncertainties associated with the firm's surplus to the capitalists. However, shedding uncertainty also encourages entrepreneurs to behave opportunistically, and thus adversely affects the firm's profit outcomes. In chapter 5 we examined the nature of this moral hazard and pointed out that, if the firm is totally leveraged, the creditors would bear the cost of the firm's failure. Under these circumstances, the entrepreneur might neglect his contractual responsibility and opt for leisure. Thus, fearing the adverse effect of moral hazards, the lenders (both bondholders and shareholders) will not permit the entrepreneurs to convert their entire claims to the firm's future stream of profits into present wealth. The entrepreneurs must remain as residual claimants in order to assure the lenders that they will carry out their decision roles faithfully.

Not only do bondholders dislike firms which rely competely on debt financing, risk-averse entrepreneurs also tend to shy away from this method of financing. Financing by bonds only, implies that the firm must make a large sum of fixed-interest payment in each period. Because the firm's revenue in each period is uncertain, this fixed payment creates a strong incentive for the firm to continue a high level of operation regardless of the level of its demand. The competitive pressure created by high constant fixed cost induces excess competition and thus accentuates the firm's profit uncertainty and increases its chance for bankruptcy. Consequently, risk-averse entrepreneurs also wish to seek equity financing so as to shift part of the firm's uncertainty to the capitalists.

Thus said, we see that the entrepreneurs perform both decision- and risk-bearing roles. However, these two roles are not equally important to the entrepreneurial function. The entrepreneur is primarily a decision-maker. Only because of the threat of moral hazard are entrepreneurs forced to serve as hostages to lenders by sharing the risk-bearing role with them. Therefore risk-bearing is an ancillary function for the entrepreneurs. The division of risk-bearing between the capitalists and the entrepreneurs, as we will see in the next section, is determined in the capital market.

The Role of the Capital Market The capital market is composed of two segments: the debt and the equity markets. In the present analysis, stocks and bonds serve three functions: they represent claims to a firm's output at a future date, they serve as a means of allocating risks among agents and as instruments to finance production. Contrary to tradition, stocks no longer endow their holders with decision-making authority.

Both capitalists and entrepreneurs use debt and equity markets to arrange for their consumption–investment portfolios. The entrepreneurs (the firms) make up the supply side of the securities and the capitalists make up the demand side. Demand and supply interact to determine the prices of stocks and bonds and their respective quantities exchanged. The determination of the bond price (interest rate) is relatively straightforward since we assume that the bond market is competitive. The determination of the stock price, however, is more complex. This complexity stems from the fact that the firm is the sole supplier of its own shares. In a later section, we will describe how the firm's share price and its capital structure are determined. Because bond and stock prices determine the cost of capital to the firm and entrepreneur, the understanding of price formation in the capital market constitutes the first step towards the understanding of profits.

The Nature of Profits

In this section we present the promised profit theory. Before proceeding, we need to define some relevant terms. Let the firm's total production cost be the sum of its outlays on land, labor, and capital goods, the firm's total surplus be its total revenue minus its total production cost, and the firm's residual be its surplus minus its total interest payments on bonds. In this section we will establish the proposition that the firm's residual minus its dividend payment is its profit. We do so in several steps.

Interest Payment is a Cost of Production   It is relatively easy to establish the proposition that interest payment is a cost of production. Assume first that the lenders are willing to lend as much as the firm wishes to borrow as long as the firm's income stream is expected to exceed the amount borrowed plus interest. The total output produced by the firm must first be distributed according to the contractual obligations to the owners of land, labor, and capital goods as well as to the owners of capital funds. Since land, labor, and capital goods are arguments in the production function, they are traditionally referred to as factors of production and their payments constitute the costs of production. The monetary capital, however, is not an argument in the production function. Payment to monetary capital is nonetheless a cost of production because, in order to make production possible in an exchange economy, the entrepreneurs must first gain command of the purchasing power – the capital funds. Only with this purchasing power will the firm be able to bid resources – land, labor, and capital goods – away from other usages and devote them to the intended production. Because a price in the form of interest must be paid in order to gain control over capital funds, the interest payment must be treated as a cost of production.

Consequently, if it were possible to secure all funds needed in production through debt financing, the firm's residual would be equivalent to its profit. Since the firm is not permitted to do this, part of the funds must be secured through the equity market. Because interest, dividend, and profit all come out of the firm's surplus, in order to understand what constitutes profits, we must first determine how the firm's capital structure is determined. We now address this issue.

Determination of the Firm's Capital Structure   Let us assume that the firm has been formed and that the sharing rule for the cooperative entrepreneurs has been established. The firm, backed up by its revenue-producing capability, offers financial instruments – stocks and bonds – to the investors. There is a demand for the firm's securities if the distribution of returns to the investors from these securities is not dominated by a linear combination of the existing securities. The distribution of returns for a given security is determined by a number of factors: (a) the product that the firm produces and the production technology it employs; (b) the composition of the entrepreneurs, the hierarchical organization of the firm, and the information structure adopted by the firm; (c) the firm's production structure, that is, its horizontal, vertical and conglomerate make-ups; (d) the firm's capital structure, that is, its debt–equity ratio; (e) the firm's profit, which is henceforth referred to as the bonus. In this section we describe how the firm's bonus rate, capital structure, and share price are endogenously determined.[2] To do this, we need to examine both the consumer's decision problem and the cooperative entrepreneurs' decision problem (that is, the firm's decision problem) in the current period.

The consumer's decision problem is relatively simple. Let the tradeable factor prices (including the interest rate), each firm's bonus rate, and each firm's share price be arbitrarily given. These, together with the expectation of the firm's product prices, define a probability distribution of returns for each security. Each investor (consumer) chooses a consumption–investment portfolio from the available commodities and securities to maximize his expected (derived) utility subject to the current-period budget constraint. This choice yields for each consumer a vector of demand functions for the commodities (including bonds) and a vector of demand functions for the firm's shares.

The firm's decision problem and the corresponding decision problem for each cooperative entrepreneur are much more complex. This complexity stems from the fact that each firm enjoys a certain degree of monopoly power over the selling of its own shares and that all firms' financial policies are interdependent. In order to describe how each firm arrives at a production-financing policy, we assume that all firms but one have arrived at their equilibrium policies and concentrate on examining how the remaining firm selects its optimal policies. We assume that the firm in question selects its policies in two steps. It first selects its production policy, and then its financial policy.

In the first step, assume that the firm's financial policy is given.[3] Let this policy be represented by the triplet (bonus rate, amount of debt, share price). The cooperative entrepreneurs of the firm in question agree in the expectation that the firm will be able to raise a certain amount of funds in the equity market. Given their expectations about the demand for the firm's product, they then jointly determine a production policy. This policy must be feasible in the sense that the total outlay for the inputs must not exceed the total funds collected from selling the firm's bonds and shares and the total entrepreneurial services required to support this production plan must not exceed the capacity of the cooperative entrepreneurs. The firm's production policy is now a function of its financial policy.

In the second step, the cooperative entrepreneurs of the firm bargain with each other, and implicitly bargain with the investors, to determine the firm's financial policy. The implicit nature of bargaining between the entrepreneurs and the investors will become apparent shortly. Here we wish only to observe that, based upon the first step described above, the selection of the firm's optimal financial policy in the second step will also lead to the adoption of an optimal production policy. This pair of policies yields the highest possible level of expected utility for each of the cooperative entrepreneurs.

The consumers and the firms interact in the bond market, the equity market, and the commodity markets to bring these markets jointly into equilibrium. Specifically, the commodity prices and the interest rate are determined competitively in their respective markets. Because each firm is a monopolist of its own shares, the firm must take into account its shareholders' reaction in order to select a price for its shares (or more precisely to select a financial policy) so that the demand for its shares equals the supply and the intake of funds is sufficient to finance its production. At equilibrium, two relevant ratios – the debt–equity ratio and the dividend–bonus ratio – are uniquely determined. We will have more to say about the dividend–bonus ratio later when we discuss the nature of profits. Here it is sufficient to mention that a firm's debt–equity ratio reflects the preferences of its cooperative entrepreneurs and the nature of the uncertainties that the entrepreneurs face. Even without tax considerations, a unique optimal debt–equity ratio exists for each firm. This result differs markedly from the standard conclusions reached in the finance literature.[4]

Having examined the derivation of the firm's production and financing policies, we are in position to develop the theme that interest and dividend payments are costs of production to the firm and are distinct from profits.

Interest and Dividend are Costs of Production   We have seen that the capitalist invests in stocks and bonds sold by firms. In a world of uncertainty, the capitalist's objective is to receive a satisfactory rate of return from a portfolio of stocks and bonds. The capitalist, as a shareholder, is not interested in gaining control of the firm's operation. Being called an owner of a firm does not mean that the shareholder has anything to do with the firm's production policy. It only means that, at the time of liquidation, the shareholder, like the bondholder, has the legal right to claim an appropriate share of the firm's assets. Both stockholders and bondholders consider themselves to be lenders of funds. As such they demand a price for the use of these funds.

The firm, however, seeks funds from both debt and equity markets. Despite the fact that payments for the use of these funds are made in different manners – fixed-interest payments for bonds with the rate determined *ex ante*, and variable dividend payments for the stock with the amount determined *ex post* – interest and dividends are the prices that the entrepreneur must pay in order to gain the privilege of using the money. Consequently, interest and dividends must both be treated as costs of production. Contrary to the claims made in the literature, a dividend is not a part of the profit; it is a cost.

Pure Profit as a Return to Entrepreneurs

Recall that under uncertainty the market fails to allocate resources by itself. Resource allocation needs the assistance of entrepreneurs. Thus the entrepreneur becomes a factor of production. Also, recall that activities associated with the entrepreneurial function cannot be evaluated *ex ante* and are subject to moral hazard; there is no market to trade entrepreneurial services. Entrepreneurs must derive their income by claiming a part of the firm's residual. Yet the dividend must also come out of the residual. Therefore profit is equal to residual minus dividend.

The entrepreneur, through the selection of the firm's financial policy, must bargain with the capitalist in the capital market to determine how the firm's surplus is to be shared between them. We have seen in the above section that this share is determined with the selection of the firm's optimal financial policy. First, the firm must offer the bondholders a market rate of return. Since the firm cannot and will not secure all its required funds from debt financing, it must offer the shareholder a distribution of return on dividends which is sufficiently attractive to secure enough funds from the equity market to supplement the proceeds derived from bond sales to make production possible.

Based upon the proposition established above, the dividend is a cost of production and is not profit. Since dividend is a return to the shareholder and the shareholder is the main risk-bearer, it is evident that returns to risk-bearing cannot be a part of the profit. Only after the dividend is deleted from the residual will the profit emerge. Profit belongs to the lone net residual claimant – the entrepreneur. Thus, despite the fact that a dividend is determined *ex post* and that the capitalist must share with the entrepreneur the risk associated with the residual, the dividend is not profit and profit is not mainly a reward for risk-bearing. Profit is a reward to entrepreneurial decision-making.

There is a common misunderstanding in the literature about the nature of the dividend. The dividend has never been treated as a cost of production. The source of this misunderstanding is historical. Recall that in the preceding chapter we observed that factor markets developed in stages over time. This pattern of development also took place among the different segments of the capital market. Before the turn of the century, capital markets generally traded bills and debt instruments; the equity segment of the capital market was not well developed. If entrepreneurs could not secure all their capital requirements through the debt market, in order to make production possible they needed to acquire funds by nonmarket means, that is, by entering into a coalition with capitalists. At the same time, the capitalist, in the absence of the equity market and thus lacking the opportunity to make a portfolio arrangement for his investments, must guarantee a satisfactory rate of return to his investment by participating in the control of the firm's operations. In this way the capitalist became an adjunct entrepreneur and confounded the capitalist and entrepreneurial roles. Under these circumstances it was not surprising that entrepreneurs were viewed synonymously with capitalists and that returns to the former became returns to the latter. This traditional view remained in the literature despite the fact that the equity segments of the capital market have become well developed and the shareholders have shed their control role. The literature stubbornly follows the convention and refers to the shareholders as owners of the firm. It insists that returns to the owners are profits, and not costs of production.

Of course this conclusion does not conform to economic reality. Owing to the proliferation of ownership, shareholders have neither the ability nor the interest to exercise control over the firm's affairs. Ownership becomes merely a legal status. Since ownership and control are now separate, profit cannot simultaneously be the return to the capitalist and to the entrepreneur. Moreover, because prices of capital are determined in the capital market, the entrepreneurs must, through the market, bid for capital services. The price paid for these services, whether determined *ex ante* as bonds or determined *ex post* as dividend, must be treated as a cost of production.

In conclusion, as land, labor, capital goods, and financial markets become well developed, the price of land, labor, capital goods, and capital funds are determined in their respective markets. Functional specialization takes place among all factors of production. The entrepreneurs are the coordinators of production. They acquire all factor services from the market. In order to gain the right to use any factor services, the entrepreneurs must pay the market-determined prices. Payments to all factors, including dividends, become the costs of production. The lone net residual is the profit which belongs to the entrepreneurs.

A Brief Digression Neither the profit theory nor the entrepreneur-centered theory of the firm can be viewed as complete until a satisfactory explanation is provided for the phenomenon that the majority shareholders can veto the firm's policies and alter its entrepreneurial control group, commonly referred to as "the management." If the shareholders hold the veto power, then what becomes of the statement "capitalists do not manage and entrepreneurs do not finance production?" Recall that this statement was made in the context that markets for all tradeable factors are competitive and that resources in these markets are perfectly mobile. Perfect mobility of capital renders it unnecessary or even uneconomical for the share-holders to intervene in the firm's production policy. Any shareholder of a firm who dislikes its policy can sell his shares without suffering a penalty.

However, the presence of monopoly elements and high transactions costs in the capital market render the shareholders immobile. A shareholder, although disliking the firm's policy, may find it un-economical to abandon the firm by selecting an alternative for his investment. His investment is stuck. Under these circumstances, the shareholder must find other means of protecting his investments. Happily, shareholders have found, or rather have inherited, a legal protection under the shareholders' majority rule. This rule gives the shareholders a veto power over "managerial decisions."

The shareholders' majority rule was originally adopted to resolve disputes among decision-makers in the days when shareholders as owners actually managed the firm's affairs. As the capital market evolved, the owner-managed firm ceased to be the sole organizational form of modern firms. Yet, owing to the fact that legal and economic institutions evolve slowly, the shareholders' majority rule continues to function in all types of firms and simply becomes a legal requirement. Although the same rule has been applied throughout history, it is important to note that the nature of the rule has changed with changes in the market enviroment. The majority shareholders' rule has changed from a method of resolving disputes among the decision-makers to a method of resolving disputes between the decision-makers (the entrepreneurs) and the shareholders (the legal owners). Disputes between the entrepreneurs and shareholders need resolution because of the high transactions costs in the capital market.

The message we wish to convey is simple and clear. The majority shareholders' veto power is not needed to ensure consistency in the firm's decision-making but rather is a legal device to protect the shareholders' interests. It serves a purpose only when the capital market is imperfect. As the capital market becomes more efficient, the market will eventually provide full protection to the shareholders. Shareholders' veto power over the entrepreneurs' decisions will become superfluous.

IMPLICATIONS OF THE PROPOSED PROFIT THEORY

We have seen that the prevailing profit theory is rooted in the belief that the entrepreneur is the capitalist and the firm is owner managed. The notable exception is Schumpeterian profit theory.

From the owner-managed firm's point of view, return to the

enterprise is return to capital. Under the premise that profit is return to capital, all enterprises are made comparable with each other. Rate of return to capital becomes a measure of the attractiveness and success of the enterprise. Since enterprises are now comparable, there is a tendency for the market to channel productive resources first to enterprises which yield the highest rate of profit, then to those which yield the next highest rate of profit, etc. In the long run, competition will bring about equalization of the rate of profits throughout all business enterprises. This observation led to two well-known and widely accepted doctrines: (a) profit is strictly a disequilibrium phenomenon; (b) at equilibrium each firm earns a normal profit and economic profit vanishes. This equilibrium phenomenon takes place because entrepreneurial activity is no longer needed at equilibrium; thus entrepreneurs cease to have claims on any rewards. Payments to all other factors of production will exhaust the value of the product.

The entrepreneur-centered theory proposed in this book is incongruent with these received doctrines. First, we agree with Schumpeter that profit is a return to the entrepreneur and not to the capitalist. Since we believe that the entrepreneur and the capitalist perform distinct functions and that there does not exist a way of measuring the marginal productivity of entrepreneurial services *ex ante*, profit is not a price paid for entrepreneurial services. It is therefore not a cost of production. Further, as the firm is a coalition of entrepreneurs with each entrepreneur using the firm to pursue his own objectives, the firm's equilibrium policy naturally reflects the composite interests of the cooperative entrepreneurs. Under these circumstances, the firm is prevented from pursuing a single objective and the performances of a firm can no longer be measured by a single measuring rod. Moreover, because the firm's composite objective is entrepreneur specific, firms pursue different objectives; the outcome of different business enterprises ceases to be comparable. Specifically, firms now pursue profits with different rigor and there does not exist a tendency towards equalization of profits among the enterprises. In the absence of this tendency, the concept of normal profit becomes irrelevant.

Second, the implications of the entrepreneur-centered theory differ sharply from those of the prevailing theories on the point that profit is strictly a disequilibrium phenomenon which vanishes whenever the economy reaches a state of equilibrium. The common belief in the literature is that profit arises from unforeseeable changes in the market. According to the Austrian economists, profit is a reward to the perceptive entrepreneur who sees profit opportunities that other agents do not see. According to Professor Knight, profit is a reward to the daring capitalist–entrepreneur who is not intimidated by unforeseeable market changes and is willing to bear uncertainties associated with production. According to Schumpeter, profit is a reward to creative entrepreneurs who inject unforeseeable changes in the market through innovation. Although the source of profit is different, all authors agree that, as time elapses, the market regains equilibrium through competition. The Austrian economists visualize the market regaining equilibrium as the entrepreneurs conquer all profit opportunities through competition. Knight believes that, with time, entrepreneurs gain experience and knowledge to cope with uncertainty and thus are able to convert uncertainties into risks. Schumpeter considers innovation as a three-stage process: invention, innovation, and imitation. Imitation increases competition and restores markets to routine operations. Thus, for all these authors, the passage of time eliminates uncertainty, intensifies competition, and returns the economy to a state of equilibrium. In this equilibrium, uncertainty is absent and profit opportunity vanishes altogether.

On the basis of the theory presented in chapter 6, we cannot agree with these assessments. Our objection to this widely received doctrine is based upon the belief that entrepreneurial decisions made under uncertainty involve judgements. The processes used by entrepreneurs to arrive at their respective decisions are highly complex and nonuniform. Thus the resulting market price fails to reveal all available market information. The failure of the price system to aggregate all available information in the market prevents the expectations of the entrepreneurs from converging. Rational expectation equilibrium ceases to be a relevant concept. The only sensible equilibrium concept is the Hicksian temporary equilibrium employed in chapter 6. Under this equilibrium concept uncertainty and equilibrium coexist.[5] The actions taken by the entrepreneur today depend not only upon current market data but also upon his expectations of future events. Given these expectations, through trading, today's decisions by all agents are made consistent in the marketplace. The current markets are in a state of equilibrium whenever all markets clear. Because today's decision depends on the entrepreneur's judgement of future events, entrepreneurial decisions necessarily involve the future. Since the future is always uncertain, decisions concerning the current policy always have an element of uncertainty even if all markets are currently in equilibrium. Consequently, entrepreneurial decisions do not vanish at equilibrium. Moreover, prodution will not take place unless the entrepreneurs expect a positive profit at equilibrium; current equilibrium and expected profit thus coexist at any point in time.

With the passage of time, the entrepreneur's decision horizon remains today and tomorrow; tomorrow never comes. The entrepreneur's decision problem repeats over time. Because the underlying market data change unpredictably from exogenous and/or endogenous sources, the entrepreneur can never learn sufficiently to convert uncertainties into risks. Uncertainties are ever present. Thus the entrepreneurial function is ongoing and never ceases. Moreover, both *ex ante* and *ex post* profits coexist. Since entrepreneurial decisions involve judgment of the future, the merit of each production decision cannot be evaluated until tomorrow. When tomorrow arrives, either a profit or a loss results. Thus, in each period, current equilibrium not only coexists with expected profit, it also coexists with actual profit (loss). Finally, because the entrepreneur's decision problem is re-current over time and entrepreneurs can never convert uncertainties into risks, profit never vanishes; it becomes a permanent market phenomenon.

Having demonstrated the coexistence of equilibrium and profit, it is perhaps constructive to further elaborate on the reason for the existence of these profits – the reason being that at any point in time entrepreneurs' expectations about future events are different.

It is well known that under certainty all decision-makers' evalu-ations about a given production situation are the same. Production decisions made under certainty are based upon technical con-siderations. Whether a firm will produce an extra unit is dependent solely upon the comparison of the known market price and the marginal cost of production. The additional unit is produced only if price exceeds marginal cost. This type of decision made by any individual can be viewed as a "decision against the market." Profit (loss) is a result of market error. When the market is competitive, perfect foresight and competition through arbitrage eliminate all market errors. No profit can result under this circumstance.

The nature of decisions made under uncertainty is different. Production decisions not only depend upon technical considerations but also upon entrepreneurial judgement. Entrepreneurs in this case not only make decisions against the market but also against each other. There are two ways in which judgements are made against each other. First, there is the wagering situation where the gain to one is identical with the loss of another. The exchange of a speculative commodity is a case in point. The buyer of this commodity gains an amount equal to the loss of a seller if the price of the commodity should rise. Second, and more generally, one can profit by betting that one's judgement of the future is superior to those of others. Suppose that one entrepreneur expects that the demand for a commodity will be higher in the future and selects the appropriate production policy to take advantage of this belief. Meanwhile, others may disagree and select the appropriate policies based upon their judgement. When the next period arrives and demand does increase, the entrepreneur with the superior judgement will collect his profit even though his gain is not entirely at the expense of his competitors.

The message we wish to convey is that profit results precisely because expectations about the future are not the same for all agents. In a wagering situation, if all agents hold the same expectations, no wager will take place and neither profit nor loss will result; there is no activity in the market. In the general case, if all entrepreneurs hold the same expectations, market outcome, that is, discrepancies between expectation and realization, reveals the information required. Market adjustment will take place in exactly the same manner as in the case under certainty. Competition and arbitrage will not only bring about equilibrium but will also eliminate uncertainties and profit. In the case where expectations are not the same and the judgements of entrepreneurs differ, temporary equilibrium will nonetheless take place. In this equilibrium, because expectations among the entrepreneurs differ, information discrepancies are disguised; not all information is revealed by the market outcome. Since economic actions taken by the entrepreneurs are based upon partial information, these actions do not have the tendency to eliminate uncertainties. Arbitrage will fall short of the extent needed to eliminate all profits. Therefore, as a rule, profit does not vanish.

NOTES

1 *The Economic Report of the President* calculates corporate profits annually. For example, see *The Economic Report of the President* US Government Printing Office, Washington, DC, 1986), pp. 351–3.
2 For a precise description of the determination of these values, see the mathematical appendix.
3 Items (a), (b), and (c) mentioned at the beginning of this subsection are also taken as fixed.
4 The standard conclusion is known as the Modigliani–Miller theorem and contends that investors are indifferent to the firm's choice of its capital structure (Modigliani and Miller, 1958).
5 Although the following discussion is based upon a two-period decision horizon, the same conclusions also hold under a multiperiod decision horizon.

11

Economy with Nonprofit Producers

In this chapter we examine the entrepreneur-centered theory in an economy which includes a voluntary sector comprising nonprofit firms. A nonprofit firm is organized under a statutory restriction prohibiting anyone from appropriating the surplus generated by the firm. This nondistribution requirement does not mean that a nonprofit firm is forever barred from making a surplus; it merely means that distribution of surplus is prohibited. Any net earnings must be retained by the firm for its own use.

A large body of literature already exists on this subject. This literature can be roughly divided into two broad categories: studies that explain the *raison d'être* of nonprofit firms, and studies attempting to analyze the behavior of nonprofit firms and draw welfare conclusions based upon this behavior. Although these studies have contributed greatly to our understanding of the roles played by nonprofit firms in the economy and how they respond to the various legal and financial constraints, many fundamental issues remain unresolved. For example, although the literature offers plausible reasons for nonprofit firms to exist, it does not offer a process for their formation. In addition, the prevailing theories invariably deduce the nonprofit firm's behavior from an assumed objective function. Welfare conclusions are drawn by comparing the market outcome implied by this behavior in the nonprofit sector with that derived in the for-profit sector. Just as we have argued in chapter 8 that there does not exist an objective function for the profit-seeking firm and that any welfare conclusion drawn from the assumed objective function must be held suspect, we argue that there also does not exist an objective function for the nonprofit firm and that the conclusions about the behavior of nonprofit firms based on an assumed objective function are unjustified and need to be reexamined. The partial equilibrium analytical procedure used to draw welfare conclusions is also questionable. We believe that, since for-profit firms and nonprofit firms serve different clienteles and operate under different constraints, they should not be compared and judged by the same criteria. In order to reach meaningful welfare conclusions, we must examine the nature of the firm's internal equilibrium and the nature of the general equilibrium involving both for-profit and nonprofit firms. Only when these equilibrium properties are well established will we be able to draw meaningful welfare conclusions.

In this chapter we again take the position that the firm does not have an objective of its own. The nonprofit firm is a coalition of entrepreneurs, each of whom uses the firm as a vehicle to pursue his own nonprofit goals. A nonprofit firm is formed whenever the cooperative nonprofit-oriented entrepreneurs, through bargaining, settle on a joint production policy, a financing policy, and a specific internal organization and reward structure. Because the entrepreneurs' goals are nonprofit in nature, the cooperative entrepreneurs are willing to abide by the nondistribution constraint required for the nonprofit organizations.

Because nonprofit firms must compete with for-profit firms in the factor markets for inputs, use the same capital pool to finance their production, and sometimes compete in the same output markets for the consumer's purchasing power, there exists a general equilibrium for both the for-profit and nonprofit sectors of the economy. We will compare the behavior of the for-profit and nonprofit firms and examine their welfare implications in this context.

Because a modern economy comprises three overlapping sectors – the private for-profit, the private nonprofit, and the public sectors – and because we have excluded the public sector from the scope of this book, the characterization of the general equilibrium of an economy given in this chapter is necessarily incomplete. Shortcomings notwithstanding, we hope that this chapter brings us a step closer to the understanding of how a modern economy functions.

Because the existing literature contributes many building blocks to the proposed general equilibrium model, we briefly summarize the relevant literature in the next section before proceeding to the main topic.

BRIEF REVIEW OF THE LITERATURE

Recently, several extensive reviews analyzing the economics of the nonprofit sector have appeared in the literature.[1] The appearance of these materials greatly lightens the burden of the present task, allowing us merely to summarize the essence of the relevant topics which lead to the development of this chapter. These topics elucidate the *raison d'être* of nonprofit firms and the analysis of their behavior.

Raison d'être *of Nonprofit Firms*

The common explanation for the existence of nonprofit firms is the failure of either the public sector or the private for-profit sector to provide some required goods and services. In responding to these failures, a new form of private business organization emerges.

Public Failures According to Weisbrod (1975), the provision of collective-consumption goods is normally made by the government and is financed through taxation. The types, quantities, and qualities of public goods that the government will supply are determined by the political process, that is, by voting. The reliance on the political process to determine the production of a public good is highly unsatisfactory. As observed by Weisbrod, "a tax-pricing system . . . does not equate, for each voter, his marginal tax with the marginal benefit he receives from each collective-consumption good" (Weisbrod, 1975, p. 24). The consumer whose marginal tax is greater (less) than his marginal benefit will want less (more) of this public good produced. In the simplest case, where production of a public good is determined by majority rule, only the median voters are satisfied. The remaining population is split into two groups: those who demand more and those who want less.

Frequently, excess demand for a public good can be met by private-good substitutes; however, these substitutes are seldom perfect. Alternatively, it can be met by a private producer of the public good. Given the free-rider problem associated with public goods, the private producer needs to be organized as a nonprofit firm and to finance its production through donations. Whenever the society's value judgement deems that a particular collective-consumption good is necessary, donation becomes a potential source of financing. We will have more to say about donation in a later section. Here we only wish to convey that donation is feasible only when the donors are assured that their contributions benefit the consumers entirely and directly and are not diverted to become profits and perquisites. The nonprofit firm operating under the nondistribution constraint serves to provide such an assurance. The voluntary nonprofit organizations thus come into being as alternatives for providing the collective-consumption goods.

Contract Failures The nonprofit firm not only serves to remedy failures in the public good sector; it may also serve as a remedy to market failures in the for-profit sector. Asymmetric information of product quality frequently exists between the buyer and the seller in favor of the seller. The existence of such information asymmetry leads to what Hansmann (1980) calls the contract failure, that is, the inability of the purchaser to ascertain whether the product of a given quality or quantity is actually produced. Contract failure leads to a reduction in the demand for the product. According to Hansmann (1980) and others, when information asymmetry exists society has the option of choosing between the for-profit and the nonprofit organization form.

Easley and O'Hara (1983) investigate these ideas with a simple game-theoretic model. They treat the selection between profit and nonprofit firms under a given market situation as the result of a noncooperative game played by the manager and society according to rules selected by society. In this game, the manager strives to maximize his utility and society attempts to maximize its collective welfare. The outcome of the game is a contract.

Not all contracts are feasible. Under information asymmetry, a feasible contract must be both individually rational and incentive compatible. That is, the contract not only provides the manager with a utility higher than his reservation level, but also makes it in the manager's self-interest to reveal his private information. Moreover, not all feasible contracts are Pareto optimal. A contract is Pareto optimal if there does not exist another contract which makes society and the manager simultaneously better off.

According to Easley and O'Hara, the terms of the optimal contract determine the type of firm that society selects. If the optimal contract does not specify the manager's reward, he will choose to maximize his own reward; the for-profit firm is chosen. Alternatively, if the optimal contract does specify the manager's reward, a "reasonable compensation constraint" applies; the nonprofit firm is selected.

Easley and O'Hara establish the *raison d'être* of nonprofit firms in three steps. First, they show that, given any set of market conditions, the game can always lead to a Pareto-optimal contract. Second, when information asymmetry is absent, that is, when consumers know the quality of the product, the for-profit firm is always chosen. The reason is simple. When consumers know the quality of the product, the contract is always incentive compatible. Society then operates only under the individual rational constraint. Even if the contract does not specify the manager's reward, society can maximize social welfare by relying on competition to limit the manager's reward to his reservation wage. Finally, in the presence of information asymmetry, the incentive-compatible constraint may not be satisfied. The for-profit firm may become nonoptimal. To demonstrate this, some specific assumptions are made. Let θ be a random variable representing the state of nature, e.g. a random cost parameter. Let the manager's utility $u(I, e)$ be increasing with his income I and decreasing with his efforts e, the consumer's utility $v(b)$ be monotonically increasing in product quality b, and the technical and resource constraint be given as $f(e, I, \theta, b) = 0$. Because there are technical and resource constraints on production and consumption, all allocations in the economy are contingent on θ. The social welfare function can be written as $W[u(I(\theta), e(\theta)), v(b(\theta))]$. Further, owing to the presence of the above-mentioned constraints, a tradeoff between I and b must exist. Assume that the seller alone knows e and θ, while all other information is common knowledge. If the optimal contract does not specify the manager's reward, he is able to pick I, e, and $b(\theta)$. Since there is a tradeoff between I and $b(\theta)$, the rational manager, in order to maximize $u(I, e)$, will always lie about θ and pick $b = 0$. No quality product will ever be produced. However, if the optimal contract specifies the manager's reward by adopting the nondistribution constraint, his income is given and he will be indifferent to which state of nature has occurred. This indifference removes the temptation for him to lie about the state of nature. Since the manager's income is given, in order to maximize his utility he will choose the minimum effort level which is required for the firm to function. This implies that the firm will now produce a product with the quality specified by the tradeoff between I and b. Thus minimum quality for the product is guaranteed. Accordingly, we can conclude that society always prefers the nonprofit firm to the for-profit firm whenever information asymmetry is present.

Demand Failures Another class of market failures exists in the for-profit sector. Frequently, because consumers' incomes are too low, it is impossible to translate their desire for a certain product into effective demand. Consequently, the market demand for the product falls everywhere below the average cost of producing the product. This product will not be produced by the for-profit firm.

Society's value judgement renders a certain class of goods and services, e.g. health services and basic education, necessary and indispensable. Their social value dictates that good citizenship requires relatively well-to-do individuals to assist those who cannot afford to purchase these goods and services. There are two ways of accomplishing this goal: first, the needy's demand for these goods and services can be augmented through public subsidy; second, the supply of these goods and services can be augmented through private donation. Since our purpose is to examine the nonprofit producers, we will center our attention on the second method. In this context, donation augments the producer's income. Whenever income derived from donation plus revenue received from the customers is sufficiently high to cover the cost of producing a required good or service, the producer will be willing to supply it.

However, an incentive problem does exist. Because a donation could end up as either profits to the firm's owners or perks to its managers, the donors will be reluctant to contribute to charities without the assurance that the contribution will be used directly to benefit the consumer. Therefore the private for-profit firm is not an incentive-compatible production organization to provide charitable products. These products will not be produced in the for-profit sector. A nonprofit firm with its characteristic nondistribution constraint serves to assure the donors; it rises to fill this market void (Hansmann, 1980).

In addition, goods and services classified as neither pure public goods nor pure private goods are also produced by nonprofit firms. The literature identifies two types of products under this category: first, religious activities, ideological pursuits and higher education; second, the fine arts. Again, the common feature of these products is that the demand curve for the product lies everywhere below the average cost curve, and that these products need to be financed by donations. However, there is a fundamental difference between the first and the second type. Regarding the products of the first type, the consumers are distinct from the donors. The donors are members of a societal subgroup whose willingness to finance the production is motivated by their belief that the consumption of such products contributes to the overall wellbeing of society. It is only with the aid of these donations that the product is produced. The products in the second type are different; the donors are also consumers of the product. Because the incomes of the consumers vary widely, production could take place by letting the seller practice price discrimination. However, the differential in prices resulting from price discrimination would be so great as to make the high priced customers resentful. A change in the producer's organization form from a for-profit firm to a nonprofit firm nullifies this resentment. The high income consumer now pays for the product not in the form of a high price but in the form of a donation. This change in practice has the advantage of making the high income consumers bear the burden for production without creating their resentment. In the end, the result of price discrimination is achieved without relying on the actual practice of price discrimination.

Despite the above-mentioned differences in the types of these products, both their productions depend on donation. Whenever donation is involved, the donor needs the assurance that his contribution is used directly and entirely towards production and is not converted into profits. The nonprofit firm emerges as the chosen form of industrial organization.

We have now examined some reasons for the existence of nonprofit firms. Just because there are reasons for nonprofit firms to exist, it does not mean that their actual existence is assured. Resources must be committed to nonprofit firms. From the above discussions, the supply of resources to the nonprofit firms apparently hinges on the altruistic behavior of the resource owners. We examine this issue in the next subsection.

Altruism and Nonprofit Firms

Conventionally, altruistic behavior is generally defined as an act of giving which involves a sacrifice, that is, the giver gives up his own enjoyment in favor of the receiver. This pure altruistic behavior, though requiring explanation, is not the subject of the present survey. Here our concern is solely with behavior in which, although it has the appearance of altruism, the giver is in fact compensated because there is an interdependence either in utilities or in production and exchange.

The economic analysis of altruistic behavior which stems from interdependence in utility has a long history.[2] The utility of individual A depends not only on his own consumption bundle but also on the consumption bundles of others. If A's utility function is monotonically increasing with regard to the consumption of B, C, . . . , then A is said to be altruistic. Some writers object to this notion of altruism and hold it as an abuse of the term because individual A has actually increased his own satisfaction by giving to those upon whom his utility depends (Kurz, 1977). A weaker definition stipulates that an individual is altruistic if his utility is enhanced not by giving to specific individuals but rather by giving to a worthy cause, knowing simply that his contribution has benefited someone else in the community.

As an alternative to the utility-interdependence approach, Kurz (1977) and Hammond (1975) sought to explain altruistic behavior by way of interdependence in production and exchange. In an environment where the cost of making and enforcing a contract is high, there is an advantage in conducting transactions by relying upon informal contracts. These informal contracts do not specify exactly what the contracting parties will do but only communicate expectations that they will do the "right thing." What constitutes the right thing depends upon the social norm. Moreover, no court of law can be relied upon to enforce informal contracts. They must be enforced collectively by society according to the prevailing social ethics. A high ethical norm needs the support of altruistic behavior. There are two reasons why altruistic behavior is consistent with egoism: first, the egoist believes that he would be given aid if he were in the place of the unfortunate; second, he believes that if he were not behaving according to the social norm, then others would do likewise, thus leading to a deterioration of the social environment. This deterioration would ultimately leave him unprotected if he were to need help in the future.

The altruistic behavior needed to support a high social ethical norm is broadly defined as "an act by one person of providing goods and services to another without an enforceable contract to receive maximum compensation for his act" (Kurz, 1977, p. 181). This definition of altruism is quite consistent with charitable giving.

Charitable contributions can take many forms. They include the supply of entrepreneurial talents needed to organize production, the supply of labor services at a reduced wage level, and the donation of capital needed to finance the nonprofit firm's production. Society collectively can practice altruism in a different manner: it can provide tax reduction or exemptions to the nonprofit firm. All told, it is the altruistic behavior of the members of society that brings nonprofit firms into existence.

Having established reasons for the existence of nonprofit firms, we are now ready to review the literature concerning their behavior and performance.

Behavior of Nonprofit Firms

The literature examines the behavior of nonprofit firms and assesses their performance by comparing them with for-profit firms. Generally, this comparison is carried out under an implicit methodological paradigm which asserts that nonprofit and for-profit firms face different operating constraints and therefore must choose to pursue different objectives. The pursuance of different objectives, in turn, leads them to behave in different ways and to produce different allocative consequences.

Specifically, nonprofit and for-profit firms face fundamentally different operating constraints. First, the nonprofit firm faces the nondistribution constraint while the for-profit firm does not. Second, nonprofit and for-profit firms use different sources to finance their production. The nonprofit firm relies on donations while the for-profit firm relies on equity financing. Finally, nonprofit firms enjoy tax advantages which are not available to for-profit firms.

These differences in operating constraints greatly influence the objectives of nonprofit and for-profit firms. As examined in chapter 4, the objectives of for-profit firms are assumed to be dominated by the profit motive. Because nonprofit firms are explicitly prevented from pursuing profits by the nondistribution constraint, different objectives for them are postulated by the different authors. These possible objectives include quality maximization, quantity maximization, and budget maximization.[3]

Quality maximization is seen as a plausible goal for nonprofit firms managed by professionals who, as observed by Hansmann, "derive strong satisfaction doing craftsman-like work" or take it as their mission to provide quality services to their clientele (Hansmann, 1987, p. 37). Thus hospitals proudly provide quality services supported by up-to-date equipment (Newhouse, 1970; Lee, 1971), theaters and orchestras perform highbrow programs catering only to the culturally elite (Hansmann, 1981), and universities emphasize graduate work and research at the expense of undergraduate teaching. Alternatively, the professional may do just as well to pursue quantity goals. They may opt to serve "as broad a segment of the public as possible" (James and Neuberger, 1981) or may be driven by the desire to build an empire in order to enjoy the prestige associated with it.

Quantity and quality maximization may not be the only way of achieving these goals. Some managers of nonprofit firms may, instead, seek to maximize the budget. Budget maximization not only provides the manager with the prestige associated with the size of the firm, it also offers the flexibility to obtain the desired tradeoff available to quantity and quality maximization (Hansmann, 1981, p. 37).

The authors of these models also explore the welfare implications of the behavior implied by the models. Generally, the property rights theorists (Alchian and Demsetz, 1972) claim that, regardless of what goal or goals the nonprofit firms pursue, the nondistribution constraint invariably makes them inefficient. The absence of ownership claims to the residual prevents anyone with a financial incentive from policing the firm's operation, thus causing the nonprofit firms to produce at a higher cost than the for-profit firms. As long as there are donations and tax subsidies to make up the difference, the nonprofit firms can afford to be inefficient and still survive the competition of their for-profit counterparts.

In addition, it is also said that, compared with for-profit firms, nonprofit firms tend to respond slowly to changes in market demand. A slow response to an increase in market demand is partly explained by the fact that nonprofit firms, facing the nondistribution constraint, are unable to finance through the equity capital market but must seek funding through donation. A perception of needs must be present before potential donors can contemplate giving. A lag in the perception of needs serves to delay the nonprofit firm's response to demand increases. The same delay in response also applies to decreases in demand. The dedicated professionals are often mission minded; the desire to serve their clientele prevents them from taking market cues in curtailing their operations. As long as the cost of production can be met by donations, the nonprofit firms will continue their rate of production.

The condemnation of nonprofit firms is by no means universal; there are others who hold favorable opinions about them. As we have seen earlier, in a market where consumers have difficulties in assessing the quality of a product, market failure occurs in the for-profit sector. Demand for the product declines which, in turn, discourages its supply. The nonprofit firm operating under the nondistribution constraint serves to assure the donor and the demander that the quality of the product will be maintained (Nelson and Krachinsky, 1973). This assurance not only has the effect of restoring demand for the product but also enhances donors' appeal; an increase in donation leads to greater production. Consequently, the nonprofit firms restore efficiency to the market whenever consumers are uncertain of their ability to judge the quality of the products.

All told, a good many controversies exist about the merits of the nonprofit firms. As always, when theoretical controversies rage, economists seek the guidance of empirical analyses. Unfortunately, empirical studies on nonprofit firms and for-profit firms, using data from Blue Cross–Blue Shield (Blair et al., 1975), nursing homes (Weisbrod and Schlesinger, 1986), and hospitals (Clarkson, 1972), yield inconclusive results. Some mildly confirm the property rights hypothesis while others negate it. To some, this conclusion is not surprising (Steinberg, 1987, p. 126). First, theoretical advantages accorded to the for-profit firm are exaggerated, and second, owing to a separation of "ownership and control," some firms in the for-profit sector may themselves not be profit-maximizers. Therefore these comparisons are, by and large, meaningless.

This controversy echoes the one that we examined in chapters 4 and 8. Recall that we have reached the conclusion that it is meaningless to deduce the behavior of a for-profit firm from an assumed objective function and that the welfare implications drawn from the deduced behavior are untrustworthy. This conclusion applies equally well here. Firms, for-profit and nonprofit alike, do not have objectives of their own. All firms are coalitions of entrepreneurs; the for-profit entrepreneurs coalesce to form for-profit firms and the altruistic-minded entrepreneurs coalesce to form nonprofit firms. The cooperative entrepreneurs each use the firm that they have formed as a vehicle to pursue their own goals. They do so by bargaining among themselves to determine a joint policy which best serves each cooperative entrepreneur's self-interest. The for-profit and the nonprofit firms then compete in the factor markets for scarce resources and in the product markets for the consumers' purchasing power. Through bargaining among the entrepreneurs and competition in the marketplace, the for-profit firms, the nonprofit firms, and the economy reach a general equilibrium. In the next section we describe this equilibrium process and examine its allocative implications.

AN ECONOMY WITH A NONPROFIT SECTOR

The hallmark of the nonprofit sector is "voluntarism, charity and community" (Young, 1986, p. 177). Based upon social ethics the members of society voluntarily mobilize their resources in an altruistic manner to assist those who are in need or to provide goods and services that are deemed necessary for the benefit of society. Thus the characteristic of the nonprofit sector is unique. Unlike the public sector and the private for-profit sector, where goods and services are provided through compulsory taxation and with the lure of pecuniary gains respectively, production in the nonprofit sector takes place in response to perceived needs and is financed by voluntary contributions. Benevolent entrepreneurs and laborers contribute their services at a sacrifice in pay, capitalists and other resource owners donate their resources without considering pecuniary returns, and the public contributes in the form of tax exemptions.

Given that there exist fundamental differences in the characteristics of the three sectors in the economy, we naturally wish to know how the various sectors coexist and come into an equilibrium. The literature has examined the coexistence of the public and the private for-profit sectors,[4] but has neglected to examine the coexistence of the private for-profit and nonprofit sectors or the coexistence of all three sectors in a general equilibrium setting. Owing to the complexity of the three-sector coexistence problem and the fact that undertaking such a project will take us away from the basic theme of this book, we will not deal with it here. In this chapter we will only endeavor to model the coexistence of the private for-profit and nonprofit sectors.

The purpose of this section is to present a general equilibrium model of an economy including both the for-profit and nonprofit sectors. The basic nature of the model is identical with that presented in chapter 6. Here we take into account the fact that the characteristics of the consumers and the entrepreneurs are now more complex. The consumer derives utility not only from consuming goods and services in the profit sector but also from consuming charitable goods and services and making charitable donations. At the same time, entrepreneurs not only seek satisfaction from endeavors associated with profit-making but also from activities associated with social services and pursuing high social ideals. These increases in the complex character of the agents naturally translate into a more complex model for the economy. However, despite the increased complexity of the economy, we wish to emphasize that the economy still operates in the manner described in chapter 6.

In this section we again use a Hicksian two-period temporary equilibrium model to describe the nature of decisions made by all agents and the process which brings the economy into a state of equilibrium. In this model, the consumer–resource owner plays a dual role and occupies the center stage. In order to carry out his consumption activities, the consumer–resource owner must convert his resources into income by participating in production. The owners of tradeable resources – land, labor, and capital – will convert their resources into income through the market. The entrepreneurs, in contrast, must convert their talents into income by organizing a firm. In this model, we assume that the entrepreneurs are divided into two distinct groups: profit-oriented entrepreneurs and nonprofit-oriented entrepreneurs.[5] Thus the activities in the economy simultaneously include the consumption– investment activities of the consumer, the coalition-formation activities of the entrepreneurs, and the production activities of the for-profit and nonprofit firms. As these activities interact to bring the economy into a state of equilibrium, not only are the structures of the for-profit and nonprofit sectors determined, but the commodity prices are also determined and the resources are channeled into optimal uses. Consequently, the formation of firms, the determination of resource utilization, and the exchange of goods and services are all an integral part of the market process. The purpose of this section is to present a model which captures this idea.[6] This model includes three components: descriptions of the consumer's behavior, the entrepreneur's activities, and the market process.

The Consumer

The consumer is assumed to possess a von Neumann–Morgenstern utility function defined on the triplet commodity set comprising the current consumption bundle of goods and services purchased in the for-profit sector, the future consumption bundle of these purchased goods and services, and the future consumption bundle of charitable goods and services as well as charitable contributions. The inclusion of future consumption of charitable goods and services in the utility function requires no justification. The inclusion of charitable givings in the utility function is based upon the notion presented in the last section that in an ethical society the giving of resources toward the production of charitable goods and services also yields the giver some utility. Charitable giving can take many forms; it can be either in kind or in money. For simplicity, we will assume that all charitable givings are made in money. This assumption is innocuous because all donations made in kind can be viewed as if the donor has received the full market value of his donated resources and then contributed the money that he has received to charity.[7]

Given the consumer's utility function, he will choose the commodity bundles, one in each period, to maximize his utility subject to the budget constraints. The nature of this choice problem will be made clear shortly; here we wish to describe the nature of the constraints.

As observed in chapter 6, the individual's budget constraints, one in each period, depend on the role he plays as a resource owner. The nature of these differences has been thoroughly discussed in chapter 6; we will not repeat the discussion here. Now we need only point out that, in the presence of nonprofit firms and charitable givings, the consumer's budget constraints undergo a change. The following is a description of these constraints in general terms.

Let a consumer's total outlay in the first period be the sum of expenditures that he has incurred for present consumption and for purchasing a stock and bond portfolio. In this model we assume that the profit-oriented entrepreneur receives a share of the firm's profit in the second period while the nonprofit-oriented entrepreneur receives a salary in the first period. Then for every consumer, except those who are nonprofit-oriented entrepreneurs, the total first-period outlay must not exceed the value of his total endowment in that period. For the consumer who is a nonprofit-oriented entrepreneur, the total outlay in the first period must not exceed the value of his first-period total endowment plus his salary as a nonprofit-seeking entrepreneur. The consumer's second-period budget constraint is slightly more complex; it also depends upon whether the consumer is a giver or receiver of charity. If the consumer is a giver of charity, his second-period outlay is his expenditure on noncharitable goods and services incurred in the second period plus his total charitable givings; if the consumer is a receiver of charity, his second-period outlay is the sum of his expenditure in both charitable and noncharitable goods and services incurred in the second period. In this model, we assume that the prices of the charitable goods and services are given exogenously by a nonmarket authority.[8] For every consumer, whether a giver or receiver of charity, the total outlay in the second period must not exceed his income for that period. However, the consumer's income crucially depends upon whether or not he is a profit-oriented entrepreneur. If the consumer is not a profit-oriented entrepreneur, his second-period income is the sum of his second-period endowment, dividend incomes, and interest incomes. If the consumer is a profit-oriented entrepreneur, his second-period income also includes his share of a firm's profit.

Having described the consumer's utility function and his budget constraints, we are ready to describe his choice problem. Because future markets do not exist, commodities for the second period cannot be traded in the first period. The consumer must make his consumption–investment decisions on the basis of some subjective expectations about second-period prices and income. On the basis of these expectations, the consumer solves his maximization problem in two stages. For any given choice of the first-period consumption bundle and resource commitments, and realized second-period prices and income, the consumer maximizes his utility by choosing the second-period consumption bundle subject to the budget constraint of that period. This second-period consumption bundle includes noncharitable goods and services, charitable goods and services, and charity donations. The resulting utility maximum, referred to as the derived utility function, is now a function of the first-period consumption bundle and the resources committed for first-period production. The derived utility is then maximized with respect to its arguments subject to the budget constraint of the first period. The outcome of this maximization problem represents the consumer's equilibrium in the current period.

The resolution of the consumer's decision problem provides us with the supply function of all tradeable factors of production and the demand functions for all products. We now need to analyze the other side of the demand and supply equations. To do this, we must investigate entrepreneurial activities.

Firm as a Coalition of Entrepreneurs

Let there be N agents in the economy. N_e of these N agents are entrepreneurs. Since not all agents are willing or able to assume the entrepreneurial role, N_e is a proper subset of N. The N_e entrepreneurs are, in turn, split into two subgroups: profit-oriented entrepreneurs, denoted by N_{e1}, and nonprofit-oriented entrepreneurs, denoted by N_{e2}. In this section we do not examine the reasons why an entrepreneur becomes either a profit-oriented or a nonprofit-oriented entrepreneur. We will investigate this issue in the next section. Here we wish to observe that the profit-oriented entrepreneurs will coalesce among themselves to form the for-profit firms, while the nonprofit-oriented entrepreneurs will coalesce among themselves to form the nonprofit firms. The two types of entrepreneurs do not mix with each other. Consequently there are potentially at most $2^{N_{e1}} - 1$ firms in the for-profit sector and $2^{N_{e2}} - 1$ firms in the nonprofit sector.

For a variety of reasons, many potential firms will not form. In chapter 6, we examined some of these reasons in connection with for-profit firms. We briefly summarize these reasons here. Some for-profit firms cannot form simply because the coalition of entrepreneurs does not possess the technical and managerial know-how to produce the product at a sufficiently low cost or cannot attract sufficient demand to make the production profitable. Other for-profit firms cannot form because the coalition of entrepreneurs fails to secure sufficient funds in the capital market to finance the intended production. Yet other for-profit firms fail to form because the potential cooperative entrepreneurs cannot agree upon a joint production policy, sharing rule, or internal organization which delineates each cooperative entrepreneur's authority and responsibility. Finally, some for-profit firms fail to form because the potential cooperative entrepreneurs cannot agree upon a cost-effective mechanism to safeguard against the potential damage caused by their opportunistic behavior.

The for-profit firms that do form are the result of a nonmarket process – a society-wide cooperative game played by the profit-oriented entrepreneurs with the production policy, the financing policy, and the sharing rule as the strategies of the game. When a group of profit-oriented entrepreneurs come together and agree upon a given set of policies which include an internal organization structure, a portfolio of stocks and bonds that the firm will issue, and a profit-sharing rule, a for-profit firm is formed.

The firm organized in the context of the present model will have a two-period decision horizon. The for-profit firm issues stocks and bonds in the first period in order to purchase inputs and commence production. In the second period, it produces its outputs and sells them in the market at the market prices. It then repays its loans with interest to its bondholders, pays dividends to its shareholders, and distributes its profits as a bonus to the cooperative entrepreneurs. Thereafter, the firm vanishes.

Likewise, not all $2^{N_{e2}} - 1$ potential nonprofit firms will form. The reasons used to explain the nonformation of for-profit firms also apply here. However, because nonprofit firms are barred from using the equity capital market but must secure sufficient funds from donations to finance their production, the financing failure described in connection with for-profit firms must be modified. Fund-raising through donation is possible only when a social need is clearly demonstrated. Thus donations customarily take place in the second period when the extent of the deficit of a nonprofit firm becomes evident. Yet, owing to the existence of a one-period production lag, production must be initiated in the first period. However, this is possible only if the firm is able to purchase the inputs required by incurring a debt. The lender is willing to finance production only under the condition that the firm's expected revenue-generating capacity plus its ability to collect donations is sufficient to repay the loan with interest. Financing failure in this context takes on a different meaning from that mentioned earlier. A nonprofit firm will not form if the cooperative entrepreneurs or lenders are not confident that the firm will be able to collect enough donations, including the cooperative entrepreneurs' own contributions, to make up the anticipated operating deficit.

Again, all the nonprofit firms that do form are the result of a society-wide cooperative game played by the nonprofit-oriented entrepreneurs with production policy, financing policy, and entrepreneur salary as game strategies. When a group of nonprofit-oriented entrepreneurs have agreed upon a given set of policies which includes the internal organization of the firm, a deficit-sharing rule, and the salary structure of the entrepreneurs, a nonprofit firm is formed.

The nonprofit firm that does form also faces a two-period planning horizon. It issues bonds in the first period in order to finance the purchase of the inputs required for production. In the second period, the firm produces its product and sells it in the market at a predetermined price level. Since the price of the charitable good or service is set intentionally below the average cost of production, a deficit results. The nonprofit-oriented entrepreneurs then solicit contributions from the public in an attempt to make up this deficit. Whenever the public contribution is not sufficient to meet this deficit, the cooperative entrepreneurs will make up this difference on the basis of the predetermined deficit-sharing rule. After this is done in a two-period setting, the nonprofit firm vanishes.

From the above descriptions of the coalition formation processes for for-profit and nonprofit firms, we observe that there is a fundamental difference between the nature of remunerations for profit-oriented and nonprofit-oriented entrepreneurs. The profit-oriented entrepreneur receives a share of the firm's profit which only becomes known in the second period. The nonprofit-oriented entrepreneur, in contrast, receives a salary which is determined and disbursed in the first period. As we have noted in chapters 5 and 10, the profit-oriented entrepreneur is prevented from claiming a salary and must retain residual claimant status in order to discourage him from acting opportunistically. Might we wonder why we are not equally concerned with the nonprofit-oriented entrepreneurs? Are the nonprofit-oriented entrepreneurs free from temptation concerning gains that may result from shirking?

There is a built-in mechanism to discourage nonprofit-oriented entrepreneurs from shirking and laxity of economic efficiency – henceforth referred to as lack of economic discipline. This built-in mechanism is associated with the way that deficits are made up in the second period. Note that greater laxity in economic discipline will lead to a greater deficit; a greater deficit, in turn, requires the nonprofit-oriented entrepreneurs to expand more effort on soliciting donations in order to make up the deficit. Consequently, there is a tradeoff between the entrepreneur's gain derived from lax economic discipline and his loss caused by the increased need to solicit donations. This tradeoff sets a limit on the ability of nonprofit-oriented entrepreneurs to enjoy shirking or excess indulgence in spending. In addition, there is a last resort for discouraging nonprofit-oriented entrepreneurs from enjoying lax economic discipline. Whenever public donations fall short of the operating deficit, the entrepreneurs must themselves make up the difference. The threat of making the nonprofit-oriented entrepreneurs personally responsible for the nonprofit firm's debt serves as a last resort for disciplining their actions.

General Equilibrium

Although the economy includes both for-profit and nonprofit sectors and the characters of the associated consumers and entrepreneurs are more complex, the market and nonmarket activities taking place in the economy remain similar to those described in chapter 6. The consumer and the owners of the tradeable resources pursue their interests through the markets by acting noncooperatively. The profit-oriented and nonprofit-oriented entrepreneurs, however, must act cooperatively in production through the formation of a firm. The agents, as both consumers and resource owners, in pursuing their own self-interest interact with each other and lead the economy into a state of equilibrium.

Because our main interest is to demonstrate that the formation of a firm is an integral part of the equilibrating process, we will center our attention on the equilibrium conditions in the first period, that is, on the determination of the following endogenous variables: (a) the structures of firms in both the for-profit and nonprofit sectors; (b) the market prices of all tradeable commodities including the interest rate; (c) the consumption–investment bundles of each consumer–resource owner; (d) the input bundle of each firm; (e) both profit-oriented and nonprofit-oriented entrepreneurial returns and commitments.[9]

Having identified the endogenous variables, we now describe the equilibrium process in a competitive economy when all agents act as price-takers in the marketplace. First, let the market prices be given. Each agent, as a consumer or as a nonentrepreneurial resource owner, chooses his own strategy so that the resulting consumption and resource commitment maximizes his derived utility subject to his first-period budget constraint. The entrepreneurs, however, in addition to choosing each of their consumption bundles, must also, through the formation of either a for-profit or a nonprofit firm, jointly choose their strategy regarding their resource commitments. This strategy can be represented by a triplet. For the profit-oriented entrepreneurs, this triplet consists of the commodity input bundle, entrepreneurial inputs, and the profit-sharing rule. For the nonprofit-oriented entrepreneurs, this triplet consists of commodity input bundles, entrepreneurial inputs, and salaries as well as the entrepreneurs' deficit-sharing rule. These choices must be made within the constraints set by the availability of funds as well as the availability of entrepreneurial talents. The availability of funds for a for-profit firm is limited by its ability to raise money in the equity capital market, and availability of funds for a nonprofit firm is set by its expected ability to raise money from donations in order to repay its debt in the second period.

From this description of the equilibrium process we again see that as a result of entrepreneurial activities a dichotomy between demand and supply emerges in the marketplace. The firm, whether for-profit or nonprofit, is the resources demander and the goods supplier. The resource owner, in contrast, is the demander for goods and supplier of resources. In this way, the demand and supply of goods and services through imputation and competition interact to determine the commodity prices. The economy constrained by the total resource endowments reaches an equilibrium when the prices of the current-period commodities are determined, all markets are cleared, and no entry or exit of firms takes place. In this state of equilibrium, no nonentrepreneur agent can improve upon his current activities by his own action, and no entrepreneur can improve his current activities by forming a new coalition. The for-profit and nonprofit firms coexist.

WELFARE ANALYSIS

Now that we have presented the model, which describes how for-profit and nonprofit firms come into existence, and also outlined the nature of a general equilibrium in an economy involving both types of firms, we are ready to investigate the welfare properties when this economy is in equilibrium.

Recall that there are controversies in the literature about the relative merits of for-profit and the nonprofit firms. The root of these controversies is the assumption that different types of firms have different objective functions and face different constraints. The property rights economist holds that, because the nonprofit firm pursues objectives other than profits and faces the nondistribution constraint, no one will have the interest and the responsibility to police its operation. Hence nonprofit firms tend to function less efficiently than for-profit firms where the owner's objective is to minimize costs so as to maximize profits. In contrast, the contract failure economist insists that, whenever information asymmetry exists between buyer and seller, it is precisely because no one is allowed to claim the residual of the nonprofit firms so that it becomes superior to the for-profit firm. In the presence of information asymmetry, the profit firm uses its private information to exploit the consumer by lying about product quality. The prevalence of such abuses discourages demand and causes the market to fail. Potentially gainful trades may not be carried out. The nonprofit firm, operating under the nondistribution constraint, will have limited incentive to lie about product quality; therefore the consumer is guaranteed a minimum quality product. This guarantee restores the demand for the product and rescues the market from failure.

Following this line of reasoning, we can no longer assert that the nonprofit firm is either inferior or superior to the for-profit firm. These firms coexist as a result of different underlying information structures within different markets. The for-profit firms have the comparative advantage in markets where information asymmetry is absent, while the nonprofit firms have the comparative advantage in markets where information asymmetry is present. For some the coexistence of for-profit and nonprofit firms thus reflects the fact that information asymmetry is present in some markets but not in others. Given the state of information asymmetry, the structural composition of the for-profit and nonprofit firms in the economy represents the optimal production structure. This conclusion suggests that the very existence of the nonprofit firms guarantees that their performances are optimal. Thus the contract failure theorist ties the existence of nonprofit firms entirely to information asymmetry. This position is, of course, too simplistic and not warranted. It is fair to say that the literature has not offered us a complete welfare assessment of the coexistence of for-profit and nonprofit firms.

As mentioned earlier, we do not believe that the welfare effect of either the for-profit or the nonprofit firm can be deduced from the assumed objective functions of these firms. This is because the firm, either for-profit or nonprofit, does not possess an objective of its own. Instead, the profit-oriented or nonprofit-oriented entrepreneurs use the firm as a stepping stone to pursuing their own objectives. The welfare implications of a particular type of firm must be found by examining the objectives of the relevant entrepreneurs and by studying how these objectives are translated into production policies and, in turn, how these policies affect the market outcomes. In short, the welfare implications of a particular type of firm must be found by examining the general equilibria involving this type of firm. In this section we investigate two distinct welfare issues. First, we take the consumers' utilities as well as the number of profit-oriented and nonprofit-oriented entrepreneurs as given and investigate the relative efficiency of the for-profit and nonprofit firms. Second, we investigate how changes in the parameters mentioned above affect social welfare.

Comparison of the Efficiency of For-profit and Nonprofit Firms

From the second section we know that a resource owner, other than the entrepreneur, can convert all his resources into income through the factor markets; he will then maximize his utility by carrying out all his consumption–investment activities in the markets. The entrepreneur, however, must convert his entrepreneurial talent into income through the formation of a firm. In order to maximize his utility, he must carry out his consumption–investment activities using both market and nonmarket means. This is true for both the profit-oriented and nonprofit-oriented entrepreneurs. Because each agent strives to maximize his own utility, at equilibrium every agent's utility is maximized even though the firms are divided into two distinct types. Moreover, if all cooperative agreements made by the cooperative entrepreneurs are binding, the equilibrium outcome is Pareto optimal. Because, as shown in the second section, the for-profit and nonprofit firms use different decision rules for production and face different constraints, we can conclude that the attainment of a Pareto optimum does not require all agents to behave in a uniform manner. As long as every agent has the opportunity of exploiting the full potential of his resources either through the markets or by nonmarket means, the resulting competitive market equilibrium will be Pareto optimal. Note that this conclusion depends crucially upon the condition that all cooperative agreements made by the entrepreneurs are binding and are fully enforceable without costs. This condition is, of course, impossible to fulfill.

As shown in chapter 7, because entrepreneurs behave opportunistically, it is impossible for cooperative entrepreneurs to attain the maximum benefit of cooperation; thus it is impossible for the economy to attain the Pareto-optimal outcome. Since social welfare is not directly affected by whether firms are organized as for-profit or as nonprofit entities but rather by the nonfulfillment of contractual obligations among the cooperative entrepreneurs, the comparison of relative efficiency between the for-profit and nonprofit firms reduces to comparison of the likelihood of contractual violations by the profit-oriented and nonprofit-oriented entrepreneurs. Because there is no a priori reason to believe that either the profit-oriented or the nonprofit-oriented entrepreneur possesses a greater self-discipline in upholding agreements, there is no reason to believe that one type of entrepreneur is more prone to opportunistic behavior than the other. Any such difference must be explained by the difference in the control mechanism of the for-profit and nonprofit firms, that is, whether the for-profit firm or the nonprofit firm as an industrial organization is more apt to curb opportunistic behavior of its cooperative entrepreneurs.

As observed earlier, both the for-profit and nonprofit firms have built-in mechanisms to safeguard against contract violations. For the profit firm, each entrepreneur receives a share of the firm's profit in the form of a bonus. Contractual violation implies a smaller profit, which in turn leads to a smaller bonus. By tying the entrepreneur's return to the profit, it is hoped that contractual violations can be avoided. In addition, the capital market also serves to discipline entrepreneurial misconduct. The firm with opportunistic entrepreneurs will have difficulty securing funds from the equity market; thus opportunistic entrepreneurs must accept a smaller share of the residual as a bonus. Therefore in order to protect the ability to secure sufficient funds to finance production, entrepreneurs must refrain from behaving opportunistically. Finally, in an imperfect capital market where the majority shareholders hold veto power over the firm's decisions, the shareholders could use this veto power as a threat to discourage the entrepreneurs from behaving opportunistically. Whenever these built-in mechanisms are not sufficient to curb opportunistic behavior, an explicit control mechanism must be introduced. It is important to note that whenever the firm relies on the control mechanism to curb the opportunistic behavior of its members, the entrepreneurs can only expect a satisfactory result of cooperation; the maximum cooperative result is no longer attainable.

For the nonprofit firm, the built-in mechanism used to discourage opportunism is different. Despite the fact that the nonprofit-oriented entrepreneur receives a fixed salary, he is not free to renege on all his contractual obligations. Greater violation of agreements leads to a larger deficit. Because the nonprofit entrepreneurs must exert greater effort to solicit donations to repay this larger deficit, they are discouraged from excessive contract violations. In addition, the donors may serve as auditors of entrepreneurial performances. Because donors desire to insure that their contributions benefit the consumers and will channel their donations to the firm organized by diligent entrepreneurs, the threat of withdrawing donations may discourage the entrepreneurs from violating contractual obligations. Finally, the nonprofit firms are subject to government regulations and audits. This government supervision also serves to discourage the nonprofit-oriented entrepreneurs from shirking their obligations. As in the case of the for-profit firm, the built-in mechanism of the nonprofit firm is insufficient to curb all opportunistic behavior. A firm-specific control mechanism must be established. Despite the fact that the nonprofit-oriented entrepreneur's decision problem is different from that of the profit-oriented entrepreneur, it can be shown that the nature of the nonprofit firm's control structure is similar to that of the for-profit firm. The reliance on control mechanisms to curb opportunistic behavior again yields for the cooperative entrepreneurs a satisfactory result of cooperation rather than the maximum result of cooperation.

Although we have failed to find a difference in the effectiveness of the control mechanism employed by the for-profit and nonprofit firms, we can still claim that one type of firm is more efficient than the other if the same opportunistic behavior produces a greater antisocial outcome under one type of firm than under the other. Because entrepreneurs can unilaterally violate the agreement by altering either the effort commitments or the action commitments, we will discuss the welfare impact of each violation in turn.

Shirking of effort, whether by profit-oriented or nonprofit-oriented entrepreneurs, will lead to a reduction in output, a reduction in each other's utility, and increased production cost. For the for-profit firm, an increase in the cost of production leads to a decrease in product supply. Shirking by profit-oriented entrepreneurs across the industry will decrease the market supply and increase the product price. This increase in price will, in turn, decrease the quantity of the product demanded and hence the utilities of the consumers. For the nonprofit firm, an increase in the cost of production leads to a greater deficit for the firm. Whether the consumer's welfare is adversely affected crucially depends upon the donors' reaction to the deficit. If donors respond negatively to the increased deficit induced by the entre-preneurs' shirking, then the firm's output will decrease and the consumer will suffer a loss in utility. However, if the increase in deficit causes the donor to believe that there now exists a greater need for the charitable product, then donations may be increased and the total output maintained. As a result, the consumer's utility will not be lowered by the entrepreneurs' shirking. At the same time, as the donor responds to the "greater needs" in charity by increasing his contribution, his utility is also increased. Thus, paradoxically, shirking by the nonprofit-oriented entrepreneur can lead to an increase in social welfare. This increase in social welfare is, of course, illusory. It is analogous to an increase in the consumer's welfare caused by the manipulative advertising taking place in the profit sector. If consumers and donors were aware of the true situation, their actions would have been reversed. Such imagined increases in social welfare do not represent a better utilization of social resources.

The welfare consequence of reneging on the agreed level of action by the entrepreneur is ambiguous. Suppose that either a profit-oriented or a nonprofit-oriented entrepreneur, after receiving private infor-mation, chooses a level of action different from that agreed upon. This course of action will affect the composition of the output produced by the firm. Such a deviation in the production plan, although increasing the utility of the perpetrator, will decrease the utilities of the other cooperative entrepreneurs. In addition, it is not clear that this deviation in the production plan will adversely affect all consumers. Suppose that a change in the production plan causes an increase in the quantity (quality) of a certain product at the expense of the other jointly produced products. Consumers who prefer the product whose quantity (quality) has been increased will experience increases in utility while consumers who prefer the other products will suffer losses in utility . Because interpersonal comparison of utility is not (theoretically) possible, the effect of reneging on the agreed level of action by a single entrepreneur is ambiguous.

However, the consequence of altering the action level by all cooperative entrepreneurs is different. These deviations from the agreed levels of action not only adversely affect the utility of all cooperative entrepreneurs but also increase production costs. Regarding the for-profit firms, this increase in production costs will lead to a decrease in their supplies and an increase in the market prices. Therefore the consumer's welfare is impaired. In contrast, an increase in the cost of production in the nonprofit firms need not lead to a decrease in the quantity (quality) of the charitable goods and services. If an increase in the cost of production were to induce a greater amount of donations, reneging on contractual agreements by the nonprofit-oriented entrepreneur might actually lead to an apparent increase in social welfare. As mentioned earlier, this increase in social welfare is illusory.

In conclusion, opportunistic behavior, whether by the profit-oriented or by the nonprofit-oriented entrepreneur, leads to a reduction in the gains derived from cooperation. There is no plausible reason for believing that either the for-profit or the nonprofit firm is an industrial organization better suited to curb deviations from agreements. The ability to uphold agreements is strictly firm specific. It depends crucially upon whether the coalition of entrepreneurs is able to create a firm-specific culture and control apparatus. Consequently, it is the ethical and the control quality in each and every firm that ultimately contributes to the level of welfare at the general equilibrium. The type of firm is not a determining factor of this outcome.

Welfare Effect of Altruism

In order to carry out a welfare comparison among systems, we must first specify what constitutes the set of all potential optimal allocations in each system. Recall that the structure of the entrepreneur-centered economy involves $N = \{1, \ldots, n\}$ agents. Each agent plays a dual role; he is simultaneously a consumer and a resource owner. Entrepreneurs are a subset of the resource owners. These entrepreneurs are further divided into two distinct groups – the profit-oriented and nonprofit-oriented entrepreneurs. The members of each entrepreneurial group coalesce to form either the for-profit or the nonprofit firms. As noted earlier, each firm possesses a coalition-specific production possibility set which is described by the set of input–output combinations. The firm's production possibility set is determined jointly by the production technology and the capabilities of the cooperative entrepreneurs. In turn, the capability of the cooperative entrepreneurs is determined not only by the endowed abilities of the entrepreneurs but also by the organization, information, and control structures they adopt. As usual, the consumer and the firms together form the coalition production economy. The activities in this economy can be described by a nonside payment game. In this book we adopt the core as the solution concept of this game, where the core is defined as the set of feasible and stable utility allocations to the agents. By a stable allocation, we mean that no other coalition exists which is capable of improving the agents' utility allocation.

Given that a coalition production economy is associated with a nonside payment game and that the equilibrium of this economy is represented by the core of that nonside payment game, the comparison of economic systems can be reduced to the comparison of the core allocations of these systems (Qin, 1987).

The comparison of the core allocations represents a game-theoretic formalization of the traditional welfare economics. According to welfare economics, as long as interpersonal comparison of utility is held to be impossible, a competitive economy does not yield a unique optimal social outcome. The set of social optimal allocations is referred to as the Pareto frontier. A unique Pareto frontier is associated with each competitive economic system. Comparison of the social desirability of the egoistic and ethical systems is reduced to a comparison of the Pareto frontiers associated with these systems. We will use an example to examine the nature of this comparison.

Let society be comprised of two individuals whose preferences are represented by the utility functions u^1 and u^2 respectively. In figure 11.1, the Pareto frontiers associated with the egoistic system and the ethical system are labeled PP and P′P′ respectively. The slope of PP is everywhere negative, reflecting that the individuals are completely egoistic. A redistribution of initial wealth from one individual to the other invariably decreases the utility of the former and increases the utility of the latter. In contrast, the slope of P′P′ is positive in some

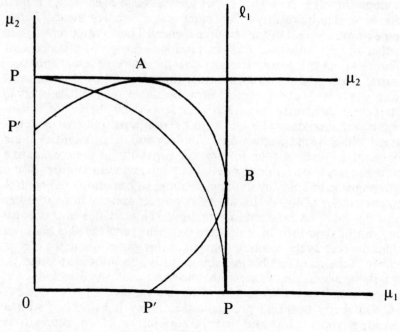

Figure 11.1

ranges and negative in others. The slopes of P'P' reflects the fact that the individual's utility functions are interdependent; that is, each individual's utility depends on both his own and the other person's consumption of each good and supply of each factor. Altruism implies that when individual I is rich and individual II is poor, individual I's utility increases if he gives part of his initial endowment to II. Thus P'A is positively sloped. However, when individual II's consumption of goods and services, with I's help, exceeds a certain level, a further increase in the consumption of these goods and services by II will reduce I's utility. Hence the slope of P'P' in the range of AB is negatively sloped. In an ethical society, if the relative endowments of I and II are reversed, II will also adopt the same benevolent attitude toward I. Thus the Pareto frontier takes on the shape P'P'. Despite the fact that positively sloped portions exist on the Pareto frontier, it is important to note that the equilibrium outcome of any competitive economy must lie on the negatively sloped portion of the Pareto frontier.

The comparison of the egoistical and ethical societies can now be

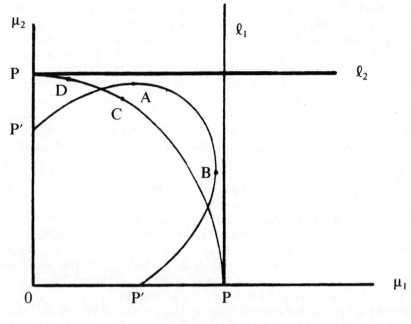

Figure 11.2

carried out by comparing the Pareto frontiers PP and P'P'. If we let the negative sloped range of P'P' curve lie everywhere to the northeast of the PP curve with the end point A not lying below ℓ_2 and the end point B not lying to the left of ℓ_1, then it is possible to say unambiguously that the ethical society is superior to the egoistical society. However, if some portion of the negative sloped P'P' curve lies inside the PP curve or outside the PP curve but with the end point A lying below ℓ_2 and the end point B lying to the left of ℓ_1 (as shown in figure 11.2), the comparison of the two systems becomes ambiguous. Under these circumstances, it only makes sense to compare specific equilibrium points belonging to the two systems. For example, if the competitive outcome under the egoistical system is represented by point C in figure 11.2 while the competitive outcome under the ethical system is represented by point A, it is possible to say that the ethical society is superior to the egoistical society. However, if the competitive outcome under the egoistic society is represented by point D, it is impossible to judge whether the ethical society is better or worse than the egoistical society.

Comparison of social welfare generated by the two systems cannot be viewed as complete unless we take into account the transfer of an individual's initial endowment through compulsory lump-sum taxation and subsidy. We again refer to figure 11.2 and assume that under the egoistical system a lump-sum tax is levied on II and a lump-sum subsidy is given to I. Let the post-transfer equilibrium be represented by point C. Clearly, by comparing C and A, we can say that the ethical society is now Pareto superior to the egoistical society. Perhaps the lesson learned from this exercise is that if an individual must give\part of his endowment to aid other members of society, a system of voluntary giving is preferred to a compulsory giving system.

SUMMARIZING REMARKS

In the second and third sections we described the simultaneous existence of for-profit and nonprofit firms by a general equilibrium model and examined the welfare properties of this two-sector production economy. The central issues emerging from this analysis differ considerably from those appearing in the literature. The issues in the literature, analyzed in a partial equilibrium framework, center around the nondistribution constraint and the difference between the objectives of the for-profit and nonprofit firms. The nondistribution constraint lost its bite in a general equilibrium setting since it is naturally satisfied. The issues associated with the firm's objective functions also become moot since we hold the view that firms are coalitions of entrepreneurs and do not possess their own objectives.

Since profit-oriented and nonprofit-oriented entrepreneurs pursue different objectives, serving different clientele and operating under different constraints, the equilibrium conditions for the for-profit and nonprofit firms are naturally different. Moreover, even equilibrium conditions of firms within each sector are different. Because each firm has a distinct collection of entrepreneurs, whose objectives, talents, and risk attitudes are different, and the firms have adopted different internal organizations and information and control structures, the profit firms exist under different profit rates and the nonprofit firms exist under different cost structures and donation patterns. Thus both for-profit and nonprofit firms coexist under diverse conditions. Comparison of efficiencies among firms can no longer be carried out by using a single-dimensional measuring rod – the profit rate. In fact, despite differences in profit rates, donation patterns, and cost structures, as long as every resource owner has exploited fully the opportunities of his resources and the entrepreneurs uphold their cooperative agreements, the resulting competitive equilibrium is

Pareto optimal. By fully exploiting the opportunities of one's resources we mean that the tradeable resource owner receives a competitive price for his resources and the entrepreneur receives a maximum return in utility to his talents by participating in production with a firm.

Because efficiency is destroyed by opportunistic behavior, it becomes necessary to establish social and ethical standards to curb opportunism. A society with a greater propensity to honor agreements will be able to achieve allocative outcomes closer to the Pareto-optimal results. In addition, a society may also improve its social welfare by shifting its resources from the for-profit sector to the nonprofit sector through the promotion of altruistic ethics. Consequently, the ethics concerning both opportunism and altruism contribute greatly to social welfare. An ethical and caring society is clearly superior to one which is egotistical and selfish.

NOTES

1 The literature reviews include Rose-Ackerman (1986), Hansmann (1987), James and Rose-Ackerman (1987), and Steinberg (1987).
2 Examples of these analyses are de von Graaf (1967), McKenzie (1968), Hockman and Rogers (1969), and Shafer and Sonnenschein (1975).
3 For a survey of this literature see Hansmann (1987).
4 For a survey of this literature, see Groves and Ledyard (1987).
5 The entrepreneurs and their types are given exogenously.
6 For a precise formulation of this model, see the mathematical appendix.
7 We assume that there is a one-period production lag; consequently, no consumption of charitable goods and services takes place in the first period. For reasons that will become clear shortly, we also assume that charitable givings are also taking place in the second period.
8 We assume that the price of a charitable good or service is set arbitrarily below its average cost of production.
9 For a precise representation of these variables, see the mathematical appendix.

Postscript

The advantage associated with the division of labor, risk-sharing, and economies of large-scale production induces members of a society to act cooperatively in joint production. Cooperative efforts can be sustained and joint production can take place only under an institutional arrangement capable of supporting the allocative mechanism chosen by society to coordinate production activities and to distribute gains derived from them.

Following the tradition of Adam Smith, economists have propagated the idea that self-interest-pursuing agents behaving individualistically in a complete and competitive market setting, supported by property rights and legally enforceable contracts, can achieve an end result which is socially optimal. The plausibility of the Smithian proposition rests crucially upon the belief that agents through trading can nullify fully the impact of uncertainty existing in the marketplace.

Contrary to this belief, uncertainties inhibit the formation of some markets and make it impossible for agents to trade away the entire impact of uncertainty. In the presence of some residual uncertainty, resource owners are no longer able to take the market cue and attain a unanimous opinion on what to produce, how to produce it, and what quantity to produce. The market breaks down. A special agent – the entrepreneur – is needed to restore production. The entrepreneurs do this by forming a coalition with each other and cooperatively managing production. Through a two-tier firm–market allocative process, the society again realizes the benefit of cooperation.

The characteristic of the market outcome derived under uncertainty differs significantly from Adam Smith's vision. First, the cooperative result of society cannot be achieved solely through noncooperative behavior of the agents; now the entrepreneurs must act cooperatively with each other. Second, the ideal cooperative outcome ceases to be an automatic market phenomenon.

286

The involvement of entrepreneurs in resource allocation injects the human element into the market. Human nature, as we know it, is full of ambiguities. On the one hand, man has the capacity to act compassionately towards others, the curiosity and courage to meet challenges, the ingenuity to solve problems, and the desire to do something good and novel. On the other hand, he is also selfish and greedy, eagerly exploits the weak, wishes to avoid risks, exaggerates his own ability and worth, and tends to shirk responsibility and live on the fruits of others' toil. This ambiguity implies that entrepreneurs may channel their efforts either creatively, constructively, and benevolently, or opportunistically and abusively. The market outcome depends crucially on the entrepreneurs' quality and vision. Because the market lacks a mechanism for fostering the noble qualities and suppressing the base character of entrepreneurs, it fails to achieve the highest potential of cooperation.

The inclusion of the human factor in economic theory alters the perception of both theoretical and institutional issues. It is not enough to say that, when public goods destroy the market, the government should intervene to provision it, that when externality destroys the market the property rights should be reassigned to internalize it, and that when monopoly destroys the market, the law should intervene to restore it. Now economists must also consider the roles played by other social institutions. Educational and cultural institutions are needed to lift individuals to a higher aspirational level; ethical institutions are needed to shape behavioral norms and enforce informal social contracts; political institutions are required to balance individual rights against collective rights. The highest potential of collective living cannot be obtained through the market institution regardless of how perfect it is. The attainment of this highest potential requires the support of all complementary social institutions.

Mathematical Appendix

The mathematical model underlying the entrepreneur-centered production economy presented in chapters 6, 7, and 11 is presented in this appendix. The basic model is a two-period general equilibrium model with many agents. Let the first period denote the present and the second period the future, and let the set of all agents be denoted by N. For our purpose, the N agents can be classified into subgroups according to two criteria: an agent is either an entrepreneur or not an entrepreneur; an agent is either a receiver or a giver of charity. Let the set of entrepreneurs be denoted N_e and the set of charity receivers be denoted N_1, where $N_e \subset N$ and $N_1 \subset N$.

There are three types of commodities: the set of all self-employed entrepreneurial services, both pure and adjunct, and the set of market-traded commodities. The traded commodities, in turn, can be divided into two subcategories: those produced for nonprofit purposes and the remainder which includes all products produced for profits and all tradeable factors of production. Let these three categories of commodities be denoted by L, Z, and M respectively. We assume $L \cap Z = L \cap M = \varnothing$, $|M| = m + 1$ (with labor as the $(m + 1)$th commodity) and $|M \cup L| = \ell$.

The special feature of the entrepreneur-centered production economy is that noncooperative and cooperative behavior exist simultaneously among agents. In a market context, all agents behave noncooperatively. Whenever a market for a factor is absent, the agents involved behave cooperatively. The model is intended to describe the market and nonmarket (entrepreneurial) activities which lead to a general equilibrium in the current period.

THE AGENTS

1   Every agent is a resource owner. At the beginning of period t, $t = 1, 2$, the agent $j \in N$ holds a marketable commodity bundle

288

$\omega^{ij} \in \mathbf{R}_+{}^M$ and some nonmarketable entrepreneurial talents $x_L{}^{ij} \in \mathbf{R}_+{}^L$. The commodity bundles at the disposal of agent j are

$$X^{1j} = \{(x_M, x_L) \in \mathbf{R}^{M \cup L}\} \qquad \text{for every } j \in N_e$$

$$X^{1j} = \mathbf{R}^M \times \{0\} \qquad \text{for every } j \in N \backslash N_e$$

$$X^{2j} \times Z^j = \mathbf{R}^{M \backslash \{m+1\} \cup Z} \times \{0\} \qquad \text{for every } j \in N_1$$

$$X^{2j} \times G^j = \mathbf{R}^{M \backslash \{m+1\}} \times \mathbf{R}_+{}^{N_{e2}} \times \{0\} \qquad \text{for every } j \in N \backslash N_1$$

where X denotes the set of commodities and entrepreneurial services, Z is the set of charitable commodities, and G^j are the monetary contributions to charity j. The last two statements reflect the present set-up that there is no production in the second period.

2   Every agent is a consumer. The characteristics of consumer j are described by (a) his consumption possibility set

$$X^{1j} \times X^{2j} \times Z^j \qquad \text{for } j \in N_1$$

$$X^{1j} \times X^{2j} \times G^j \qquad \text{for } j \in N \backslash N_1$$

(b) his von Neumann–Morgenstern utility function

$$u^j: X^{1j} \times X^{2j} \times Z^j \rightarrow \mathbf{R} \qquad \text{for } j \in N_1$$

$$u^j: X^{1j} \times X^{2j} \times G^j \rightarrow \mathbf{R} \qquad \text{for } j \in N \backslash N_1$$

and (c) his initial endowments $(\omega^{1j}, \omega^{2j}) \in X^{1j} \times X^{2j}$ for $j \in N$. The set $X^{1j} \times X^{2j} \times Z^j$ or $X^{1j} \times X^{2j} \times G^j$ consists of all commodity–entrepreneurial bundles agent j can consume in both periods.

3   Every agent can be a stockholder of any for-profit firm and bondholder for any firm. Let $\mathscr{S}_1$ ($\mathscr{S}_2$) be the set of all potential for-profit (nonprofit) firms in the economy. ($\mathscr{S}_1$ and $\mathscr{S}_2$ will be defined shortly.) A portfolio of agent j is a point $(c_j, B_j) \in \mathbf{R}_+{}^{\#\mathscr{S}_1} \times \mathbf{R}_+{}^{\#(\mathscr{S}_1 \cup \mathscr{S}_2)}$, where $c_j{}^S$ is the number of shares of firm S that agent j owns and B_j is his investment in bonds issued by all firms. Let firm S's share price be denoted q^S; therefore $s_j{}^S = q^S c_j{}^S$ signifies the nominal value of firm S's stock held by agent j and $B_j{}^S$ signifies the nominal value of firm S's bonds held by agent j if firm S is formed.

4   The agents, as entrepreneurs, enter into a cooperative agreement with each other and commit themselves to a joint policy (to be defined later) under a particular organizational structure. There are two classes of entrepreneurs N_{e1} and N_{e2}. Members of N_{e1} are

devoted to organizing for-profit firms and members of N_{e2} are devoted to organizing nonprofit firms. We assume that $N_{e1} \cup N_{e2} = N_e$ and that $N_{e1} \cap N_{e2} = \varnothing$. The entrepreneurs in N_{e1} finance their production through the debt and equity markets. They seek to create a surplus from the production activities and then each claims a share of the firm's profit derived from this surplus in the second period. The entrepreneurs in N_{e2}, however, finance their production through debts and through public and private donations. They bargain for an *ex ante* determined salary and are responsible for soliciting donations as well as for making up the deficit incurred in production in the second period.

Two concepts referred to as coalition structure and hierarchical coalition structure describe the formation and coexistence of firms. Let a set of S entrepreneurs ($S \subset N_{e1}$) form the for-profit firm S. There are potentially $2^{N_{e1}} - 1$ firms, denoted by $\mathcal{N}_{e1}$. A *coalition structure* $\mathcal{T}_1$ is a partition of N_{e1} where the relative positions of the entrepreneurs in the coalition are deemed unimportant. When $\mathcal{T}_1$ prevails, the firms $(S|S \in \mathcal{T}_1)$ coexist. Let $\mathcal{T}_1$ denote the family of all admissible coalition structures. A *hierarchical coalition structure* takes into account the internal relationship among the $|S|$ entrepreneurs. Let the set of admissible internal structures among the S entrepreneurs be denoted by Π^S with elements π^S. Define

$$\mathcal{H}_1 := \{(S, \pi^S)_{S \in \mathcal{T}_1} | \pi^S \in \Pi^S \text{ and } \mathcal{T}_1 \in \mathcal{T}_1\}$$

$\mathcal{H}_1$ is the set of all admissible hierarchical coalition structures. The generic element of $\mathcal{H}_1$ is denoted $\mathcal{H}_1$. Denote (S, π^S) by H_1. Then $j \in H_1(j) \in \mathcal{H}_1$ signifies that the entrepreneur j plays a specific role in the firm $H_1(j)$ of S entrepreneurs. $\mathcal{H}_1$ induces a partition of N_{e1} and the firms $(H_1|H_1 \in \mathcal{H}_1)$ coexist.

The concepts $\mathcal{N}_{e2}, \mathcal{T}_2, \mathcal{H}_2, \mathcal{T}_2$, and $\mathcal{H}_2$ pertaining to the nonprofit firm sector are similarly defined. A typical firm with a distinct internal organization in the nonprofit sector is denoted by H_2 where $H_2 = (T, \pi^T)_{T \in \mathcal{T}_2}$.

THE FIRM AS A COALITION OF ENTREPRENEURS

The firm is a coalition of entrepreneurs. It purchases resources from the resource owners, converts these resources into outputs, and then sells the outputs to consumers. Specifically the firm's inputs are a commodity–entrepreneur bundle. The firm's ability to convert inputs into outputs depends on the production technology, its internal organization, and its capacity to acquire funds to finance production.

The precise structure of this production problem depends on whether the firm is organized as a for-profit or a nonprofit entity.

The For-profit Firm

Let S be a coalition of profit-seeking entrepreneurs organized in the hierarchical form π^S. The firm's production set is

$$Y(S,\pi^S) \subset \mathbf{R}_+{}^{M \cup L} \times [\mathscr{M}(\mathbf{R}_+{}^M)]^{\#S}$$

where $\mathscr{M}(\mathbf{R}_+{}^M)$ is a probability measure, one for each entrepreneur. Let the firm's production activity be denoted by

$$(y,\xi) = (y,(\xi^j)_{j \in H_1}) \in Y(H_1)$$

The S entrepreneurs organized in the hierarchical form H_1 control the inputs and determine the firm's production policy. This choice of policy is indirectly influenced by the firm's financial policy (B^{H_1}, q^{H_1}) which determines the firm's budget constraint $(B^{H_1} + \Sigma_{j \in N} S_j{}^{H_1})$.

The entrepreneurs' sharing rule is described by the bonus rate set

$$\mathbf{b}(H_1) := \left\{ b \in \mathbf{R}_+^{H_1} \mid \sum_{j \in H_1} b_j{}^{H_1} \leq 1 \right\}$$

whose generic element is b^{H_1}. When a bonus rate bundle b^{H_1} is chosen and the total surplus of H_1, say $v(H_1)$, is realized in the second period, the entrepreneur $j \in H_1$ receives[1] the bonus

$$b_j{}^{H_1} [v(H_1) - (1 + r) B^{H_1}]$$

and the shareholders $i(\in H_1)$ receive the dividend

$$\theta_{iH_1} \left(1 - \sum_{j \in H_1} b_j{}^{H_1} \right) [v(H_1) - (1 + r) B^{H_1}]$$

where

$$\theta_{iH_1} = \frac{c_i^{H_1}}{\Sigma_{j \in N} c_j^{H_1}}$$

is the fraction of firm H_1's share value held by the stockholder i.

When a set S of entrepreneurs comes together and agrees to organize in the hierarchical form $H_1 \in \mathscr{H}_1$ and to adopt a strategy $[y^{H_1}, (B^{H_1}, q^{H_1}), b^{H_1}]$, the for-profit firm H_1 is formed. If the hierarchical coalition structure $\mathscr{H}_1$ prevails, the firms $(H_1 | H_1 \in \mathscr{H}_1)$ coexist.

The Nonprofit Firm

Let T be a coalition of nonprofit-seeking entrepreneurs organized in the hierarchical form π^T. Denote (T, π^T) by H_2. Firm H_2's production set is

$$Y(T, \pi^T) \subset \mathbf{R}_+{}^{M \cup L} \times [\mathscr{M}(\mathbf{R}_+{}^Z)]^{\#T}$$

The firm's production activity is denoted by

$$(y, \xi) = (y, (\xi^j)_{j \in H_2}) \in Y(H_2)$$

The T entrepreneurs organized in the hierarchical form H_2 control the inputs and determine the firm's production policy. The choice of policy is influenced by the firm's internal organization H_2 and its financial policy (B^{H_2}, d^{H_2}), where d^{H_2} is the deficit-sharing rate bundle for the entrepreneurs in H_2.

The sharing rule for the nonprofit-seeking entrepreneurs is described by the salary structure w^{H_2} with the generic element $w_j^{H_2}$. The salaries are distributed in the first period. For two reasons, we are not concerned about the moral hazard issues here. First, the members in N_{e2} cannot claim profit and are assumed to be altruistic and therefore not apt to behave opportunistically. Second, the entrepreneurs in T are responsible for making up deficits incurred in production in the second period according to the deficit-sharing rate d^{H_2} determined in the first period. Let this deficit be

$$v(H_2) - (1+r) B^{H_2} + \sum_{j \in N} G_j^{H_2}$$

where $G_j^{H_2}$ is the amount of donations collected from agent j in the second period. The presence of this deficit inhibits shirking.

Again, when a set of T entrepreneurs comes together, agrees to organize in the hierarchical form $H_2 \in \mathscr{H}_2$, and agrees to adopt a given policy $[y^{H_2}, (B^{H_2}, d^{H_2}), w^{H_2}]$, the nonprofit firm H_2 is formed. If the hierarchical coalition structure H_2 prevails, the firms $(H_2 | H_2 \in \mathscr{H}_2)$ coexist.

Let $\mathcal{H} = \mathcal{H}_1 \times \mathcal{H}_2$ be a family of admissible hierarchical coalition structures. The nonempty set $\mathcal{H}$ is an a priori datum.[2] The main purpose of this appendix is to explain which member of $\mathcal{H}$ is realized in equilibrium.

ENDOGENOUS VARIABLES

The model under construction is intended to formulate market and nonmarket mechanisms which determine the values of the following first period endogenous variables: the hierarchical coalition structures

$$(\mathcal{H}_1, \mathcal{H}_2) \in \mathcal{H}_1 \times \mathcal{H}_2$$

the market prices and interest rate

$$(P, r) \in \Delta^{m+1} \times \{0\} \times \mathbf{R}_+^1$$

the consumption–investment bundles

$$(x^{1j}, c_j, B_j)_{j \in N} \in \prod_{j=1}^{N} X^{1j} \times C_j \times \mathbf{B}_j$$

the input bundles

$$(y^H, \xi^H)_{H \in \mathcal{H}_1 \cup \mathcal{H}_2} \in Y(H)$$

the entrepreneurial returns and commitments

$$(b^{H_1})_{H_1 \in \mathcal{H}_1} \in \underset{H_1 \in \mathcal{H}_1}{\times} b(H_1)$$

$$(w^{H_2})_{H_2 \in \mathcal{H}_2} \in \mathbf{R}_+^{H_2}$$

$$(d^{H_2})_{H_2 \in \mathcal{H}_2} \in \mathbf{d}^{H_2} = \left\{ d^{H_2} \in \mathbf{R}_+^{H_2} \,\middle|\, \sum_{j \in H_2} d_j^{H_2} = 1 \right\}$$

where b^{H_1} is the bonus rate bundle for entrepreneurs in the for-profit firm H_1, w^{H_2} is the wage rate bundle for entrepreneurs in the nonprofit firm H_2, and d^{H_2} is the deficit-sharing rate bundle for entrepreneurs in the nonprofit firm H_2, and the share-price vector

$$(q^{H_1})_{H_1 \in \mathcal{H}_1} \in \mathbf{R}_+^{\mathcal{H}_1}$$

These variables satisfy the conditions

$$Px^{1j} + \sum_{H_1 \in \mathcal{H}_1} q^{H_1} c_j^{H_1} + \sum_{H \in \mathcal{H}_1 \cup \mathcal{H}_2} B_j^H \le \begin{cases} P\omega^{1j} & \forall j \in N \backslash N_{e2} \\ P\omega^{1j} + w_j^{H_2} & \forall j \in N_{e2} \end{cases} \quad \text{(A.1)}$$

$$Py^{H_1} \le B^{H_1} + \sum_{j \in N} q^{H_1} c_j^{H_1} \qquad \forall H_1 \in \mathcal{H}_1$$

$$\text{(A.2)}$$

$$y_L^{H_1} \le \sum_{j \in H_1} x_L^{1j}$$

$$\sum_{j \in H_2} w_j^{H_2} + Py^{H_2} \le B^{H_2} \qquad \forall H_2 \in \mathcal{H}_2$$

$$\text{(A.3)}$$

$$y_L^{H_2} \le \sum_{j \in H_2} x_L^{1j}$$

$$\sum_{j \in N} x_M^{1j} + \sum_{H \in \mathcal{H}_1 \cup \mathcal{H}_2} y_M^H \le \sum_{j \in N} \omega^{1j}$$

$$\text{(A.4)}$$

$$P\left(\sum_{j \in N} x_M^{1j} + \sum_{H \in \mathcal{H}_1 \cup \mathcal{H}_2} y_M^H\right) = P\left(\sum_{j \in N} \omega^{1j}\right)$$

$$\sum_{j \in N} B_j^H = B^H \qquad \forall H \in \mathcal{H}_1 \cup \mathcal{H}_2 \qquad \text{(A.5)}$$

Each agent is a price taker. First, let (P, r) be given. Each j as a consumer–investor chooses the consumption–investment strategy (x_M^{1j}, c_j, B_j) subject to the budget constraint (A.1). These strategies are chosen noncooperatively. Second, the entrepreneurs of the realized for-profit firm H_1 jointly choose their strategies $\{(y^{H_1}, \xi^{H_1}), b^{H_1}, q^{H_1}, B^{H_1}\}$ subject to the budget constraint (A.2). The entrepreneurs of the realized non-profit firm H_2 jointly choose their strategies $\{(y^{H_2}, \xi^{H_2}), w^{H_2}, B^{H_2}, d^{H_2}\}$ subject to the budget constraint (A.3). Third, the price vector (P, r) is determined in the market so that the market clearance conditions (A.4) and (A.5) are satisfied. Thus cooperative behavior among the entrepreneurs, noncooperative behavior among agents as consumers and investors, and the price-adjusting mechanism of the market exist simultaneously. In order to analyze the agents' behavior, both cooperative and noncooperative, it is necessary to discuss the incentive of each agent. However, before doing so, we need to identify the firm sector structure.

FIRM SECTOR STRUCTURE

A *firm sector structure* Ξ_f is a list of specific values of the endogenous variables which describes the activities in the realized firms, the financial structure of the firms, and the current price interest rate vector. Symbolically,

$$\Xi_f = [(\mathcal{K}_1, \mathcal{K}_2), (c_j, B_j)_{j\in N}, \{(y^{H_1}, \xi^{H_1}), B^{H_1}, q^{H_1}, b^{H_1}\}_{H_1\in\mathcal{K}_1},$$

$$\{(y^{H_2}, \xi^{H_2}), B^{H_2}, w^{H_2}, d^{H_2}\}_{H_2\in\mathcal{K}_2}, P, r]$$

Marks can be used to distinguish one firm sector structure from another. For example, $\bar{\Xi}_f$ stands for the prevailing firm sector structure.

AGENT'S CHOICE PROBLEMS

Since our primary objective is to determine the equilibrium values for the endogenous variables in the first period, we need to obtain the derived utility function for each agent. For this purpose we first describe the formation of each agent's expectations in the first period about the second-period prices and outputs and then describe the agent's second-period decision problem. Both the agent's expectations about the future variables and his second-period choice problem depend crucially on whether he is or is not an entrepreneur and whether he is a giver or receiver of charity.

Agents as Nonentrepreneurs

An agent $j \in N \backslash N_e$ is a price-taker and is incapable of affecting the firm sector structure. As such, agent j perceives that anything he does will not affect the market environment. Consequently, in making his future choices, he will take $\bar{\Xi}_f$ as given and will passively form a subjective belief about the future variables (P^2, y^2). The function

$$\hat{\mu}^j : [\bar{\Xi}_f] \to \mathcal{M}\{\Delta^m \times (\mathbf{R}_+^M)^{\#\bar{\mathcal{K}}_2}\} \qquad \text{for } j \in \bar{N}\backslash\bar{N}_e$$

describes the formation of j's belief. This function is an exogenously given datum of the model.

In order to obtain agent j's derived utility function, we also need to describe his second-period decision problem. Given his choice (X^{1j}, c_j, B_j) made in the first period, and the (P^2, y^2) realized in the second period, the nonentrepreneur agent j will choose the second-period consumption bundle from the budget set which offers him the highest satisfaction. His choice problem, however, depends upon whether he is a giver or a receiver of charity. Let the charitable commodities be denoted by the vector z and their prices by the vector P_z, and let the expected value of a variable be denoted by a circumflex and the value at which it is held constant be denoted by a bar. If it is assumed that the charitable commodities are fixed exogenously at $\bar{P}_z$, a nonentrepreneur's second-period choice problem can be expressed as follows. For $j \in N_1 \backslash N_e$

$$\max_{\langle x^{2j}, z^j \rangle} u^j(x^{1j}, x^{2j}, z^j)$$

subject to

$$P^2 x^{2j} + \bar{P}_z z^j \leq \hat{I}^{2j} \quad \text{and} \quad (x^{1j}, x^{2j}, z^j) \in X^{1j} \times X^{2j} \times Z^j$$

For $j \in N \backslash (N_1 \cup N_e)$

$$\max_{\langle x^{2j}, m^j \rangle} u^j(x^{1j}, x^{2j}, g^j)$$

subject to

$$P^2 x^{2j} + \sum_{H_2 \in \mathcal{K}_2} g_j^{H_2} \leq \hat{I}^{2j} \quad \text{and} \quad (x^{1j}, x^{2j}, g^j) \in X^{1j} \times X^{2j} \times G^j$$

where

$$\hat{I}^{2j} = P^2 \omega^{2j} + \sum_{H_1 \in \mathcal{K}} \theta_{jH_1} \left(1 - \sum_{i \in H_1} \bar{b}_j^{H_1} \right) [P^2 y^{2H_1} - B^{H_1}(1+\bar{r})]$$

$$+ \sum_{H \in \mathcal{K}_1 \cup \mathcal{K}_2} B_j^H(1+\bar{r})$$

and

$$\theta_{jH_1} = c_j^{H_1} \Big/ \sum_{i \in N \backslash \{j\}} \bar{c}_i^{H_1} + c_j^{H_1}$$

The above maximization problems yield $\hat{x}^{2j}(x^{1j}, \hat{I}^{2j})$ and $\hat{z}^j(x^{1j}, \hat{I}^{2j})$

for $j \in N_1 \backslash N_e$, and $\hat{x}^{2j}(x^{1j}, \hat{I}^{2j})$ and $\hat{g}^j(x^{1j}, \hat{I}^{2j})$ for $j \in N \backslash (N_1 \cup N_e)$. With these solutions in hand, agent j's derived utility function can be written as

$$
\hat{U}^j(x^{1j}, c^j, B^j; \Xi_f) =
\begin{cases}
\displaystyle\int_{\langle P^2, y^2 \rangle} u^j(x^{1j}, \hat{x}^{2j}, \hat{z}^j) \, d\hat{\mu}^j [\bar{\Xi}_f] (P^2, y^2) & \text{if } j \in N_1 \backslash N_e \\[20pt]
\displaystyle\int_{\langle P^2, y^2 \rangle} u^j(x^{1j}, \hat{x}^{2j}, \hat{g}^j) \, d\hat{\mu}^j [\bar{\Xi}_f] (P^2, y^2) & \text{if } j \in N \backslash N_1 \cup N_e
\end{cases}
$$

Agents as Entrepreneurs

The derivation of the derived utility function for an entrepreneur is more complex because the formation of expectations by the entrepreneur and the resulting entrepreneurial behavior may affect firms' choice of strategy and the firm sector structure. These changes, in turn, affect the agent's expectations about the future variables. Because a difference in expectation formation exists between entrepreneurs in the for-profit sector and those in the nonprofit sector, we will divide this section into two subsections.

Agents as For-profit Entrepreneurs Suppose that entrepreneurs in some $H_1 \in \mathcal{N}_{e1}$ reject the prevailing coalition structure and want to form a firm of their own. In order to calculate whether such a move is desirable, each conspiring entrepreneur in H_1 must estimate his resulting income caused by such a move. This involves the estimation of outsiders' reactions to this move and requires the formulation of subjective probabilities on the future events. Suppose that the conspiring entrepreneurs change their portfolio from $(\bar{c}_j, \bar{B}_j)_{j \in H_1}$ to $(c_j, B_j)_{j \in H_1}$ and agree on a joint strategy $(B^{H_1}, q^{H_1}, b^{H_1})$. Each entrepreneur $j \in H_1$ must form expectations on other agents' reactions to the income-determining variables. For each $j \in H_1$, these expectations are postulated as follows:

$$
(\hat{\mathcal{H}}_1^{(j, H_1)}, \hat{\mathcal{H}}_2^{(j, H_1)}) : (B^{H_1}, q^{H_1}, b^{H_1}; \Xi_f) \to \mathcal{H}_1 \times \mathcal{H}_2 \tag{A.6}
$$

$$
\hat{b}^{H(j, H_1)} : (B^{H_1}, q^{H_1}, b^{H_1}; \Xi_f) \to [0, 1] \tag{A.7}
$$

$$
\hat{q}^{H(j, H_1)} : (B^{H_1}, q^{H_1}, b^{H_1}; \Xi_f) \to \mathbf{R}_+^{1} \tag{A.8}
$$

$$
\hat{c}^{H(j, H_1)} : [(c_i, B_i)_{i \in H_1}, B^{H_1}, q^{H_1}, b^{H_1}; \Xi_f] \to \mathbf{R}_+^{1} \quad \forall H \in \hat{\mathcal{H}}_1^{(j, H_1)} \tag{A.9}
$$

Although it is perfectly acceptable for agents in H_1 to hold different expectations about other firms' choices which may affect each of their income-determining parameters, in order to arrive at a cooperative choice of the input bundle for H_1, all entrepreneurs in H_1 must hold consistent expectations about the variables in (A.7) and (A.9). Accordingly, we impose the following consistency conditions:

$$\hat{c}^{H_1(j, H_1)} = \hat{c}^{H_1}, \; \hat{b}^{H_1(j, H_1)} = \sum_{j \in H_1} \hat{b}_j^{H_1} \quad \text{for all } j \in H_1 \qquad (\text{A.10})$$

If these expectations lead to a higher expectation in income for all $j \in H_1$, the entrepreneurs in H_1 could bargain for a joint strategy $\{B^{H_1}, q^{H_1}, b^{H_1}, (y^{H_1}, \xi^{H_1})\}$. After this strategy is chosen, each entrepreneur in H_1 forms his subjective expectation on the probability distribution of the future events. This expectation is postulated by

$$\hat{\mu}^{(j, H_1)} : \left((c_i, B_i)_{i \in H_1}, B^{H_1}, q^{H_1}, b^{H_1}, \xi^{H_1}; \Xi_f \right) \to \mathscr{M}[\Delta^m \times (\mathbf{R}_+{}^M)^{\#\hat{\mathscr{R}}_1(j, H_1)}]$$

Again, given j's choice of (x^{1j}, c_j, B_j) in the first period and $(P^2, (y^{2H_1})_{H_1 \in \hat{\mathscr{R}}_1(j, H_1)})$ realized in the second period, he will choose a feasible consumption bundle which gives him the highest level of satisfaction. His choice problem depends on whether he is a giver or a receiver of charity. Specifically, for $j \in N_1 \cap N_{e_1}$ the agent will

$$\max_{\langle x^{2j}, z^j \rangle} u^j(x^{1j}, x^{2j}, z^j)$$

subject to

$$P^2 x^{2j} + \bar{P}_z z^j \leqslant \hat{I}^{2j} \quad \text{and} \quad (x^{1j}, x^{2j}, z^j) \in X^{1j} \times X^{2j} \times Z^j$$

and for $j \in (N \backslash N_1) \cap N_{e_1}$ the agent will

$$\max_{\langle x^{2j}, m^j \rangle} u^j(x^{1j}, x^{2j}, g^j)$$

subject to

$$P^2 x^{2j} + \sum_{H_2 \in \hat{\mathscr{R}}_2(j, H_1)} g_j^{H_2} \leqslant \hat{I}^{2j} \quad \text{and} \quad (x^{1j}, x^{2j}, g^j) \in X^{1j} \times X^{2j} \times G^j$$

where

$$\hat{I}^{2j} = P^2\omega^{2j} + \sum_{H_1 \in \hat{\mathscr{H}}_1^{(j, H_1)}} \hat{\theta}_{jH_1} (1 - \int^{H_1(j, H_1)}) [P^2 y^{2H_1} - B^{H_1}(1 + \bar{r})]$$

$$+ b_j^{H_1} [P^2 y^{2H_1} - B^{H_1}(1 + \bar{r})] + \sum_{H \in \hat{\mathscr{H}}_1^{(j, H_1)} \cup \hat{\mathscr{H}}_2^{(j, H_1)}} B_j^H (1 + \bar{r})$$

$$\hat{\theta}_{jH_1} = c_j^{H_1} / \hat{c}^{H_1(j, H_1)} \quad \text{for each } H_1 \in \mathscr{H}_1^{(j, H_1)}$$

The above maximization problems yield the solutions $\hat{x}^{2j}(x^{1j}, \hat{I}^{2j})$ and $\hat{z}^j(x^{1j}, \hat{I}^{2j})$ for $j \in N_1 \cap N_{e_1}$, and $\hat{x}^{2j}(x^{1j}, \hat{I}^{2j})$ and $\hat{g}^j(x^{1j}, \hat{I}^{2j})$ for $j \in (N \backslash N_1) \cap N_{e_1}$. Accordingly, agent j's derived utility function becomes

$$\hat{U}^{(j, H_1)}(x^{1j}, (c_i, B_i)_{i \in H_1}, B^{H_1}, q^{H_1}, b^{H_1}, y^{H_1}, \xi^{H_1}; \Xi_f)$$

$$= \begin{cases} \displaystyle\int_{\langle P^2, y^2 \rangle} u^j(x^{1j}, \hat{x}^{2j}, \hat{z}^j) \, \mathrm{d}\hat{\mu}^{(j, H_1)}(P^2, y^2) & \text{if } j \in N_1 \cap N_{e_1} \\[4mm] \displaystyle\int_{\langle P^2, y^2 \rangle} u^j(x^{1j}, \hat{x}^{2j}, \hat{g}^j) \, \mathrm{d}\hat{\mu}^{(j, H_1)}(P^2, y^2) & \text{if } j \in (N \backslash N_1) \cap N_{e_1} \end{cases}$$

Agents as Nonprofit Entrepreneurs Assume that the entrepreneurs in some $H_2 \in \mathscr{N}_{e2}$ reject the prevailing coalition structure and wish to form a nonprofit firm of their own. In order to calculate whether such a move is desirable, each $j \in H_2$ must estimate his expected income following such a move. As in the previous case, this calculation involves j's estimation of outsiders' reactions to this move and requires the formation of his subjective probability over the future events. Suppose that the conspiring entrepreneurs change their portfolio from $(\bar{c}_j, \bar{B}_j)_{j \in H_2}$ to $(c_j, B_j)_{j \in H_2}$ and agree on a joint strategy (B^{H_2}, d^{H_2}). Each entrepreneur $j \in H_2$ must form expectations on other agents' reactions which affect his own income in the second period. For each $j \in H_2$, these expectations are

$$(\hat{\mathscr{H}}_1^{(j, H_2)}, \hat{\mathscr{H}}_2^{(j, H_2)}) := (B^{H_2}, d^{H_2}; \Xi_f) \to \mathscr{H}_1 \times \mathscr{H}_2 \tag{A.11}$$

$$\hat{c}^{H(j, H_2)} : ((c_i, B_i)_{i \in H_2}, B^{H_2}, d^{H_2}; \Xi_f) \to \mathbf{R}_+^{1} \tag{A.12}$$

$$\int^{H(j, H_2)} : (B^{H_2}, d^{H_2}; \Xi_f) \to [0, 1] \quad \forall H \in \hat{\mathscr{H}}_1^{(j, H_2)} \tag{A.13}$$

In addition, since H_2 is a monopolist producer for z_{H_2}, each $j \in H_2$ must also form an expectation on the demand for his own firm's output:

$$\hat{z}_{H_2}^{(j, H_2)} : (B^{H_2}, d^{H_2}; \Xi_f) \to \mathbf{R}_+^{\,1} \tag{A.14}$$

If these expectations lead to favorable expectations on income for all $j \in H_2$, the cooperative entrepreneurs in H_2 can choose a joint strategy $[B^{H_2}, d^{H_2}, w^{H_2}, (y^{H_2}, \xi^{H_2})]$. After this strategy is chosen, each entrepreneur $j \in H_2$ forms his subjective expectations on the amount of donations that H_2 will collect in the second period and on the probability distribution of the future events. For each $j \in H_2$, these expectations are given respectively as

$$\hat{D}^{(j, H_2)} : (B^{H_2}, d^{H_2}, y^{H_2}, g_j^{H_2}; \Xi_f) \to \mathbf{R}_+^{\,1} \tag{A.15}$$

$$\hat{\mu}^{(j, H_2)} : [(c_i, B_i)_{i \in H_2}, B^{H_2}, d^{H_2}, \xi^{H_2}; \Xi_f] \to \mathscr{M}[\Delta^m \times (\mathbf{R}_+^M)^{\#\mathscr{H}_1(j, H_1)} \times \mathbf{R}_+^{\,1}] \tag{A.16}$$

where $g_j^{H_2}$ denotes the jth entrepreneur's donation to his own firm in the second period.

Given entrepreneur j's choice of (x^{1j}, c_j, B_j) in the first period and $(P^2, (y^{2H_1})_{H_1 \in \mathscr{H}_1}^{(j, H_2)}, z_{H_2})$ realized in the second period, where z_{H_2} denotes H_2's output level, j will choose a feasible consumption bundle to maximize his level of satisfaction. Assume that all $j \in H_2$ are givers of charity; entrepreneur j's second-period choice problem becomes

$$\max_{\langle x^{2j}, m^j \rangle} u^2 (x^{1j}, x^{2j}, g^j)$$

subject to

$$P^2 x^{2j} + \sum_{H_2 \in \mathscr{H}_2^{(j, H_2)}} g_j^{H_2} \leq \hat{I}^{2j} \quad \text{and} \quad (x^{1j}, x^{2j}, g^j) \in X^{1j} \times X^{2j} \times G^j$$

where

$$\hat{I}^{2j} = P^2 \omega^{2j} + \sum_{H_1 \in \mathscr{H}_1^{(j, H_2)}} \hat{\theta}_{jH_1} \left(1 - b^{H_1 (j, H_2)}\right) \{P^2 y^{2H_1} - B^{H_1} (1 + \bar{r})\}$$

$$+ \sum_{H \in \mathscr{H}_1^{(j, H_2)} \cup \mathscr{H}_2^{(j, H_2)}} B_j^H (1 + \bar{r})$$

$$+ d_j^{H_2} \min \left\{ \hat{D}^{(j, H_2)} + \bar{P}_{z_{H_2}} \min (\hat{z}_{H_2}^{(j, H_2)}, z_{H_2}) - B^{H_2} (1 + r), 0 \right\}$$

and

$$\hat{\theta}_{jH_1} = c_j^{H_1}/\hat{c}^{H_1(j, H_2)} \qquad \forall H_1 \in \mathscr{H}_1^{(j, H_2)}$$

The above maximization problem yields the solution $\hat{x}^{2j}(x^{1j}, \hat{I}^{2j})$ and $\hat{g}^j(x^{1j}, \hat{I}^{2j})$. Accordingly, entrepreneur j's derived utility function becomes

$$\hat{U}^{(j, H_2)}(x^{1j}, (c_i, B_i)_{i \in H_2}, B^{H_2}, d^{H_2}, (y^{H_2}, \xi^{H_2}); \Xi_f)$$

$$= \int\limits_{\langle P^2, y^2, z_{H_2} \rangle} u^j(x^{1j}, \hat{x}^{2j}, \hat{g}^j) \, d\mu^{(j, H_2)}(P^2, y^2, z_{H_2})$$

THE ECONOMY AND AN EQUILIBRIUM

We now state explicitly the endogenous data for the model.

Definition 1 An economy $\mathscr{E}$ is a list of specific data

$$\{N, \dot{N}_{e1}, N_{e2}, N_1, [X^{1j} \times X^{2j} \times Z^j, u^j, (\omega^{1j}, \omega^{2j})]_{j \in N_1}$$

$$[X^{1j} \times X^{2j} \times G^j, u^j, (\omega^{1j}, \omega^{2j})]_{j \in N \setminus N_1}, (\hat{\mu}^j)_{j \in N}, [Y(H)]_{H \in \mathcal{N}_{e1} \cup \mathcal{N}_{e2}},$$

$$[\mathscr{H}_1^{(j, H_1)}, \mathscr{H}_1^{(j, H_2)}, \hat{q}^{H(j, H_1)}, \hat{c}^{H(j, H_1)}, \beta^{H(j, H_1)}, \hat{\mu}^{(j, H_1)}, \hat{B}^{H(j, H_1)}]_{j \in H_1 \in \mathcal{N}_{e1}, H \in \mathcal{N}_{e1}}$$

$$[\mathscr{H}_2^{(j, H_1)}, \mathscr{H}_2^{(j, H_2)}, \hat{q}^{H(j, H_2)}, \hat{c}^{H(j, H_2)}, \beta^{H(j, H_2)}, \hat{D}^{(j, H_2)}, \hat{\mu}^{(j, H_2)}, \hat{B}^{H(j, H_2)}]_{j \in H_2 \in \mathcal{N}_{e2}, H \in \mathcal{N}_{e1}}\}$$

which satisfy the consistency conditions (A.10).

The endogenous variables of the model were given earlier. In this section, we present the economic mechanism which determines the equilibrium value of these variables.

Definition 2 An equilibrium of an economy $\mathscr{E}$ is a quintuple

$$(\mathscr{H}_1^*, \mathscr{H}_2^*) \in \mathscr{H}_1 \times \mathscr{H}_2$$

$$(P^*, r^*) \in \Delta^m \times \mathbf{R}_+^1$$

$$(x^{1j*}, c_j^*, B_j^*) \in X^{1j} \times \mathbf{R}_+^{\mathscr{H}_1^*} \times \mathbf{R}_+^{\mathscr{H}_1^* \cup \mathscr{H}_2^*} \qquad \text{for } j \in N$$

$$[(y^{H_1*}, \xi^{H_1*}), B^{H_1*}, q^{H_1*}, b^{H_1*}] \in Y(H_1) \times \mathbf{R}_+^1 \times \mathbf{R}_+^1 \times \mathbf{b}^{H_1} \text{ for } H_1 \in \mathscr{H}_1^*$$

$$[(y^{H_2*}, \xi^{H_2*}), B^{H_2*}, d^{H_2*}, w^{H_2*}] \in Y(H_2) \times \mathbf{R}_+^1 \times \mathbf{d}^{H_2} \times \mathbf{R}_+^{H_2} \text{ for } H_2 \in \mathscr{H}_2^*$$

which has the following properties.

1   It satisfies conditions (A.1)–(A.5).

2   For any nonentrepreneur j ($\in N \backslash N_e$) and any

$$(x^{1j}, c_j, B_j) \in X^{1j} \times \mathbf{R}_+{}^{\mathscr{K}^*_1} \times \mathbf{R}_+{}^{\mathscr{K}^*_1 \cup \mathscr{K}^*_2}$$

satisfying the budget constraint

$$P^* x^{1j} + \sum_{H_1 \in \mathscr{K}^*_1} q^{H_1} c_j^{H_1} + \sum_{H \in \mathscr{K}^*_1 \cup \mathscr{K}^*_2} B_j^H \leqslant P^* \omega^{1j} \qquad (A.17)$$

it follows that

$$\hat{U}^j(x^{1j}, c_j, B_j; \Xi_f^*) \leqslant \hat{U}^j(x^{1j*}, c_j^*, B_{j_i}^*; \Xi_f^*) \qquad (A.18)$$

3   For any $H_1 \in \mathscr{K}_{e1}$, any $(x^{1j}, c_j, B_j)_{j \in H_1}$, and any

$$[(y^{H_1}, \xi^{H_1}), B^{H_1}, q^{H_1}, b^{H_1}] \in Y(H) \times \mathbf{R}_+{}^1 \times \mathbf{R}_+{}^1 \times \mathbf{b}^{H_1}$$

satisfying

$$P^* x^{1j} + \sum_{H_1 \in \mathscr{K}_1^{(j, H_1)}} \hat{q}^{H_1(j, H_1)} c_j^{H_1} + \sum_{H \in \mathscr{K}_1^{(j, H_1)} \cup \mathscr{K}_2^{(j, H_1)}} B_j^H$$

$$\leqslant P^* \omega^{1j} \quad \forall j \in H_1 \qquad (A.19)$$

$$P^* y^{H_1} \leqslant q^{H_1} \hat{c}^{H_1} + B^{H_1} \qquad \forall H_1 \in \mathscr{K}_1 \qquad (A.20)$$

$$y_L^{H_1} \leqslant \sum_{j \in H_1} x_L{}^{1j}$$

it is not true that

$$\hat{U}^{(j, H_1)}[x^{1j}, (c_i, B_i)_{i \in H_1}, B^{H_1}, q^{H_1}, b^{H_1}, (y^{H_1}, \xi^{H_1}); \Xi_f^*]$$
$$> \hat{U}^{(j, H^*(j))}[x^{1j*}, (c_i^*, B_i^*)_{i \in H_1}, B^{H^*(j)}, q^{H^*(j)}, b^{H^*(j)}, (y^{H^*(j)}, \xi^{H^*(j)}); \Xi_f^*]$$
$$(A.21)$$

where $H^*(j) \in \mathscr{K}^*_1$ with $j \in H^*(j)$ for each $j \in H_1$.

4   For any $H_2 \in \mathscr{N}_{e2}$, any $(x^{1j}, c^j, B_j)_{j \in H_2}$ and any

$$[(y^{H_2}, \xi^{H_2}), B^{H_2}, d^{H_2}, w^{H_2}] \in Y(H_2) \times \mathbf{R}_+{}^1 \times \mathbf{d}^{H_2} \times \mathbf{R}_+{}^{H_2}$$

satisfying

$$P^*x^{1j} + \sum_{H_1 \in \mathscr{H}_1^{(j,H_2)}} \hat{q}^{H_1(j,H_2)} c_j^{H_1} + \sum_{H \in \mathscr{H}_1^{(j,H_2)} \cup \mathscr{H}_2^{(j,H_2)}} B_j^H$$

$$\leqslant P^*\omega^{1j} + w_j^{H_2} \quad \forall j \in H_2 \tag{A.22}$$

$$\sum_{j \in H_2} w_j^{H_2} + P^*y^{H_2} \leqslant B^{H_2} \quad \forall H_2 \in \mathscr{H}_2 \tag{A.23}$$

$$y_L^{H_2} \leqslant \sum_{j \in H_2} x_{Lj}^{1j}$$

it is not true that

$$\hat{U}^{(j,H_2)}\left[x^{1j}, (c_i, B_i)_{i \in H_2}, B^{H_2}, d^{H_2}, w^{H_2}, (y^{H_2}, \xi^{H_2}); \Xi^*\right]$$

$$> \hat{U}^{(j,H^*(j))}\left[x^{1j*}, (c_j^*, B_j^*)_{i \in H_2}, B^{H^*(j)}, d^{H^*(j)}, w^{H^*(j)}, (y^{H^*(j)}, \xi^{H^*(j)}); \Xi^*\right] \tag{A.24}$$

where $H^*(j)$ is defined as in condition (3) for each $j \in H_2$.

The right-hand sides of inequalities (A.18), (A.21), and (A.24) are the expected utility levels currently enjoyed by agent j as a nonentrepreneur, as an entrepreneur in the profit sector, and as an entrepreneur in the nonprofit sector respectively. Condition (2) thus implies that nonentrepreneur j cannot improve his expected utility by altering his own behavior. The left-hand side of (A.21) represents the expected utility level that entrepreneur j in the profit sector would obtain if he were to participate in the new firm H_1 and agree to the joint strategy $[B^{H_1}, q^{H_1}, b^{H_1}, (y^{H_1}, \xi^{H_1})]$. Condition (3) implies that no such new coalition among entrepreneurs in the profit sector can improve each of their expected utilities. Likewise, the left-hand side of (A.24) represents the expected utility that the entrepreneur j in the nonprofit sector would receive if he were to participate in a new coalition and agree to a joint strategy $[B^{H_2}, d^{H_2}, w^{H_2}, (y^{H_2}, \xi^{H_2})]$. Condition (4) implies that no such new coalition in the nonprofit sector can improve each entrepreneur's expected utility.

The economic mechanism formulated here reflects the mixture of noncooperative and cooperative behavior of agents. First, each agent as a consumer and as an owner of tradeable resources behaves noncooperatively. He takes the market prices (P, r) as given and chooses his strategy by himself so that conditions (1) and (2) of definition 2 are satisfied. Second, the activities of both for-profit and nonprofit firms are determined by the economy-wide cooperative game played by the entrepreneurs. Given any price vector (P, r), stable (core) strategies emerge as an outcome of this game satisfying conditions (3) and (4). Finally, the market mechanism works through demand and supply to adjust the prices (P, r) until all markets are cleared, that is, conditions (A.4) and (A.5) are satisfied.

NOTES

1 Strictly speaking we should say here that $j \in S$ where $(S, \pi^S) = H_1$. Because this notation is rather cumbersome, we will henceforth simplify it by saying $j \in H_1$.
2 We assume for simplicity that N_{e1} and N_{e2} are exogenous. However, it is possible to construct a model with them determined endogenously.

References and Bibliography

Akerlof, G. A. 1970: The market for "lemons:" quality and the market mechanism. *Quarterly Journal of Economics*, 84, 488–500.

Alchian, A. A. 1950: Uncertainty, evolution and economic theory. *Journal of Political Economy*, 58, 211–21.

Alchian, A. A. and Demsetz, H. 1972: Production, information costs and economic organization. *American Economic Review*, 62, 777–95.

Aoki, M. 1980: A model of the firm as a stockholder–employee cooperative game. *American Economic Review*, 70, 600–10.

Armour, H. O. and Teece, D. 1978: Organizational structure and economic performance. *Bell Journal of Economics*, 9, 106–22.

Arrow, K. J. 1951: An extension of the basic theorem of classical economics. *Proceedings of the 2nd Berkeley Symposium on Mathematics, Statistics and Probability*. Berkeley, CA: University of California Press.

Arrow, K. J. 1963a: *Social Choice and Individual Values*, new edn. New Haven, CT: Yale University Press.

Arrow, K. J. 1963b: Uncertainty and the welfare economics of medical care. *American Economic Review*, 62, 941–73.

Arrow, K. J. 1971a: *Essays in the Theory of Risk-bearing*, Chicago, IL: Markham.

Arrow, K. J. 1971b: The firm in general equilibrium theory. In R. Marris and A. Woods (eds), *The Corporate Economy: Growth, Competition and Innovative Potential*, Cambridge, MA: Harvard University Press.

Arrow, K. J. 1971c: The role of securities in the optimal allocation of risk-bearing. In K. J. Arrow (ed.), *Essays in the Theory of Risk-bearing*, Chicago, IL: Markham, chaper 4.

Arrow, K. J. 1974a: Limited knowledge and economic analysis. *American Economic Review*, 64, 1–10.

Arrow, K. J. 1974b: *The Limits of Organization*. New York: W. W. Norton.

Arrow, K. J. 1975: Vertical integration and communication. *Bell Journal of Economics*, 6, 173–83.

Arrow, K. J. 1977: Extended sympathy and the possibility of social change. *American Economic Review*, 67, 219–25.

Arrow, K. J. 1981: Futures markets: some theoretical perspective. *Journal of Futures Markets*, 1, 107–15.

Arrow, K. J. and Debreu, G. 1954: Existence of equilibrium for a competitive economy. *Econometrica*, 22, 269–90.

Ashton, T. S. 1962: *The Industrial Revolution, 1760–1830*, revised edn. Oxford: Oxford University Press.

d'Aspremont, C. and Gevers, L. 1977: Equity and the information basis of collective choice. *Review of Economic Studies*, 44, 199–209.

Azzi, C. 1978: Conglomerate mergers, default risk, and homemade mutual funds. *American Economic Review*, 68, 161–72.

Baiman, S. 1982: Agency research in managerial accounting: a survey. *Journal of Accounting Literature*, 1, 154–213.

Balch, M. S. and Wu, S. Y. 1974: Some introductory remarks on behavior under uncertainty. In M. S. Balch, D. McFadden, and S. Wu (eds), *Essays on Economic Behavior Under Uncertainty*, New York: Elseiner, 1–22.

Barnard, C. I. 1938: *The Functions of the Executive*. Cambridge, MA: Harvard University Press.

Baron, D. P. 1970: Price uncertainty, utility and industrial equilibrium in pure competition. *International Economic Review*, 11, 463–80.

Baron, D. P. 1979: On the relationship between complete and incomplete financial market models. *International Economic Review*, 20, 105–17.

Baumol, W. J. 1965: *The Stock Market and Economic Efficiency*. New York: Fordham University Press.

Baumol, W. J. 1967: *Business Behavior, Value and Growth.* New York: Harcourt, Brace and World.

Baumol, W. J. 1968: Entrepreneurship in economic theory. *American Economic Review*, 58, 64–71.

Beard, C. A. 1969: *The Industrial Revolution*. New York: Greenwood Press.

Berle, A. A. and Means, G. C. 1932: *The Modern Corporation and Private Property*. New York: Macmillan.

Bernard, J. 1971: Trade and finance in the Middle Ages, 900–1500. In C. M. Cipolla (ed.), *The Fontana Economic History of Europe*, vol. 1, London: Fontana.

Blair, R. D. and Kaserman, D. L. 1978: Uncertainty and incentive for vertical integration. *Southern Economic Journal*, 45, 266–72.

Blair, R. D., Ginsburg, P. B. and Vogel, R. J. 1975: Blue Cross–Blue Shield administration costs: a study of nonprofit health insurers. *Economic Inquiry*, 13, 55–70.

Bull, C. 1983: Implicit contracts in the absence of enforcement and risk aversion. *American Economic Review*, 73, 658–71.

Calvo, G. and Wellisz, S. 1978: Supervision, loss of control, and the optimum size of the firm. *Journal of Political Economy*, 86, 943–52.

Cantillon, R. 1964: *Essay on the Nature of Trading in General*. New York: Augustus M. Kelley.

Cass, D. and Stiglitz, J. E. 1970: The structure of investor preferences and asset returns, and separability in portfolio allocation: a contribution to the pure theory of mutual funds. *Journal of Economic Theory*, 2, 122–60.

Cassels, G. 1932: *The Theory of Social Economy*. London: T. F. Unwin.

Casson, M. 1982: *The Entrepreneur*. Totawa, NJ: Barnes and Noble.

Caves, R. E. 1980: Industrial organization, corporate strategy and structure. *Journal of Economic Literature*, 18, 64–92.

Chandler, A. D., Jr. 1962: *Strategy and Structure*. Cambridge, MA: MIT Press.

Chandler, A. D., Jr. 1977: *The Visible Hand: The Managerial Revolution in American Business*. Cambridge, MA: Harvard University Press, chapter 13 and Conclusion.

Cheung, S. 1969: *The Theory of Share Tenancy*. Chicago: Chicago University Press.

Clark, J. B. 1891: Distribution as determined by a law of rent. *Quarterly Journal of Economics*, 5, 289–318.

Clark, J. B. 1899: *The Distribution of Wealth*. New York: Macmillan.

Clark, R. 1981: The four stages of capitalism: reflections on investment management treatises. *Harvard Law Review*, 94, 561–83.

Clarke, R. N. 1982: Endogenous mergers in stochastic Cournot–Nash oligopoly. *SSRI Working Paper*, University of Wisconsin–Madison, Madison, WI.

Clarke, R. N. 1983: Coalition and the incentive for information sharing. *Bell Journal of Economics*, 14, 383–94.

Clarkson, K. 1972: Some implications of property rights in hospital rights and hospital management. *Journal of Law and Economics*, 15, 363–84.

Clemence, R. V. and Doody, F. S. 1950: *The Schumpeterian System*. Cambridge, MA: Addison-Wesley.

Coase, R. H. 1937: The nature of the firm. *Economica* (NS), 4, 386–405. Reprinted in K. E. Boulding and G. J. Stigler (eds), *Readings in Price Theory*, Homewood, IL: Richard D. Irwin, 1965; also 2nd edn, 1975.

Cohen, J. S. 1978: The achievements of economic history: The Marxist School. *Journal of Economic History*, 38, 29–57.

Cohen, J. S. and Weitzman, M. L. 1975: A Marxian model of enclosures. *Journal of Developmental Economics*, 1, 287–336.

Cohen, K. J. and Cyert, R. M. 1965: *Resource Allocations in a Market Economy*. Englewood Cliffs, NJ: Prentice-Hall; also 2nd edn, 1975.

Cole, A. H. 1968: The entrepreneur: introductory remarks. *American Economic Review*, 58, 60–3.

Cox, J. C., Ingersoll, J. E., Jr. and Ross, S. A. 1981: The relationship between forward prices and futures prices. *Journal of Financial Economics*, 9, 321–46.

Cyert, R. M. and Hedrick, C. L. 1972: Theory of the firm: past, present and future: an interpretation. *Journal of Economic Literature*, 10, 398–9.

Cyert, R. M. and March, J. G. 1963: *A Behavioral Theory of the Firm*. Englewood Cliffs, NJ: Prentice-Hall.

Day, R. 1964: Review of Cyert and March "A behavioral theory of the firm." *Econometrica*, 32, 461–5.

Day, R. and Tinney, E. H. 1968: How to cooperate in business without really trying: a learning model of decentralized decision making. *Journal of Political Economy*, 76, 583–600.

Debreu, G. 1952: A social equilibrium existence theorem. *Proceedings of the National Academy of Sciences of the United States of America*, 38, 886–93.

Debreu, G. 1959: *Theory of Value: An Axiomatic Analysis of Economic Equilibrium*. New York: Wiley.

DeGroot, M. 1970: *Optimal Statistical Decisions*. New York: McGraw-Hill.

Demsetz, H. 1968: The cost of transacting. *Quarterly Journal of Economics*, 82, 33–53.

Demsetz, H. 1969: Information and efficiency: another viewpoint. *Journal of Law and Economics*, 12, 1–22.

Demsetz, H. 1983: The structure of ownership and theory of the firm. *Journal of Law and Economics*, 26, 383.

Demski, J. and Feltham, G. 1976: *Cost determination: a conceptual approach.* Ames, IA: Iowa State University Press.

Diamond, P. 1967: The role of a stock market in a general equilibrium model with technological uncertainty. *American Economic Review*, 57, 759–76.

Diamond, P. and Maskin, E. 1979: An equilibrium analysis of search and breach of contracts. *Bell Journal of Economics*, 10, 282–316.

Dobb, M. H. 1925: *Capitalist Enterprise and Social Enterprise.* London: Routledge.

Doeringer, P. and Piori, M. 1971: *Internal Labor Markets and Manpower Analysis.* Boston, MA: D. C. Heath.

Dow, G. 1988: Information, production decisions and intrafirm bargaining. *International Economic Review*, 29, 57–80.

Drèze, J. H. 1974: Investment under private ownership: optimality, equilibrium and stability. In J. H. Drèze (ed.), *Allocation under Uncertainty: Equilibrium and Optimality*, New York: Halsted Press, 129–66.

Drèze, J. H. 1976: Some theory of labor management and participation. *Econometrica*, 44, 1125–39.

Drèze, J. H. 1982: Decision criteria for business firms. *CORE Discussion Paper no. 8211*, Université Catholique de Louvain.

Drèze, J. H. 1984: (Uncertainty and) the firm in general equilibrium theory. *CORE Discussion Paper no. 8426*, Université Catholique de Louvain.

Eagly, R. V. 1974: *The Structure of Classical Economic Theory.* New York: Oxford University Press.

Easley, D. and O'Hara, M. 1983: The economic role of the nonprofit firm. *Bell Journal of Economics*, 14, 531–8.

The Economics Report of the President: 1986. Washington, DC: U. S. Government Printing Office, 351–3.

Edgeworth, F. Y. 1881: *Mathematical Psychics.* London: Kegan Paul.

Ekern, S. 1974: Some aspects of firms' decision making in an economy with incomplete markets. *Swedish Journal of Economics*, 5, 117–30.

Ekern, S. and Wilson, R. 1974: On the theory of the firm in an economy with incomplete markets. *Bell Journal of Economics and Management Science*, 5, 171–80.

Fama, E. F. 1971: Risk, return and equilibrium. *Journal of Political Economy*, 79, 30–55.

Fama, E. F. 1980: Agency problems and the theory of the firm. *Journal of Political Economy*, 88, 288–307.

Fama, E. F. and Jensen, M. 1983: Separation of ownership and control. *Journal of Law and Economics*, 26, 301–25.

Fisher, I. 1925: *Mathematical Investigations in the Theory of Value and Prices.* New Haven: Yale University Press.

Forsythe, R. and Suchanek, G. 1984: Collective decision mechanisms and efficient stock market allocations: existence of a participation equilibrium. *International Economic Review*, 25, 21–43.

Fudenberg, D. and Tirole, J. 1983: Sequential bargaining with incomplete information. *Review of Economic Studies*, 50, 221–47.

Geanakoplos, J. and Milgrom, P. 1985: A theory of hierarchies based on limited managerial attention. *Cowles Foundation Paper no. 775*, Yale University, New Haven, CT.

Gilson, R. J. and Mnookin, R. H. 1985: Sharing among the human capitalists:

an economic inquiry into the corporate law firm and how partners split profits. *Stanford Law Review*, 37, 313–90.

Gjesdal, F. 1982: Information and incentives: the agency information problem. *Review of Economic Studies*, 49, 373–90.

Goldberg, V. P. 1974: Institutional change and the quasi-invisible hand. *Journal of Law and Economics*, 17, 461–92.

Gordon, R. A. 1966: *Business Leadership in the Large Corporation*. Berkeley, CA: University of California Press.

van de Graaf, J. 1967: *Theoretical Welfare Economics*. London: Cambridge University Press.

Grossman, S. J. and Hart, O. D. 1979: A theory of competitive equilibrium in stock market economics. *Econometrica*, 47, 293–329.

Grossman, S. J. and Hart, O. D. 1982: Corporate financial structure and managerial incentives. In J. J. McCall (ed.), *The Economics of Information*, Chicago, IL: University of Chicago Press, 107–40.

Grossman, S. J. and Hart, O. D. 1986: The costs and benefits of ownership: a theory of vertical and lateral integration. *Journal of Political Economy*, 94, 691–719.

Grossman, S. J. and Stiglitz, J. E. 1976: Information and competitive price systems. *American Economic Review*, 66, 246–53.

Groves, T. 1973: Incentives in teams. *Econometrica*, 41, 617–31.

Groves, T. and Ledyard, J. D. 1971: Risk, return and equilibrium. *Journal of Political Economy*, 79, 30–5.

Groves, T. and Ledyard, J. D. 1980: The existence of efficient and incentive compatible equilibria with public goods. *Econometrica*, 48, 1487–506.

Groves, T. and Ledyard, J. D. 1987: Incentive compatibility since 1972. In T. Groves, R. Radner and S. Reiter (eds), *Information, Incentives and Economic Mechanisms: Essays in Honor of Leonid Hurwicz*, Minneapolis, MN: University of Minnesota Press.

Hammond, P. J. 1975: Charity: altruism or cooperative egoism. In E. S. Phelps (ed.), *Altruism, Morality and Economic Theory*, New York: Russell Sage Foundation.

Hammond, P. J. 1979: Straightforward individual incentives compatibility in large economies. *Review of Economic Studies*, 46, 263–82.

Hammond, P. J. 1985: Welfare economics. In G. R. Feiwel (ed.), *Issues in Contemporary Microeconomics and Welfare Economics*, Albany, NY: State University of New York, 405–34.

Hansmann, H. 1980: The role of nonprofit enterprise. *Yale Law Journal*, 89, 835–901.

Hansmann, H. 1981: Nonprofit enterprise in the performing arts. *Bell Journal of Economics*, 12, 341–61.

Hansmann, H. 1987: Economic theories of nonprofit organization. In W. W. Powell (ed.), *The Nonprofit Sector*, New Haven, CT: Yale University Press.

Harris, M. and Townsend, R. 1981: Resource allocation under asymmetric information: an introduction. *Review of Economic Studies*, 50, 3–36.

Hart, O. D. 1975: On the optimality of equilibrium when the market structure is incomplete. *Journal of Economic Theory*, 11, 418–43.

Hayek, F. 1945: The use of knowledge in society. *American Economic Review*, 35, 519–30.

Hayek, F. 1948: *Individualism and Economic Order*. Chicago, IL: University of Chicago Press.

Heal, G. M. and Silbertson, A. 1972: Alternative managerial objectives: an explanatory note. *Oxford Economic Papers*, 24, 137–253.

Heflebower, R. B. 1960: Observations of decentralization in large enterprise. *Journal of Industrial Economics*, 9, 7–22.

Henderson, J. M. and Quandt, R. E. 1971: *Microeconomic Theory: A Mathematical Approach*. New York: McGraw-Hill.

Hicks, J. R. 1939: Foundation of welfare economics. *Economic Journal*, 49, 696–712.

Hicks, J. R. 1946: *Value and Capital*, 2nd edn. London: Oxford University Press.

Hicks, J. R. and Allen, R. G. D. 1934: A reconsideration of the theory of value. *Economica* (NS), 1, 55.

Hildebrand, W. 1970: Existence of equilibria for economies with production and a measure space of consumers. *Econometrica*, 38, 608–23.

Hirschleifer, J. 1971: The private and social value of information and the rewards to inventive activity. *American Economic Review*, 61, 561–79.

Hockman, H. and Rogers, J. 1969: Pareto optimal redistribution. *American Economic Review*, 59, 542–57.

Holmstrom, B. 1979: Moral hazard and observability. *Bell Journal of Economics*, 10, 74–91.

Horen, J. and Wu, S. Y. 1988: Vertical integration under uncertainty. In T. B. Fomby and Tae Kun Seo (eds), *Studies in the Economics of Uncertainty: In Honor of Josef Hadar*, New York: Springer.

Hoselitz, B. F. 1951: The early history of entrepreneurial history. *Explorations in Entrepreneurial History*, 3, 193–220.

Hurwicz, L. 1972: On informationally decentralized systems. In C. B. McGuire and R. Radner (eds), *Decision and Organization*, Amsterdam: North-Holland, 297–336.

Hurwicz, L. 1979: Outcome functions yield Walrasian and Lindahl allocations at Nash equilibrium points. *Review of Economic Studies*, 46, 217–25.

Ichiishi, T. 1977: Coalition structure in a labor-managed market economy. *Econometrica*, 45, 341–60.

Ichiishi, T. 1981: A social coalition equilibrium existence lemma. *Econometrica*, 49, 369–77.

Ichiishi, T. 1982: Management vs. ownership I. *International Economic Review*, 23, 323–36.

Ichiishi, T. 1985: Management vs. ownership II. *European Economic Review*, 27, 115–38.

James, E. and Neuberger, E. 1981: The university department as a nonprofit labor cooperative. *Public Choice*, 36, 585–612.

James, E. and Rose-Ackerman, S. 1987: The private non-profit firm. In M. Montias and J. Kornai (eds), *Economic Systems*, New York: Harvard Academic Publishers.

Jenner, R. A. 1966: An information version of pure competition. *Economic Journal*, 76, 786–805.

Jensen, M. and Meckling, W. H. 1976: Theory of the firm: managerial behavior, agency costs and ownership structure. *Journal of Financial Economics*, 3, 305–60.

Jensen, M. and Meckling, W. H. 1979: Rights and production functions: an application to labor-managed firms and codetermination. *Journal of Business*, 52, 469–506.

Johnson, H. G. 1967: *Essays in Monetary Economics*, Cambridge, MA: Harvard University Press, chapter IV.

Kai Ma 1984: A theory of the firm; the bargaining approach. *Dissertation*, University of Iowa.

Kaldor, N. 1934: Equilibrium of a firm. *Economic Journal*, 44, 60.

Kaldor, N. 1939: Welfare proportion in economics. *Economic Journal*, 49, 549–52.

Kirkland, E. C. 1961: *Industry Comes of Age; Business, Labor and Public Policy: 1860–1897.* New York: Holt, Rinehart and Winston.

Kirkstand, B. S. 1953: *Theory of Profits and Income Distribution.* Oxford: Oxford University Press.

Kirzner, I. M. 1973: *Competition and Entrepreneurship.* Chicago, IL: University of Chicago Press.

Kirzner, I. M. 1979: *Perception, Opportunity and Profit.* Chicago, IL: University of Chicago Press.

Klein, B. and Leffler, K. B. 1981: The role of market forces in assuring contractual performance. *Journal of Political Economy*, 89, 615–41.

Klein, B., Crawford, R. G. and Alchian, A. A. 1978: Vertical integration, appropriable quasi-rents and the competitive contracting process. *Journal of Law and Economics*, 21, 297–326.

Klein, B., Crawford, R. G. and Alchian, A. A. 1983: Contractual costs and residual claims: the separation of ownership and control. *Journal of Law and Economics*, 26, 273.

Knight, F. H. 1956: *On the History and Method of Economics.* Chicago, IL: University of Chicago Press.

Knight, F. H. 1971: *Risk, Uncertainty and Profit.* Chicago, IL: University of Chicago Press. (First published 1921.)

Koopmans, T. 1957: *Three Essays on the State of Economic Science.* New York: McGraw-Hill.

Koopmans, T. 1974: Is the theory of competitive equilibrium with it? *American Economic Review*, 64, 325–9.

Kriedte, P., Medick, H. and Schlumbohm, J. 1981: *Industrialization before Industrialization: Rural Industry in the Genesis of Capitalism.* Cambridge: Cambridge University Press.

Krouse, C. G. 1966: The optimality of risk allocation. *Southern Economic Review*, 56, 762–77.

Kurz, M. 1977: Altruistic equilibrium. In B. Balassa and R. Nelson (eds), *Economic Progress, Private Values and Public Policy: Essays in Honor of William Fellner*, Amsterdam: North-Holland, 177–200.

Lambert, R. 1983: Long-term contracting and moral hazard. *Bell Journal of Economics*, 14, 441–52.

Lange, O. and Taylor, F. M. 1938: *On the Economic Theory of Socialism.* Minneapolis, MN: University of Minnesota Press.

Ledyard, J. 1987: Market failure. *Social Science Working Paper 623*, California Institute of Technology, Pasadena, CA.

Lee, M. L. 1971: A conspicuous production theory of hospital behavior. *Southern Economic Journal*, 38, 48–58.

Leibenstein H. 1968: Entrepreneurship and development. *American Economic Review*, 58, 72–83.

Leibenstein, H. 1978: *General X-Efficiency Theory and Economic Development.* Oxford: Oxford University Press.

Leibenstein, H. 1979: A branch of economics is missing: micro-micro theory. *Journal of Economic Literature*, 17, 477–502.

Leland, H. 1972: Theory of the firm facing random demand. *American Economic Review*, 62, 278–91.

Leland, H. 1974: Production theory and the stock market. *Bell Journal of Economics and Management Science*, 5, 125–44.

Lewellen, W. 1971: *The Ownership Income of Management.* New York: Columbia University Press.

Lewellen, W. and Huntsman, B. 1970: Managerial pay and corporate performance. *American Economic Review*, 60, 710–20.

Machlup, F. 1957: Theories of the firm: marginalist, behavioral, managerial. *American Economic Review*, 57, 1–33.

Malmgreen, H. B. 1961: Information, expectation and the theory of the firm. *Quarterly Journal of Economics*, 75, 399–421.

Mantoux, P. 1962: *Industrial Revolution in the Eighteenth Century.* New York: Harper and Row.

Marglin, S. 1974: What do bosses really do? The origins and functions of hierarchy in capitalist production. *Review of Radical Political Economics*, 6, 60–112.

Margolis, J. 1958: Analysis of the firm: rationalism, conventionalism and behaviorism. *Journal of Business*, 31, 187–99.

Marris, R. 1963: A model of the managerial enterprise. *Quarterly Journal of Economics*, 77, 185–209.

Marris, R. 1964: *The Economic Theory of Managerial Capitalism.* New York: Free Press.

Marris, R. 1972: Is the corporate economy a corporate state? *American Economic Review*, 62, 103–15.

Marris, R. and Mueller, D. C. 1980: The corporation and competition. *Journal of Economic Literature*, 18, 32–63.

Marris, R. and Wood, A. 1971: *The Corporate Economy: Growth, Competition, and Innovative Potential.* Cambridge, MA: Harvard University Press.

Marschak, J. and Radner, R. 1972: *Economic Theory of Teams.* New Haven, CT: Yale University Press.

Marshall, A. 1953: *Principles of Economics*, 5th printing. New York: Macmillan. (First published 1891).

Marx, K. 1967: The process of capitalist production. In K. Marx, *Capital, A Critique of Political Economy*, vol. I, 3rd German edn, ed. F. Engels, transl. S. Moore and E. Aveling, New York: International Publishers. (First published 1867.)

Mason, E. 1939: Price and production policies of large scale enterprise. *American Economic Review*, 29, 61–74.

Masson, R. 1971: Executive motivation, earnings and consequent equity performances. *Journal of Political Economy*, 79, 1278–92.

McAndrews, J. 1985: First-mover organizations. Working Paper, University of Iowa.

McEachern, W. 1975: *Managerial Control and Performances.* Lexington, MA: D. C. Heath.

McGuire, J., Chiw, J. and Elbing, A. 1962: Executive income, sales and profits. *American Economic Review*, 52, 753–61.

McKenzie, L. 1959: On the existence of general equilibrium for a competitive market. *Econometrica*, 27, 54–71.

McKenzie, L. 1968: Competitive equilibrium with dependent consumer preferences. In P. Newman (ed.), *Readings in Mathematical Economics I*, Baltimore: Johns Hopkins Press, 125–46.

Meeks, G. and Whittington, G. 1975: Director's pay, growth and profitability. *Journal of Industrial Economics*, 24, 1–14.

Mill, J. S. 1976: *Principles of Political Economy*. New York: Augustus M. Kelley. (First published 1848).

Mingay, G. E. 1968: *Enclosure and the Small Farmer in the Age of the Industrial Revolution*. London: Macmillan.

Mirrlees, J. A. 1976: Optimal structure of incentives and authority within an organization. *Bell Journal of Economics*, 7, 105–31.

von Mises, L. 1949: *Human Action*. New Haven, CT: Yale University Press.

von Mises, L. 1962: *The Ultimate Foundation of Economic Science*. New York: Van Nostrand.

Modigliani, F. and Miller, M. H. 1958: The cost of capital, corporation finance and the theory of investment. *American Economic Review*, 48, 261–97.

Monsen, R. J., Chiw, J. S. and Cooley, D. E. 1968: The effect of separation and control on the performance of the large firm. *Quarterly Journal of Economics*, 82, 435–51.

Morgenstern, O. 1976: Perfect foresight and economic equilibrium. In A. Schotter (ed.), *Selected Economic Writings of Oskar Morgenstern*, New York: New York University Press, 169–83.

Morishima, M. 1977: *Walras' Economics: A Pure Theory of Capital and Money*. Cambridge: Cambridge University Press.

Myerson, R. 1979: Incentive compatability and the bargaining problem. *Econometrica*, 47, 61–73.

Nash, J. F. 1950: The bargaining approach. *Econometrica*, 18, 155–62.

Nash, J. F. 1951: Non-cooperative games. *Annals of Mathematics*, 54, 289–95.

Nelson, R. R. 1981: Assessing private enterprise: an exegesis of tangled doctrine. *Bell Journal of Economics*, 12, 93–111.

Nelson, R. R. and Krachinsky, M. 1973: Two major issues of policy: public policy and organization of supply. In R. Nelson and D. Young (eds), *Public Subsidy for Day Care for Young Children*, Lexington, MA: D. C. Heath.

Nelson, R. R. and Winter, S. 1978: Forces generating and limiting concentration under Schumpeterian competition. *Bell Journal of Economics*, 9, 524–48.

Nelson, R. R. and Winter, S. 1982: *An Evolutionary Theory of Economic Change*. Cambridge, MA: Harvard University Press.

Newhouse, J. 1970: Toward a theory of nonprofit institutions: an economic model of a hospital. *American Economic Review*, 60, 64–74.

Ng, Y. 1974: Utility and profit maximization by an owner–manager: toward a general analysis. *Journal of Industrial Economics*, 23, 97–108.

Nordquist, G. L. 1965: The breakup of the maximization principle. *Quarterly Review of Economics and Business*, 5, 33–46.

North, D. 1981: *Structure and Change in Economic History*. New York: W. W. Norton.

Obrinsky, M. 1983: *Profit Theory and Capitalism*. Philadelphia, PA: University of Pennsylvania Press.

Palmer, J. P. 1973: The profit performance effects of the separation of ownership from control in large U.S. corporations. *Bell Journal of Economics*, 4, 293–303.

Papandreou, A. G. 1952: Some basic problems in the theory of the firm. In B. F. Haley (ed.), *A Survey of Contemporary Economics*, vol. II, Homewood, IL: R. D. Irwin, 183–222.

Pareto, V. 1971: *Manual of Political Economy*, transl. A. Schwier, New York: Augustus M. Kelley. (First published 1913).

Penrose, E. T. 1959: *The Theory of the Growth of the Firm*. Oxford: Oxford University Press; New York: Wiley.

Piore, M. 1986: Corporate Reform in American Manufacturing and the Challenge to Economic Theory. Mimeograph, Massachusets Institute of Technology.

Piore, M. and Sabel, C. 1985: *The Second Industrial Divide*. New York: Basic Books.

Powell, E. T. 1966: *The Evolution of the Money Market: 1385–1915*. New York: Augustus M. Kelley.

Prescott, E. and Visscher, M. 1980: Organizational capital. *Journal of Political Economy*, 88, 446–61.

Purdy, H. L., Lindahl, M. L., Carter, W. A. 1950: *Coporation Concentration and Public Policy*. New York: Prentice-Hall.

Putterman, L. 1982: Some behavioral perspectives on the dominance of hierarchical over democratic forms of enterprise. *Journal of Economic Behavior and Organization*, 3, 139–60.

Putterman, L. 1984: On recent explanations of why capital hires labor. *Economic Inquiry*, 22, 171–87.

Putterman, L. 1986: *The Economic Nature of the Firm*. Cambridge: Cambridge University Press.

Qin, Cheng-Zhong 1987: Comparison of Welfare Situations: A Game Theoretic Approach. Mimeograph, University of Iowa.

Radner, R. 1962: Team decision problems. *Annals of Mathematical Statistics*, 33, 857–81.

Radner, R. 1968: Competitive equilibrium under uncertainty. *Econometrica*, 36, 31–58.

Radner, R. 1972: Existence of equilibrium plans, prices, and price expectations in a sequence of markets. *Econometrica*, 40, 278–91.

Radner, R. 1974: A note on unanimity of stockholders' preferences among alternative production plans: a reformulation of the Ekern–Wilson model. *Bell Journal of Economics*, 5, 181–4.

Radner, R. 1975: Satisficing. *Journal of Mathematical Economics*, 2, 253–62.

Radner, R. 1981: Monitoring cooperative agreements in a repeated principal–agent relationship. *Econometrica*, 49, 1127–48.

Radner, R. and Rothschild, M. 1975: On the allocation of effort. *Journal of Economic Theory*, 10, 358–76.

Reekie, W. D. 1984: *Markets, Entrepreneurs and Liberty: An Austrian View of Capitalism*. Brighton: Wheatsheaf Books.

Ricardo, D. 1951–1955: *The Works and Correspondence of David Ricardo*, eds P. Sraffa and M. Dobb. Cambridge: Cambridge University Press. (First published 1817.)

Richardson, G. B. 1972: The organization of industry. *Economic Journal*, 82, 883–96.

Riley, J. G. 1979a: Information equilibrium. *Econometrica*, 47, 331–53.

Riley, J. G. 1979b: Noncooperative equilibrium and market signaling. *American Economic Review*, 69, 303–7.

Rima, I. H. 1967: *Development of Economic Analysis*. Homewood, IL: R. D. Irwin.

Roberts, D. R. 1959: *Executive Compensation*. Glenco: Free Press.

Robertson, R. M. and Walton, G. M. 1979: *History of the American Economy*, 4th edn. New York: Harcourt Brace Jovanovich.

Robinson, A. 1934: The problem of management and the size of the firm. *Economic Journal*, 44, 242–53.

Robinson, J. 1950: *Economics of Imperfect Competition*. London: Macmillan.

de Roover, R. 1963: The organization of trade. In E. Miller, M. M. Postan, and E. E. Rich (eds), *Cambridge Economic History of Europe*, vol. 3, Cambridge: Cambridge University Press, 42–118.

Rose-Ackerman, S. (ed.) 1986: *The Economics of Non-Profit Institutions*. New York: Oxford University Press.

Rosen, S. 1972: Learning by experience as joint production. *Quarterly Journal of Economics*, 86, 366–82.

Ross, S. 1973: The economic theory of agency: the principal's problem. *American Economic Review*, 63, 134–9.

Ross, S. 1977: The determination of financial structure: the incentive signaling approach. *Bell Journal of Economics*, 8, 23–40.

Rothschild, M. and Stiglitz, J. E. 1976: Equilibrium in competitive insurance markets: an essay on the economics of imperfect information. *Quarterly Journal of Economics*, 90, 628–49.

Rubin, P. H. 1973: The expansion of firms. *Journal of Political Economy*, 81, 936–49.

Samuelson, P. 1947: *Foundations of Economic Analysis*. Cambridge, MA: Harvard University Press.

Samuelson, P. 1957: Wages and interest: a modern dissection of Marxian economic models. *American Economic Review*, 47, 887–912.

Sandmo, A. 1971: On the theory of the competitive firm under price uncertainty. *American Economic Review*, 61, 65–73.

Say, J. B. 1804: *Treatise on Political Economy*. Philadelphia, PA: Lippincott, 1860; also 4th edn, New York: John Grigg, 1830.

Scherer, F. M. 1980: *Industrial Market Structure and Economic Performance*, 2nd edn. Chicago, IL: Rand McNally.

Schneider, E. 1935: *Theorie der Production*. Vienna: Springer.

Schotter, A. 1981: *The Economic Theory of Social Institutions*. New York: Cambridge University Press.

Schotter, A. and Schwödiauer, G. 1980: Economics and the theory of games: a survey. *Journal of Economic Literature*, 18, 479–527.

Schultz, T. W. 1975: The value of the ability to deal with disequilibria. *Journal of Economic Literature*, 13, 827–46.

Schumpeter, J. A. 1934: *The Theory of Economic Development*. Cambridge, MA: Harvard University Press. (First published 1910.)

Schumpeter, J. A. 1939: *Business Cycles*. New York: McGraw-Hill.

Schumpeter, J. A. 1942: *Capitalism, Socialism and Democracy*. New York: Harper and Row.

Schumpeter, J. A. 1947: The creative response in economic history. *Journal of Economic History*, 7, 149–59.

Schumpeter, J. A. 1958: Theories of decision making in economics and behavioral science. *American Economic Review*, 48, 607–17.

Schumpeter, J. A. 1965: Economic theory and entrepreneurial history. In H. G. Aiken (ed.), *Explorations in Enterprises*, Cambridge, MA: Harvard University Press.

Scitovsky, T. 1943: A note on profit maximisation and its implications. *Review of Economics Studies*, 11, 57–60.

Sen, A. K. 1970: *Collective Choice and Social Welfare*. San Francisco, CA: Holden Day.

Senior, N. W. 1965: *An Outline of the Science of Political Economy*. New York: Augustus M. Kelley (First published 1836.)

Shafer, W. and Sonnenschein, H. 1975: Some theorems on the existence of competitive equilibrium. *Journal of Economic Theory*, 1, 83–93.

Sharpe, W. F. 1964: Capital asset prices: a theory of market equilibrium under conditions of risk. *Journal of Finance*, 19, 425–52.

Shubik, M. 1959: *Strategy and Market Structure*. New York: Wiley, chapter 4.

Shubik, M. 1984: *Game Theory in the Social Sciences*. Cambridge, MA: MIT Press.

Silver, M. and Auster, R. 1969: Entrepreneurship, profit, and the limits on firm size. *Journal of Business*, 42, 277–82.

Simon, H. A. 1951: A formal theory of the employment relationship. *Econometrica*, 19, 283–305.

Simon, H. A. 1952: A comparison of organizational theories. *Review of Economic Studies*, 20, 40–8.

Simon, H. A. 1957a: A formal theory of the employment contract. In H. A. Simon, *Models of Man: Social and Rational*, New York: Wiley.

Simon, H. A. 1957b: *Models of Man: Social and Rational*. New York: Wiley.

Simon, H. A. 1959: Theories of decision-making in economics and behavioral science. *American Economic Review*, 49, 253–83.

Simon, H. A. 1962: The architecture of complexity. *Proceedings of the American Philosophical Society*, 106, 467–82.

Slutsky, E. 1965: On the theory of the budget of the consumer. *American Economic Association Readings in Price Theory*, Homewood, IL: R. D. Irwin, 27–56. (First published 1915.)

Smith, A. 1937: *The Wealth of Nations*. New York: Random House, Modern Library Edition. (First published 1776.)

Soltow, J. H. 1968: The entrepreneur in economic history. *American Economic Review*, 58, 84–92.

Stein, J. 1971: *Money and Capacity Growth*. New York: Columbia University Press.

Steinberg, R. 1987: Nonprofit organizations and the market. In W. W. Powell (ed.), *The Nonprofit Sector*, New Haven, CT: Yale University Press.

Stigler, G. J. 1941: *Production \and \Distribution\ Theory. |* New York: Macmillan.

Stigler, G. J. 1951: The division of labor is limited by the extent of the market. *Journal of Political Economy*, 49, 185–93.

Stiglitz, J. E. 1974: Incentives and risk sharing in sharecropping. *Review of Economic Studies*, 41, 219–55.

Stiglitz, J. E. 1975: Incentive, risk and information: notes toward a theory of hierarchy. *Bell Journal of Economics*, 6, 552–71.

Teece, D. J. 1980: Economies of scope and the scope of the enterprise. *Journal of Economic Behavior and Organization*, 1, 223–45.

Telser, L. G. 1972: *Competition, Collusion and Game Theory*. Chicago, IL: Aldine.

Telser, L. G. 1979: *Economic Theory and the Core*. Chicago, IL: Chicago University Press.

Telser, L. G. 1980: A theory of self-enforcing agreements. *Journal of Business*, 53, 27–44.

Thrupp, S. L. 1963: The guilds. In E. Miller, M. M. Postan and E. E. Rich (eds), *Cambridge Economic History of Europe*, vol. III, Cambridge: Cambridge University Press, 230–80.

von Thunen, J. H. 1951: *Ausgewahlte, Texte*, transl. W. Walker. Germany: West Kulturverlag Anton Hairin.

Tisdell, C. 1963: Uncertainty, instability, expected profit. *Econometrica*, 31, 243–7.

Tobin, J. 1965: Money and economic growth. *Econometrica*, 33, 671–84.

Townsend, R. M. 1979: Optimal contracts and competitive markets with costly state verification. *Journal of Economic Theory*, 21, 265–93.

Usher, A. P. 1920: *Introduction to the Industrial History of England*. Boston, MA: Houghton.

Vanek, J. 1970: *The General Theory of Labor-managed Economies*. Ithaca, NY: Cornell University Press.

Walras, L. 1954: *Elements of Pure Economics*, transl. W. Jaffe. Homewood, IL: R. D. Irwin. (First published 1874.)

Ward, B. 1958: The firm in Illyria: market syndication. *American Economic Review*, 48, 566–89.

Weisbrod, B. A. 1975: Toward a theory of the voluntary non-profit sector in a three-sector economy. In S. Rose-Ackerman (ed.), *The Economics of Nonprofit Institutions*, New York: Oxford University Press, 1986.

Weisbrod, B. A. and Schlesinger, M. 1986: Public, private, nonprofit ownership and the response to asymmetric information: the case of nursing homes. In S. Rose-Ackerman (ed.), *The Economics of Nonprofit Institutions*, New York: Oxford University Press.

van Werveke, H. 1963: The rise of the towns. In E. Miller, M. M. Postan and E. E. Rich (eds), *Cambridge Economic History of Europe*, vol. III, Cambridge: Cambridge University Press, chapter 1.

Wicksell, K. 1935: *Lectures on Political Economy*. New York: Macmillan. (First published 1901.)

Wicksteed, P. 1894: *An Essay on the Coordination of the Laws of Distribution*. London: Macmillan.

Wicksteed, P. 1935: *The Common Sense of Political Economy*, ed. L. Robbins. London: Routledge. (First published 1910.).

Williamson, O. E. 1957: Hierarchical control and optimum firm size. *Journal of Political Economy*, 75, 123–38.

Williamson, O. E. 1963a: *The Economics of Discretionary Behavior: Managerial Objectives in a Theory of the Firm*. Englewood Cliffs, NJ: Prentice-Hall.

Williamson, O. E. 1963b: Managerial discretion and business behavior. *American Economic Review*, 53, 1031–57.

Williamson, O. E. 1963c: A model of rational managerial behavior. In Cyert, R. M. and March, J. G. (eds), *A Behavioral Theory of the Firm*, Englewood Cliffs, NJ: Prentice-Hall, 237–52.

Williamson, O. E. 1970: *Corporate Control and Business Behavior*. Englewood Cliffs, NJ: Prentice-Hall.

Williamson, O. E. 1971a: Managerial discretion, organization form and the multidivision hypothesis. In R. Marris and A. Wood (eds), *The Corporate Economy*, Cambridge, MA: Harvard University Press.

Williamson, O. E. 1971b: The vertical integration of production: market failure considerations. *American Economic Review*, 61, 112–23.

Williamson, O. E. 1975: *Markets and Hierarchies: Analysis and Antitrust Implications: A Study in the Economics of Internal Organization*. New York: Free Press.

Williamson, O. E. 1979: Transaction cost economics: the governance of contractual relations. *Journal of Law and Economics*, 22, 233–61.

Williamson, O. E. 1981: The modern corporation: origin, evaluation, attributes. *Journal of Economic Literature*, 19, 1537–68.

Williamson, O. E. 1983: Organizational form, residual claimants and corporate control. *Journal of Law and Economics*, 26, 365.

Williamson, O. E., Wachter, M. L. and Harris, J. E. 1975: Understanding the employment relation: the analysis of idiosyncratic exchange. *Bell Journal of Economics*, 6, 250–78.

Wilson, R. 1968: The theory of syndicates. *Econometrica*, 36, 119–32.

Wilson, R. 1975: Informational economies of scale. *Bell Journal of Economics*, 6, 184–95.

Winter, S. G. 1964: Economic "natural selection" and the theory of the firm. *Yale Economic Essays*, 4, 225–72.

Winter, S. G. 1971: Satisficing, selection and the innovating remnant. *Quarterly Journal of Economics*, 85, 237–61.

Wu, S. Y. 1979: An essay on monopoly power and stable price policy. *American Economic Review*, 69, 60–72.

Yarrow, G. K. 1973: Managerial utility maximization under uncertainty. *Economica* (NS), 40, 155–73.

Yarrow, G. K. 1976: On the predictors of managerial theories of the firm. *Journal of Industrial Economics*, 24, 267–79.

Young, D. 1981: Entrepreneurship and the behavior of nonprofit organizations. In S. Rose-Ackerman (ed.), *The Economics of Nonprofit Institutions*, New York: Oxford University Press, 1986, 161–84.

Name Index

Subject Index